Frantz Fanon and Emancipatory Social Theory

Studies in Critical Social Sciences Book Series

Haymarket Books is proud to be working with Brill Academic Publishers (www.brill.nl) to republish the *Studies in Critical Social Sciences* book series in paperback editions. This peer-reviewed book series offers insights into our current reality by exploring the content and consequences of power relationships under capitalism, and by considering the spaces of opposition and resistance to these changes that have been defining our new age. Our full catalog of *SCSS* volumes can be viewed at https://www.haymarketbooks .org/series_collections/4-studies-in-critical-social-sciences.

Frantz Fanon and Emancipatory Social Theory

A View from the Wretched

Edited by

Dustin J. Byrd
Seyed Javad Miri

Haymarket Books
Chicago, IL

First published in 2019 by Brill Academic Publishers, The Netherlands.
© 2019 Koninklijke Brill NV, Leiden, The Netherlands

Published in paperback in 2020 by
Haymarket Books
P.O. Box 180165
Chicago, IL 60618
773-583-7884
www.haymarketbooks.org

ISBN: 978-1-64259-353-2

Distributed to the trade in the US through Consortium Book Sales and Distribution (www.cbsd.com) and internationally through Ingram Publisher Services International (www.ingramcontent.com).

This book was published with the generous support of Lannan Foundation and Wallace Action Fund.

Special discounts are available for bulk purchases by organizations and institutions. Please call 773-583-7884 or email info@haymarketbooks.org for more information.

Cover design by Jamie Kerry and Ragina Johnson.

Printed in United States.

10 9 8 7 6 5 4 3 2 1

Library of Congress Cataloging-in-Publication Data is available.

Contents

Notes on Contributors

Mumia Abu-Jamal
is an acclaimed writer, commentator, and journalist, whose politically motivated incarceration has generated worldwide attention and support. He is the author of ten books, written from within America's carceral state. They include: *Live from Death Row* (Perennial, 1995), *Death Blossoms: Reflections from a Prisoner of Conscience* (The Plough Publishing House, 1997), *We Want Freedom: A Life in the Black Panther Party* (South End Press, 2004), *Have Black Lives Ever Mattered?* (City Lights Books, 2017), and *Murder Incorporated: Empire, Genocide, Manifest Destiny. Book One: Dreaming of Empire* (Prison Radio, 2018). For over twenty years he has delivered weekly radio commentaries, focusing on issues of race, racism, politics, economics, history, colonialism, war, and a variety of other topics. He continues to fight for his freedom.

Syed Farid Alatas
is Professor of Sociology at the National University of Singapore. He is also appointed to the Department of Malay Studies at NUS and headed that department from 2007 to 2013. He lectured at the University of Malaya in the Department of Southeast Asian Studies prior to joining NUS. In the early 1990s, he was a Research Associate at the Women and Human Resource Studies Unit, Science University of Malaysia. Prof. Alatas has authored numerous books and articles, including *Ibn Khaldun* (Oxford University Press, 2013); *Applying Ibn Khaldun: The Recovery of a Lost Tradition in Sociology* (Routledge, 2014), and (with Vineeta Sinha) *Sociological Theory Beyond the Canon* (Palgrave, 2017) and "The State of Feminist Theory in Malaysia" in *Feminism: Malaysian Reflections and Experience* (special issue of *Kajian Malaysia: Journal of Malaysian Studies*) Maznah Mohamad and Wong Soak Koon, eds. 12, 1–2 (1994): 25–46. His areas of interest are the sociology of Islam, social theory, religion and reform, intra- and inter-religious dialogue, and the study of Orientalism.

Rose M. Brewer
is The Morse Alumni Distinguished Teaching Professor and past chairperson of the Department of African American & African Studies, University of Minnesota-Twin Cities. She also is an affiliate faculty member in Sociology and Gender Women and Sexuality Studies. She received her M.A. and Ph.D. degrees in sociology from Indiana University and did post-doctoral studies at the University of Chicago. An activist scholar, Brewer publishes extensively on

Black feminism, political economy, social movements, race, class, gender and social change. She is a University of Minnesota College of Liberal Arts Dean's Medalist, a member of the Academy of Distinguished Teachers, a winner of the American Sociological Association's Distinguished Teaching award, and a Josie Johnson Social Justice Award recipient. For over fifteen years she was a member of the board of Project South: Institute for the Elimination of Poverty and Genocide; a past board member of United for a Fair Economy, and a founding member of the Black Radical Congress. As a core organizer of the 2007, 2010, and 2015 US Social Forums, the struggle for social change for her has been centered in the local and global. Her current work focuses on Black life in the U.S. today examining the impact of late capitalism and racism on the Black population in cities such as Minneapolis, Milwaukee, the broader Midwest and the nation.

Dustin J. Byrd

is a specialist in political philosophy, the Frankfurt School's "Critical Theory of Religion," and contemporary Islamic thought. He is an Associate Professor of Philosophy, Religion, and Arabic at Olivet College in Michigan, USA. He is the Editor-in-Chief of the *Islamic Perspective Journal,* published by the London Academy of Iranian Studies. Along with dozens of articles, Dr. Byrd has published numerous books, including *Unfashionable Objections to Islamophobic Cartoons: L'affaire Charlie Hebdo* (Cambridge Scholars Publishing, 2017), and *Islam in a Post-Secular Society: Religion, Secularity, and the Antagonism of Recalcitrant Faith* (Brill, 2017). The latter was translated into Arabic by Dr. Mohammad 'Aafif and published by Mominoun Without Borders (Rabat, Morocco) in 2019. Along with Seyed Javad Miri, he has co-edited the following books: *Malcolm X: From Political Eschatology to Religious Revolutionary* (Brill, 2016), *Ali Shariati and the Future of Social Theory: Religion, Revolution, and the Role of the Intellectual* (Brill, 2018). He is currently researching the philosophical and religious origins of the West's anti-liberal "Traditionalism."

Sean Chabot

is a Professor in Sociology at Eastern Washington University. His intellectual work focuses on decolonizing the strategy and study of nonviolent resistance, entanglements of violence and nonviolence, subaltern movements in the global South, and transnational connections among different activist communities. Recent publications include the book *Transnational Roots of the Civil Rights Movement: African American Explorations of the Gandhian Repertoire* (Lexington Books, 2011), "The Violence of Nonviolence" in *Societies without Borders* 8 (2): 205–232 (2013, with Majid Sharifi), and "Decolonizing Civil Resistance" in *Mobilization: An International Quarterly* 20 (4): 517–532 (2015, with Stellan Vinthagen).

Richard Curtis

holds a Ph.D. from Claremont Graduate University's School of Religion. He has taught throughout the Seattle, Washington area. Currently Dr. Curtis is Professor of Philosophy and Editor for the Existential and Psychoanalytic Institute and Society (at the University of Montana) and Visiting Professor for the OLLI Program (at the University of Washington). He is currently working on a book developing a post-theistic Reform Jewish theology.

Nigel C. Gibson

is an activist and academic specializing in the work of the Algerian revolutionary Frantz Fanon. Gibson is author of *Fanon: The Postcolonial Imagination* (Polity Press, 2003), which won the 2009 Caribbean Philosophy Frantz Fanon Outstanding Book Award and was translated into Arabic in 2013, and *Fanonian Practices in South Africa: From Steve Biko to Abahlali baseMjondolo* (University of Kwa Zulu-Natal Press and Palgrave MacMillan, 2011). Gibson has also edited and co-edited collections of work on Adorno, Biko, Fanon, African Studies and Social Movements in South Africa. His latest work is *Fanon: Psychiatry and Politics*, co-authored with Roberto Beneduce (Rowman and Littlefield and University of Witwatersrand Press, 2017). He teaches at Emerson College, Boston, USA and is Honorary Professor in the Humanities Unit at the University currently known as Rhodes, South Africa.

Ali S. Harfouch

is a Lecturer at the American University of Beirut where he also received his Master of Arts (2017) in Political Studies. His publications include "Towards a Groundwork for the Metaphysics of an Islamic Decoloniality" (Researching Islam in the Global Village, Center for Educational Research and Training, 2017) and "The Illusion of Realism: What is the Future of Muslim Politics?" (Milestones: Commentary on the Islamic World, Milestones, 24 July 2017, www .milestonesjournal.net/). He specializes in contemporary Islamic thought, political theory and is a commentator on politics in the Muslim world.

Timothy Kerswell

is Assistant Professor of Government and Public Administration at the University of Macau, China. He is the author of *Worker Cooperatives in India* (Palgrave MacMillan, 2018). His research interests include the global division of labor, international class structure, labor politics in India and China, labor and migration policy, and Marxist political thought. He previously worked for Australia's Department of Immigration and Citizenship on labor market policy, and for the trade union United Voice as a researcher.

Seyed Javad Miri

holds a Ph.D. from the Institute of Humanities and Cultural Studies, and is Professor of sociology and history of religions at that Institute in Tehran. He has published more than fifty books and a hundred articles on various issues related to philosophy, religion, sociology, and social theory. His latest book is *Reimagining Malcolm X: Street Thinker Versus Homo Academicus* (University Press of America, 2016).

Pramod K. Nayar

teaches at the Department of English, University of Hyderabad, India. Among his newest books are *Brand Postcolonial* (de Gruyter, 2018), *Bhopal's Ecological Gothic* (Lexington, 2017), *The Extreme in Contemporary Culture* (Rowman and Littlefield, 2017), *Human Rights and Literature* (Palgrave Macmillan, 2016), among others. His *Frantz Fanon* appeared in the Routledge Critical Thinkers Series in 2013.

Elena Flores Ruíz

is an Assistant Professor of Philosophy and Global Studies at Michigan State University. She received her Ph.D. in Philosophy and M.A. in Social and Political Theory from the University of South Florida. Prior to joining MSU, Dr. Ruíz was a research fellow at Institut de Hautes études Internationales et du Développement in Geneva, Switzerland. Her primary areas of research are in political philosophy and feminisms of the global south. Her work examines the philosophical foundations of violence, structural oppression, and theories of harm (cultural, epistemic, linguistic) in the context of violence affecting women and marginalized populations in the Global South. Her work has appeared in *Hypatia, Feminist Philosophy Quarterly, The Routledge International Handbook to Contemporary Social and Political Theory*, as well as in edited collections and trade journals.

Majid Sharifi

is Associate Professor in Political Science Department and Director of International Affairs Program at Eastern Washington University. He is the author of *Imagining Iran: the Tragedy of Subaltern Nationalism*. His book breaks new grounds in connecting what he calls subaltern nationalism to the imperial nature of global governance. Sharifi's current research explores the intersection between security and violence on the one hand, and social movements on the other hand. His most recent article, "The Violence of Nonviolence" was published by *Societies without Borders* 8 (2): 205–232 (2013, with Sean Chabot). Presently, Sharifi is co-authoring a book titled, *Security/Insecurity Communities in the Muslim World*. The book is under contract with Manchester Press, and it is to be published by August 2019.

Mohamed Imran Mohamed Taib

is director of Centre for Interfaith Understanding (CIFU) in Singapore. He was formerly an associate research fellow at the Studies in Interreligious Relations in Plural Societies programme, S Rajaratnam School of International Studies (RSIS), and was working for the Islamic Religious Council of Singapore (Muis) in research and policy, the Muis Academy and the Harmony Centre. He was also founding member of Leftwrite Center, a dialogue initiative in Singapore on multicultural issues; and former board member of Centre for Contemporary Islamic Studies. He writes on issues of multiculturalism, interfaith relations and Muslim reform, published in dailies such as *The Straits Times*, *Today, Channel NewsAsia* and *South China Morning Post*. His co-edited books are *Islam, Religion and Progress: Critical Perspectives* (2006), *Moral Vision and Social Critique: Selected Essays of Syed Hussein Alatas* (2007) and *Budi Kritik* (2018). He was also chief editor of Malay socio-religious journal, *Tafkir*.

Esmaeil Zeiny

is a Research Fellow at the Institute of Malaysian and International Studies (IKMAS), National University of Malaysia (UKM). He has received his PhD in Postcolonial Literature in English from the National University of Malaysia. His research interests lie at the intersection of literary studies, political theory, and cultural studies. He has recently co-edited *Seen and Unseen: Visual Cultures of Imperialism* (Brill, 2018, with Sanaz Fotouhi) and *Reconstructing Historical Memories* (UKM Press, 2018, with Richard Mason).

Introduction

In his seminal work, *The Wretched of the Earth*, Frantz Fanon, the revolutionary psychiatrist and theorist, wrote: "Each generation must out of relative obscurity discover its mission, fulfill it, or betray it."[1] This important passage, which has been endlessly quoted, lays out a challenge. Taken in light of Fanon's own life and work, it appears as a clarion call for revolutionary theory and praxis in an unjust world – an emancipatory task that each successive generation must either commit itself to or turn away from in cowardice. To "betray" a cause is to know it is right and nevertheless flee from it. Fanon's statement, of course, assumes that there will be a need for future revolutionary projects, just as there was a need for such in Fanon's own lifetime. In the post-September 11th world, which has seen a global financial collapse, the weakening of the neo-liberal hegemonic world order, and the reemergence of a second superpower with Putin's Russia, the world has experienced an era of political, economic, and cultural *erlebnisse*. These traumatic and sometime apocalyptic events have not only shaken the confidence of the Western middle classes, who are so often blissfully ignorant of the state of the world amidst the phantasmagoria of necrophilic consumorism, they have compounded the wretchedness of the *still-wretched*, both in the West and in the East. The Western middle classes, who in the 20th century rose out of the proletariat to become middle management, have become the new "precariat," nervously guarding the what's left of their "American dream" against those they are told are coming to take it from them: the foreigner, the immigrant, and the refugee. At the same time, neo-liberal democracy, as it is exported in the rest of the world, has yet to fulfill its promise of universal prosperity. Rather, it has left more and more of the world's population in the ditch of history – scrambling for the scrapes of the few who prosper. Whether it be the waste-pickers in the "trash mountains" of India, South Pacific islanders losing their homelands to sea level rise in the Indian Ocean, the coal miners in West Virginia dying of Black Lung disease, Yemeni civilians constantly being killed by Saudi warplanes with American-made bombs; whether it be the Muslim Rohingya being ethnically cleansed in Myanmar, the Syrian refugees being harassed and accosted in Europe while seeking safety from the civil war, Central American families pleading for asylum at the United States' southern border, the young Nigerian girls being kidnapped and raped by Boko Haram, or the citizens of Flint, Michigan, still forced to consume Governor

---

1   Frantz Fanon, *The Wretched of the Earth*, trans. Constance Farrington (New York: Grove Press, 1963), 206.

Rick Snyder's "poisoned water," the *still-wretched* are waiting for their liberation. In other words, they still wait for the present generation to discover its emancipatory mission and "fulfill it."

When one reads the works of Frantz Fanon today, one reads him amidst two different emotive states: First, he is read in sadness – sadness because the reader knows that since Fanon lived the world has yet to alleviate the plight of the wretched despite having the resources to do so. In fact, new forms of wretchedness are invented with each passing year, and new ideological excuses are invented to justify the maintenance of their wretchedness. Yet, that sadness must not be debilitating. That is why we read Fanon, secondly, with hope – a form of hope that is not optimistic, but nevertheless continues to harken back to the victories won by liberation movements throughout the world as they attempted to decolonize their lands from the domination of others. This future-oriented remembrance of such revolutionary successes reminds the reader that history is not pre-determined; it is not only made by powerful elites; it is not the toy of the wealthy; it is not fate. Rather, Fanon's works remind us that history is shaped by those who claim as their task the shaping of history – those who "discover their mission… and fulfill it."[2] In reading Fanon, we find the strength and fortitude to thusly remain "prisoners of hope."

The works of Frantz Fanon cause us to reflect on academic life, coming to the conclusion that it must be more than just teaching, writing, and making presentations at conferences. His books, lectures, and letters, galvanize us to realize that the seeds of a new and more justice-filled tomorrow need only the fertile soil that we have yet to till. Frantz Fanon's example, as a revolutionary and theorist, combining both theoretical and practical wisdom, serves as a catalyst for scholars in the 20th century to reject the complacency in the academic life, and move their protests to the streets, the bazaars, the parliaments, and to the temples, synagogues, churches, and mosques; they must translate their insights into the conditions that create the ever-recycled wretched into liberational movements, as was done by Fanon. Philosophically, he has already done much of the theoretical work. He has emancipated the act of writing, the act of thinking, and the act of speaking, from its eremitic tendencies, transforming it into a cenobitic exercise, with the intent to animate revolutionary praxis within the Third World and also within the "internal colonies" in the metropoles.

This book represents a step in the direction towards understanding the nature, history, and present condition of colonialism, class domination, racism,

---

2 Ibid.

gender oppression, and other forms of oppression, as was understood by Frantz Fanon. Additionally, the scholars represented in this book seek to determinately negate Fanon's work, allowing certain critical potentials in his revolutionary philosophy to migrate into the present struggle against neo-colonialism, neo-fascism, and the hegemony of the neo-liberal world order. Fanon is not treated as an untouchable dogma; he is not a "museum piece" that we lovingly gaze upon. Rather, his work is viewed as an elastic source of insight, some of which remain hopelessly locked within his own particular time and circumstance, while others easily affix themselves to contemporary struggles.

The various scholars in this book come from different backgrounds: sociology, history, religious studies, philosophy and theology. Included is even a political prisoner, Mumia Abu-Jamal, whose own prophetic voice narrates the consciousness of many revolutionaries today, much like Fanon's did in the 1960s. Although authorities have tried to break his determined-will for decades, Mumia Abu-Jamal continues to deeply embody the recalcitrant spirit of Fanon from within the penal palace of the carceral state. Like Mumia Abu-Jamal, each contributor sees Fanon from his or her own parallax view; they offer the reader a variety of ways of interpreting Fanon, of understanding his continual significance to history, and of the bearing he has on present conditions. His potential to continually fertilize contemporary struggles with his critique of capitalism, colonialism, racism, and class domination appears limitless. Thus, the chapters in this book are multifaceted, just as Fanon's work itself was multifaceted.

We would like to thank the many talented contributors to this volume. Their theoretical insights, critiques, and perspectives have augmented our understanding of Frantz Fanon and his continual significance for a more human world. Once you think you know enough about a given subject that you can competently write on it, you encounter other scholars whose work blows apart your own, and in doing so creates whole new avenues of understanding. Each scholar in this book has done nothing less than force me to reorder and reconsider my own thinking on Fanon, and for that I'm eternally grateful.

We would especially like to thank Mumia Abu-Jamal for agreeing to write a chapter for this book. Unlike the rest of us, he is writing under difficult conditions. Although no longer on death row, he continues to be incarcerated in Pennsylvania due to his Fanon-like struggle for the full emancipation of humanity, especially for the *still-wretched* in the United States. Someday a change will come, and justice will prevail.

We would also like to thank Dr. David Fasenfest, the series editor of Brill's *Studies in Critical Social Sciences*. He and the editors at Brill's Leiden offices make the difficult and sometimes maddening task of academic publishing enjoyable and rewarding.

Lastly, we would like to thank Jamie Groendyk for reviewing the text. In between caring for little Alexander James, she spent hours reading and rereading the chapters of this book and offering helpful suggestions. She deserves more appreciation that we can possibly give her.

Dustin J. Byrd, Ph.D.

Why should we study Frantz Fanon in the 21st century? Is there any authentic need to re-visit him, and if the answer to this question is affirmative, then within what kind of parameters should we re-consider his intellectual legacy? There are various ways in which readers encounter the legacy of Fanon, and by looking through the historical record we can find many important ways in which Fanon's insights have been appropriated by activists and freedom fighters around the globe. These engagements with Fanon are important, yet, what is of greater significance in the current context is the relevance of Fanon in terms of social theory. It is time to read Fanon outside of a Eurocentric frame of reference in regards to social theory, and reflect upon conceptual contributions of his without confining him *merely* within racial theories. In other words, it seems Fanon has been appropriated exclusively by certain social theorists within the post-colonial tradition, but these singular readings of Fanon do not do justice to Frantz Fanon as a social theorist *par excellence*. In light of his observation, the question inevitably becomes: how to read Fanon? If we bring Malcolm X's influential approach, where he talks about the fate of Afro-Americans in the United States of America, to Frantz Fanon's discourse, then we may be able to refashion our understanding of his theoretical contributions. Malcolm X employed two concepts, "House Negro" and "Field Negro," or "House Slave" and "Field Slave," and by these two concepts he referred to two different mentalities that an enslaved individual displayed. In the form of a "House Negro," the enslaved had no sense of autonomous subjectivity; he experienced himself merely as an extension of his master. In the second form, the "Field Negro," while the slave endured all kinds of torturous punishments at the hands of the Master, he nevertheless retained his own sense of subjectivity vis-à-vis the Master. In other words, by using the metaphorical categories of Malcolm X in relation to Frantz Fanon and how we read his intellectual legacy, we can argue that it is possible to study Fanon in two broad forms, i.e. in terms of a "House Narrative" and in terms of "Field Narrative." That's to argue that we need a kind of approach whereby Fanon is not conceptualized as an extension of Eurocentric categories and forms of subjectivities, but rather within the boundaries of a "Field Narrative" (à la Malcolm X). If reading Fanon in such a way is at all possible, then I would consider his intellectual legacy as one of the most significant paradigms in social theory. If this is the case, why then is Fanon not represented as one of the most important works of social theory in sociological textbooks around the world? In my view, one of the main reasons for such systematic negligence is the way through which the Fanonian discourse has been conceptualized, especially in terms of a "House Narrative." In this book, we have tried to look at Fanon in a different fashion. For instance, my own contribution is focused on how Fanon has been reinterpreted outside Euro-American traditions. I have argued that we can read Fanon through various forms, one of which was demonstrated through the work of Ali Shariati. In my view, *Restern interpretations* have been rarely discussed within the social sciences, and this lack itself has resulted in the under-theorization of *Restern* approaches vis-à-vis *western* outlooks in academia. If we could develop *Restern* approaches within academia, then gradually more progressive forms of social theories could be made possible, wherein the world is not viewed solely through a Eurocentric prism, but rather multiple foci of subjectivities can emerge within the frames of academia and by extension around the globe. If we are really honest about breaking epistemic boundaries of Eurocentrism and capitalist forms of knowledge production, and its accompanying necrophilic modes of being, then dominant mentalities must be debunked and overcome. Along with many other critical thinkers, Frantz Fanon plays a pivotal role in achieving a future where injustice does not rule supreme. In other words, Frantz Fanon is important for furthering the critique of the status quo, but it should be borne in mind that all readings of Fanon are not critical or critical enough. Said differently, we need to reflect upon the critical ways in which we read the emancipatory legacy of Frantz Fanon; one of the most important ways is the kind of interpretative approach conceptualized by Malcolm X vis-à-vis the slave mentality in the United States of America. Of course, I do not use Malcolm X's concepts in a literal fashion, but I think of them metaphorically, as the "House Narrative" and "Field Narrative" concepts could open up venues for more theoretical debates among sociologists and social theorists, especially among those who have not reflected upon the Fanonian discourse in terms of Field Narrative. By stepping outside the sociological canon, we have demonstrated the will to go beyond the dominant vision of social theory, which can be verified by examining the content of this work and the analyses that we present. In other words, we have attempted to demonstrate that other interpretive paradigms are possible and even desirable, and that it is time to move the social sciences and social theoretical concepts and images beyond the Eurocentric canonical pantheon.

I would like to express my gratitude to the numerous contributors to this book, the editorial staff at Brill, Dr. David Fasenfest, and Jamie Groendyk for all their hard work putting this volume together. Without them it would never have happened.

Seyed Javad Miri, Ph.D.

CHAPTER 1

Frantz Fanon and His Influence on the Black Panther Party and the Black Revolution

Mumia Abu-Jamal

For the mostly teenaged members of the Black Panther Party for Self-Defense (BPP), the name Fanon was a familiar one. For every Panther was told it was his/her duty to read *The Wretched of the Earth*. It mattered little that it was difficult, given its translation from the original French to English. Fanon, a revolutionary psychiatrist, influenced by his professional knowledge and its concomitant jargon, had a deep penchant to view the world through his psychiatric and psychological lenses.

Luckily, BPP co-founder, Bobby Seale, early elected to share his copy of *The Wretched of the Earth* with his fellow co-founder, Huey P. Newton. Huey, who almost finished high school while being an active illiterate, was so moved by the work that he read and reread *Wretched* six times.[1] If one has spent his formative years as an illiterate, and does so clandestinely, he must utilize his memory to determine what has transpired in his life and relationships. When one subsequently acquires literacy, this does not extinguish that extraordinary recall, but rather understandably, it is strengthened thereby.

As such, Fanon's text was mulled over as a valued resource, which found its way into the canons of the Party, and the fundament of BPP ideology and political thought.

Fanon was, to say the least, a deep thinker, who contemplated the future of neocolonial African and global societies, and sought to inject his insights into revolutionary and post-colonial states the ability to defend and protect itself from imperial penetration and economic exploitation.

From Fanon's work (including his subsequently published *Toward the African Revolution* [ca. 1964]), BPP cadre acquired tremendous insights into the notion of viewing Black communities as colonies of an external, repressive White state power. Newton built on these concepts, as well as the justification to utilize paramilitary force to resist the empire. This essential insight, that

---

1   Bobby Seale, *Seize the Time: The Story of the Black Panther Party and Huey P. Newton.* (New York: Vintage Books, 1970), 25.

the African American community was an oppressed colony of the empire, was surely something Newton learned from Fanon, but it was not Newton's alone.

The late theologian, activist/scholar, Dr. James H. Cone, quotes none other than Rev. Dr. Martin Luther King, Jr., as observing: The Black ghetto is "a system of internal colonialism... The slum is little more than a domestic colony which leaves its inhabitants dominated politically, exploited economically, segregated and humiliated at every turn."[2]

Few observers saw points of convergence between King, the avatar of peace, and Newton, the advocate of revolution, but on the question of the actual status of Black America and its most populous communities, the two are almost indistinguishable. For who could deny that the vast majority of Black Americans lived in a profoundly separate living space, which reflects Fanon's insights about the Manichaean differences between the spaces dwelt in by the colonizer and the colonized? These recognitions suggest that Fanon was read by far more than the typical Black militants of the imperial, urban core.

BPP Central Committee member and Communications officer, Kathleen Neal Clever has written widely about the "profound" influence of Fanon's *The Wretched of the Earth.* In her article, "Back to Africa," an exposition on her times as a leader of the International Section of the BPP in Algiers, she writes:

> The crucible of civil war forged the writings of Frantz Fanon, the Black psychiatrist from Martinique who fought alongside Algerian revolutionaries for independence from France. His books became available in English just as waves of civil violence engulfed the ghettoes of America, reaching the level of insurrection in the wake of the assassination of Dr. Martin Luther King, Jr. in 1968. Fanon died in 1961, a year before Algeria obtained the independence he had given his life to win, but his brilliant, posthumously published work *The Wretched of the Earth* became essential reading for Black revolutionaries in America and profoundly influenced their thinking. Fanon's analysis seemed to explain and to justify the spontaneous violence ravaging Black ghettoes across the country, and linked the incipient insurrections to the rise of a revolutionary movement.[3]

---

2 James H. Come, *Martin & Malcolm & America: A Dream or a Nightmare.* (New York: Orbis Books, 1991), 223.

3 Kathleen N. Cleaver, "Back to Africa: The Evolution of the International Section of the Black Panther Party (1969–1970)," in *Black Panther Party Reconsidered,* ed. Charles E. Jones (Baltimore, MD: Black Classic Press, 1998), 214.

With precision and conciseness, Cleaver has illustrated the enlightenment that Fanon's work awakened in the Black World.

Fanon, some two years before the publication of *Les damnés de la terre*, speaking at a conference of Black writers in Rome, called for a "literature of combat." It seems safe to assume that he was working to complete what would become an international sensation: *The Wretched of the Earth*.

While Fanon doubtlessly made a major contribution to the African and Black world(s), his edification of colonialism was, by no means, his only – or even major – contribution. To that question we will now turn.

1   The Rise of the Lumpenproletariat

Dr. Frantz Fanon's *Wretched* was many things; an exposé of French colonialism, an examination of Arab resistance to said colonialism, the psychological analysis of the oppressed, colonized Arab communities, torture, the dual effects of state torture, the liberating effects of violence against colonial forces, and the like.

It is also, in some ways, an ideological primer that teaches anti-colonial rebels to build their forces by utilizing *lumpenproletariat* figures as first line militants against the state forces through guerilla war. In traditional Marxist thought, the revolutionary movement depends on the proletariat as the mass force that can upend the state's elite power. Fanon, writing of the Algerian colony, relies upon the *lumpen* strata of society to spearhead attacks against the colonial state. Fanon writes:

> It is among these masses, in the people of the shanty towns and in the lumpenproletariat that the insurrection will find its urban spearhead. The lumpenproletariat, this cohort of starving men, divorced from tribe and clan, constitutes one of the most spontaneously and radically revolutionary forces of a colonized people.[4]

In the Chinese independent and national liberation struggle, Mao made much of their rural masses – more pointedly, its peasantry – to propel the revolutionary struggle forward:

---

4 Frantz Fanon, *The Wretched of the Earth,* trans. Richard Philcox (New York: Grove Press, 2004), 81.

The ruthless economic exploitation and political oppression of the peasants by the landlord class forced them into numerous uprisings against its rule... it was the class struggles of the peasants, the peasants uprisings and peasant wars that constituted the real motive force of historical development in Chinese feudal society.[5]

Both historical examples made Black militants and revolutionaries in the American milieu look with significant interest at *lumpenism* as a viable bed of anti-state, revolutionary ferment. BPP Chairman Bobby Seale, recalled how important Fanon's insights were, as often explained and explicated by Newton:

We would sit down with *Wretched of the Earth* and talk, go over another section or chapter of Fanon, and Huey would explain it in depth... Huey understood the meaning of what Fanon was saying about organizing the lumpen proletariat and give a base for organizing the brother who's pimping, the brother who's hustling, the unemployed, the downtrodden, the brother who's robbing banks, who's not politically conscious – that's that lumpen proletariat means – that if you don't relate to these cats, the power structure would organize these cats against you.[6]

What we learned is that various national liberation movements elected to differentiate their struggles from the Marxist ideal to the reality of the populations and proportions of their sites of struggle. Where were the populations that would be most hostile and alienated from the central or colonialist governments? Where was the heaviest concentration of social forces likely to align with the liberating forces?

Fanon wrote critically about who the "colonialist bourgeoisie" were, arguing that they were "partisans... of order," who don't want social change, as much as they want a bigger slice of the imperialist pie.[7]

What of the peasants, the rural masses who form the biggest slice of the population? Fanon sees them as, "in colonial countries only the peasantry is revolutionary."[8] Why? "It has nothing to lose and everything to gain."[9] Mao's China seemingly made a similar conclusion.

---

5 Mao TseTung, *Quotations from Chairman Mao TseTeung,* (Peking: Foreign Language Press, 1972), 9.

6 Seale, *Seize the Time,* 26, 30.

7 Fanon, *The Wretched of the Earth,* 22.

8 Ibid., 23.

9 Ibid.

It is therefore not surprising that African American militants and revolutionaries, like Newton and Seale, viewed the lowest lumpen strata as possessive of similar qualities and promise. Fanon and Mao were searching for fighters – not conversationalist. The same could be said of Newton and Seale, who sought to assemble young militants who were willing to fight against the System, and move toward a revolution.

Mao rather famously uttered the following:

A revolution is not a dinner party, or writing an essay, or painting a picture, or doing embroidery; it cannot be so refined, so leisurely and gentle, so temperate, kind, courteous, restrained and magnanimous. A revolution is an insurrection, an act of violence by which one class overthrows another.[10]

This was, after all, a revolutionary age, when African, Asian, and other (then called Third World) states were engaged in a liberational and anti-colonial existence for national liberation and freedom.

Ultimately, that is the question before us; what works against the System? What configuration of social forces is best suited to challenge and disable the System? Who will fight? Those are the questions that will prove fundamental in any serious struggle against the rigor mortis of the status quo.

For members of the Black Panther Party, both Mao and Fanon were figures of great, global significance. Mao led the Communist Party to state power in the biggest (by population) country in the world: China. Fanon lent his considerable talents to help the FLN (*Front de libération nationale*) win their anti-colonial struggle against a great European power: France. And while both figures were admired for their roles in these struggles, Fanon – as a Black man from the Americas (Martinique) – to help stage and win a revolution was a deeply moving figure.

His writing therefore, sank deeper into Black consciousness in the colonies of North America.

2   Time and Fate

Dr. Fanon, his body wracked by leukemia, went to America's Johns Hopkins University Hospital, in a last ditch effort to find some relief and perhaps suppression of his cancer, but this was not to be. In October 1961, publisher

10   Mao, *Quotations*, 11–12.

François Maspero releases *Les Damnés de la terre* to the French-reading population. On December 6th, Dr. Fanon succumbs to his illness. On December 7th, 1961, police in Paris seize copies of *Les Damnés de la terre*. In 1963, the work appeared in English as *The Wretched of the Earth*. In October, 1966, Seal would give a copy of the book to Newton, and the two men would, during a two-week period, decide to form a Black freedom group: The Black Panther Party for Self-Defense.

Fanon, although he was certainly aware of black militant groups in America, did not live long enough to see the rise of the Black Panther Party.[11] However, his thinking was integral to the group's rise into consciousness. He therefore played a pivotal role in the party's formation and ideology.

While each Panther was required to acquire and read *The Wretched of the Earth*, BPP officers and staff read more deeply, and read *Black Skin, White Masks, A Dying Colonialism*, and *Toward the African Revolution*, soon after their publications in English. *The Wretched of the Earth* is unquestionably Fanon's masterwork, and the source of much of his renown and global fame, for it reveals many facets of Fanon; the psychiatrist, the ethnologist, the philosopher, and the historian. His subsequent *Toward the African Revolution*, a thinner, tighter work, is closer to his March 1959 call for a "literature of combat."[12] For here one finds Fanon performing as the Voice of the FLN, published as *El Moujahid*, a publication of Algerian anonymity. These columns constitute perhaps two-thirds of the book's total text. They are acerbic, witty, cutting, and directed to two audiences: The French Left and its intelligentsia. He prods, probes, and slices the French Left, enraging many, no doubt, while playing the contradictions between the French at home.

In *El Moujahid* of December 1957, Fanon sends searing prose to Parisians who support the state's tortures and terrors against the Algerian nationalists. Fanon writes:

From 1956 onward the Algerian war was accepted by the nation. France wants the war, as Mr. Guy Mollet and Mr. Bourgés-Maunoury have explicitly stated; and the people of Paris, on July 14th, 1957, conveyed to Massu's parachutist torturers the country's deep gratitude. The liberals abandoned the struggle at this stage. The accusation of treason to which the adversaries of the Algerian war exposed themselves became a formidable weapon in the hands of the French government. Thus in early 1957, many

---

11   See Fanon, *The Wretched of the Earth*, 39: "...black radicals in the U.S. have formed armed militia groups."

12   Jean Khalfa and Robert J.C. Young (eds.), *Frantz Fanon: Alienation and Freedom*, trans. Steven Corcoran. (London: Bloomsbury Academic, 2018), 781.

democrats ceased their protests or were overwhelmed by the clamor for vengeance, and a clumsily constructed elementary patriotism manifest-ed itself, steeped in racism – violent, totalitarian, in short, fascist.

The French government was to find its second argument in what is called terrorism. Bombs in Algiers have been exploited by the propaganda ser-vice. Innocent children who got hurt, who did not answer to the name of Borgeaud or who did not fit the classic definition of the "ferocious co-lonialists," created unexpected problems for French democrats. The Left was staggered: Sakamody accentuated this reaction. Ten French civilians, in this case, were killed in an ambush and the entire French Left, in a unanimous outburst, cried out: we can no longer follow you! The pro-paganda became orchestrated, wormed its way into people's minds and dismantled convictions that were already crumbling. The concept of bar-barism appeared and it was decided that France in Algeria was fighting barbarism.[13]

Fanon, speaking anonymously in *El Moujahid*, the official voice of the FLN, was stirring the pot, and dividing the ostensible Left of French polity to decide where it stood on the Algeria question. The choice wasn't Right/Left; it was actually pro-or-anti-colonialism, placed in sharp, clear focus.

Although Fanon isn't generally seen or remembered as a journalist (colum-nist), he played that role for years on behalf of the FLN. As journalists for the rebels, his job was to provoke, antagonize, and play the contradictions.

Fanon, in both *The Wretched of the Earth* and *Toward the African Revolution*, especially when writing for the FLN, spoke in the voices of the oppressed – either as an Arab or an Algerian. He expressed this clearly, by literally saying "we Arabs" and/or "We Algerians." His commitment to the revolution, and to the liberation movement was total and all-encompassing. And just as his writ-ing was uncompromising, so too was his activities on behalf of the FLN.

Fanon was an active revolutionary. He carried arms to FLN safe-houses. His chapter entitled "This Africa to Come," covers his efforts to send arms to the Provisional Government of the Republic of Algeria (GRPA).[14] He sought routes to the Algerian interior, and plans for bases where Algerian troops could train their forces.

Who can doubt that Fanon was a profoundly committed revolutionary? Who can doubt that he proved invaluable to senior members of the Black Panther

---

13   Frantz Fanon, *Towards the African Revolution*, trans. Haakon Chevalier (New York: Grove Press, 1964), 78–79.

14   Ibid., 177–190.

Party? Dr. Fanon was a revolutionary, who, while no longer alive, yet taught others to see the world through his revolutionary eyes.

David F. Greenberg, who edited the 1981 anthology, *Crime and Capitalism*, wrote an article towards the end of this text which demonstrates the limits of Marxism, citing Marx himself for how theory should be handled. Writes Greenberg:

> Praxis in turn changes conditions and so reveals new information to the theorist... [it] permits theory to be modified or extended, and makes new phenomena accessible to theorizing. Theory, then, is not dogma. It does not descend to the earth from on high, or from the brow of Karl Marx. Marx himself always insisted that his ideas were not fully worked out, and they were not to be taken as unchangeable doctrine. That some of his followers have transformed Marx's writings into "Articles of Faith" is a drastic departure from his own intentions. For Marx, theory is not an unquestioned doctrine, but something that develops dialectically, in interaction with empirical knowledge.[15]

Huey P. Newton, who emerged as the BPP's principal theorist, has written similar messages in his writings, as well as spoken thus in his public appearances before media.

Fanon, brilliant, in many ways self-assured of his genius, felt fully confident in breaking with Marxist tradition. He was, without question, a man of prodigious energy and production. He was also a man driven by a liberational vision: a free Algeria; a free, post-colonial Africa; a Free Africa!

He was born in the colonies, a man raised in a world awash with French language; French ideas; the ubiquity of a French Empire. France was the Mother Civilization, of completion and of reason. Her colonies were perpetual students of French Masters. For France was the teacher; the center of a global universe.

3   Fanon's Beginnings at Home

In *Toward the African Revolution*, Fanon writes about his origins in the island of Martinique, at the northern range of the Windward Islands. Its major claim to French history is that it was the birthplace of Napoleon's first wife, Empress

---

15   David F. Greenberg, ed., *Crime and Capitalism: Readings in Marxist Criminology*. (Palo Alto, CA: Mayfield Publishing Co., 1981), 485.

Josephine. Its population is primarily descendants of African slaves. To be Martiniquais was to be a Negro, but what was that? It was a people opposed to the Africans, the Senegalese, the Ghanaians, and the like. Fanon writes:

> At every level of West Indian society an inescapable feeling of superiority over the African develops, becomes systematic, hardens. In every West Indian, before the war of 1939, there was not only the certainty of a superiority over the African, but the certainty of a fundamental difference. *The African was a Negro and the West Indian a European.*[16]

What was this war of 1939? How could a Black people consider themselves European? The war was, of course, the opening of World War II, when France suffered Nazi occupation and the rise of Vichy-France, servants of Nazi power. That breaking, that shattering of the power of the French empire was also the time of the shattering of colonial worship of France, and the opening of new possibilities of freedom for those under French suzerainty.

For Fanon, the fall of free France was conterminous with the rise of Black consciousness in Martinique, in the person of one of Fanon's teachers at the lycée: Monsieur Amié Césaire, then a 27-year-old who was considered quite mad by Martiniquais for his proud embrace of his dark skin, its African origin, and a doctrine he espoused: négritude. Fanon was in his 15th year of life. He would later write:

> The downfall of France, for the West Indian, was in a sense the murder of the father. This national defeat might have been endured as it was in the metropolis, but a good part of the French fleet remained blockaded in the West Indies during the four years of the German occupation.[17]

These lessons, learned in one's youth, were also lights of learning for national liberationists and anti-colonial thinkers the world over, for it showed chinks in the imperial armor. French capitulation to Hitler's *Wehrmacht,* and British cities under the whim of Germany's *Luftwaffe,* all demonstrated the limits of European imperial power.

Fanon wasn't born a revolutionary. He wasn't born a Marxist. He wasn't born African. He wasn't born an anti-colonialist. He was born into a middling family in Fort-de-France, capital of Martinique, at 33 Rue de la République. He was

---

16   Fanon, *Toward the African Revolution,* 20. Emphasis added.
17   Ibid., 22.

born in a world where people considered themselves either West Indians, or Martiniquais, living in an overseas department of the French République.

As a teenager, his exposure to an extraordinary teacher, "an educated man, a man with a diploma," forced him to rethink a great many things – especially his dark complexion – and the place of people in a new Black world.[18] He was moved by his life experiences there, and after he moved to France to new vistas of what it meant to be alive and conscious during those times.

Surely, the utter defeat of France by Nazi forces was an awakening experience. Similarly, the weakening of empires in the ashes of the Second World War brought light to the world of colonials the world over, not merely of France, but of Britain as well. Egyptians saw Britain stumble; Senegalese saw Paris fall, and this, after colonials served in the defense of their colonial masters.

As Fanon demonstrates with his underground life as a revolutionary, that some lessons are never forgotten.

While not explanative, it is of interest to note that another revolutionary leader, Malcolm X, was born in the same year that Fanon was born: 1925. This speaks of the zeitgeist of the times, of Black self-assertion, Black consciousness, and Black resistance and pride. Beyond that, of course, is what people actually see in their lives and personal experience. For Fanon, the world changed when the knees of France buckled to greater power. For Newton and Seale, they had to experience similar insights when the United States fell to little, Asian Vietnam. That said, Vietnam had an even greater impact when the empire's troops were bested by Vietnamese guerillas at Dien Bien Phu in 1954, another marker of the limits of Empire. For African Americans, Vietnam was a rite of passage, for many Panthers (like the late Geronimo Ji-Jiaga Pratt, LA Chapter) fought in Vietnam for the US empire.

A small, Asian country wasn't supposed to beat France, much less the world's most prominent superpower, the USA. But this was a time of ferment, of revolutionary states taking power. This was an Age of Revolution.

As the Algerian War split France in twain, so too did the Vietnam War split the American state. Friendships, business relationships, and even marriages were cut apart because of the rigors of war, and how people fell on one side or the other of these conflicts. And the mind-numbing spectacle of loss seeped into the political culture, changing society in fundamental ways.

That's why, over a generation after Vietnam, the American President George H.W. Bush, found it necessary to exclaim, "We've finally whipped that Vietnam Syndrome!" (or words to that effect). That exclamation, coming after the 1st

---

18   Ibid., 21.

Gulf War in Iraq, gives us some sense of the power of the Vietnam years after its passage into national memory and imperial psychosis.

The incidence, of course, wasn't the same between Fanon and his philosophical descendants. For what Fanon saw as a teen differed considerably from what the adults Newton and Seale saw in their mature years. Fanon saw the world change in 1939, the first days of the World War II. Newton and Seale and the first Panther generation saw Vietnam emerge victorious in 1973, when the U.S. departed from Indochina. The U.S. suffered a profound, historical defeat. France suffered at least two such defeats, for Algeria's victory was followed by France's defeat in Vietnam. For both the empires and those held in its claws, the world had changed.

What kind of man was Frantz Fanon? A proud one.

In his works are the drops of blood of his life. There, in each line, are his revolutionary rage and fury. But there are other things beside this. There is indignity, angered responses to ignorance, and a fierce hunger for justice against the injustice that he grew up in, and that he imbibed in the imperial air. This, we must recognize, was fueling him in his earlier, pre-revolutionary life, spawned by dreams of a Free France.

When he was but a youth, around seventeen years old, he escaped from Martinique, traveled to nearby Dominica, and joined the Free France forces. Meanwhile, back at home, Martinique was led by French Admiral Georges Robert. The admiral announced his support for the Vichy government and its head, H. Philippe Pétain. He declared an armistice with Germany, and his government ran the country's affairs from 1940 to 1944.

After Germany lost the war in 1944, a Provisional Government led by Charles de Gaulle took power, both in France and in her colonies. Fanon repatriated back to Martinique from Dominica, and, against his family's wishes, formally joined the Free France forces. He was young, true, but how could the man now known as one of the world's greatest revolutionaries act so French? The answer is actually quite simple. For at that time, in the bloom of his youth, he *was* French – French in language, French in orientation, French in worldview.

For this Free France (while not actually free for millions in its Asian, African, and Caribbean colonies), was anti-Nazi, and profoundly pro-French in independence. So, in many ways, these sons and daughters of French culture responded to France's needs. Fanon was one among millions. It is also true that he had not yet become the Fanon we have come to know, for his greatest works were yet to come. That Fanon was beginning to study in Medical school in Paris.

While in the Free French forces, he was deployed to Casablanca (*al-dār al-bayḍā'* in Arabic), in Morocco. Was it there that he really saw the rigors of colonialism among Arab populations? Was it there that the seeds of becoming Fanon were being planted in the soul? It is said that travelers see deeper into foreign societies than those who were born there, for the traveler asks questions that natives rarely notice.

We know, reading his works, that Paris is where he heard a child passing by in the City of Lights to watch out for the nigger, referring to Fanon. We know, reading of him by those in his orbit, that such events did not stand alone. When he was named Chief Doctor of the Blida-Joinville Psychiatric Hospital in Algeria, his French colleagues there reportedly called him "Médicin Negre" (Dr. Nigger). As he would later write in *The Wretched of the Earth*, many of his psychiatric colleagues assisted the security forces in the torture of Algerians.[19]

Fanon, the man who penned *The Wretched of the Earth* and *Toward the African Revolution* writes with identification with the Arabs of colonized societies, and Africans of Black Africa. They are not "they"; "they" are "we." His fierce intellect, his searing critiques of his writings, were for the oppressed: *Les damnes de la terre*.

How do we interpret that young lad who joined the Free French Forces in comparison with the man who helped oust the French from North Africa? That man concentrated on freedom – not France. Also that young man experienced something that millions did during the mid-20th century: when you know more, you grow up. Fanon grew up. He grew into an inspiration to people around the world, yearning for freedom from oppression, tyranny, and colonialism.

4   Fanon: the Philosophy of Revolutionary Violence

Frantz Fanon entered his service as a psychiatrist (and chief doctor) at the psychiatric facility at Bilda-Joinville in November 1953. A year later, the anti-colonial war began between the FLN and the French colonial government. By early 1955, Fanon makes his first contact with the FLN, and soon functioned in a public role by appearing at an FLN press conference circa 1957. In late January 1957, Fanon is expelled from Algeria. He returns to Paris, and then travels to Tunis. There he opens a day clinic for psychiatric patients.

As a psychiatrist at a hospital during the war, he became intimate with the violence of the state against suspected insurgents and their families. His case studies, excerpted in *The Wretched of the Earth*, reveal the psychological damage suffered by militants who had been tortured or whose families were tortured by state colonial police. In Section 5 of the text, "Colonial War and

---

19   Fanon, *The Wretched of the Earth*, 213.

Mental Disorders," Fanon makes note of a series of cases, for example, of an FLN supporter who avoided detection and escaped arrest. Fanon writes:

Case No. 1 – Impotence in an Algerian following the rape of his wife.
B----- is a twenty-six-year-old man. He has been referred to us by the Medical Services of the National Liberation Front for persistent migraines and insomnia. A former taxi driver, he has been a militant in the nationalist parties since the age of eighteen. In 1955, he became a member of an FLN (Front de Libération Nationale) unit. On several occasions he used his taxi to carry propaganda leaflets and political leaders. Confronted with a widening crackdown, the FLN decided to wage war in the urban centers. B----- was then assigned to driving commandos close to the point of attack, and fairly often having to wait for them.

One day, however, right in the middle of the European sector, following a fairly extensive commando raid, the sector was sealed off, forcing him to abandon his taxi and compelling the commando unit to break up and disperse. B-----, who managed to escape the enemy's surveillance, took refuge in a friend's house, and a few days later, on orders from his superiors, went underground to join the nearest resistance unit without ever going home.

For several months he went without news of his wife and his twenty-month-old daughter. He did learn, however, that the police had been looking for him for weeks in the city. After two years in the resistance movement he received a message from his wife asking him to forget her. She had brought shame on herself. He must no longer think of coming back to live with her. Extremely worried, he requested permission from his commander to make a secret trip back home. It was refused. However, steps were taken for a member of the FLN to contact B-----'s wife and parents.

Two weeks later a detailed report reached the commander of B-----'s unit. Soon after his abandoned taxi had been discovered (with two machine gun magazines inside) a group of French soldiers and policemen had gone to his home. Finding him absent, they took away his wife and kept her for over a week.

She was interrogated about the company her husband kept and slapped fairly violently for two days. On the third day a French soldier – she was unable to say whether he was an officer – he ordered the others out and raped her. Shortly thereafter a second solider, this time in this presence of the others, raped her, telling her: "If you ever see that bastard your husband again, don't forget to tell him what we did to you." She remained another week without undergoing further interrogation. She was then escorted home.[20]

This insidious picture of colonialist violence show that it was collective, and not individual, designed to destroy Algerian families and consciousness. Fanon's case study subject suffered profound depression, disassociation from the liberation movement, and associated his wife and daughter with rotting meat. He experienced anorexia and insomnia. When he tried to initiate sexual relations with other women, he repeatedly failed. The state, by raping his wife, severely damaged his psyche, and his familial relations.

The French colonial forces were not shy about wreaking violence against the Algerian people. They raided and wiped out whole villages, or, on occasion, took the men from villages and massacred them. For their objective wasn't just to kill, but to terrorize communities, by crippling them into psychological paralysis. Fanon, the psychiatrist, reasoned that only counter-violence, which increased the cost of administering the colony, would convince them that the costs were too high.

Fanon peppers his prose with massacres throughout Algerian history, especially predating the emergence of the FLN. Sétif. Kenya. Korea. His is a geography of imperialism, the unchecked, uncondemned mega-violence of imperial states, designed to open the road to the inevitable economic exploitation of colonized territories and peoples. Given these realities, who can seriously question his observation: "between oppressors and the oppressed, force is the only solution."[21]

In *The Wretched of the Earth,* Fanon offers succinct equations of power, always in the context of the colonized vis-à-vis the colonizer, arguing: "Violence among the colonized will spread in proportion to the violence exerted by the colonial regime."[22] For, once national consciousness emerges in a colonized people, it begins to create space to oppose, reject, and expel the foreign colonial power. This consciousness fuels the core of resistance, and heightens the contradiction between the colonized and the colonizer.

It is henceforth only a matter of time before that resistance becomes martial, explosive and of a military nature. In his early chapter, "Grandeur and Weakness of Spontaneity," Fanon turns to the rural masses, who remember

20   Fanon, *The Wretched of the Earth*, 185–186.
21   Ibid., 32.
22   Ibid., 46–47.

the precolonial times, when heroes and heroines of the tribe stood against the foreign threats. Their spontaneous attacks are energizing and enervating – that is, of course, until the state evokes its monstrous repression.

Political parties emerge, but they do little more than produce verbiage which fails to energize rural peoples. An anti-colonial paramilitary force comes into being, and in the name of the People, the new Nation, battles against the colonial foreign power. What Fanon demonstrates, in his best-known texts, is the inherent violence of the imperialist forces, which begins, sustains, and ends in exploitation over the colonized. That violence gives rise to responsive, liberational violence, which gives shape and meaning of the new State power being born.

In his opening chapter, Fanon cites the deep yearning of the colonized to literally replace the colonizer by seizing his space. This is done, of course, through violence, Fanon noted:

> The colonized subject thus discovers that his life, his breathing and his heartbeats are the same as the colonist's. He discovers that the skin of the colonist is not worth more than the "native's." In other words, his world receives a fundamental jolt. The colonized's revolutionary new assurance stems from this. If, in fact, my life is worth as much as the colonist's, his look can no longer strike fear into me or nail me to the spot and his voice can no longer petrify me. I am now no longer uneasy in his presence. In reality, to hell with him. Not only does his presence no longer bother me, but I am already preparing to waylay him in such a way that soon he will have no other solution but to flee.[23]

Dr. Fanon has been the subject of considerable critique for his unabashed support – and yes, violent support – of the decolonization project. Many of his critics condemn his philosophical positions, while accepting colonization itself, as if this development is a natural social function. As Fanon explains, colonization is a violent phenomenon from its very inception,

> Decolonization, we know, is an historical process: In other words, it can only be understood, it can only find its significance and become self-coherent insofar as we can discern the history-making movement which gives it form and substance. Decolonization is the encounter between two congenitally antagonistic forces that in fact owe their singularity to the kind of reification secreted and nurtured by the colonial situation. Their first confrontation was colored by violence and their cohabitation – or

---

23   Ibid., 10.

rather the exploitation of the colonized by the colonizer – continued at the point of the bayonet and under cannon fire. The colonist and the colonized are old acquaintances. And consequently, the colonist is right when he says he "knows" them. It is the colonist who *fabricated* and *continues to fabricate* the colonized subject. The colonist derives his validity, i.e., his wealth, from the colonial system.[24]

Colonialism, then, is the opening salvo of an economic attack on the soon-to-be colonized population, one begun in violence, and from which one can only truly escape by way of revolutionary, redemptive violence. This view, which is but a logical statement no less unremarkable than the simple call for self-defense, only sparks apprehension because it condemns the violence of colonialism, imperialism, and capitalism.

Terms like "colonialism" and "imperialism" are not commonly used in American daily newspapers or in the corporate media. Similar, the writings of Fanon, while undoubtedly familiar to radical and revolutionary readerships, are not commonly exposed to regular audiences. These are sad but true realities which limit deep exposure to communities which may find value and clarity if the opportunity was given to widen such exposures.

Fanon, in the first page of his first chapter of *The Wretched of the Earth*, defines his target with clinical precision. He writes of the foreigners who have come to Algiers from afar to build a system of economic exploitation and racist domination. He calls them, *Colons*, a French word derived from Latin, meaning settler, farmer, or plantation owner. It is the root of the term colonialism, a system of control over others.

For "imperialism," we humbly offer Michael Parenti's text *The Face of Imperialism*, where he writes:

> Imperialism is defined as follows: The process whereby the dominant investor's interests in one country bring to bear military and financial power upon another country in order to expropriate land, labor, capital, natural resources, commerce and markets of that other country.[25]

Beneath these benign-sounding terms lies the reality of their operation, with all of its intensity and violence. Beneath these words live the global impacts of repression.

---

24   Ibid. 2.
25   Michael Parenti, *The Face of Imperialism* (Boulder, CO: Paradigm Publishers, 2011), 23.

Black Panther leader, Kathleen Neal Cleaver, has studied Fanon's text, and expressed its value to members of the Party and other Black Revolutionaries. She wrote:

> The opening sentence of *The Wretched of the Earth* said, "National libera-tion, national renaissance, the restoration of nationhood to a people... whatever may be the headings used or the new formulas introduced, decolonization is always a violent phenomenon." Fanon's penetrating dis-section of the intertwining of racism and violence in the colonial scheme of domination was compelling to Blacks fighting in America; it provided a clearly reasoned antidote to the constant admonition to seek change peacefully. Fanon explained how violence was intrinsic to the imposition of White colonial domination, and portrayed the oppressed who violently retaliate as engaged in restoring human dignity they were stripped of by the process of colonization. His analysis of the tortured mentality of the colonized person and the therapeutic nature of fighting to destroy colo-nial domination provided radical Blacks in America with deep insights – into both their own relationship to a world-wide revolution underway and to the profound kinship between their status in America and that of colonized people outside America.[26]

Members and officers of the Black Panther Party read Malcolm X, Mau Tse Tung, Ernesto "Che" Guevara, Kwame Nkrumah, Mikhail Bakhunin, Robert E. Williams, and, of course, Frantz Fanon. Some advanced cadre read Karl Marx, or V.I. Lenin, but neither were required. For many Panthers, however, we read to understand the dimensions of a world in transformation, and to succeed in our tasks. *The Wretched of the Earth* taught many of us what was possible in [North] Africa, and what a man with a will could accomplish.

Many years after the Party's demise, ex-Panthers, in personal/political dis-cussions, would bring up quotes remembered from the Party's brightest days, which still had purchase in Black hearts. Former BPP Philadelphia chapter Captain, Reggie Schell, at almost every visit with the writer, would unfailingly quote Fanon's dictum on the task for youth in an oppressed colony: "Each gen-eration must discover its mission, fulfill it or betray it..."[27]

That kind of staying power in consciousness speaks about the significance of *The Wretched of the Earth,* and what it means as elders of the Black Revolu-tion still utilize Fanon to interpret the present.

---

26   Cleaver, "Back to Africa," 214.
27   Fanon, *The Wretched of the Earth*, 145.

5   Conclusion

We began this project by examining the Fanonist theory of lumpenism as a tool of revolutionary, anti-colonial sparks of resistance. BPP co-founder, Huey Newton, in the latter years of the Party, would critique that decision as well as other early strains of the organization. Much of this critique arose from his disenchantment with Eldridge Cleaver, whom he believed had too much influence over the membership.

In a 1971 article entitled "On the Relevance of the Church," Newton wrote the following:

> The Black Panther Party was formed because we wanted to oppose the evil in our community. Some of the members in the Party were not refined – we were grasping for organization. It wasn't a college campus organization; it was basically an organization of the grassroots, and anytime we organize the most victimized of the victims we run into a problem. To have a Party or a church or any kind of institution, whether we like it or not, we have to have administrators. How an institution, organization, or the Party in this case, functions, as well as how effective it is, depends upon how knowledgeable and advanced in thinking the administrators are. We attempt to apply the administrative skills of our grassroots organization to the problems that are most frequently heard in the community.
>
> History shows that most of the parties that have led people out of their difficulties have had administrators with what we sometimes call the traits of the bourgeoisie or declassed intellectuals. They are the people who have gone through the established institutions, rejected them, and then applied their skills to the community. In applying them to the community, their skills are no longer bourgeoisie skills but people's skills, which are transformed through the contradiction of applying what is usually bourgeoisie to the oppressed. That itself is a kind of transformation.
>
> In our Party we are not so blessed. History does not repeat itself; it goes on also transforming itself through the dialectical process. We see that the administrators of our Party are victims who have not received that bourgeois training. So I will not apologize for our mistakes, our lack of a scientific approach to use and put into practice. It was a matter of not knowing, of learning, but also of starting out with a loss – a disadvantage that history has seldom seen. That is, a group attempting to influence and

change the society so much while its own administrators were as much in the dark much of the time as the people that they were trying to change.[28]

Dr. Huey P. Newton, a man not given to apologies, felt that one was necessary to the community's religious persons.

Dr. Frantz Fanon and Dr. Huey P. Newton could hardly appear more dissimilar. The former was, above all things, the quintessential student: born to study, born to learn. The latter, however, began his political life as a petty criminal, a thief, and perhaps surprisingly, an illiterate. Fanon grew up in a middle class home, in his country's capital. He attended the finest schools and attained a diplomate in medicine, specializing in psychiatry. Newton was a diffident student, who taught himself to read after he reached 10th grade. Yet, beyond their externalities, both men were from the periphery of their nations, for Fanon dwelled in an overseas territory, while Newton was raised in a Black American ghetto. Fanon would acquire his doctorate in medicine as a relatively young man. Newton would acquire his doctorate in philosophy while middle aged, and after a lifetime of leading the Black Panther Party.

Both men would have a revolutionary impact far beyond the land of their birth.
Both men inspired those around them by their own deep commitment to revolution.
Both were Black revolutionaries.
Both will long be remembered for their dedication to Freedom.

Bibliography

Cleaver, Kathleen Neal. "Back to Africa: The Evolution of the International Section of the Black Panther Party (1969–1970)." In *The Black Panther Party Reconsidered.* Edited by Charles E. Jones, 211–254. Baltimore, MD: Black Classic Press, 1998.

Cone, James. *Martin and Malcolm and America: A Dream or a Nightmare.* New York: Orbis Books, 1991.

Fanon, Frantz. *The Wretched of the Earth.* Translated by Richard Philcox. New York: Grove Press, 1963/2004.

Fanon, Frantz. *Toward the African Revolution.* Translated by Haakon Chevalier. New York: Grove Press, 1964.

---

28   Huey P. Newton, *The Huey P. Newton Reader,* ed. David Hilliard and Donald Weise (New York: Seven Stories Press, 2002), 216–217.

Greenberg, David F., ed. *Crime and Capitalism: Readings in Marxist Criminology.* Palo Alto, CA: Mayfield Publishing Co., 1981.

Khalfa, Jean and Robert J.C. Young, eds. *Frantz Fanon: Alienation and Freedom.* Translated by Steven Corcoran. London: Bloomsbury Academic, 2018.

Mao TseTung. *Quotations from Chairman Mao TseTung.* Paking: Foreign Language Press, 1972.

Newton, Huey P. *The Huey P. Newton Reader.* Edited by David Hilliard and Donald Weise. New York: Seven Stories Press, 2002.

Parenti, Michael. *The Face of Imperialism.* Boulder, CO: Paradigm Publishers, 2011.

Seale, Bobby. *Seize the Time: The Story of the Black Panther Party and Huey P. Newton.* New York: Vintage Books, 1970.

CHAPTER 2

Alatas, Fanon, and Coloniality

Syed Farid Alatas

1   Introduction

This chapter looks at coloniality through the works of Frantz Fanon and Syed Hussein Alatas. Both recognized the physically and discursively violent nature of colonialism, the impact that colonialism had on the colonized, and the debilitating effect it had on the possibilities for liberation, even after formal independence. The writings of Fanon and Alatas complement each other and together provide an approach towards understanding the continuing coloniality in the so-called "post-colonial" world. Both Alatas and Fanon would say that colonialism is not merely an order of the past, but rather persists today through mimesis and mental captivity. Heightened consciousness of this problem is necessary for a more liberated or autonomous mind.

The chapter proceeds as follows: First we will discuss the specific context of coloniality that Alatas and Fanon were speaking in, namely, colonial capitalism. Reading the two of them brings us to the themes of alienation and racism as central features of colonialism. This is followed by a discussion of the post-colonial situation, which is ironically characterized by a continued coloniality. This section elaborates on the nature of a sustained coloniality in the post-colonial era with specific attention paid to Fanon's indictment of the irrelevance of intellectuals and Alatas' notion of the captive mind. This section discusses the phenomenon of the native's internalization of the colonizers' view of the colonized that defines the cultural and intellectual life in so-called post-colonial societies. This then leads to a discussion in the subsequent section on the "rule of the fool," which can be understood in the context of the absence of the intellectual. The final section concludes with some thoughts on the implications of Alatas' and Fanon's views concerning the tasks of native intellectuals in confronting coloniality.

2   The Context of Colonial Capitalism

The formative period of the thought of Syed Hussein Alatas and Frantz Fanon was European colonialism. For Alatas, the context was above all British Malaya and the Dutch East Indies, while for Fanon it was French Algeria. The nature of these societies can be captured through the concept of "colonial capitalism," an idea which was discussed by Alatas in his demystifying and deconstructing work, *The Myth of the Lazy Native*.[1] Here, we find that the work of Alatas and Fanon complement each other. While Alatas conceptualizes colonial society in terms of colonial capitalism, Fanon is interested in understanding the condition of coloniality in what Alatas would understand as colonial capitalist society. For Alatas, certain European ideas pertaining to the natives functioned as constituent parts of colonial ideology to advance the interests of colonial capitalism. For Fanon, such European ideas formed the basis for what he called the "double alienation of the native." Both were concerned with the nature and perniciousness of colonial depictions and images of the native and how these images affected the colonized to the point of being internalized by them.

Capitalism, as defined by Alatas, takes into account its historically contingent aspects, which are distinguished from capitalism's universal features. The Western-bound concept of historical capitalism may include free wage labor as a determinate feature, but 19th century Dutch capitalism in Java was not founded on free labor.[2] An understanding of colonial capitalism cannot simply be derived from European history. For example, free labor was a historical trait of capitalism, not a universal feature, and was specific to a certain period of European history. The historical configuration of capitalism in the colonies differed from that in Europe and warrants the reference to colonial capitalism.[3]

Colonial capitalism itself was characterized by a number of features including the control of and access to capital by an alien power, highest levels of trade and industry dominated by an alien community, a bias towards agrarian production as opposed to industry, production around semi-free labor, minimal scientific and technological expansion, and a set of antitheses in the colonized society that can be best described by the term "dualism."[4]

---

1   Syed Hussein Alatas, *The Myth of the Lazy Native: A Study of the Image of the Malays, Filipinos and Javanese from the 16th to the 20th century and its Function in the Ideology of Colonial Capitalism* (London: Frank Cass, 1977).

2   Ibid., 4–5.

3   Ibid., 5.

4   Ibid., 2. The term dualism was in reference to the Dutch economist, J.H. Boeke's notion of "dualistic economics." For Boeke, capitalism did not have the same impact in the colonies as it did in the West. The destruction of social and economic institutions by capitalism in the colonies forced the native population to fall back on small-scale farming. Native production, trade, and system of distribution were destroyed to make way for Western industries. See J.H. Boeke, "Dualistic Economics," in *Indonesian Economics* (The Hague: W. van Hoeve, 1961), 172, cited in Alatas, *The Myth of the Lazy Native*, 31–32, n5.

The ideology of colonial capitalism emerged to justify Western rule or the interests of colonial capitalism. A central feature of this ideology was the denigration of the natives and their history. They were held to be unintelligent, lazy, evil, and unfit to rule.[5] It was the victims of colonial rule who were blamed rather than the colonial masters, the exploiters. The ideologues of colonial rule, that is, colonial administrators and scholars, made no mention of injustices and atrocities committed by the Europeans against the natives or other non-Europeans. This was done in the name of dispassionate, objective scholarship.[6] Neither did they consider that the ostensible laziness of the native was actually a conscious sabotage on his part against colonialism. As Fanon put it:

> How many times – in Paris, in Aix, in Algiers, or in Basse-Terre – have we not heard men from the colonized countries violently protesting against the pretended laziness of the black man, of the Algerian, and of the Viet-Namese? And yet is it not the simple truth that under the colonial regime a *fellah* who is keen on his work or a Negro who refuses to rest are nothing but pathological cases? The native's laziness is the conscious sabotage of the colonial machine; on the biological plane it is a remarkable system of auto-protection; and in any case it is a sure brake upon the seizure of the whole country by the occupying power.[7]

As noted by Said in his discussion on *The Myth of the Lazy Native*, Alatas details how colonialism created an object, that is, the lazy native.[8] The purpose of the colonial image of the lazy native was to maintain the natives in an intellectual and moral state that left them inferior to the Europeans, although their numbers were far greater.[9]

Concomitant with the colonial discourse on the lazy native was their subjection to "[g]ambling, opium, inhuman labor conditions, one-sided legislation, acquisition of tenancy rights belonging to the people, [and] forced labor..." all of which were part of the fabric of colonial ideology.[10] While subjected to all kinds of human degradation, the natives were also labelled as ingrates when they critiqued the colonizer, as pointed out by Fanon.[11]

---

5   Alatas, *The Myth of the Lazy Native*, 8, 10–11.

6   Ibid., 12.

7   Frantz Fanon, *The Wretched of the Earth*, trans. C. Farrington (London: MacGibbon & Kee, 1965), 294.

8   Edward Said, *Culture and Imperialism* (New York: Vintage, 1993), 296.

9   Alatas, *The Myth of the Lazy Native*, 56.

10 Ibid., 96.

11 Frantz Fanon, *Black Skin, White Masks*, trans. Charles Lam Markmann (New York: Grove Press, 1967), 35.

As Said put it, "the myth of the lazy native is synonymous with domination, and domination is at bottom power."[12] Said perceptibly notes that Alatas' work did not merely focus on the discursive effect of power but revealed its total and devastating consequences.[13] As Alatas noted, taking the example of the Dutch East Indies:

> Power falling into Dutch hands was different from power falling into the hands of an indigenous successor. An indigenous power was generally more liberal in trade. It did not destroy its own trading class throughout the whole area, and continued to use the products of its own industry. It built its own boats and last but not least was incapable of imposing a monopoly throughout the major part of Indonesia. It promoted the abilities of its own people even though a tyrant was on the throne.[14]

In Alatas' description of colonial ideology, he cites Fanon:

> Native society is not simply described as a society lacking in values. It is not enough for the colonist to affirm that those values have disappeared from, or still better never existed in, the colonial world. The native is declared insensible to ethics; he represents not only the absence of values, but also the negation of values. He is, let us dare to admit, the enemy of values, and in this sense, he is the absolute evil. He is the corrosive element, destroying all that comes near him; he is the deforming element, disfiguring all that has to do with beauty or morality; he is the depository of maleficent powers, the unconscious and irretrievable instrument of blind forces.[15]

In *Black Skin, White Masks*, Fanon says that his analysis is psychological. In fact, his discussion on the psychology of the colonized complements Alatas' critique of colonial ideology. Whereas Alatas focused on the nature of colonial ideology and its function in advancing the interests of capital, Fanon was interested in the development of an inferiority complex among the colonized. Fanon speaks of alienated or duped blacks. He refers to the Negro professional as intellectually alienated when he "conceives of European culture as a means

---

12   Said, *Culture and Imperialism*, 307.
13   Ibid., 307–308.
14   Alatas, *The Myth of the Lazy Native*, 200.
15   Fanon, *The Wretched of the Earth*, 33–34. Cited in Alatas, *The Myth of the Lazy Native*, 24.

of stripping himself of his race...".[16] Dis-alienating the black man requires the recognition of the social and economic realities that created the alienation as well as the process by which he internalizes a sense of inferiority. In other words, the inferiority is the outcome of a double process.[17] Subsequently, the black man has to wage a war at both the psychological and material levels.[18] As Fanon says, the inferiority complex had been created in colonized people by the death and burial of their original local cultural and their being confronted by the culture of the colonizers. The colonized individual is subsequently elevated above his savage status in proportion to the degree to which he adopts the colonizers cultural standards.[19] These standards are sometimes literally applied. Fanon refers to the "black man who wants to turn his race white..."[20] This has been referred to as lactification:

> Lactification, making skin look lighter and acting 'more like the white man' is the desire for whiteness at the EXPENSE of blackness. (The) inferiority complex is created by colonizers to place people in positions of degradation and reinforced to make people believe that they are inferior to their colonizers (their 'superiors') and becomes intra-psychic: internalized inferiority. Deliverance comes through admiring whiteness and 'all things good that come with being white.'[21]

Fanon also notes that "[i]t is not possible to enslave men without logically making them inferior through and through. And racism is only the emotional, affective, sometimes intellectual explanation of this inferiorization."[22] The native admits his misfortunes; his inferiority is the direct result of his cultural and racial characteristics.[23] He is intellectually and culturally alienated. Part of the experience of alienation is a pejorative judgement of the native toward the self. Drawing lessons from psychoanalysis, Fanon describes the symptoms

---

16   Fanon, *Blacks Skin, White Masks*, 29, 223–224.
17   Ibid., 12–13.
18   Ibid., 13–14.
19   Ibid., 18.
20   Ibid., 10–11.
21   Arnold Itwaru, "Caribbean Studies Lecture on Psychic Torture," 17 October 2011. Cited in Susan Enberg, The "Epidermalization of Inferiority and the Lactification of Consciousness," 2011. <https://www.researchgate.net/publication/281902045_The_Epidermalization_of_Inferiority_and_the_Lactification_of_Consciousness>. Accessed 20 June 2018.
22   Frantz Fanon, *Towards the African Revolution: Political Essays*, trans. Haakon Chevalier (New York: Grove Press, 1964), 40.
23   Ibid., 38.

of the inferiorization of the Negro as anguish, aggression and the devaluation of self, that is, the symptomatology of neurosis.[24]

The European image of the native was founded on colonial racism. The general incapacities associated with the natives were explained in racist terms. Alatas noted that while capitalism in Europe undermined and eventually overcame the forces of feudalism, in the colonies, colonial capitalism preserved aspects of the feudal order, underlying it with racism. A race dominated status system was created.[25] This reflected the derogatory views the Europeans had of the natives. For example, British colonial officers such as Thomas Stamford Raffles and John Crawfurd regard the Malays as being rude and uncivilized in character, of feeble intellect, and at a low stage of intellectual development, indolent, submissive, and prone to piracy. Furthermore, much of their backwardness and negative traits were blamed on the religion of Islam.[26] European civilization and its best representatives, not just the petty officials, small traders, adventurers and politicians, were responsible for colonial racism.[27]

For Alatas, the internalization of the European image of the native by the natives themselves and the concomitant development of an inferiority complex among them is a vital consequence of colonial rule and a key feature of the post-colonial condition. This internalization began in the colonial period.

> In discussing the image which the indigenous people had of themselves we must bear in mind that some 20th century converts to this aspect of the colonial ideology are present among the indigenous people. An ideology is never confined to its originating group. It is also shared by those who are dominated by the system of which the ideology is the rationalization. During the time when slavery was current there were many slaves who believed in it. They shared the false consciousness inherent in the ideology.[28]

In the post-colonial period, it becomes a condition of coloniality without colonialism. There is only one destiny for the black man. He wants to be like the white man. He has long admitted "the unarguable superiority of the white man, and all his efforts are aimed at achieving a white existence."[29]

---

24   Fanon, *Black Skin, White Masks*, 73.
25   Alatas, *The Myth of the Lazy Native*, 18.
26   Ibid., 38–41.
27   Fanon, *Black Skin, White Masks*, 90–91.
28   Alatas, *The Myth of the Lazy Native*, 132.
29   Fanon, *Black Skin, White Masks*, 11, 63, 228.

Fanon and Alatas highlighted how colonialism sought to control the colonized by devaluing their history and distorting their past. Fanon says:

> Perhaps we have not sufficiently demonstrated that colonialism is not simply content to impose its rule upon the present and the future of a dominated country. Colonialism is not satisfied merely with hiding a people in its grip and emptying the native's brain of all form and content. By a kind of perverted logic, it turns to the past of the oppressed people, and distorts, disfigures and destroys it. This work of devaluing pre-colonial history takes on a dialectical significance today.[30]

Complementing the above, Alatas says:

> One need not be a Marxist to recognize that a dominant ruling elite upholding a definite social, economic and political order will utilize all channels of influencing thought and behaviour to impart its ideology to the minds of the people. The higher seats of learning, the press, the church, the party, the school, the books, all have been used for this purpose. The vigorous outburst of colonialism in the 19th century was accompanied by intellectual trends which sought to justify the phenomenon. Colonialism, or on a bigger scale, imperialism, was not only an extension of sovereignty and control by one nation and its government over another, but it was also a control of the mind of the conquered or subordinated.[31]

This is the ideological context in which the black man has been prepared and conditioned to "rule."

3   The Coloniality of the Post-colonial

It is this ideological configuration that the native was allowed to be master by the white man: "The Negro is a slave who has been allowed to assume the attitude of a master. The white man is a master who has allowed his slaves to eat at his table."[32] For his part, the native intellectual frantically assimilates the culture of the colonized and enthusiastically criticizes his own national culture.[33]

---

30   Fanon, *The Wretched of the Earth*, 210.
31   Alatas, *The Myth of the Lazy Native*, 17.
32   Fanon, *Black Skin, White Masks*, 219.
33   Fanon, *The Wretched of the Earth*, 236–237.

As mentioned above, for Alatas, the internalization of the European image of the native and the inculcation of an inferiority complex among the natives are defining features of post-colonial societies and suggest the continuing co-loniality of the post-colonial world. The impact of colonial rule was such that it reproduced its false consciousness among the Malay elite that assumed con-trol of the country upon independence.

> The false consciousness distorts the reality. The Malay ruling party in-herited the rule from the British without a struggle for independence such as that which took place in Indonesia, India and the Philippines. As such, there was also no ideological struggle. There was no intellectual break with British ideological thinking at the deeper level of thought. The leadership of this party were recruited from the top hierarchy of the civil service trained by the British, and middle class Malay school teach-ers and civil servants. The few professionals associated with it did not set the pattern.[34]

The native elite was manufactured by the Europeans. Promising young natives were picked out and had inculcated in them the principles of Western cul-ture. They may have had a short stay in the mother country, but they returned "whitewashed," as it were.[35]

In this context, national consciousness was an empty shell.[36] The native elite, like their former colonial masters, continued to propagate the notion of native incapacities. An example cited by Alatas is the work, *Revolusi Mental*[37] (*Mental Revolution*), authored by members of the then ruling party, the United Malay National Organization (UMNO). It was compiled by Senu Abdul Rah-man, who was at the time Secretary-General of the party as well as ex-Minister of Information and a former ambassador to Indonesia. The book details a very unflattering image of the Malays. The Malays are not honest with themselves, lack the courage to fight for the truth, consistently fail to resist against exploi-tation and oppression, adopt a fatalistic attitude, do not think rationally, are uninterested in science and technology, have no spirit of perseverance, lack frugality, are ill-disciplined, are unoriginal and unimaginative, and generally backward.[38]

---

34   Alatas, *The Myth of the Lazy Native*, 152.
35   Fanon, *The Wretched of the Earth*, 7.
36   Ibid., 148.
37   Senu Abdul Rahman, *Revolusi Mental*. Kuala Lumpur: Penerbitan Utusan Melayu, 1971.
38   Ibid., 75, 119, 158, 159, 161–162, 351. Cited in Alatas, *The Myth of the Lazy Native*, 147–148.

Although laziness as a trait is not explicitly discussed, Alatas notes that the attitude of *Revolusi Mental* to the problem is ambivalent and that it is inclined to view the Malays as lazy. The book notes that Malay farmers and fisherman are thought of as lazy but neither denies no confirms this.[39] Alatas expresses his astonishment at the fact that the book characterizes the Malays in "negative terms unexcelled in the history of colonialism. While many British colonial writers stressed the laziness of the Malays they did not strip the Malays of so many other qualities which the *Revolusi Mental* did."[40] *Revolusi Mental* is a confirmation of colonial capitalist ideology, although its intention was to assess the problems of the Malays and suggest the way towards progress.[41]

The internalization of the ideology of the colonizer, in this case, the ideology of colonial capitalism, is a reflection of the ubiquity of the captive mind. Alatas developed the idea in order to understand the nature of scholarship in the developing world, particularly in relation to Western dominance in the arts and social sciences. Alatas defines the captive mind as an "uncritical and imitative mind dominated by an external source, whose thinking is deflected from an independent perspective."[42] The external source is Western knowledge. Such uncritical imitation influences all the constituents of scientific activity such as problem-selection, conceptualization, analysis, generalization, description, explanation and interpretation.[43] Among the traits of the captive mind are the inability to be creative and raise original problems, the inability to devise original analytical methods, and alienation from the main issues of indigenous society. The captive mind is trained almost entirely in the Western sciences, reads the works of Western authors, and is taught predominantly by Western teachers, whether in the West itself or through their works available in local centres of education. Mental captivity is also found in the suggestion of solutions and policies. Furthermore, it reveals itself at the theoretical level and through empirical work. Alatas had also suggested that the mode of thinking of colonized peoples paralleled political and economic imperialism. Hence, the expression "academic imperialism," the context within which the captive mind appears.[44]

---

39   Alatas, *The Myth of the Lazy Native*, 149.
40   Ibid., 150.
41   Ibid.
42   Syed Hussein Alatas, "The Captive Mind and Creative Development," *International Social Science Journal* 36, 4 (1974): 691–699, p. 692.
43   Syed Hussein Alatas, "The Captive Mind in Development Studies," *International Social Science Journal* 34, 1 (1972): 9–25, p. 11.
44   Syed Hussein Alatas "Academic Imperialism," Lecture delivered to the History Society, University of Singapore, 26 September 1969; Syed Hussein Alatas, "Intellectual

For Fanon, colonialism prepares the ground for the captive mind by uprooting the native, by alienating him from his culture. Colonialism is able to do this because its form of domination is total. Its totality enables it to disrupt the cultural life of the colonized.[45] Further resonating with these ideas are Fanon's statements on the underdeveloped and imitative middle class after independence:

> After independence this underdeveloped middle class, reduced in numbers and without capital, which refuses to follow the path of revolution, will fall into deplorable stagnation. It is unable to give free rein to its genius, which formerly it was wont to lament, though rather too glibly, was held in check by colonial domination.[46]

Furthermore, Fanon notes that the middle class after independence has nothing to do with transforming the nation. Rather, it takes upon itself the task of mediating between the nation and a neo-colonialist capitalism. It is content to play the role of the Western bourgeoisie's business agent.[47] It has, in fact, assimilated the most corrupt aspects of colonialist thought, including its racial philosophy. Speaking of Africa, Fanon says that the laziness and the will to imitate by the middle class results in its promoting a racism that was characteristic of the colonial period.[48] Fanon laments that the middle class had enthusiastically adopted the mode of thinking of the colonizer and has become alienated from its own thought.[49] The native intellectual's "writings correspond point by point with those of his opposite numbers in the mother country. His inspiration is European and we can easily link up these works with definite trends in the literature of the mother country. This is the period of unqualified assimilation."[50] Fanon also remarked that intellectual alienation is a product of middle class society, a society that is "rigidified in predetermined forms, forbidding all evolution, all gains, all progress, all discovery."[51] Where mental captivity is the norm, the intellectual is irrelevant.

   Imperialism: Definition, Traits, and Problems," *Southeast Asian Journal of Social Science* 28, 1(2000): 23–45.

45   Fanon, *The Wretched of the Earth*, 236.
46   Ibid., 151.
47   Ibid., 152–153.
48   Ibid., 162.
49   Ibid., 178.
50   Ibid., 222.
51   Fanon, *Black Skin, White Masks*, 224.

It is interesting to note that Fanon himself may have manifested some degree of mental captivity. In his discussion of the "wretched of the earth," he fails to name their anti-colonial culture as Islamic, although it is known that the Islamic Association of Scholars in Algeria in both city and countryside played an important role in anti-colonial resistance. Fanon was certainly familiar with the Association. In a letter to Ali Shariati, he expresses his appreciation for the Association's contribution to the anti-French struggle, although he had disagreements with them.[52] As noted by Slisli, while the work of the Association is cited extensively by Fanon, it is "stripped of its Islamic references and never attributed to the Association."[53] Slisli even suggests that Fanon at times "degenerates into an orientalism reminiscent of Joseph Conrad's Heart of Darkness" when he compares the "wretched of the earth" to "hordes of rats moved by primordiality of the bush, jungle or dessert rather than an Islamic-inspired ideology."[54]

4   The Rule of the Fool

Fanon perceptively spoke of the irrelevance of the native intellectual in the society of the colonized. Alatas would explain this irrelevance in terms of the dominance of the captive mind in intellectual life. Fanon refers to the anxiety felt by the native intellectual in trying to be relevant to his people:

> The native intellectual nevertheless sooner or later will realise that you do not show proof of your nation from its culture but that you substantiate its existence in the fight which the people wage against the forces of occupation. No colonial system draws its justification from the fact that the territories it dominates are culturally non-existent. You will never make colonialism blush for shame by spreading out little-known cultural treasures under its eyes. At the very moment when the native intellectual is anxiously trying to create a cultural work he fails to realise that he is utilizing techniques and language which are borrowed from the stranger in his country. He contents himself with stamping these instruments with a hall-mark which he wishes to be national, but which

---

52   Sara Shariati, Le Fanon connu de nous. http://1libertaire.free.fr/FFanon29.html Accessed 18 June 2018. Cited in Fouzi Slisli, "Islam: The Elephant in Fanon's *The Wretched of the Earth*," *Critique: Critical Middle Eastern Studies* 17, 1 (2008): 97–108.

53   Slisli, "Islam: The Elephant in Fanon's *The Wretched of the Earth*," 104.

54   Fanon, *The Wretched of the Earth*, 130. Cited in Slisli, "Islam: The Elephant in Fanon's *The Wretched of the Earth*," 104–105.

is strangely reminiscent of exoticism. The native intellectual who comes back to his people by way of cultural achievements behaves in fact like a foreigner. Sometimes he has no hesitation in using a dialect in order to show his will to be as near as possible to the people; but the ideas that he expresses and the preoccupations he is taken up with have no common yardstick to measure the real situation which the men and the women of his country know. The culture that the intellectual leans towards is often no more than a stock of particularisms. He wishes to attach himself to the people; but instead, he only catches hold of their outer garments. And these outer garments are merely reflections of a hidden life, teeming and perpetually in motion.[55]

The native intellectual is irrelevant because he is like a foreigner, having only bookish, superficial, and abstract knowledge of the people. Also, the native intellectual runs the risk of being irrelevant by being out of date. Fanon gives the example of the artist who, in his bid to create a national work of art and construct the principles of national art, confines himself to the stereotypical reproduction of details, turning his back on foreign culture and searching for an authentic national culture. He forgets that the people themselves have changed in their way of thinking about what national culture means, their minds having being dialectically reorganized by modern ideas and techniques, language and so on. The artist, on the other hand, in trying to portray the truth of the nation, turns away from actual events toward the past. As Fanon put it, what the artist comes to know are actually the shells and corpses of tradition. He fails to recognize that the truths of a nation are not to be found in an abstract and static past but in the current realities of the present.[56] A national culture cannot be reduced to a folklore or an abstract populism in which the true nature of a people can be discovered. Fanon views the national culture in far more concrete terms as "the whole body of efforts made by a people in the sphere of thought to describe, justify, and praise the action through which that people has created itself and keeps itself in existence."[57]

The irrelevance of the intellectual and their marginalization in society, so articulately described by Fanon, also presents another problem, that is, the emergence and prevalence of the fool.

Alatas, in one of his last publications, suggested that the International Sociological Association organize a session at the World Congress of Sociology on

---

55   Fanon, *The Wretched of the Earth*, 223–224.
56   Ibid., 225.
57   Ibid., 233.

the issue of an autonomous sociological tradition in order to "alert sociologists throughout the world to pool their attention on this extremely vital need for the development of sociology," and, therefore, to counter the influence of the captive mind.[58] Indeed, the South is not lacking in creative and original thinkers. Many examples of alternative discourses can be cited from various countries in Asia and Africa. But, the question is whether a tradition of autonomous thinking in the social sciences can develop. According to Alatas:

> A tradition can be expected to emerge. By tradition it is not meant the mere presence of disparate studies of local or regional subjects by indigenous scholars. Apart from the traits we have earlier cited, there is one significant overriding trait of a tradition, that is, the continuous discussion of a set of major problems and ideas in the course of long duration, decades or centuries, reflecting the cumulative development of knowledge concerning particular subjects. An example is the discussion on the French Revolution or periodization in European history.[59]

But, whether such a tradition can emerge in much of the South will depend on our ability to make changes in policy, change the reward systems in institutions of learning, reduce corruption and inefficiency, and remove national and local politics from the centers of learning. In other words, this requires nothing short of the non-interference of the fools in the entire art, science, and business of education. But, the fools are dominant.

Alatas, in fact, had also suggested the creation of sessions on a new theme – the sociology of the fools. By this, he meant the sociological fool as opposed to its counterpart, the sociological intellectual. Sociologists should not only be interested in the sociology of the intellectual but also in the sociology of the opposing type, the fool. The concept of the fool is not only an original concept and an example of the type of creativity needed for an autonomous social science tradition, it also points to a diagnosis of the problems that alternative discourses face in societies dominated by fools in positions of leadership.[60]

Alatas had started discussing the topic of the fool in his book *Intellectuals in Developing Societies*.[61] Fourteen characteristics for the definition of the sociological concept of the fool and the concrete consequences of power-wielding

58 Syed Hussein Alatas, "The Autonomous, the Universal and the Future of Sociology," *Current Sociology* 54, (2006): 7–23, p. 17.

59 Ibid., 15.

60 Ibid., 17.

61 Syed Hussein Alatas, *Intellectuals in Developing Societies* (London: Frank Cass, 1977), Chapter 4.

fools were discussed. Leaders and administrators who are fools stamp their own peculiar foolish imprint on whatever thinking and practices they undertake. For example, in their corrupt practices, "their corruption bears the imprint of the fool. When they are honest, their honesty can be naïve and immature."[62] Among the traits of the fools are: (1) the inability to recognize a problem; (2) the inability to solve a problem if told to them; (3) the inability to learn what is required; (4) the inability to learn the art of learning; and (5) not admitting that they are fools.[63]

5   The Task of Native Intellectuals

For Alatas and Fanon, the native became nothing more than a colonial category along with the condition or attributes of laziness and other incapacities. These were internalized by the native elite. Reflecting on the Malaysian context, Alatas would have added that grafted on to that is an exclusivist and legalistic interpretation of Islam that the Malay is supposed to identify with. Therefore, there are two dominant discourses, a colonial one and an internalized, authoritarian Islamic one. What is the task of native intellectuals in this context? Both Fanon and Alatas would argue that the categories of the colonizer have to be rejected. For Fanon:

> Colonialism, which has not bothered to put too fine a point on its efforts, has never ceased to maintain that the Negro is a savage; and for the colonist, the Negro was neither an Angolan nor a Nigerian, for he simply spoke of 'the Negro.' For colonialism, this vast continent was the haunt of savages, a country riddled with superstitions and fanaticism, destined for contempt, weighed down by the curse of God, a country of cannibals – in short, the Negro's country. Colonialism's condemnation is continental in scope. The contention by colonialism that the darkest night of humanity lay over pre-colonial history concerns the whole African continent.[64]

Here, Fanon makes an important point, that "[t]he efforts of the native to rehabilitate himself and to escape from the claws of colonialism are logically inscribed from the same point of view as that of colonialism."[65] In other words,

---

62   Alatas, "The Autonomous, the Universal and the Future of Sociology," 17.
63   Alatas, *Intellectuals in Developing Societies*, 45.
64   Fanon, *The Wretched of the Earth*, 211–212.
65   Ibid., 212.

the native intellectual has to reject the very categories of colonialism. This is no easy task. The native intellectual has to go through three phases, as far as the relationship with colonialism is concerned. In the first phase, the intellectual is adamant to prove that he has assimilated the culture of the colonizer. He is up to date on the latest trends in literature in the mother country and his writings correspond with those of his counterparts there. In the second phase, a period of greater creativity than the first, the intellectual feels disturbed that he had forgotten what he was and attempts to re-discover and re-call the local culture. Nevertheless, he is looking at his own heritage as an outsider, "in the light of a borrowed estheticism and a conception of the world which was discovered under other skies."[66] The third phase is that of a revolutionary and fighting literati in which the need to speak to the nation and the desire to express what is in the hearts of the people is strongly felt.[67] However, the effectiveness with which this can be done is constrained by the native intellectual's mental captivity and his tendency to view his own society as an outsider, worse still is his internalization of the colonial image of the native, as discussed above. For Fanon, there seems no way out of this conundrum.[68]

For Alatas, writing thirty years after the independence of Malaysia, the state of mental captivity and the prevalence of the fool require the constructive role of an intellectual community, which is needed for "demand for change in the fundamental forms of society."[69]

Since the 1950s, Alatas had devoted a great deal of his attention to the absence of a functioning group of intellectuals in Malaysia and other developing societies. The task of the intellectual is to think, consider specific problems of society, and attempt to arrive at their solutions. He defined the intellectual as a "person who is engaged in thinking about ideas and non-material problems using the faculty of reason." Furthermore, "knowledge of a certain subject or the possession of a degree does not make a person an intellectual although these often coincide. There are many degree holders and professors who do not engage in developing their field or trying to find the solution to specific problems within it. On the other hand, a person with no academic qualifications can be an intellectual if he utilizes his thinking capacity and possesses sufficient knowledge of his subject of interest."[70]

---

66   Ibid., 222.
67   Ibid., 222–223.
68   Mohammed A. Bamyeh, "On Humanizing Abstractions: The Path Beyond Fanon," *Theory, Culture and Society* 27, 7–8 (2010): 52–65, 61.
69   Alatas, *Intellectuals in Developing Societies*, 52.
70   Ibid., 8.

The inquiry in *Intellectuals in Developing Societies* centered on three issues: (1) why intellectuals are needed in developing societies; (2) what type of intellectuals best answer the need; and (3) what are the obstacles in the way of the emergence and functioning of this group.[71] I may add here that the problems addressed by the group of intellectuals can be divided into two. These are theoretical and practical problems. Theoretical problems refer to problems that are found in the area of knowledge. For Alatas, the foundational theoretical problem of our time was that of the captive mind. This has been discussed above.

The problem of the captive mind is also connected with problems of a practical nature. Examples of practical problems dealt with by Syed Hussein Alatas include Muslim extremism, irrational thought and behavior, and corruption.[72] Because the captive mind is not aware of its conditions of mental captivity and does not think in an autonomous fashion, it is unable to comprehend and analyze problems that afflict its society; on the contrary, it brings problems to its society.

The result of his concern with such practical problems was several proposals that he forwarded to solve some of our problems. This is certainly an area of research that needs to be developed as far as the work of Syed Hussein Alatas is concerned. But, in the hierarchy of factors established by him as requiring attention with a view towards dealing effectively with our problems, what stands at the apex is the problem of leadership. This problem was discussed in a number of works including *Kita dengan Islam* and *Cita Sempurna Warisan Sejarah*.[73] In *Cita Sempurna,* four types of leadership based on the ideals of excellence are discussed. The characteristics of these types of leadership are derived from historical personalities such as Sayyidina Ali (*karramallah wajh-hu*), Khalifah Umar ibn Abd al-Aziz and Sultan Salah al-Din Ayyubi. These are contrasted with the ideals of destruction, which are exemplified in personalities such as the Caliph Al-Kahir, Sultan Ghiyasuddin Balban, and Muhammad Tughluk. In today's society, there are types of leaders that are guided by the ideals of excellence as well as those that are guided by the ideals of destruction.[74]

---

71   Ibid.

72   Syed Hussein Alatas, *Kita dengan Islam: Tumbuh Tiada Berbuah* (*Islam and Us: Growing without Fruits*), Singapore: Pustaka Nasional, 1979; Syed Hussein Alatas, *The Sociology of Corruption: The Nature, Function, Causes and Prevention of Corruption*, Singapore: Donald Moore, 1968; *The Problem of Corruption*, Singapore: Times, 1986; *Corruption: Its Nature, Causes and Functions*, Avebury: Gower, 1990; *Corruption and the Destiny of Asia*, Petaling Jaya: Prentice Hall, 1999.

73   Alatas, *Kita Dengan Islam*, Chap. 8; Syed Hussein Alatas, *Cita Sempurna Warisan Sejarah* (*The Ideals of Excellence as Historical Legacy*), Bangi: Penerbit Universiti Kebangsaan Malaysia, 2000.

74   Alatas, *Cita Sempurna*, 46.

From what has been said above, we can conclude that in the thought of Alatas, the main factor in the hierarchy of cause and effect is the principle of morality. For example, in his writing on the sociology of corruption, he stressed that structural changes in the administration of government would not have the desired effects if not accompanied by the emergence of leaders with high moral principles.

Throughout his intellectual life, Alatas lived in fear of our society being taken over by the fools. He wrote,

> The revolution of the fools which had occurred in many developing societies was to a great extent due to the colonial period. The colonial government did not pay much attention to the creation of high-caliber administrators in the colonies. During that time all the thinking at national levels was done by the colonial government abroad. The commercial and industrial houses were similarly foreign-based. Education in the colonies was mainly geared to provide clerical service or tasks at a subsidiary level. After independence following the Second World War, there was a sudden increase in the volume and intensity of administration and other decision-making centres covering diverse projects which were introduced in increasing number by the newly independent states. During this period there was a shortage of intelligent manpower to deal with the sudden increase of planning and administration, both in the official and in private realms, in the newly independent states. Hence the rise to power of the fools. Once the fools came to power, they perpetuate their own breed. With the fools came nepotism, provincialism, parochial party politics, to condition selection and ascent in the hierarchy of administrative power. Fools cannot cope with a situation where merit and hard work are the criteria of success, and so corruption is the hallmark of the rise to power of the fools, making a farce of government tenders and leading to bureaucratic intrigues to gain office or promotion. Where fools dominate it is their values which become society's values, their consciousness which becomes society's consciousness.[75]

The weakness or non-existence of intellectuals "prolongs the revolution of the fools."[76] Fanon would have been very agreeable with such an assessment for he

---

75   Alatas, *Intellectuals in Developing Societies*, 45–46.
76   Ibid., 69.

too feared the fools. If asked why he wrote *Black Skin, Whites Masks*, his reply would be that "there are too many idiots in this world."[77]

Such is the context within which our society's sense of morality decays. Fanon said that in ex-colonies, there always exist a few honest intellectuals who reject the competition for positions and pensions, and express contempt for profiteers and schemers. Fanon's plea was for the nation to use such intellectuals.[78] Does our society have the leadership of sufficient integrity, resolve, and bravery to combat the ideals of destruction? If there is one big question that Alatas and Fanon left for us to answer, it is that.

Fanon has not been seriously encountered in the Malay world by scholars and activists.[79] *The Wretched of the Earth* is read by the character, Orked, a bourgeois Malay girl in Yasmin Ahmad's film, *Sepet*. Even here, as much as Orked is able to understand the complexities of colonialism and its effects on the psychology of the colonizer and the colonized through reading Fanon, she is unable to connect all of that to the realities of Malaysia.[80]

Even more perplexing is the relative neglect in Malaysia of Alatas' anti-colonial writings and his plea for an autonomous social science tradition as a response to academic imperialism and mental captivity. These point to the continuing coloniality in the post-colonial world. As Mahatma Gandhi said, "it would not be proper for you to say that you have obtained Home Rule if you have merely expelled the English."[81]

---

77   Fanon, *Black Skin, White Masks*, 1.

78   Fanon, *The Wretched of the Earth*, 177.

79   Among the few exceptions are Azhar Ibrahim, *Orientalisme dalam Pengajian Melayu* (Orientalism in Malay Studies), Persidangan Antarabangsa Bahasa, Sastera dan Kebudayaan Melayu ke-2 bertemakan "Ke arah bitara kesarjanaan Melayu", Singapore, 1–3 September, 2002; Mohamed Imran Mohamed Taib, *The Pathology of Race and Racism in Postcolonial Society: A Reflection on Frantz Fanon's Black Skin, White Masks.* https://dialogosphere.wordpress.com/2015/09/15/the-pathology-of-race-and-racism-in-postcolonial-society-a-reflection-on-frantz-fanons-black-skin-white-masks/; and Adeline Koh and Frieda Ekotto, "Frantz Fanon in Malaysia: Reconfiguring the Ideological Landscape of Negritude in Sepet," in Frieda Ekotto and Adeline Koh, eds, *Rethinking Third Cinema: The Role of Anti-Colonial Media and Aesthetics in Postmodernity*, Berlin: Lit Verlag, 2009, pp. 120–138.

80   Koh and Ekotto, "Frantz Fanon in Malaysia."

81   Mohandas. K. Gandhi, "Hind Swaraj," in M.K. Gandhi, *The Collected Works of Mahatma Gandhi: November 1909 – March 1911.* (Ahmedabad: The Publications Division, Ministry of Information and Broadcasting, Government of India, 1963), 6–68.

Bibliography

Alatas, Syed Hussein. *The Sociology of Corruption: The Nature, Function, Causes and Prevention of Corruption.* Singapore: Donald Moore, 1968.

Alatas, Syed Hussein. "Academic Imperialism," Lecture delivered to the History Society, University of Singapore, 26 September 1969.

Alatas, Syed Hussein. "The Captive Mind in Development Studies." *International Social Science Journal* 34, 1 (1972): 9–25.

Alatas, Syed Hussein. "The Captive Mind and Creative Development." *International Social Science Journal* 36, 4 (1974): 691–699.

Alatas, Syed Hussein. *The Myth of the Lazy Native: A Study of the Image of the Malays, Filipinos and Javanese from the 16th to the 20th century and its Function in the Ideology of Colonial Capitalism.* London: Frank Cass, 1977.

Alatas, Syed Hussein. *Intellectuals in Developing Societies.* London: Frank Cass, 1977.

Alatas, Syed Hussein. *Kita dengan Islam: Tumbuh Tiada Berbuah. (Islam and Us: Growing without Fruits).* Singapore: Pustaka Nasional, 1979.

Alatas, Syed Hussein. *The Problem of Corruption.* Singapore: Times, 1986.

Alatas, Syed Hussein. *Corruption: Its Nature, Causes and Functions.* Avebury: Gower, 1990.

Alatas, Syed Hussein. *Corruption and the Destiny of Asia.* Petaling Jaya: Prentice Hall, 1999.

Alatas, Syed Hussein. "Intellectual Imperialism: Definition, Traits, and Problems." *Southeast Asian Journal of Social Science* 28, 1 (2000): 23–45.

Alatas, Syed Hussein. *Cita Sempurna Warisan Sejarah (The Ideals of Excellence as Historical Legacy).* Bangi: Penerbit Universiti Kebangsaan Malaysia, 2000.

Alatas, Syed Hussein. "The Autonomous, the Universal and the Future of Sociology." *Current Sociology* 54 (2006): 7–23.

Azhar Ibrahim. *Orientalisme dalam Pengajian Melayu* (Orientalism in Malay Studies), Persidangan Antarabangsa Bahasa, Sastera dan Kebudayaan Melayu ke-2 bertemakan "Ke arah bitara kesarjanaan Melayu", Singapore, 1–3 September, 2002.

Bamyeh, Mohammed A. "On Humanizing Abstractions: The Path Beyond Fanon." *Theory, Culture and Society* 27, 7–8 (2010): 52–65.

Boeke, J.H. "Dualistic Economics." In *Indonesian Economics.* The Hague: W. van Hoeve, 1961.

Enberg, Susan. "The Epidermalization of Inferiority and the Lactification of Consciousness." 2011. <https://www.researchgate.net/publication/281902045_The_Epidermalization_of_Inferiority_and_the_Lactification_of_Consciousness>.

Fanon, Frantz. *Towards the African Revolution: Political Essays.* Translated by Haakon Chevalier. New York: Grove Press, 1964.

Fanon, Frantz. *The Wretched of the Earth*. Translated by C. Farrington. London: MacGibbon & Kee, 1965.

Fanon, Frantz. *Black Skin, White Masks*. Translated by Charles Lam Markmann. New York: Grove Press, 1967.

Gandhi, Mohandas. K., "Hind Swaraj." In M.K. Gandhi, *The Collected Works of Mahatma Gandhi: November 1909 – March 1911*. Ahmedabad: The Publications Division, Ministry of Information and Broadcasting, Government of India, 1963.

Itwaru, Arnold. "Caribbean Studies Lecture on Psychic Torture." 17 October 2011.

Koh, Adeline Koh and Frieda Ekotto. "Frantz Fanon in Malaysia: Reconfiguring the Ideological Landscape of Negritude in Sepet." In *Rethinking Third Cinema: The Role of Anti-Colonial Media and Aesthetics in Postmodernity*. Edited by Adeline Koh and Frieda Ekotto. Berlin: Lit Verlag, 2009.

Mohamed Imran Mohamed Taib, *The Pathology of Race and Racism in Postcolonial Society: A Reflection on Frantz Fanon's Black Skin, White Masks*. https://dialogosphere .wordpress.com/2015/09/15/the-pathology-of-race-and-racism-in-postcolonial -society-a-reflection-on-frantz-fanons-black-skin-white-masks/.

Said, Edward. *Culture and Imperialism*. New York: Vintage, 1993.

Senu Abdul Rahman, *Revolusi Mental*. Kuala Lumpur: Penerbitan Utusan Melayu, 1971.

Shariati, Sara. "Le Fanon connu de nous." http://1libertaire.free.fr/FFanon29.html.

Slisli, Fouzi. "Islam: The Elephant in Fanon's *The Wretched of the Earth*." *Critique: Critical Middle Eastern Studies* 17, 1 (2008): 97–108.

CHAPTER 3

Fanon, Black Lives, and Revolutionary Black Feminism: 21st Century Considerations

Rose M. Brewer

> *Europe is literally the creation of the Third World. The riches that choke her are that which was stolen from underdeveloped peoples. The ports of Holland, the docks of Bordeaux and Liverpool Specialized in the slave trade and owe their renown from millions of deported slaves.*
> ~ FRANTZ FANON

1 Introduction

While Fanon is clear about the source of Europe's wealth in his interrogation of colonialism, accumulation, and violence, what, in fact, are the implications for revolutionary Black feminism's 21st century expression of this interrogation? What are the transformational implications of Fanon's theory and practice for today's U.S. struggles for Black liberation? The paper is a call for a deeper interrogation of how knowledge is produced and how political change is catalyzed, centering the theory and practice of revolutionary Black feminism while drawing upon some of the insights of Frantz Fanon. Indeed, whose theory and practice are guideposts for 21st century Black emancipation? This chapter takes a look at Fanon's thought in the context of revolutionary Black feminism, which is now undergirding some articulations of Black Lives Matter and the Black Lives movement in general in the United States and beyond.

One key lesson from Fanon's analysis of European colonialism is the fact that the United States is the child of Europe. The U.S. society grew out of white settler colonialism and the enslavement of Africans. Land theft and labor expropriation are foundational. The dye was already caste by the time the American Revolution occurred. Slavery was incorporated into the U.S. constitution and the slavocracy of the new nation would build the wealth of the country in the context of a deeply instantiated white supremacy. This would establish the hierarchy of race for generations, including the present period. U.S. imperialism extended its reach with so-called "westward expansion": The removal and genocide of Native Americans.[1] The new nation would expand its vision of empire with the colonization of Hawaii in 1893, then Cuba, Puerto Rico, Guam, and the Philippines. The American apartheid order, which was already in place, was further cemented by the *Dred Scott v. Sandford* decision of 1857, when Supreme Court Justice Roger B. Taney ruled that Black people "had no rights which the white man was bound to respect."[2] Anti-Black racism was solidified further in the post-slavery period with another Supreme Court decision, *Plessy v. Ferguson* in 1896. This decision institutionalized formally "separate but equal" which, of course, was separate but never equal. Thus, globally and domestically, a white supremacist and patriarchal society was hardened. The political fight continues into the current era with the fight for Black lives.

Once again, resistance to colonial assumptions and Black dispossession are folded into today's social movement struggles. The very systems that originally colonized are still in motion under late capitalism. Of course, racial monopoly capitalism has shifted in crucial features such as intense financialization, but global appropriation from the global South to North continues.[3] Thus, the call is for neo-colonized voices to be heard in today's struggles for Black liberation. What is clear regarding this call is that we must think of simultaneity, articulating mutually constitutive systems decentering the traditional ways of delineating radical social change. While not a theorist of the simultaneity of oppressions, Fanon articulates a revolutionary praxis that should be lifted up given today's revolutionary Black feminism.[4] While critiqued for his masculinist, some would argue misogynist approach to colonialism/anti-colonialism, Fanon offers lessons important to the contemporary project of Black liberation in the U.S., and the praxis of revolutionary Black feminism. Critical here is the call for revolutionary decolonization – internal and external – to stop the cultural and literal killing of Black people. It is imperative to build a new social order. So, the revolutionary Black feminist project is this: we must dismantle heteropatriarchy colonialisms (neo-settler and internal), in the context of neo-liberal global capitalism.[5] This resistance is expressed in the current uptick in Black insurgency in the United States and the re-centering of Black struggle

1   Dunbar-Ortiz, *Indigenous People's History of the United States.* (Boston: Beacon Press, 2001), 162.

2   U.S. Supreme Court, *Dred Scott v. Sandford.* 1857.

3   Moody, *On New Terrain: How Capitalism is Reshaping the Battleground of Class War.* (Chicago: Haymarket Books, 2017), 5.

4   Frantz Fanon, *The Wretched of the Earth,* trans, Richard Philcox. (New York: Grove Press, 2004), 3.

5   Combahee River Collective Statement. https://americanstudies.yale.edu/sites/default/files/files/Keyword%20Coalition_Readings.pdf.

through a revolutionary Black feminist lens. Black people in rebellion in the U.S. and beyond have recognized and lived the violence of the system, the inherent violence of capitalism. This state violence lit a response in Ferguson, Baltimore, New York, London, Durban, and so on. The demand was made for Black lives. Fanon lives in the articulation and re-articulation of this fundamental fact. This state violence is at the heart of police murders, male and female, in the current period. Bringing it to an end is the clarion call of today's Black radicalism.

2   Political Economy and Black Life Today

Understanding the inequality of the Black world lodged within the violent history of enslavement, colonialism, capitalism, and patriarchy is foundational. Fanon, of course, is quite theoretically impactful in this regard. The U.S., the African continent, and the Black diaspora are all imbricated in global white supremacy and the attendant anti-Black racism which it catalyzes. My analysis of revolutionary Black feminism means making sense out of a number of complexities. While race is anchored materially, as well as in the realm of ideology and culture, it is also deeply rooted in the interstices of advanced capitalism. Racism and capitalism are at the same time interpenetrating, working in deep relationality to patriarchy. Connecting male domination to racism and capitalism is often unstated in analyses of the Black world, but the inter-relationality of these systems of imperialism, racism, and patriarchy, as revolutionary Black feminism theorizes, best captures the current realities.

While the impacts of capitalist crises today have been especially harsh, I contend that political economy as unmediated economics is not sufficient to explain its impact on a society in which race is a central organizing principle. As is quite clear by Fanon, revolution must be about the transformation of the entire system. Clearly, revolutionary Black feminism, found for example in the articulations of Claudia Jones, Assata Shakur, and The Combahee Collective, understands this.[6] Revolutionary Black feminists put front and center the complete transformation of the social order. Yet, this is not only a racial question. Racism is deeply enmeshed in sexism through which the modality of class is lived – to rearticulate the words of Stuart Hall. These realities are rooted materially and have profound consequences. Profits fueled by derivatives, cutbacks

---

6   Assata Shakur, *Assata: An Autobiography* (Chicago: Chicago Review Press, 2001), 1–36; Claudia Jones, "An End to the Neglect of the Negro Woman," https://libcom.org/library/end-neglect-problems-negro-woman. Accessed July 2, 2018.

in the social wage, the exploitation of women as cheap labor, and the increasing dispossession of large numbers of the population continue to be rooted in North/South expropriation. From outsourcing to the cheapest labor possible to the expropriation of land, water, and resources, the imperial labor market is part and parcel of late capitalist logics. It embodies a racist, sexist, classist logic, and it is an anti-Black logic, framed around a narrative of individual not system blame. This is anti-black rhetoric flowing into a naturalized notion of who is worthy. This goes to the heart of the impact of Fanon on revolutionary Black feminism as the demand for the validation of all Black life. It reveals the current mystification, a discursive space that does not name capitalism as the source of the crisis or the fundamental fact that a small elite possesses the majority of the wealth and resources of earth as the majority of humanity lives in poverty and want. Violence is the constitutive element that keeps the system functioning, often targeting blackness. This anti-Blackness under colonialism was quite clear to Fanon. He understood the depth of it for the colonizer and the colonized. Indeed, as Duggan skillfully points out under conditions of the current capitalist world order,

> The goal of raising corporate profits has never been pursued separately from the rearticulation of hierarchies of race, gender, and sexuality in the United States and around the globe. Neoliberals, unlike many leftists and progressives... make use of identity politics to obscure redistribution aims, and they use 'neutral' economic policy terms to hide their investments in identity-based hierarchies, but they don't make the mistake of fundamentally accepting the ruse of liberalism – the assertion of a clear boundary between the politics of identity and class.[7]

And for the poorest Black people in advanced Western capitalist societies such as the U.S., the dismantling of the social wage through destruction of the welfare state, the attack on public education, the incarceration and imprisonment of Black men and women, and the structural consequences of wealth concentration are part and parcel of racialized neoliberal capitalism. The more than five hundred years of economic underdevelopment of African people by the capitalist world system is clearly understood by Fanon, as noted by Stephens,

> It is instructive to remind ourselves of Fanon's perspective over fifty years ago, the degree to which he understood his 'blackness' as articulated within blacks shared political-economic condition globally, but also their shared place in the unconscious, cultural-discursive structures of

---

7 Lisa Duggan, *Twilight of Equality* (New York: Beacon Press, 2004), 15.

modernity across both Old and New Worlds. Such structures both transcend nationality and work simultaneously to resituate the discursive
products of global, racial history *within the structure of nationality*.[8]

These material and ideological facts are intertwined in the underpinnings
of 21st century race think – changed but deeply intractable when it comes
to Blackness. As Nikhil Singh has argued, the core of this racism is "distance
from Blackness," as "the national articulation of citizen [is] intertwined with
capital's value differentiation."[9] Anti-Black racism has been intractable, deeply
rooted, and very difficult to extricate because it is constitutive of both symbol
and material systems, state, and economy. Indeed, it is a capitalist system that
enshrines a property rights regime within nation-states in a way that guaran-
tees the removal of dispossession from the discourse. It is a system embedded
in white supremacy, patriarchy, core-capitalist-dependency in nationalist projects, and a dynamic mix of national and international policies. This interpenetration brings the Black world and other parts of the African diaspora into a
deep interconnectivity with the Black population in the U.S. This is cemented
ideologically in 21st century ideas of color blindness, post racialism in dialectic
with so-called Black incapacity. Thus, the deep entanglement of racism with
capitalism is a fact of the matter. This entanglement is being expressed in the
current white nationalist anti-immigrant upsurge in the European context.

As Valluvan and Penny speak to this,

> When seen along the terms of optimal economic citizenry–those who are
> able to convey the ideals of Independence, enterprise and offer premium
> skills–darker-skinned people and the stereotypes fixed to their bodies al-
> ready constitute a symbolic antithesis.[10]

We are in fact dealing with global white supremacy. The narrative of who constitutes the "model citizen" and faux colorblindness exists side by side with
an older language of unworthiness. It is a racialized language, an anti-black
rhetoric, dog whistled as too much government support for certain groups of
people. It flows into a naturalized set of assumptions about who "those people
are." No name is necessary.

---

8   Michele Stephens, "Black Transnationalism and the Politics of National Identity: West In-
    dian Intellectuals in Harlem in the Age of War and Revolution." http://www.virginia.edu/
    woodson/courses/aas102%20(spring%2001)/articles/stephens.html.
9   Nikhil Pal Singh, *Black is a Country*. Cambridge, MA: Harvard University Press, 2004.
10 Sivamohan Valluvan and Eleanor Penny, "The New Undesirables." October 20, 2018.
    https://www.redpepper.org.uk/the-new-undesirables/ Accessed August 3, 2018.

3   The Political Economy of White Supremacy, Patriarchy,
       and Anti-blackness after Fanon

Globalization, the logic of transnational capital in search for international profits, the reality of global financial capital free of any impediments to its hegemony, expresses the political economy of the current moment. It still articulates an imperialism of rich nations over poor nations, as well as a link between the dispossessed of the global north and global south. Technology figures strongly in this equation, with computerization and the growth of electronics labor expressing the realities of the current period. Imperialism is a logic and a practice that expropriates the resources of the world and shifts these resources, i.e. land, labor, mineral, human etc., into the coffers of a global elite. The face of imperialism is still racialized but many of the elite beneficiaries are in reality indigenous to oppressed cultures. Nonetheless, this sector represents a class integrated into the logic of transnational capital to the benefit of global capital and their own wealth expropriation. The $124 billion salary of Amazon CEO Jeff Bezos is more than the salaries of 2 million others in the U.S.[11] The outsourcing of millions of jobs from the North to the South in the search for the cheapest labor possible is part and parcel of today's globalization.

These processes in the economically dominant North are mirrored in the South through the capitalist governance structure of the International Monetary Fund (IMF) and World Bank. These institutions, which are support systems of transnational corporations and their maintenance of inequality, extract resources, wreck cultural havoc through cultural imperialism, and exploit humans for generations in pursuit of transnational profits. Race and class are deeply entangled in gender, sexuality and nation; they are simultaneously being shaped and constructed by political economy and ideology. Such institutions in the service of capital express its transnational organization. The transnationals are supranational entities with their own laws transcending those of any particular nation state. Imperial globalization may not be new, but the degree of transnational integration is an important shift. The intense global financialization of the system is a leading dynamic. In this context, the significance for Blacks throughout the diaspora expresses the five-hundred-year history of justifications of expropriation.

The working class here are those women who are at the center of the global economy. The focus here is on those women in general and Black women

---

11   David Carrig, "Jeff Bezos' Wealth is now Equal to 2.3 Million Americans." https://www
       .usatoday.com/story/tech/news/2018/03/06/how-much-jeff-bezos-worth-centibillionaire
       -wealth/352082002/ Accessed August 3, 2018.

in particular across the United States, Africa, and the African diaspora. Their labor is undervalued, deeply exploited, and used to enrich a small male economic elite. As Marxist feminists such as Angela Davis have delineated, value is extracted not only in the realm of production but in uncompensated socially reproductive work.[12] This socially productive and reproductive work is low paid care work, unpaid cleaning, cooking, nurturing. This socially necessary work is central to the labor exploitation of the international division of labor. Surplus value expropriation is inherent in the gender division of labor under capitalism. In its public and cultural expression, the female incorporation into the logic of transnational capital often means the disruption of the traditional women's informal economic sectors. African women's informal markets across the continent have been heavily destabilized by global capital. As these women's economic networks are destroyed, so are the foundations of communal life – communities with some degree of economic and cultural autonomy. Networks of Black women have been central to community construction. Women in general and poor women, in particular, are expected to perform unpaid labor in the home while surplus value is systematically extracted in the formal labor force. Through the U.S.'s system of mass incarceration, Black women as well as Black men are exploited as virtually uncompensated labor, i.e. prison labor. They are an important factor in the growth of the prison industrial complex. Their labor is extracted for profit. So, whether in Africa, the Caribbean, or the U.S., there is an interplay between violence, coercion, and incarceration, and state violence is used to manage these realities.

Understanding the centrality of gender extends Fanon's interpolation of the violence inherent in anti-Black racism. Indeed, global white supremacy, in the context of transnational capital, interconnects the inequality experienced by continental African and Black women throughout the diaspora. In response, the Black Lives Matter Global Network has extended its reach transnationally. Intimate violence, state violence, and the dynamics of gender, race, and class are predicated on the structural commonalities in the positioning of these women globally. What is increasingly referred to as the linkages and dispersal of African women (or the diaspora) means locating and articulating the impact of current capitalist policies on African diaspora women as well as African women on the continent. Basically, this is a period of global economic restructuring and crisis with consequences for all African descent women.

The contention here is that the historical experiences of exploitation are expressed contemporarily through the shared realities of neoliberalism, racism, and deeply embedded gender inequities. Although Black women of Africa

---

12   Angela Davis, *Women, Race, and Class* (New York: Random House, 1982), 1–48.

and the African diaspora are situated in nation-state contexts, gender and class shape state racial practice of Black women throughout the African world.

Cultural imperialism is expressed in consciousness. As Angela Davis observes, we know (or are conditioned to think we know) what crime looks like, and it is the face of Blackness, often female. Marlon M. Bailey goes on to argue that

> blackness tends to occupy – no matter the community – the very bottom of every domain in society as first observed by Cathy Cohen. Overall, for black gender and sexual minorities, racial blackness, womanizes, transient, and queerness constitute multiple and simultaneous forms of socio-political disqualification and oppression... the means through which black is equated with nonnormativity and pathology.[13]

The power of race and racism continues to loom large in current white nationalist and white supremacist upsurges in the United States and Europe and leads us to relook at what Fanon understood as the violence of colonialism. Most palpably today, this occurs in the U.S. context of Black engagement with the police. Entire communities are sites of police occupation. Racial inequality through broad-scale economic exclusion was a powerful organizing force in Detroit 50 years ago; and in Ferguson and Baltimore today. It is in this context that 21st century Black insurgency in the U.S. is catalyzed. Most importantly, radical Black feminist resistance has shaped the leadership of this insurgency. A good deal of the leadership is queer Black feminists. This frame demands gendering sexual orientation across the insurgency. Revolutionary Black feminism asserts there should be no illusions that enslavement, colonialism, patriarchy capitalism, no matter how intertwined, have created devastating psychological and social consequences for the peoples of the world, and Black life in particular. Anti-Black racism is a particular expression of "othering," deeply rooted in the history of racism since the 16th century and well into the current period.

Indeed, over the last five-hundred-years of history, there has been a deep and profound othering of the African; both factually defined as other and raced as nonhuman or subhuman. Yet, no one has been left out of the snare of white supremacism, which is the foundational element of racism in the modern world; it is both central and constitutive of the American social order since its inception. We know that state violence is built into the very fiber of

---

13   Marlon M. Bailey and Rashad Shabazz, "Gender and Sexuality of Blackness." https://asu.
       pure.elsevier.com/en/publications/gender-and-sexual-geographies-of-blackness-new-
       black-cartographie. Accessed August 3, 2018.

American society, from its foundational white settler colonialism, born in the genocide of indigenous peoples, and the brutal, genocidal, and forced enslavement of Africans, to the state-violence that is deeply intertwined in policing and mass incarceration. The protection of private property for the ultimate purpose of accumulating profits is expressed in police violence, mass incarceration, war, and militarism. Additionally, structural racism remains deeply embedded with transnational capital. As the disposability of Black men and women becomes ever more visible in the everyday operation of the economy, state-violence intensifies ideologically and materially. In short, Black life is expendable and much of Black labor is no longer needed. Here, the linked fortunes of the global Black world are evident; Black disposability in the heart of empire is not disconnected from hyper-exploitation and 21st century plunder of the African continent.

To secure this, all but one country of the 54 African nations now have *Africa Command* (Africom), a set of U.S. military bases "protecting" U.S. interests. In short, the relations of production under these increasingly militarized conditions do not benefit Africans, nor African diaspora women, but represent the face of global capital. Profits generated are in the hands of a global elite. This leads to deep poverty and immiseration for Africans and African diasporic women. Traditional economies have been disrupted by monocrop demands articulated in "structural adjustment" programs as dictated by the IMF and the World Bank. African women on the continent then attempt to carve out alternative economic spaces just to feed themselves, their children, and their extended families. Indeed, global restructuring, the logic of transnational capital in search of profits internationally, expresses continued wealth transfer: from the poor to the rich in the form of multinational profits. Thus, the expropriation of human and material resources continues unabated on the African continent in this era of "New Empire." The global south is pressed into policies that destroy the social wage and consequently restructure the nation to operate in such ways that it maximizes transnational profits. These "structural adjustment" programs have been the key tools of the IMF to accomplish this agenda, and Africa has been the poster child of these policies.

Given this, we must be clear that the problems for women of African descent have never been simply the expression of class exploitation, but rather are deeply conditioned by racial practices *and* gender ideologies *and* the division of labor. This complicated race/class/gender history reflects how these inequalities multiply, not just as race or gender, but also in relation to these systems. As articulated earlier, race, class, and gender, operate together and influence one another as systems of inequality. This is the meaning of "relationality." This means that racism is redefined in the context of the changed political economy of advanced capitalism, and gender is realigned by this same system – expressed in neoliberal practices. Thus, Black women are members of an intensely exploited working class. It is within this conceptual "multiplicity of oppression" framework that Black women's continued exclusion, economic exploitation, and violation must be understood. As such, this theoretical point structures revolutionary Black feminist thought. Black life can be marginalized or excluded from the economy and other institutions as long as capitalism generates a surplus population, coupled with an organized ideology of white entitlement that protects its interests. In addition to the global search for cheap labor, the internal Third World languishes while the external Third World is paid 80 cents a day to increase the hyper-profits of American corporations.

This is how imperialism plays out in the context of today's global capitalism. As Sarah Bracking and Graham Harrison point out, "imperialism is a useful starting point to understand Africa's global relations: structures of inequality reproduced through a capitalist system of both political and economic power."[14]

Fanon was sure about organizing a revolutionary struggle against imperialism. This is a lesson for 21st century Black feminist insurgency. This is not simply the centering of gender but the demand for an anti-imperialist struggle across the Black world. The issue is *revolutionary decolonization*. Despite the tremendous national diversity, Black women of Africa and the African diaspora must be catalyzed into a joint struggle. These struggles are cultural, political, economic, whether they are on the continent or in the United States. Given this 21st century reality, sectors of Black women in the U.S., the Caribbean, Europe, Africa, and the diaspora in general, are in social, economic, and political crises. In advanced western capitalist societies such as the U.S., the dismantling of the social wage is just one example of such crises. It entails the destruction of welfare state supports that reach the poorest women and children. The fact that a disproportionate percentage of those women and children are Black is part and parcel of present day dispossession. Moreover, the increasingly white nationalist direction of the U.S. racial state under Trumpism is of grave concern.

The integration of rightwing ideology with increasingly repressive economic policies, signals a deep move to the right. The liberal welfare state of the New Deal has literally been dismantled, and its remnants are on the chopping block under the current regime. This, of course, took flight under "dismantling welfare as we know it" as stated by then President Bill Clinton. Clinton signed into law welfare reform in 1996. These "welfare to work" policies, predicated on the heavy vilification of Black women, forced them to work. This intense

---

14   Sarah Bracking and Graham Harrison, "Africa, Imperialism & New Forms of Accumulation," *Review of African Political Economy* 30 (2003): 5.

privatization continues apace in education, mass incarceration, food stamps, disability, and health care. Much of the current "full employment" rhetoric masks the reality of work in the 21st century U.S. economy. Much of this work is low pay with few if any benefits. Working conditions are often unsavory and even dangerous. Wages are pushed downward generating greater profits for corporations that employ these workers. Women are working for their poverty under the onerous conditions of low pay, few benefits, and no prospect for advancement. Even for those women working fulltime, poverty is the ultimate outcome. As such, multiple jobs are required just to fulfill basic needs. Thus, the neoliberalism of the global order is reflected internally within U.S. state decision-making, which locates African American women and men within the political economy as being exploitable and/or expendable labor. Today, neo-liberals of the American capitalist state operate in accordance with Black expendability, if not in word, certainly in deed. The continuing vilification of Black women as drains on the state continues to be an ideologically potent discourse undergirding privatization. Indeed, the triple oppressions of economic exploitation, sexism, and racism are in play.

Culturally, even as new cooperative initiatives are emerging, other indigenous Black community structures are under attack. Funding for citizens' agencies ended long ago. Local YMCA's and YWCA's, which focused on Black life, have been phased out. These are aspects of the old order that sustained Black people. Certainly, the most damaging impact has come with the increase in police violence, the growing militarization of local police, as well as police occupation of Black communities. The lack of universal child care facilities, the lack of solidary wage policies – which raise the wages of all workers – and the lack of universal health care are all contributing factors in Black community life. Blacks are an economic surplus population. Cheap labor is available all over the world, and thus the process of neo-imperialism continues.

Black Lives Matter arose during the Obama presidency. And, as it stands, different sectors of the Black leadership class are proposing fundamentally different strategies for social change. The liberal Democrats are compromised politically. The NAACP has increasingly argued for a greater piece of the private enterprise pie. As the welfare state is being reshaped, it is apparent that a more systematic dismantling for social programs such as Social Security, Medicare, and Medicaid are on the agenda. On the other side of the political spectrum, Black conservative thinkers have argued for a massive infusion of free enterprise into Black communities. This is a strategy critiqued several decades ago by W.E.B. DuBois in his call for Black cooperative structures.

A generation of 18- to 34-year-old young Black women has been born under the rules of capitalism, and a reconstituted racism that is coded "colorblind."

They have dismissed this characterization and have become the core of the activists in the Black Lives Matter movement. As such, the struggle for dignified work and substantive meaning is central for these young women. They have entered a domestic economy comprised mainly of low-paid service work or no work at all. They have experienced police violence that often goes unnamed. They assert the need to #Sayhername, in order to give light to all the unnamed Black women who are also the victims of police killings. Many of these unknown names are Trans, lesbian, and bisexual youth. Sex trafficking is, of course, global in the diaspora. Nonetheless, in the U.S., it is these gender nonconforming Black women who are often heavily exploited, coerced, and even enslaved into sex slavery to survive.[15]

Patriarchal dynamics infuse reality with the logic of racism and capitalism. Both political and economic realities are infused with cultural and ideological meaning, embedded within a discursive terrain that says that these women deserve to be at the bottom. These economic, political, and social processes are remade in the contemporary context, and are intimately tied to the capitalist economy.

4   Black Lives Today: Fanon Redux

Given this broad political economic and ideological context, what are we to make of the current period and the forces in motion on the ground? Clearly a reconfiguration of struggle is in motion. The ever potent words of Frantz Fanon hold great meaning in this context: "Each generation must, out of relative obscurity, discover its mission, fulfill it, or betray it."[16]

As noted, at the center of Black life today is a twenty-first century transnational economy and the social forces that keep the dream of Black radical transformation alive. The ideological nature of neoliberal capitalism eliminates racism through the discourses of colorblindness and post racialism, fueled by the imagery of a nation that once elected a Black president. The discourse is reflected in the disappearance of even a moderate public articulation of racial fairness and justice. In fact, the direction is in the complete dismantling of affirmative action. Strikingly, from within Black life, a segment of the Black leadership elite has strongly embraced this neoliberal position. The most visible exemplar of the neoliberal turn in Black life was President Barack Obama

---

15   "Meaningful Work Transgender Experiences in the Sex Trade" https://www.transequality. org/sites/default/files/Meaningful%20Work-Full%20Report_FINAL_3.pdf Accessed December 28, 2018.

16   Frantz Fanon, The *Wretched of the Earth*, 145.

who carried out the policies of neoliberal capitalism under his watch. Ideologically, on more than one occasion, he chided Black fathers for not taking responsibility without ever pushing an economic agenda which would address high levels of Black male dispossession. Organizations such as the NAACP and National Urban League have followed a corporate strategy which positioned them in the neoliberal camp.[17]

They and their white counterparts argue that this is now a "colorblind society." The impact of this powerfully placed group of Black pundits, centrists, conservatives, and liberals is telling; it is an articulation rejected by this generation of Black activists.

As argued earlier, the global economic order of the 21st century looms large in this equation. Significant here is the continued economic marginalization or exclusion of large numbers of the Black population from the formal economy and the growth of the prison industrial complex in the U.S., earmarked by a prison population of 2.2 million people, half of whom are African American males and a growing number of African American women. With the prison economy, comprised in part of "for-profit prisons," or the "illegal economy," 21st century neoliberalism has hit Black America hard. The number of incarcerated individuals reflects the harsh reality of 21st century racism/sexism/classism, the illumination of an unfinished revolution. So, Fanon's generational command looms large in this era of Black Lives Matter. A new generation struggles to take its place in the pantheon of those who fight for Black liberation. This holds across the Black world, whether in South Africa or in the U.S.

In assessing the Black struggle in the 21st century, one thing is quite clear: the intellectual and political agendas of those committed to human liberation are stretched thin as humanity confronts the logic of transnational crises: ecological, economic, and social. Moreover, the current period requires complex theoretical understanding of the emerging intersectional and movement-building energies as Black revolutionary feminism asserts. It's in that spirit that the call to struggle recognizes the deeply entangled realities of the current period, patriarchy, imperialism, racism, and state violence. This captures a fundamental organizing idea that African peoples are in the crosshairs of a capitalist order that is itself in transformation. Revolutionary Black feminism insists that we understand and contend with the fundamental fact of deadly transnational capitalism, hetero-patriarchal, white supremacist dispossession. And, twenty-first century anti-Black racism means holding in check or removing a population of people who are deemed a threat to the status quo. When communities become dumping grounds for guns not made there, drugs that

---

17   For a fuller discussion of Black neoliberal governability, see Lester K. Spence, "The Neoliberal Turn in Black Politics," *Souls* 14:3–4 (2012): 139–159.

are imported, and locked out of opportunities in education, employment, housing, and healthcare, transformational change is required. When deep levels of disrespect and inhumanity are business as usual, the demand and the struggle must be for social transformation. And, of course, advanced capitalism continues to be deeply shaped by racism, as the poorest people on the face of the earth are disproportionately Black, young, elder, female and queer. It is within this "multiplicity of oppression" framework that Black Lives Matter can best be understood.

Given this simultaneity of oppression, the Hashtag #blacklivesmatter, emerges in a complicated and violent context of police killings of young Black men. Alicia Garza, one of the Black Lives Matter (BLM) founders clearly states:

> Black Lives Matter is an ideological and political intervention in a world where Black lives are systematically and intentionally targeted for demise. It is an affirmation of Black folks' contributions to this society, our humanity, and our resilience in the face of deadly oppression.[18]

Although perhaps submerged, the profound contradictions of living Black in a white supremacy society beg a radical response. In an advanced Western capitalist society such as the United States, the dismantling of the social wage, the defunding public education, and the outsized incarceration and imprisonment as well as murder of Black women and men, demands a radical response. As the movement for Black lives asserts, the assault on Black people is relentlessly cultural and transnational. Black Lives Matter has taken a stand by creating a global network, and Black women across the African diaspora are linked in. The Brazilian queer Black woman activist, Marielle Franco, who was assassinated in March of 2018, was recognized in the statement below released by the Black Lives Matter network:

> On March 14th, 2018 Marielle Franco an Afro-Brazilian council member was brutally assassinated in Rio de Janeiro, Brazil. She was a human rights advocate raised in the favelas, and thousands have gathered to mourn her. Black organizers in Brazil reached out to the Black Lives Matter Global Network, who along with the rest of the Movement for Black Lives, have issued the following statement in support of our family in Brazil, and all those who stand for the liberation of all Black people everywhere.
> We are outraged and devastated by the political assassination of Marielle Franco, a powerful freedom fighter and defender of the rights of Black people, favela dwellers, and other targets of police violence in

---

18   Black Lives Matter. https://blacklivesmatter.com/ Accessed July 2, 2018.

Brazil. Marielle was a lesbian, Afro-Brazilian council member from Rio de Janeiro who was assassinated on Wednesday, March 14th in her car for courageously fighting against police violence and corruption. Just two weeks ago, on Sunday, March 11th, Marielle denounced recent actions of military police terrorizing residents of the Favela de Acari; many believe that this was the final motivator of her murder.

In April and November of last year, Black organizers from across the U.S. met and spoke directly with Marielle about our collective need to build Black power and solidarity beyond borders. We are clear that throughout the world, Black people face similar patterns of violence, so this injustice is personal. We grieve her death because she is one of our own, fighting for the liberation of all Black people, even when separated by superficial borders.

This is not a time to be silent or afraid. Marielle's death, and those we have lost in the struggle before her, is a call for more action. Black people of Brazil, our bond is one that is deep and ancestral. When you call on us, we will stand ready. We will honor your leadership in the days, months, and years that follow until we have built a movement for all Black people to achieve self-determination and safe communities worldwide.[19]

The global commitment to worldwide Black liberation is captured in the last sentence: "We will honor your leadership in the days, months, and years that follow until we have built a movement for all Black people to achieve self-determination and safe communities worldwide."

5   Conclusions

There are a series of key points to lift up given this interrogation of revolutionary Black feminism in view of some of the key insights of Frantz Fanon. Several of these insights are summed up below:

(1)   Fanon's correct naming of empire, colonialism, materialism, and violence remains analytically powerful in what he would call the "neocolonial" world of today. The state/economy has been restructured under global capitalism with the continued expropriation of human and natural resources. Processes of political economy shape the exclusion, inclusion, and fracturing of economic and civil life along race/nation lines. It is also in this terrain that heterosexism is most tangible. It is the space where fear and loathing and anti-Black racism is articulated as a discursive

---

19   Ibid.

space that divides and fragments workers. This is the space in which African women's productive and reproductive capacities are heavily exploited. Yet, this centering the lives of Black women extends Fanon's analysis.

(2)   Given capitalism's crises today, Black women across the African diaspora
        remain in its cross hairs. As Fanon recognized, these are internal as well
        as external fissures. For African and African diaspora women, there are
        tensions between those who possess and those who are the dispossessed
        within Black life; Class formation internally and the shifting of wealth up-
        ward in the national and global economies figure centrally in class forma-
        tion. Simultaneously, the gendering of poverty, Black and female, is real
        even as Black men are also likely to be impoverished. African and African
        diasporic women and children are some of the poorest people on earth.

(3)   It is the restructuring of the state and economy, the economic and tech-
        nical logic of transnational capital and new imperialism, matched by the
        resistance and political struggles of the global and local Black dispos-
        sessed, that must be articulated. Indeed, the complexities of civil soci-
        ety, identities, and the everyday are significant. For example, while the
        public face of Blackness is commodified and rendered one-dimensional
        through the discourses of criminality and unworthiness, the internal fab-
        ric of Blackness is complicated along a number of dimensions of gay and
        straight, young and old. Revolutionary Black feminism articulates these
        multilayered complexities. Indeed, sexuality, gender, race, and class are
        simultaneous and deeply imbricated.

(4)   Fanon understood something beyond a narrow, misogynist nation-
        alism as Reiland Rabaka aptly notes. The demand was "rather a na-
        tional consciousness that would lead to internationalism and social
        democracy."[20] Nonetheless, the Black world continues to live out the
        legacies of colonialism, neocolonialism, imperialism, and the current in-
        equalities of global capital.

(5)   Within the advanced capitalist logic of the global North, white national-
        ism is on the rise. The event that occurred in Charlottesville, Virginia, in
        August of 2017,[21] was the visible space where the reemergence of overt
        racism, xenophobia, and anti-Semitism was on full display.

---

20   Reiland Rabaka. "Revolutionary Fanonism: On Frantz Fanon's Modification of Marxism
        and Decolonization of Democratic Socialism." *Socialism & Democracy* 25, 1 (June, 2011):
        126–145.

21   The Unite the Right rally of white supremacist nationalists was held in Charlottesville,
        Virginia, August 12, 2017. They spewed hatred, racist and anti-Semitic venom, to protest
        the removal of the Robert E. Lee statue. Anti-racist activists were attacked. One anti-racist

(6)   As another generation, as Fanon exhorted, struggles to resist, #Blacklives-
       matter has been the most visible expression of this resistance. The depth
       of this insurgency was fully evident in the uprisings in Ferguson and
       Baltimore.[22] At the same time, the struggle against inequalities occurs
       in other spaces: labor organizing, protests, rebellion, and cultural resis-
       tance. The internationalism that Fanon asserted is in need of fuller devel-
       opment in the current struggle. Nonetheless, the global network of the
       Black Lives Matter movement has been impactful across the globe, from
       South Africa to England and France, and from Brazil to other parts of
       the global South. Beyond Fanon, this resistance extends into the realm of
       class, race, as well as gender and sexuality struggles. It is arrayed against
       state violence, police violence, as well as male domination and hetero-
       sexism. In turn, these fights have the potential to reshape state/economy/
       cultural practices. Black struggles must be considered an essential ele-
       ment in the transnational realities of the current period. Nevertheless,
       race/class/gender struggles in the U.S. and outside the U.S., have chal-
       lenged but never completely transformed this political-economy.

6   Social Transformation: What Now?

Revolutionary Black women struggle for a new society, a society free of racism, classism, sexism, heterosexism, colonialism, and imperialism. But this
struggle, and the social transformation it strives for, must encompass a vision:
it must struggle against these oppressions simultaneously and in recognition if
their deep relationality. We have struggled along racial lines, while some have
struggled against class exploitation. Others have struggled against race and
class, but the Revolutionary Black feminist tradition demands social transformation: A new society. That is, we must struggle simultaneously against capitalism, imperialism, white supremacy, and heteropatriarchy.

---

activist, Heather Heyer was killed when James Alex Fields, Jr., used his car as a weapon to
ram into the anti-racist protestors.

22 Michael Brown's police murder on August 9, 2014 catalyzed days of protest in Ferguson,
Missouri, in 2014. The rebellion drew worldwide attention and was one of the clearest
expressions of Black rebellion against police violence in the United States. The Freddie
Gray death in a police van after his arrest on April 12, 2015, sparked Black rebellion in
Baltimore, Maryland, for a number of days. The rebellion against police occupation and
violence struck a chord nationally and beyond. Black Lives Matter was the rallying cry and
organizing form of much of the resistance.

Indeed, this period, which encompasses the intense internationalization of capital, represents a new moment for peoples of Africa and the African diaspora. Perhaps most importantly, the tensions generated by the current crisis and global restructuring demonstrates the substantive potential for a collective struggle in order to alter the given situation. Yet the elites have made a gamble; they are invested in the idea that their stringent policies can be imposed without organized resistance. However, the recent upsurge in Black resistance in the U.S. – and beyond – proves that the people will respond. There is, and will continue to be, a concerted effort to organize and struggle for Black humanity, for Black lives. Social transformation demands fighting for a truly democratic, just, and transformed world. Fanon stood for this humanist vision.

Since Frantz Fanon did not advocate a narrow, misogynist nationalism, but rather a national consciousness that would lead to internationalism and social democracy, the antiracist and anti-capitalist consciousness, which is at the core of Fanon's theorization, remains a beacon for today's Black liberation movements. This thinking is embedded in radical Black feminism: antiracism and the struggle for Black life. For Revolutionary Black feminism, the demand requires the destruction of *all* systems of oppressions. This was articulated over 40 years ago by the Combahee River Collective.[23] The new struggles for Black life must be able to articulate the complex theoretical and practice spaces in which global racialized imperialism connects with gender and class. This is what the Combahee River Collective recognized as precursor to today's revolutionary Black feminism. That is, transforming transnational hetero-patriarchal white supremacist capitalism must be at the center of this revolutionary theory and practice. This is the profound and imperative lesson of revolutionary struggles all over the world. Indeed, Fanon reminds us that the need for total liberation encompasses the decolonization of activist-intellectuals. Black women radicals must take this seriously. Revolutionary struggle by definition *is* connected to those struggles on the ground: the women most exploited by racist capitalist patriarchy. Fighting back requires not only theory, but also a strong collaboration with women who are organizing to create a different social order. The need is to put front and center the inversion of othering – defining the lived experience through the lives of that experience. It requires shifting the lens of racial othering. Indeed, it is the deep refusal to be defined from without, even in the context of highly determinative structural inequalities, that the seeds of a new society are planted.

---

23   Taylor, Keeanga-Yamahtta. *How We Get Free: Black Feminism and the Combahee River Collective*. Chicago: Haymarket Books, 2017.

Bibliography

Bailey, Marlon M. and Rashad Shabazz, Gender and sexual geographies of Blackness. https://asu.pure.elsevier.com/en/publications/gender-and-sexual-geographies-of -blackness-new-black-cartographie.

Black Lives Network. https://blacklivesmatter.com/.

Bracking, Sarah and Graham Harrison, "Africa, Imperialism & New Forms of Accumulation," *Review of African Political Economy* 30 (2003): 5–10.

Brewer, Rose M. "21st Century, Austerity, and Black Economic Dispossession," *Souls: A Critical Journal of Black Politics, Culture, and Society* 14 (2012):227.

Carrig, David. "Jeff Bezos' wealth is now equal to 2.3 million Americans." https://www.usatoday.com/story/tech/news/2018/03/06/how-much-jeff-bezos-worth -centibillionaire-wealth/352082002/.

Combahee River Collective Statement https://americanstudies.yale.edu/sites/default/ files/files/Keyword%20Coalition_Readings.pdf.

Dahms, Harry F. *Transformations of Capitalism: Economy, Society, and the State in Modern Times*. New York: New York University Press, 2000.

Darity, William A. "History, Discrimination and Racial Inequality." In *The Impact of Color-Consciousness in the United States: The State of Black America,* edited by William Spriggs. New York: The National Urban League, 1999.

Davis, Angela. *Women, Race, and Class*. New York: Random House, 1982.

Davis, Angela. *Abolition Democracy*. London: Seven Stories Press, 2005.

Duggan, Lisa. *The Twilight of Equality*. New York: Beacon Press, 2004.

Dunbar-Ortiz, Roxanne. *An Indigenous People's History of the United States*. Boston: Beacon Press, 2001.

Fanon, Frantz. *The Wretched of the Earth*. Translated by Richard Philcox. New York: Grove Press, 2004.

Fanon, Frantz. *Toward The African Revolution*. Translated by Haakon Chevalier. New York: Grove Press, 1967.

Fanon, Frantz. *Black Skins, White Masks*. Translated by Richard Philcox. New York: Grove Press, 2008.

Garza, Alicia. A Herstory of the #BlackLivesMatter Movement. https://thefeministwire .com/2014/10/blacklivesmatter-2/ Last modified March 24, 2018.

Gordon, Lewis R., T. Denean Sharpley-Whiting, and Renee T. White. eds. *Fanon: A Critical Reader*, Oxford: Blackwell, 1996.

Gordon, Lewis R. *What Fanon Said: A Philosophical Introduction to his Life and Thought*. New York: Fordham University Press, 2015.

hooks, bell. *ain't i a woman*. Boston: South End Press, 1981.

Jones, Claudia. "An End to the Plight of the Negro Woman" https://libcom.org/library/ end-neglect-problems-negro-woman.

Kelley, Robin D.G. *Freedom Dreams: The Black Radical Imagination.* Boston: Beacon Press, 2002.

Kuenychia, Akua. "The Impact of Structural Adjustment Programs on women's international human rights: the example of Ghana." *Human Rights of Women: National and International Perspectives,* ed. Rebecca J. Cook. Philadelphia: University of Pennsylvania Press, 1994.

Marable, Manning. *How Capitalism Underdeveloped Black America.* Boston: South End Press, 1983.

Meaningful Work Transgender Experiences in the Sex Trade Reportt https://www.transequality.org/sites/default/files/Meaningful%20Work-Full%20Report_FINAL_3.pdf.

Mies, Maria. *Patriarchy and Accumulation on a World Scale.* London: Zed Books, 1986.

Mohanty, Chandra Talpade. *Feminism Without Borders: Decolonizing Theory, Practicing Solidarity,* Durham: Duke University Press, 2003.

Moody, Kim. *On New Terrain: How Capitalism is Reshaping the Battleground of Class War.* Chicago: Haymarket Books, 2017.

Mwaria, Cheryl Benois, and Silvia Federici. *African Visions: Literary Images, Political Change and Social Struggle in Contemporary Africa.* Westport: Greenwood Press, 2000.

Nya, Nathalie. "Sarte and Fanon: On Men and Women, and Gender and Race Intersection as They Relate to French Colonial Resistance," *Journal of General Philosophy* 2(2015): 61.

Rabaka, Reiland. *Africana Critical Theory.* Lanham: Rowland and Littlefield, 2010.

Rabaka, Reiland. "Revolutionary Fanonism: On Frantz Fanon's Modification of Marxism and Decolonization of Democratic Socialism," in *Socialism and Democracy*, edited by John H. McClendon III and Yusuf Nuruddin. New York: Routledge, 2011.

Rodney, Walter. *How Europe Underdeveloped Africa.* Washington, DC: Howard University Press, 1982.

Shakur, Assata. *Assata: An Autobiography.* Chicago: Chicago Review Press, 2001.

Sharpley-Whiting, T. Denean. *Frantz Fanon: Conflicts and feminisms.* Lanham: Rowman and Littlefield, 1998.

Singh. Nikhil Pal. *Black is a Country.* Cambridge, MA: Harvard University Press, 2004.

Spence, Lester K. "The Neoliberal Turn in Black Politics," *Souls* 14:3–4 (2012):139–159.

Stephens, Michelle A. "Black Transnationalism and the Politics of National Identity: West Indian Intellectuals in Harlem in the Age of War and Revolution." http://www.virginia.edu/woodson/courses/aas102%20(spring%2001)/articles/stephens.html.

Taylor, Keeanga-Yamahtta. *How We Get Free: Black Feminism and the Combahee River Collective.* Chicago: Haymarket Books, 2017.

Valluvan, Sivamohan and Eleanor Penny. "The New Undesirables." October 20, 2018. https://www.redpepper.org.uk/the-new-undesirables/.

CHAPTER 4

On the Possibility of a Post-colonial Revolutionary: Reconsidering Žižek's Universalist Reading of Frantz Fanon in the Interregnum

Dustin J. Byrd

In 2013, Santiago Zabala wrote a short essay for Aljazeera.com entitled "Slavoj Žižek and the Role of the Philosopher." Hamid Dabashi, the Columbia University Professor of Iranian Studies and Comparative Literature, dismayed by Zabala's "lovely little panegyric" to the Slovene public intellectual, and the Eurocentric assumptions that he and Žižek make about philosophy, responded with his own essay entitled "Can Non-Europeans Think."[1] Walter Mignolo, an Argentinian literary theorist, responded in-kind to Dabashi's article, adding strength to the already bold criticisms of Žižek. Mignolo, aping a passage from Žižek's 1998 essay, "A Leftist Plea for Eurocentrism," wrote,

> When one says Eurocentrism, every self-respecting decolonial intellectual has not as violent a reaction as Joseph Goebbels had to culture – to reach for a gun, hurling accusations of proto-fascist Eurocentrist cultural imperialism. A self-respecting decolonial intellectual will reach instead to Frantz Fanon: Now, comrades, now is the time to decide to change sides. We must shake off the great mantle of night, which has enveloped us, and reach, for the light. The new day, which is dawning, must find us determined, enlightened and resolute. So, my brothers, how could we fail to understand that we have better things to do than follow that Europe's footsteps.[2]

---

1 Hamid Dabashi, *Can Non-Europeans Think? What Happens with Thinkers Who Operate Outside the European Philosophical Pedigree.* January 15, 2013. https://www.aljazeera.com/indepth/opinion/2013/01/2013114142638797542.html.

2 This is a play on Žižek's essay, wherein he wrote the following: "When one says Eurocentrism, every self-respecting postmodern leftist intellectual has a violent a reaction as Joseph Goebbels had to culture – to reach for a gun, hurling accusations of proto-fascist Eurocentrist cultural imperialism. However, is it possible to imagine a leftist appropriate of the European political legacy?" See Walter Mignolo, *Yes, We Can: Non-European Thinkers and Philosophers.* February 19, 2013. https://www.aljazeera.com/indepth/opinion/2013/02/20132672747320891.html.

Of course, Žižek, ever the Lacanian and Marxist, responded in kind. In a lecture at the Birkbeck Institute of Humanities, on February 28, 2013, Žižek criticized Mignolo's peculiar use of Fanon against him, arguing that Mignolo engages in a "version of Baudrillard's battle cry": "forget Europe, we have better things to do than deal with European philosophy, better things than endlessly deconstructing."[3] Yet, Žižek retorts, "the irony here is that this battle cry did not hold for Fanon himself" as it did for Mignolo, since Fanon "dealt intensively [with European philosophy] and was proud of it. The first obscenity seems to me how dare he to quote Fanon!"[4]

In addition to his response to Walter Mignolo, Žižek takes on other uses (or postmodern abuses) of Fanon, including Harvard's premiere post-colonial studies scholar, Homi K. Bhabha's, and his taming of Fanon's radical revolutionary philosophy of violent emancipation. Žižek rejects Bhabha's attempt to explain away Fanon's avocation of violence in service to human emancipation, arguing that Bhabhba's interpretation of Fanon "neutralizes" the Martinique revolutionary. Žižek objects to the line of thinking that would state: "he [Fanon] didn't really mean it, with killing and violence; he meant some sublime gesture where there is no blood and nobody is really hurt and so on." Žižek, rather, accepts Fanon in all his violent radicality. In other words, Žižek endorses Fanon's "reach for the gun" in the cause of human emancipation.

My task here is not to rehash the merits of this enflamed debate; all those involved had valid arguments that are worth contemplating, and in many cases I suspect there is more of an overlapping consensus on Fanon between them

---

3   Žižek responds to his Critics. http://www.critical-theory.com/zizek-responds-to-his-critics/.
4   Ibid. It could be argued that Fanon argues for a "forgetting" of Europe in the conclusion of
     The Wretched of the Earth, wherein he writes, "let us waste no time in sterile litanies and
     nauseating mimicry... leave this Europe where they are never done talking of Man... how is it
     that we do not understand that we have better things to do than to follow that same Europe...
     we do not imitate Europe, so long as we are not obsessed by the desire to catch up with
     Europe... Let us decide not to imitate Europe... we have no more to fear; so let us stop envy-
     ing her," etc. However, it's clear that Fanon never meant to abandon all that Europe is, as even
     he worked through (and with) European philosophy all his adult life. Rather, Fanon argues
     against the Third World's blind mimicry of Europe, especially since Europe has forcefully ar-
     gued for universal values, principles, and ideals, but has always failed to achieve them, or has
     made a mockery out of them with bourgeois liberalism, colonialism, imperialism, fascism,
     authoritarian communism, etc. As Fanon writes, "All the elements of a solution to the great
     problems of humanity have, at different times, existed in European thought. But the action of
     European men has not carried out the mission which fell to them..." (p. 314) The "new man"
     (pg. 316), which Fanon argues for, should not make the same mistakes as Europe. Rather, it
     should actualize the very "elements of a solution" for humanity's problem that Fanon himself
     says "existed in European thought." See Frantz Fanon, *The Wretched of the Earth,* trans. Con-
     stance Farrington (New York: Grove Press, 1963), 311–316.

than not. I set as my task rather, to rethink what it was that Žižek was trying to get at when he quoted various passages in Frantz Fanon's *Black Skin, White Masks,* when he defended his understanding of Fanon against that of Dabashi, Mignolo, and Bhabha. I'm especially interested in the post-colonial revolutionary that Žižek depicts as being *authentically* Fanon, and why such a post-colonial, or de-particularized, revolutionary is so important in the 21st century, especially in light of the abrupt turn towards Alt-Fascism and *retrotopian* thought that is now taking place in much of the West. Juxtaposed to Bhabha's domesticated non-threatening Fanon-with-a-friendly-face, I want to use the same passages that Žižek invokes in order to clarify that which was only hinted at: The urgent need for post-colonial revolutionary theory (and praxis), which is already a constitutional part of Fanon's thought, but gets buried by those whose own pre-political foundations cause them to claim Fanon selfishly for themselves.[5] In this, I hope to emancipate Fanon from the petty ghettoization that so many attempt to lock him in, while at the same time avoid dispersing him to the point where he becomes meaningless.

1   Whose Fanon?

Clearly the work of Frantz Fanon does not belong to any one particular racial, ethnic, or religious group, be they African, North African, African America, Caribbean, Algerian, Muslim, etc. His recalcitrant, revolutionary, and emancipatory thought has fertilized the work of many important philosophers, sociologist, political figures, activists and revolutionaries around the world. Much like Che Guevara, those committed to a "universal" human emancipation discovered in their study of Fanon, regardless of their own pre-political foundations, a source of liberational theory and praxis. That Fanon's matrix of particularities includes him being Black, from Martinique, a subject of French colonialism, a soldier, a student in – and observer of – the French metropole

---

5   I use the phrase "pre-political foundations" in the way Jürgen Habermas defines it, as those characteristics that historically define a *Volk,* i.e. race, ethnicity, shared history, language, shared religion, etc. At one point in history, nations were almost always defined by such pre-political foundations: The *Volksgemeinschaft* – the "people's community." However, since the Enlightenment, some Western nations, as well as in their former colonial territories, chose to define the nation by shared *political* foundations, i.e. those values, principles, and ideals that (ideally) any person of any pre-political foundation could ascribe to via an act of their will. This sort of nation is a *willensgemeinschaft* – a "willed community," or "intentional democratic community." See Jürgen Habermas, *Between Facts and Norms,* trans. William Rehg. (Cambridge, MA: The MIT Press, 1996), 494–495.

(including its persistent racism), a psychiatrist, an author, and a revolutionary in a North African struggle, does not stop the African, Asian, European, North, Central, or South American from learning from his thought and biography, as well as interpreting and adapting his work to their conditions, whether they were contemporaries of Fanon or activists/revolutionaries in the 21st century. Fanon is relevant in colonial Algeria, just as much as he is relevant in today's North America; he is relevant in the industrialized prisons of the United States as much as he is in the slums of Cairo, Calcutta, and Johannesburg, not to mention the de-industrialized and forgotten cities of Detroit and Flint. No one owns Fanon, for his intellect and praxis was a "slave" – to use his own word – to no *single* cause. As such, he remains an open book – an encyclopedia of revolt for all those who are committed to a *universal* cause: human emancipation.

Nevertheless, our interpretations of Fanon are wide and varied. This was so demonstrated by the rigorous defense of "my Fanon" displayed by Žižek and Dabashi. "How dare he quote Fanon," said Žižek, "Fanon is *my* hero, that's why I defend him...," to which Dabashi writes, "Žižek can have *his* Fanon all to himself. There is plenty of Fanon left for *others*," as if there are other Fanons that are reserved for only certain people with particular pre-political foundations, or as if Fanon can be segmented – parted from himself.[6] Our interpretations vary, but Fanon as a thinker, despite his shortcomings, is relatively consistent, is holding up through time, and is continuing to be relevant in various fields.[7] Yet, there is a plethora of Fanon(s) – "on the market" – to choose from. To invoke Feuerbach, Fanon seems to be the revolutionary deity into which we project ourselves. Thus, the Fanon we witness in his writing often depends on what we witness in ourselves, leading to the variety of Fanons that are then argued for amidst scholars ("my hero," "his Fanon"). This is not a novel situation, as other thinkers, activists, revolutionaries, especially figures like Jesus of Nazareth, Prophet Muhammad, Martin Luther King Jr., and Malcolm X, are subject to this kind of subjective projection. When we ensnare Fanon within our own exclusionary perspectives, especially reading him merely through our own pre-political foundations, which are not the product of our will, but rather of our "thrownness" (*geworfenheit*), we diminish the capacity for Fanon's work and legacy to contribute effectively to the very goal of Fanon: emancipation of the wretched.[8] This I think is why Žižek quotes the particular passages that

---

6   Hamid Dabashi, *Can Non-Europeans Think?* (London: Zed Books, 2015), 7. Emphasis added.

7   For a critical "reassessment" of Fanon's work, see Anthony C. Alessandrini, *Frantz Fanon: Critical Perspectives*. New York: Routledge, 1999.

8   I do not think the same is true for philosophical commitments, which I think are proper and productive to read Fanon through. How would a Marxists, a libertarian, a Catholic, a Muslim, a nationalist, etc., interpret Fanon? How can Fanon's work critique various social, political, religious, and economic systems and dogmas? How can his work contribute to other systems

he quotes in *Black Skin, White Masks* in his Birkbeck lecture; he is attempting to let Fanon define himself outside of his immediacy by reminding the reader that Fanon argues for his own transcendence beyond his pre-political foundations, especially when speaking in terms of his liberational mission.

2   Žižek's Universal Fanon, or Fanon's Universalism

In his Birkbeck lecture on Fanon, Žižek said, "when I read lines like Mignolo's, I reach not for the gun but for Fanon."[9] To evidence this claim, the Fanon that Žižek reaches for is the Fanon that appears most powerfully in the last chapter of *Black Skin, White Masks*. Without abandoning the reality of Fanon's pre-political foundations, nor diminishing their significance, Žižek interconnects a narrative from Fanon's last chapter that emphasizes the *universal* over the *particular*, the *ultimate* over the *immediate*, the *essence* over the *appearance*, as a way of restoring Fanon above the temptation to locate him merely within a given community defined by non-European pre-political foundations.[10] He begins by quoting a statement of Fanon that expresses his most basic *humanistic universalism*:

> I am a man, and I have to rework the world's past from the very beginning. I am not just responsible for the slave revolt in Saint Dominque.

> Every time a man has brought victory to the dignity of the spirit, every time a man has said no to an attempt to enslave his fellow man, I have felt a sense of solidarity with his act.

> In no way does my basic vocation have to be drawn from the past of peoples of color.

---

of thought? That seems to be a justifiable exercise. However, to delineate Fanon within certain struggles because of the reader's own pre-political foundations – the "my Fanon" perspective – I think is problematic for Fanon himself, as it distorts the *universal* element of his critique.

9   Žižek responds to his Critics. http://www.critical-theory.com/zizek-responds-to-his-critics/.
10   In his book *Can Non-Europeans Think*, Hamid Dabashi makes a colossal mistake. The quote of Fanon that Žižek cites in his Birkbeck lecture is attributed to Žižek himself by Dabashi. Thus, when Fanon expresses his humanistic universalism, coming directly out of *Black Skin, White Masks*, Dabashi assumes it is Žižek speaking in the first person, thus giving the impression that Žižek is rejecting concerns for people of color. This is a clear misreading of Žižek's interpretation of Fanon. Dabashi forgets that Žižek is "reaching for Fanon" in response to Bhabha's obfuscation of Fanon's radicality, and thus is quoting Fanon directly. See Dabashi, *Can Non-Europeans Think*, 8–11.

In no way do I have to dedicate myself to reviving a black civilization unjustly ignored. I will not make myself the man of any past. I do not want to sing the past to the detriment of my present and my future.[11]

Using Fanon's own words, Žižek lays out the basic contours of Fanon's revolutionary universalism, and by consequence his appeal for what can be described as a *post-colonial revolutionary*: a revolutionary untethered to the restrictive particulars of any given struggle. Fanon argues that simply as a "man," a mere member of humanity, he must concern himself with the reality and history of oppression and human-caused unnecessary suffering, which encompasses all forms of tyranny, including slavery, indentured servitude, racism, colonialism, imperialism, and genocide, for the entire "world's past." For Fanon, he finds himself in solidarity with all those who have fought for human emancipation from such tyranny and injustice, regardless of the matrix of pre-political foundations that are relevant within such struggles. Thus, the Thracian Spartacus, who led the Third Servile War (slave revolt) against the Roman Republic, to Nat Turner, who led a slave revolt in 1831 against the slaveholders of Southampton County, Virginia, onto Ernesto "Che" Guevara, who attempted to liberate Latin America from North American imperialism, and many others, immediately conjure a sense of co-fraternity with Fanon, regardless of their particularities in time, place, race, ethnicity, or religious background. He feels a "sense of solidarity" with all of their actions against the unjust conditions they find themselves in, and in doing so, their struggles are on principle his struggles, as each struggle is an episode within the much larger project of human emancipation. As such, Fanon's sense of justice is *universally* applied; it includes Europe; it is not trapped within particularity; it is not merely a sensitivity for the suffering of his segment of humanity, for that only reproduces the idolization of "pure identity" that the philosopher Theodor W. Adorno thought Auschwitz confirmed to be "death," for it privileges one segment of humanity over another, and seeks "absolute integration" of the other via death.[12] Thus, Fanon's "basic vocation" need not be derived merely from only the "past of peoples of color," but from the globalized categories of the "wretched" in general, which, according to Marx, can be found throughout the history of the world, and in

---

11   Frantz Fanon, *Black Skin, White Masks,* trans. Richard Philcox. (New York: Grove Press,
      2008), 201. The version of Fanon's book that Žižek quotes from is not the same as Philcox,
      nor is it the same as the Charles Lam Markmann translation. Thus, he most likely is using
      his own translation. Throughout this essay, I will use the Philcox translation unless otherwise noted.
12   Theodor W. Adorno, *Negative Dialectics.* (New York: Continuum, 1999), 362.

all human societies.[13] As such, according to Fanon, his sensitivity for the suffering of the finite individual is not racialized, ethnicized, or religionized, etc.
Such particularized pasts cannot, as Fanon argued, become the narrow vision
through which his revolutionary praxis is viewed. It can be the *starting point*,
as it was with him in Martinique, France, and Algeria, but the struggle for human liberation in those particular territories does not reach the level of *universal* emancipation; such success would merely be a local affair if it only liberates
the victims of those particular struggles. Žižek, invoking Fanon, seems to call
for something much more radically profound.

   In order to build his case for a *post-colonial revolutionary*, Žižek continues
to further quote Fanon,

> It is not the black world that governs my behavior. My black skin is not a
> repository for specific values.

> Haven't I got better things to do on this earth than avenge the Blacks of
> the seventeenth century?[14]

Against the confining contours of identity-thought, which presumes one's pre-
political foundations determine one's subjectivity and subjective values, as if
geworfenheit is "will" or "fate," Fanon argues that his "black skin" does not au-
tomatically construct a preconceived value system, although it keenly informs
him of the unjust nature of tyranny and oppression, especially in a colonized
condition. He is black, and the systemic racism of the colonial situation forcefully reminds him of his blackness – and how such blackness is systematically
defined and denigrated by its opposition: *white supremacy.* Yet, Fanon states,
such blackness is not an intrinsic "repository" of values, as it is assumed to be
by his racist opposition. As such, it doesn't lead him to attempt to redeem the
Black victims of the seventeenth century, no more than white victims of class
oppression in the industrialized nineteenth century. From a materialist point of
view, such victims are long dead and therefore unredeemable. Unlike other revolutionary thinkers, such as Walter Benjamin, there is no sense of redemptive-
messianism in Fanon's understanding in his emancipatory project. There is no

---

13   Karl Marx and Friedrich Engels, "Manifesto of the Communist Party" in *The Marx-Engels
      Reader*, ed. Robert C. Tucker. (New York: W.W. Norton & Co., Inc., 1978), 473.
14   Again, reading these quotes knowing it is Fanon speaking, tilts them towards a "universal-
      ized" meaning, whereas if a reader thought it came from the white European philosopher
      Žižek, whom Dabashi assumed it came from, the meaning appears racially insensitive or
      even dismissive.

"weak messianism" that can redeem the innocent victims of history.[15] Thus, there is no hope for an *apocatastasis* in Fanon's revolutionary political praxis.[16] With the weight of the present and the future in front of him, the dead of the past are not his immediate concern; the living – the *now-and-still-wretched of the earth* – is his primary concern.

Žižek continues to quote Fanon's attempt to liberate himself from the ensnarement of pre-political foundations,

> I have not the right as a man of color to wish for a guilt complex to crystallize in the white man regarding the past of my race.
>
> I have not the right as a man of color to be preoccupied with ways of trampling on the arrogance of my former master.
>
> I have neither the right nor the duty to demand reparation for my subjugated ancestors.
>
> There is no black mission; there is no white burden.
>
> I do not want to be the victim of the Ruse of a black world.
>
> Am I going to ask today's white men to answer for the slave traders of the seventeenth century?
>
> Am I going to try by every means available to cause guilt to burgeon in their souls?[17]

I read these set of passages in two ways, (1) Fanon's insistence that the reality of race does not heteronomically assign members of a given race a "basic vocation," nor a pre-ordained "repository of values": such matters are subjects of the autonomous will, and that will, regardless of race, acting on its own convictions, can be revolutionary, reactionary, or apathetic. (2) We can also read these passages in light of Fanon's philosophical tendencies towards political

---

15   Walter Benjamin, *Illuminations: Essays and Reflection,* ed. Hannah Arendt, trans. Harry Zohn. (New York: Schocken Books, 1968), 254.

16   *Apocatastasis* refers to a restitution of a primordial condition – a return to the original state of being. Although it has its roots in Greek philosophy, this term became an important feature within the Abrahamic traditions. In the Vulgate Bible, the Greek was translated as "in tempora restitutionis omnium quae locutus est Deus" (the restitution of all things of which God has spoken).

17   Fanon, *Black Skin, White Masks,* 203–204.

and philosophical realism. What meaningful purpose would it serve for him to insist that "white" people feel guilty about the actions of their ancestors, when they can no more redeem (or punish) their ancestors from the horror and terror they perpetrated upon Fanon's black ancestors, than Fanon can redeem the victims of such horror and terror? Should such guilt be passed along from generation to generation like original sin, or should knowledge of the past injustices be transfigured into something more emancipatory? What purpose would it serve to attack the *arrogance* of the dead former master, other than to increase one's dedication to negate the master's negation, and hopefully bring about the positive: a more just and reconciled society? That dedication can be increased in much more productive ways.

As for the dead masters themselves, they are no longer subject to earthly judgment, although they cannot escape history. At best, one can long for *ultimate* justice for the innocent victim of the slave masters in an afterlife, but what concern has Fanon ever displayed for such an eschatological longing? His materialist metaphysics brooks no sensitivity for such a hopeful eschatology. Additionally, what could reparations do to redeem the "subjugated ancestors"? What meaningful recognition would that bring to the living descendants of those subjugated ancestors? It appears that Fanon rejects the idea that he's somehow privileged, as a descendent of the *wretched* of Martinique, to speak in their name. But if not the descendent, who should speak in their name? Fanon seems to have already answered that question in a universalized way: "I am a man, and I have to rework the world's past from the very beginning. I am not just responsible for the slave revolt in Saint Dominque." By virtue of being a man (a human), concerned with the condition of my fellow humans, "I" am charged with speaking and acting against the continual debasement of my wretched brothers and sisters, including, but not limited to, the wretched of Martinique. It cannot be the case, Fanon is implying, that only the descendants of the wretched speak for the wretched, but the descendants of the victors must also speak for and act on the behalf of their victims, whilst not forgetting what is most important: *Jetztzeit* – time impregnated with revolutionary potential.[18] In light of Fanon's universal humanism, it would not be

---

18   One of the most powerful examples of a descendent of the victors speaking and acting on behalf of the descendants of the victims (and the victims themselves), was the white American abolitionist John Brown, whom Malcolm X, while still in the Nation of Islam, thought to be the only redeemable white man in American history. Frederick Douglass said of John Brown, that while "I could live for the slave, but he could die for him." Brown transcended the concerns of his own white *volksgemeinschaft* and made his concern the emancipation of the oppressed, regardless of their pre-political foundations. For his efforts, he was murdered by the U.S. government in Charles Town, Virginia, on December 2nd, 1859.

wrong to interpret the "I" in "I am charged" as being the "universal I," meaning "all of us," not just Fanon.

Fanon seems to resist the quicksand of reading the history of injustice through bourgeois historicism, and keeps his mind squarely on the injustice that is in front of him, for it is only through the conquering of the present injustice that makes the historical injustice meaningful. Historical injustice reveals the entrenched mechanisms of present injustices. As such, Fanon writes, I "have not the right to confine myself in a world of retroactive reparations," especially in light of the depth of injustice that is ever-growing in the modern world.[19]

Furthermore, what universal emancipatory mission can be determined simply by *blackness*; what burden can be eternally carried simply because of *whiteness*? From his experiences of Bourgeois "freedom," in Martinique, France, and colonial Algeria, Fanon realized that "universal emancipation" cannot be viewed (or fought) merely through the prism of race; a much more comprehensive prism is required: a distant messianic-like perspective, that reveals the full totality of history as horror, terror, suffering, alienation, and destructiveness.[20] The unarticulated yet powerful presence of pre-political particularities in revolutionary struggles is an abiding factor for Fanon. For example, the Bourgeois revolution, although made in the name of universal emancipation, proved only to be in the interest of a segment of humanity. Having guillotined the monarchs of Europe, the Bourgeois revolutions led only to the freedom of the shopkeepers and the oligarchs: the aristocracy of wealth. Thus, politically, the "demos" were in fact only those who *owned* the nation, not the wretched masses who toiled and fought *for* the nation. The communist revolutions, while criticizing their bourgeois forebears for their failure to realize the promised *liberté, fraternité, et equalité*, liberated the working class from material deprivation, but stripped them of their political rights and freedoms. Such a regimented existence resulted in Stalin's "red fascism", which deprived millions of their lives, and many millions more from their ability to actualize their potentials. These revolutions were hypocritical, in that they were in service to the few (mainly European), despite the rhetoric of "universal applicability." As such, they perpetuated the class struggle, they perpetuated racial struggles, they perpetuated colonial domination, and they used religion, tribe, and nationhood to divide the workers, the peasants, the poor, and the colonial "subjects." In other words, the *particularity* of the Western revolutions betrayed

---

19   Fanon, *Black Skin, White Masks*, 205.
20   Adorno writes in his *Minima Moralia*, that in the face of history, such perspectives "must be fashioned that displace and estrange the world, reveal it to be, with its rifts and crevices, as indigent and distorted as it will appear one day in the messianic light." Theodor W. Adorno, *Minima Moralia: Reflections on a Damaged Life*. (New York: Verso, 2005), 247.

their stated universality. They were frauds. The claim of universality was but the ideological cover for particular interests.

Even to the extent that it has been abused, "universality" mustn't be abstractly negated and consigned to the dustbin of history. Rather, the *ideological fraud* perpetrated by particular interests in the name of "universal emancipation" must be identified, arrested, and expunged. By rejecting the temptation to particularize his emancipatory project, Fanon avoids the fraud that lay at the heart of the bourgeois and communist revolutions in the West, thus resuscitating emancipatory universalism. Žižek continues to quote Fanon,

> I am not a slave to slavery that dehumanized my ancestors.

> ...it would be of enormous interest to discover a black literature or architecture from the third century before Christ. We would be overjoyed to learn of the existence of a correspondence between some black philosopher and Plato. But we can absolutely not see how this fact would change the lives of eight-year-old kids working in the cane fields of Martinique or Guadeloupe.[21]

Here, Fanon refuses to be continually defined by, and trapped in, the legacy of slavery and colonialism. To merely be concerned with the emancipation of the descendants of the slaves, privileged above all other victims of history simply because of his personal intimacy with that struggle, perpetuates the legacy of racism, as it continues to define Fanon and his subjective concerns merely by his Afro-Caribbean heritage and the definition thereof by white supremacy. By rejecting the privileging of this particular struggle, he consequently rejects the racism that animates this particular struggle, as from a racist perspective, Fanon's own race should determine his concerns, thus localizing him within the struggle of his own particularity, i.e. the "black struggle" in Martinique, the Caribbean, or in metropole France. Fanon, no longer a "slave to the slavery that dehumanized [his] ancestors," rejects such a diminishment of his humanity to mere race. "As a man," as he stated earlier, he has to "rework the world's past from the *very beginning*." He is not "just responsible for the slave revolt of Saint Dominique," but is rather, in the fullness of his humanity, concerned with all of humanity's unjust suffering – even though that universal concern is iterated within his particular concern for the emancipation of the subjects of France's colonial empire.

The last sentence that Žižek quotes from Fanon's final chapter in *Black Skin, White Masks*, comes oddly enough not from the last page, but rather from the middle of the chapter. It is not Fanon's final statement in his book, rather it

---

21   Fanon, *Black Skin, White Masks*, 205.

is Žižek's final statement about Fanon from Fanon's closing thoughts: an exclamation point on Žižek's argument about Fanon's post-colonial universalism and his final rebuttal of the ghettoization of Fanon within certain intellectual circles. He quotes him saying, "I find myself one day in the world, and I acknowledge one right for myself: *the right to demand human behavior from the other.*"[22]

It is important to note that the "otherness" that Fanon invokes lacks determination; it isn't bound to any articulated pre-political particularity. He leaves ambiguous who the "other" is, thus implying that the other is by default the "universal other." Such indeterminate "otherness" implies the totality of others. This not only includes the obvious other, those who created the colonial condition, the European ruling classes, and the proletariats who faithfully served their master's needs and demands, but also the collaborators who share Fanon's own pre-political foundations. By universalizing the "other," Fanon implies that he stands with *all the wretched of the earth*, even amidst his abiding concern for those presently in front of him. Thus, in standing with the wretched, he takes sides; his universal solidarity is paradoxically particularized. It is universally with the victims of history, not the triumphant victors, who remain outside of his immediate concern. From Fanon's body of work, we can see that there is no meaningful "solidarity" with those African, Caribbean, Middle Eastern, and Asian ruling-classes, just because they belong to a pre-political foundation that has been historically mistreated, marginalized, and exploited by European empires.[23] Along with the European and Euro-American ruling-classes, such non-white ruling classes (the "native elite") are engaged in the oppression, suppression, exploitation, and genocidal destruction of the wretched, even though, as Jean-Paul Sartre pointed out, they too are often manufactured by the European elites.[24] Thus Fanon's solidarity with the other is not completely universalized, as it remains anchored in the framework of class struggle. He is, by this logic, universally concerned with the *wretched of the earth*, not the *wretched-makers of the palaces, penthouses, and parliaments.*

But by what right does Fanon have to "demand human behavior" from the other? This too can be argued within a universalistic framework, as the "human" within "human behavior" is *fully* universal, encompassing all within the species. As such, on the principle of equality, it demands something from *all* of those within the bounds of humanity, as it is prepared to reciprocate to *all*

---

22   Fanon, *Black Skin, White Masks*, 204.

23   See Fanon's discussion of the "national bourgeoisie" or "native bourgeoisie" in the chapter "The Pitfalls of National Consciousness," in Frantz Fanon, *The Wretched of the Earth*, 148–205.

24   Jean-Paul Sartre, "Preface," in *The Wretched of the Earth*, Frantz Fanon. (New York: Grove Press, 1963), 7.

within those bounds. Without spelling out succinctly what he means by "human behavior," one can rightly assume from any number of sources what he means: mutual-recognition, inter-subjective respect, equal moral consideration, etc. This *demand,* which exempts no individual, group, race, or class, regardless of their pre-political foundations, is a universal demand that Fanon not only rhetorically advanced, but was willing to shed blood for, as the Algerians were not *his people* (according to pre-political foundations), but like the Argentinian Che Guevara and the Cubans, he made their liberation *his cause* as part of a broader revolutionary project. Žižek rightly includes Fanon's statement here as his exclamation mark precisely because of this point; that final statement is Fanon's demand for universal justice and emancipation, within which belongs the long and brutal struggle for the rights, respect, and equality of the non-European *wretched of the earth.* As such, Fanon is not *merely* a Martiniquais, a male, of African descent, or a revolutionary in North Africa, but one that represents the struggle for *universal* emancipation within the *particular* struggles in which he participated: the *post-colonial revolutionary.*

3   Ideological Perversion of Universalism: the Truth as Lie's
     Camouflage

While we can argue that Fanon places an emphasis of universal emancipation throughout his writings, especially in his *Black Skin, White Masks,* it would be wrong to assume that all appeals to the "universal" are emancipatory. Take for example the Black Lives Matter movement. When the phrase "Black Lives Matter" is *not* countered with the phrase "Black Lives Don't Matter" Rather, it is countered with the phrase "All Lives Matter." Such rendering of the universal is ideological camouflage. It is clear that the former phrase "Black Lives Matter" is a particular claim, rooted in the black *erlebnis* (traumatic experience) of American history.[25] In essence, it means that black folk warrant moral consideration, respect, and the fullness of rights due to all citizens, and that the systematic violence of the police against young black men is an egregious violation of those values. Implicitly within the *particular* claim is the *universal* claim; black lives matter *just as much* as any other lives, and as such, black lives should be incorporated into the universal concern for human life. Nevertheless, the ideological function of saying "All Lives Matter" is to *neutralize* the reality of the particular. It is as if to say, "your suffering matters, but it matters no more than any other groups' suffering." This of course is true on the

---

25   See Fanon, *Black Skin, White Masks,* 123, 128.

one hand; concern for the suffering of the finite individual has universal significance, regardless of time, place, race, religion, etc. However, within a given
context, wherein one group is systematically oppressed, historically under-
served, the subject of random violence and subjugation, denied their human
and civil rights, as well as dehumanized and demonized, the secret intention
of the universal claim becomes apparent: it is an attempt to bury the grotesque
reality of the particular underneath the *truth* of the universal, thus denying
the immediacy of black suffering. Truth itself is ideologically appropriated and
functionalized, resulting in an intentional distortion of truth. It is an attempt
to use the universal claim to conceal their own "negrophobia," by distorting the
particular claim into appearing to privilege the particular over the universal,
which in reality it does not.[26]

Additionally, elevating the false-universal ideologically transforms those
who are not the historical subject of imperialism and colonialism into "victims," giving them a share in the "privilege of the victim" – the right, legitimacy,
and authority to speak from the perspective of one who has been systemically
and systematically wronged. From a White Nationalist perspective, the white
population in the West is the victim of "modernity" (the creation of white liberals and Jews), for it has lost its own civilization, land, and culture to foreigners. Thus, in elevating the false-universal, in which the White Nationalist can
claim victimhood on behalf of the entire West, they augment their ideological
claim; they too can speak with authority against the crimes of their oppressors:
Blacks, Muslims, immigrants, refugees, and other marginalized groups within
the West.

Such functionalization of the universal must be rejected, as it fundamentally distorts and disfigures the emancipatory intention of the universal claim
for the benefit of the unjust, unequal, and necrophilic status quo, while rendering the truth of the particular moot. The unifying essence of the universal
claim must be preserved in its undistorted state, as it is what produces universal solidarity amongst the global wretched. As Fanon stated, "I am fighting for
the birth of a *human world*, in other words, a world of *reciprocal recognitions*."[27]

4   Post-colonial Mind

European colonialism ideologically defined the colonial subject as merely a
small conglomerate of particularities; the slave was *merely* "a black," *merely* "a

---

26   Ibid., 138.
27   Ibid., 193. Emphasis added.

woman" or "a breeder," *merely* "a beast of burden," a *mere* piece of "property," *merely* a "living tool." Being such, the "colonized mind," which absorbed the imposed *mere-ness*, could not escape the degradation of the *mere* particularities; they were enchained within them, both in the colonizers' law, and more painfully, in their damaged psyche.[28] Universalism, to be able to think beyond the immediate, beyond the given, beyond the isolated appearances, with few exceptions, was not a trait that the *merely* particular could easily ascend to, especially when they were overwhelmed by their own particular experiences of oppression. Who could fault the American slave for not concerning himself/herself with the plight of European Serfs or the Aboriginals in Australia? Their world was brutally immediate and overwhelming, and they struggled to maintain their own existence on a daily basis. Universal thought, we can deduce, was the privilege of those who could afford, in time and resources, universal thought, not those struggling to survive daily whippings, rape, starvation, deprivations, and torture, both psychological and physical. Because they *appeared* to not think beyond the immediate, it was assumed the wretched were "incapable" of thinking. Thus, abstract thought, we are told by the master-class, was the work of the superior, the colonial masters, the metropole: the civilizational *übermenschen*. Yet this was merely a reflection of the way society was constructed and maintained: the masters and the slaves; the oppressor and the oppressed; the exploiter and the exploited. Fanon, by rejecting the enslavement of humanity to the pre-determined "capabilities" associated with pre-political foundations, which were ideologically created by the master-classes, also rejected the racist ideologies that attempt to chain him to the *mere-ness* of the colonized and enslaved subject.[29] Thus, he reclaims his full humanity

---

28   See Na'im Akbar, *Breaking the Chains of Psychological Slavery.* Tallahassee, FL: Mind Productions & Associates, Inc., 1996. I base my understanding of the "colonized mind" from the Malaysian scholar Syed Hussein Alatas' notion of the "captive mind," wherein the captive mind is defined as being uncritical, merely imitative, and dominated by a heteronomic source, predominately Western, and therefore lacking any internal autonomy. Alatas is primarily speaking of non-Western academics who reflexively imitate their Western counterparts, while simultaneously neglect the work of their non-Western peers. In our use of the phrase "colonized mind," we're speaking of those individuals of the former (and still) colonies that retain (or even embrace) the colonizers false-ideology within their own minds, and are thus determined by such false-ideology, therein sharing a consciousness with their masters. In doing so, they perpetuate the very damaging notions, ideas, and principles that were imposed upon them to maintain their colonized state of being for the benefit of the colonizers.

29   On racist ideologies, which were meant to legitimate self-interested policies, see Ibram X. Kendi, *Stamped from the Beginning: The Definitive History of Racist Ideas in America.* New York: Nation Books, 2016.

when he, in Žižek's words, "dealt intensively [with European philosophy] and was proud of it... he dealt extensively with Hegel, psychoanalysis, Sartre, even Lacan."[30] To be sure, his humanity was not reclaimed because the philosophy he dealt with was predominately *European*: European philosophy has no such elevating power; it couldn't even compel Europe to realize its own humanistic ideals, values, and principles. Rather, it was because he transcended that which European colonialism defined him as – simple *mere-ness*. Such imposed *mere-ness* would not have allowed him the possibility of engaging intensely with the philosophy of the "superior civilization," for the "natural capability" for a Black man to engage such thought was denied in fact (via self-interested policies), and denied in theory (via legitimating ideologies).[31] That he mastered, expanded upon, and applied Europe's Marxist and existentialist philosophy, that by his race he was supposed to be incapable of, and determinately negated it into his own revolutionary philosophy, is both poetic justice and the forceful dissolution of a racist ideology that says a Black man is incapable of such thought. Thus, what helped him realize the fullness of humanity was his ascent to the universal – in his case, the universal concern for matters beyond the *mere-ness* that his subaltern status was meant to cage him in. And like Toussaint L'Ouverture's revolution in Haiti from 1791 to 1794, Denmark Vesey's rebellion in South Carolina in 1822, Nat Turner's rebellion in Virginia in 1831, Frederick Douglass and his fight with the "slave-breaker" Edward Covey, MOVE Organization's standoffs with the Philadelphia Police Department, and many other revolts against oppression, Fanon's participation in the violent struggle for a people's emancipation concretely liberated him from such mere-ness, as the dignity of the struggle itself relieved him of the master's dehumanizing ideology.

In transcending the *mere-ness* of the colonial mind, along with an embracing and adopting the universal concern, Fanon invented his own subjectivity: his own "post-colonial mind." He was not an imperfect Black copy of the European colonial, but rather a universal man demanding universal humanity from the rest of humanity. In such an emancipated state, he saw how the struggle for human liberation in his Caribbean island was intimately tied with the struggle for emancipation in Europe, in Vietnam, in Africa, even in the slums and prisons of North America, wherein the hypocrisy of the Liberal Bourgeois "revolution" is intimately felt every day. As such, he rejected what Žižek called "Baudrillard's

---

30   Dabashi, *Can Non-Europeans Think*, 7.
31   Kendi, *Stamped from the Beginning*, 1–11.

battle cry: forget Europe," for forgetting Europe was no more possible then forgetting any other part of the earth wherein the wretched are made.[32]

5   Reversing Fanon in the Interregnum: the New Colonial Project

In the last decade, especially with the election of Barack Obama and the "white-lash" election of his nationalist and faux-populist successor, Donald J. Trump, a virulent form of fascism, rooted in a longing for racial "retrotopia" – yet clothed in the aesthetics and technology of the 21st century – has made its loud appearance on the world-historical stage, both in the United States and in Europe.[33] This strain of fascism, or "Alt-Fascism" as we're describing it here, is a re-articulation of what the British political theorist Roger Griffin describes as *palingenetic ultra-nationalism*. It is rooted partly in neo-liberal economic anxiety, post-modern nihilism, cultural alienation within multiculturalism, the fear of "white genocide," and the assumed culture of political correctness, which, according to White Nationalists, represses obvious "truths" in the name of "cultural sensitivity." According to Griffin, such palingenetic ultra-nationalist movements also includes the "forces [of] militarism, racism, charismatic leadership, [and] populist nationalism."[34] It is determined by "fears that the nation or civilization as a whole [is] being undermined by the forces of decadence," and is plagued with a "deep anxiety about the modern age and longing for a new era to begin."[35] In addition to these ingredients, what has forcefully birthed fascism back in to the public sphere is the growing fear of *Le grand remplacement* (The Great Replacement), which is understood by far-right traditionalists, paleo-conservatives, and White Nationalists as being the inevitable outcome of the Liberal-Socialist pro-immigration agenda – one that works to the advantage of immigrants at the expense of white natives.[36] The xenophobic fear of being replaced has once again mutated into an irrational hatred for all things perceived to be "other" – for the other is the agent of the demise of the white "natives."

---

32   Žižek, http://www.critical-theory.com/zizek-responds-to-his-critics/.
33   Zygmunt Bauman, *Retrotopia.* Malden, MA: Polity Press, 2017.
34   Roger Griffin, *The Nature of Fascism.* (New York: Routledge, 1993), viii.
35   Ibid.
36   Joakim Andersen, *Rising from the Ruins: The Right of the 21st Century.* (London: Arktos Media Ltd., 2018), 120; Greg Johnson, *The White Nationalist Manifesto.* San Francisco: Counter-Currents Publishing Ltd., 2018; John Tirman, *Dream Chasers: Immigration and the American Backlash.* Cambridge, MA: The MIT Press, 2015.

Coined by the French polemical author, Renaud Camus, the "great replace-ment" theory, as it pertains to France, argues that the "ethnic French," those belonging to the historical community of France and their matrix of pre-political foundations, will inevitably be replaced by those who lack such an ethnic foundation for their French identity, predominately the immigrants of Northern Africa and the Middle East.[37] Such critics argue that the Bourgeois Enlightenment's (as well as post-colonial liberals') preference for *jus soli* (right of the soil, or "birthright citizenship") over the pre-political *jus sanguinis* (right of blood), which limits citizenship to those who share in the pre-political ma-trix of a historical "blood-bound" nation (*volksgemeinschaft*), is the Trojan Horse that allows the ethnically and culturally non-French to claim French citizenship. In obtaining *political* citizenship, these foreign "outsiders" claim that their cultural "otherness" is also rightfully considered French, for within the post-modern condition, "Frenchness" is without content, and thus merely formal. Consequently, all manner of things can find an equal home within this post-modern amorphic "French," which renders "Frenchness" meaningless, as it has no distinguishable substance; it is just an empty form. As such, the "in-tentional democratic community," the *willensgemeinschaft*, comprised of rep-resentatives of all nations and cultures claiming "Frenchness," is the concep-tual flank for these "invaders" to destroy what is left of historic French cultural and genetic particularity. Without the strength of French cultural particularity, France becomes incapable of asserting its identity against the so-called "hordes of invaders." Thus, pre-modern traditional French culture, the basis of French identity, they believe, is dying a slow and agonizing death under the weight of multiculturalism, with the ultimate outcome of France being replaced by a cultural amalgamation: Eurabia.[38]

Fanon himself wrote about the process of *déculturation* in his book *Toward the African Revolution,* when he discussed the colonial power's ability to strip native peoples of their sense of self, their identity, their cultural patterns, and systems of reference, all through systematic racism. He writes, the "racialized group tries to imitate the oppressor and thereby to deracialize itself. The 'infe-rior race' denies itself as a different race. It shares with the 'superior race' the convictions, doctrines, and other attitudes concerning it."[39] In the perspective

---

37   See Renaud Camus, *Le Grand Remplacement: Introduction au remplacisme global.* France: Chez l'auteur, 2017. Also see Renaud Camus, *You Will Not Replace Us!* France: Chez l'auteur, 2018.

38   "Eurabia" was coined by Bat Ye'or (Gisele Littman) in her book *Eurabia: The Euro-Arab Axis.* Cranbury, NY: Associated University Presses, 2005.

39   Frantz Fanon, *Toward the African Revolution,* trans. Haakon Chevalier (New York: Grove Press, 1967), 38.

of Alt-Fascists, a similar yet perverted process is happening among Whites in the West. Because of white-guilt, i.e. ethnomasochism, Whites attempt to de-racialize themselves by imitating the culture of their former colonial subjects, by adopting their cultural patterns and systems of reference (*negrification*). In this case, it is not the "inferior race" that "denies itself as a race," but rather the "guilty race" that "denies itself as a race," for in deracializing itself, it absolves it-self of the sins of its colonial forefathers, the knowledge of which is repeatedly hammered into the younger generation by ethnomasochistic educators. In this process, European *hochkultur* (high culture) is replaced by African-inspired pop culture, pushed by the power of the *lügenpresse* (lying press), resulting in the evaporation of Europe's primordial identity and traditional culture. As Fanon knew, *déculturation*, or *Umvolkung* ("de-people-ing" in German), is a way of making space between a people and their historical culture, thus de-priving them of the vital resources needed to maintain their distinct identity and resist capitulation to the colonial invader. Without such a strong sense of self, the invader can impose upon them the identity of their choosing, which is always a submissive and subservient identity. From the perspective of the anti-immigrant Far-Right, *überfremdung* (over-foreignization), leads to *décultura-tion*, which is a precondition for the subaltern to replace their former masters in the former masters' own fatherland.

For the White Nationalists, it is not just the liberal bourgeois state of France, or in immigrant friendly Germany, that are now under the threat of losing their historic (and racial) identity, but the entire West is threatened by post-modern "globalism."[40] The West, it is charged, exports its nihilistic consumerist culture and neo-liberal economic system abroad while it imports its population from the *tiers monde* (third world), thus destroying both the Third World and the First World. True multiculturalism, it is argued, is the opposite of the form of multiculturalism found within the pluralist democracies of the West; it is leav-ing traditional cultures intact within their traditional geographical boundar-ies: the sovereign and "pure" ethno-states. For the Alt-Fascists, the right not to have a people's traditional culture undermined by a foreign culture includes modern Europe. Thus, the "world of reciprocal recognition," as Fanon so de-sired, is assented to by the Alt-Fascists, but it is a world wherein people do not interpenetrate each other territorially.[41] Rather, this imagined world is governed bi-laterally through sovereign *nation-states* (in the strict biological

---

40   Guillaume Faye, *The Colonisation of Europe*. London: Arktos Media Ltd., 2016. These same
       arguments in the American context can be found in Greg Johnson's *The White Nationalists
       Manifesto*, 9–57.
41   Fanon, *Black Skin, White Masks*, 193.

sense of the phrase), whose membership within the nation-state is determined by pre-political foundations. As it would be a transgression of the biologically determined nation-state for an individual to become a citizen of another nation-state, individuals do not go beyond their historical geographical borders. It is the end of the *willensgemeinschaft*. As such, mutual-reciprocity and mutual-recognition is a matter between the ethnically bound nation-states, not individuals of different ethnic, religious, and racial groups cohabitating within one state.

Being against such cultural and racial interpenetration, the Alt-Fascists criticize *neo-liberal capitalist globalization* – the economics of modernity, as it is capitalism's relentless pursuit of profit that forces cultures to interpenetrate each other, either through immigration, business partnerships, pursuit of education, and the inevitable brain-drain from the Third World to the First World. This, it is argued, undermines each peoples' *eigentlichkeit* (authenticity), and therefore it must be replaced with an economic system that allows various nation-states to remain undisturbed by the influences of foreign cultures.

In addition to neo-liberal capitalism, Alt-Fascists criticize Marxism, socialism, and other forms of Left-wing "globalist" thought, for it too diminishes Western cultural superiority to the level of the inferior others, all in the name of "egalitarianism."[42] From the perspective of the Alt-Fascists, equality, as such, is unjust, as it fails to recognize the genius – and thus superiority – of the West. By operating on the principle of equality of cultures, the Left gives equal space within Western societies to foreign and "degenerate" cultures, thus weakening the West's ability to stabilize, rejuvenate, and reproduce its own identity (and biology). Additionally, the insistence on equality of peoples is an affront to the psychological well-being of those who see themselves as superior, as it denies the very the uplifting yet false-consciousness that gives them a sense of superiority: "superiority" being a psychological defense mechanism against their own sense of insecurity, alienation, and isolation.[43]

Within the "interregnum" between modernity and the rise of postmodernity, White Nationalists, Nationalist Populists, Paleoconservatives, Traditionalists, Archeofuturists, and other Alt-Fascists, have appropriated Fanon's insights into colonialism and its psychological destructiveness. They seek to demonstrate how the descendants of Europe's colonial subjects have returned to the metropoles, and with the help of Cultural Marxists, Liberals, Jews, and non-conforming left-wing intellectuals (the "collaborators," or European "native elites" to use a Fanonian phrase), have begun to colonize liberal Europe

---

42   Joakim Andersen, *Rising from the Ruins*, 86–87.
43   See Erich Fromm, *Escape from Freedom*. New York: Henry Holt and Company, 1994.

under the cover of equality, tolerance, and diversity. While such a "coloniza-tion" is a catastrophe for European civilization as a distinct civilization, its death culminates in a palingenetic opportunity: the creation of a stronger and more vibrant Europe: *The Fourth Age of European Civilization,* as the New Right philosopher Guillaume Faye calls it.[44] In order to avoid civilization death via "involution" – the regression of civilization due to dysgenic forces – and bring about this rebirth of Europe, Europeans must, according to Faye, "unite in self-defense, expel the colonizers, throw off the American yoke, and regenerate themselves biologically and morally."[45] Anything less than a *totalen krieg* (total war) against their invading foreigners will leave Europe vulnerable to complete colonization, and colonization means collapse – a dystopic and apocalyptic end to a distinctly Christian-inheritance Enlightenment civilization.

Although immigration of Muslims and Africans is seen as the primary dys-genic force in Europe, various Alt-Fascists have once again seized upon a fa-miliar target: *Der Jude* (The Jew). The Jewish community plays a particularly insidious role in this new iteration of White Nationalism. In his essay "The Populist Temptation," Slavoj Žižek shed light on this new formulation of anti-Semitism. First, Žižek rejects the idea that the Muslims are the "new Jews" of Europe, as some on the Left have claimed. Rather, he argues, *Der Jude* is seen now, as was before, as being the "secret master that pulls the strings."[46] While it was the strings of international finance, the media, and pop culture, that the Jews pulled in Europe in the 1920s and 1930s, today, his work is done primarily through immigration. Žižek writes, "if one suspects a secret plot in their [the Muslims] 'invasion of Europe,' then Jews have to be behind it," since the Mus-lims are "too visible" and "clearly not integrated into our societies."[47] By way of

---

44 Guillaume Faye, *Why We Fight: Manifesto of the European Resistance,* trans. Michael O'Meara. (London: Arktos Media Ltd., 2011), 178–179. The other three ages of European civilization, according to Faye, are Antiquity, the Middle Ages, and Modernity, which the latter is now coming to its conclusion. Faye has a particular disdain for American style democracy, as it is the most prominent example of a *willensgemeinschaft.* America is also the guardian of the neo-liberal world order, which imposes a multiculturalist-democratic form of political-economics on European countries.

45 Ibid.

46 Slavoj Žižek, "The Populist Temptation," in *The Great Regression,* ed. Heinrich Geiselberg-er. (Malden, MA: Polity Press, 2018), 186.

47 Ibid. This anti-Semitic trope was on full display when Robert Gregory Bowers, a 46-year-old White Nationalist, attacked the Tree of Life Synagogue on October 27, 2018, in the Spring Hill neighborhood in Pittsburgh, Pennsylvania. Bowers was enraged that the Jew-ish community sponsored Muslim refugees, who were "invaders" and would "kill our people." Although he was a supporter of Donald J. Trump, he criticized the President for being a "globalist, not a nationalist," because he wasn't hard enough on the Jews. "There is no MAGA (Make America Great Again) as long as there is a kike infestation," he wrote on

his social invisibility, "the Jew" is undetected as he makes Europe comfortable for his own existence by transforming Europe into a "multicultural dystopia" akin to the United States. Through this unseen string pulling, he slowly removes the particularity of Europe; he subjects its economy to global forces; he denigrates Europe *hochkultur* (high culture) with dysgenic pop-culture (negrification); he fills its cities with people who do not belong to Europe, cannot integrate with its people, nor assimilate its libertine (or its traditional) culture. In doing so, the Jew, who is otherwise the perpetual other, creates the conditions for his own flourishing at the expense of the native.[48] Additionally, through liberal institutions, he has removed Europe's ability to remove him.[49]

From the perspective of White Nationalists, Jews can blend in European society, but they cannot be absorbed or integrated into the distinct *geist* of Europe, with its Christian inheritance, no matter how diminished that *geist* is. Thus, they must ally themselves with those who have the ability to deconstruct that *geist*: The Muslims. Anything outside of this complete deconstruction of European distinctiveness leaves Europe's small Jewish community vulnerable to a new and more complete *Endlösung* (final solution): the absolute integration of the Jews via extermination of the Jews. Thus, in order to secure their own existence, Europe must become Americanized – a hodgepodge of peoples without clearly defined cultural inheritances.

Žižek is right to point out here the dangerous nature of this new form of Alt-Fascism; it successfully combines Islamophobia and traditional Anti-Semitism. The Muslims are the *weapons* used against the Europeans and the Jews are the *agents* through which the "invading hordes" accomplish their colonizing task. Through their demographics, such a Jewish-Muslim alliance will conquer Europe and colonize it under the guise of multiculturalism and cultural Marxism, which will inevitably lead to "white genocide."[50] Although the legitimacy of

---

a Gab post. Eleven worshippers were killed in the attack and seven more were injured. He was later hailed as a patriot by many White Nationalist groups.

48   Ibid.

49   Although White Nationalists see this supposedly friendly Jewish-Muslim alliance as being detrimental to Europe, the recent rise of anti-Semitism in Europe has mainly come from disaffected Muslim youths, who have directed their anger about their own conditions, and the conditions of the Palestinian people, against the small Jewish communities that still remain in Europe. Anti-Semitism from Muslims, most of which are not religious, but are mainly second generation sons of immigrants, have driven many Jews from Europe to Israel.

50   Using the language of the biological sciences, Johnson attributes "white genocide" to four causes: "habitat loss, invasive species, hybridization, and predation." See Johnson, *The White Nationalist Manifesto*, 23, 17–22.

this claim is dubious, it is not unbelievable among those who've experienced the growing Muslim presence in Europe as, to use Fanon's word, an *erlebnis*.

6 Erlebnis as Civilizational Trauma; Retrotopia as Ersatz Utopia

In discussing the psychopathology of the Black Man in *Black Skin, White Masks*, Fanon quotes Freud's understanding of the lasting effects of trauma on the psyche, as being the basis of an individual's neuroses.[51] Since here we are not speaking of one single individual, but rather a collectivity of individuals – Western society – we can philosophically appropriate this concept from Freud/ Fanon and apply it to the traumatic experience of modernity and how it has contributed to the conditions from which Alt-Fascism becomes a credible alternative in the eyes of otherwise rational Westerners.

Fanon quotes Freud as saying that the symptoms associated with an erlebnis are the "residue of emotional experiences... psychic traumas," that are not always caused by a "single event," but on the contrary, arise from "multiple traumas, frequently analogous and repeated."[52] Thus, says Fanon, "there is a determined *Erlebnis* at the origin of every neurosis."[53] The West is currently suffering from such a neurosis. On the one hand, it publically remains committed to the values of the Enlightenment, while at the same time it doubts whether or not those values can keep an increasingly disparate people together. Those who advocate for an ethno-state, like Greg Johnson, Jared Taylor, and Wilmot Robertson, have seized on this troubling fissure. According to Greg Johnson,

> ethnonationalism is contrasted with civic nationalism, in which the principle of unity is subjection to a common system of laws or the profession of a shared civic creed. Civic nationalism need not exist in a multiracial or multicultural society, but the primary reason that civic nationalist creeds are promulgated is to deal with the absence of organic, ethnic unity in a society.[54]

If the liberal *willensgemeinschaft* is to remain intact, it must replace what it lacks – "organic" or "ethnic unity" – with some other form of social adhesive. This is usually done with civic religion, national myths, and political institutions and

---

51   Fanon, *Black Skin, White Masks*, 123.
52   Freud, as quoted by Fanon, *Black Skin, White Masks*, 122–123.
53   Ibid., 123.
54   Johnson, *The White Nationalist Manifesto*, 49.

ideologies. However, globalized modernity has (1) revealed the limits of such sources of social unity, (2) eroded what is left of those sources, and (3) has constructed a political-economic and cultural reality that is perceived by the Western precariat to be incapable of being solved by such liberal sources. The traumatic erlebnis of modernity has ruptured the modern Westerners from their "organic" and "ethnic unity"; it has severed it from its Christian cultural inheritance; the ravages of aggressive neo-liberal capitalism have undermined its own promise of working class prosperity; and its scientism, metaphysical materialism, instrumental reason, pervasive nihilism, and necrophilic consumerism as a comprehensive way-of-being-in-the-world, have ciphered any sense of inherent meaningfulness and hopefulness in life. In this existential void, many in the West have sought to overcome the civilizational *entzauberung* (disenchantment) and recover their "lost utopia" with its ersatz: *retrotopia*.

According to the Polish philosopher Zygmunt Bauman, retrotopias exist when societies abandon their confidence in future progress, when societies in decline no longer look forward to the "not-yet-born," but begin to look backwards in nostalgia towards an imaged ideal type of the *status quo ante* (the way it used to be), before modernity brought about the polyethnic, multicultural, and dispersed society.[55]

In *Black Skin, White Masks*, Fanon reminds us that in "every society, in every community, there exists, must exist, a channel, an outlet whereby the energy accumulated in the form of aggressiveness can be released."[56] In the 21st century post-secular and multicultural societies of Europe, such accumulated aggressiveness has been filtered through palingenetic ultra-nationalism and directed towards a singular ideologically constructed culprit: The Immigrant/ Refugee, the "invading hordes" determined to colonize Europe.[57] Whilst retrotopia remains aspirational, a mere ersatz meant to satisfy the longing for an idealized past age, when such aspirations take concrete form in citizen groups in civil society, and metastasize into political parties determined to take power, then the retrotopian vision of a purified and authentic society becomes a great danger to those who are outside of the "in-group" dynamic: the unintegrated and unassimilated other – especially those who nevertheless claim "westernality" despite their abiding otherness. Through palingenetic ultra-nationalism, the West engages in the "collective catharsis," which Fanon believed "every society naturally acquir[es]."[58] Thus, the struggle to actualize the retrotopic

---

55   Bauman, *Retrotopia*, 5, 9.
56   Fanon, *Black Skin, White Masks*, 124.
57   Guillaume Faye, *The Colonisation of Europe*.
58   Fanon, *Black Skin, White Masks*, 124.

vision of a future society is the way the West "defends" itself from the colonizing project of the immigrants and refugees. It is the bringing forth of the
Ragnarök.[59]

7   Beyond the Flaschenpost: the Call for the Post-colonial Revolutionary

The Frankfurt School's post-World War II critical theory of society, especially
its analyses of nationalism, authoritarianism, and anti-Semitism, was meant to
be a *flaschenpost* – a "message in a bottle" – for those who mistakenly believed
that such forces had been defeated. According to Leo Löwenthal, one of the
early members of the Frankfurt School, the *flaschenpost* arose in the aftermath
of World War I, "out of the feeling that one could contribute to change, that the
message would get through to the right people, that possibilities would once
again arise."[60] Indeed, such possibilities did arise again, as fascism, responding
to the failures of liberalism and the threat of Soviet communism, brought upon
World War II, the greatest of world-historical catastrophes. Yet, what people
optimistically thought was finally destroyed in World War II, fascism, was only
destroyed militarily. As a political philosophy, it was merely repressed, awaited
the right opportunity – the right time for another "collective catharsis" – to
explode back onto the canvas of history, albeit in a new "alternative" form.

   In the interregnum between modernity and post-modernity, with the collapse of the socialist Left as a world-historical force, and the reemergence of
virulent forms of palingenetic ultra-nationalism, it is time for the post-colonial
revolutionaries, those committed to universal emancipation, to once again
take their places among the barricades. The post-colonial revolutionary –
those revolutionaries who've emancipated themselves from their pre-political
foundations as limiting factors in their revolutionary politics – are uniquely
qualified for this struggle. For the "colonial" and "anti-colonial" struggle is no
longer happening in the *tiers monde* (at least not according to the Alt-Fascists),
but rather it is happening in the West, which is comprised of numerous post-
secular societies that are multiethnic and multi-confessional. Building bridges
and bonds between the various marginalized communities, as opposed to

---

59   In Norse mythology, a *Ragnarök* is an apocalyptic sweeping away of an old order. Either
      through natural disaster or through a man-made cleansing of the old, a new order as-
      cends from the ashes of the old.
60   Leo Löwenthal, *The Unmastered Past.* (Berkeley: University of California Press, 1987), 257.
      Also See Rudolf J. Siebert, *From Critical Theory to Critical Political Theology: Personal Au-
      tonomy and Universal Solidarity.* (New York: Peter Lang, 1994), 15.

defining their struggle simply on the basis of their communities' particularities, is absolutely necessary if the push to eradicate the non-integrative "other" from the society is to be halted, if Fanon's truly human world, "a world of reciprocal recognitions," is to come about.[61]

Liberalism has shown itself to be incapable of realizing its own "universal" creed (*Liberté, Equalité, and Fraternité*); it has shown that it will continue to produce the very political, economic, and cultural conditions that call for its own destruction – either by a reactionary retrotopian move, which comes at the expense of all those who cannot be integrated into the singular identity of the imagined community, or through a post-modernity that seeks as its goal the reconciliation of the fundamental antagonisms that currently plague humanity – class, race, gender, culture, not through the dissolution of human differences through haphazard amalgamation, but through a radical realization of humanity's oneness *within* its differences: Its *E pluribus unum*. Fanon's universalism, his commitment to the wretched of the earth, which Žižek highlighted in his Birkbeck lecture, is a prime example of what is needed in today's disfigured and distorted social relations. It is not time to retreat with Fanon into our own local struggles; rather, it is time to invoke Fanon in those struggles, and connect them with the broader struggle for human emancipation. *Divide et impera*, (divide and conquer) the Romans used to say; it would be foolish if we let Fanon be functionalized as a tool for that division.

To end with Fanon, again from his finale in *Black Skin, White Masks*:

> Only conflict and the risk it implies can, therefore, make human reality, in-itself-for-itself, come true. This risk implies that I go beyond life toward an ideal which is the transformation of subjective certainty of my own worth into a universally valid objective truth.

Bibliography

Adorno, Theodor W. *Minima Moralia: Reflections on a Damaged Life*. New York: Verso, 2005.

Adorno, Theodor W. *Negative Dialectics*. New York: Continuum, 1999.

Akbar, Na'im. *Breaking the Chains of Psychological Slavery*. Tallahassee, FL: Mind Productions & Associates, Inc., 1996.

Alessandrini, Anthony C. *Frantz Fanon: Critical Perspectives*. New York: Routledge, 1999.

---

61   Fanon, *Black Skin, White Masks*, 193.

Andersen, Joakim. *Rising from the Ruins: The Right of the 21st Century*. London: Arktos Media Ltd., 2018.

Bauman, Zygmunt. *Retrotopia*. Malden, MA: Polity Press, 2017.

Benjamin, Walter. *Illuminations: Essays and Reflection*. Edited by Hannah Arendt. Translated by Harry Zohn. New York: Schocken Books, 1968.

Camus, Renaud. *Le Grand Remplacement: Introduction au remplacisme global*. France: Chez l'auteur, 2017.

Camus, Renaud. *You Will Not Replace Us!*. Chez l'autuer, 2018.

Dabashi, Hamid. *Can Non-Europeans Think?* London: Zed Books, 2015.

Dabashi, Hamid. *Can Non-Europeans Think? What Happens with Thinkers Who Operate Outside the European Philosophical Pedigree*. January 15, 2013. https://www.aljazeera .com/indepth/opinion/2013/01/2013114142638797542.html.

Fanon, Frantz. *Black Skin, White Masks*. Translated by Richard Philcox. New York: Grove Press, 2008.

Fanon, Frantz. *Toward the African Revolution*. Translated by Haakon Chevalier. New York: Grove Press, 1967.

Fanon, Frantz. *The Wretched of the Earth*. Translated by Constance Farrington. New York: Grove Press, 1963.

Faye, Guillaume. *The Colonisation of Europe*. Translated by Roger Adwan. London: Arktos Media Ltd., 2016.

Faye, Guillaume. *Why We Fight: Manifesto of the European Resistance*. Translated by Michael O'Meara. London: Arktos Media Ltd., 2011.

Fromm, Erich. *Escape from Freedom*. New York: Henry Holt and Company, 1994.

Griffin, Roger. *The Nature of Fascism*. New York: Routledge, 1993.

Habermas, Jürgen. *Between Facts and Norms*. Translated by William Rehg. Cambridge, MA: The MIT Press, 1996.

Johnson, Greg. *The White Nationalists Manifesto*. San Francisco: Counter-Currents Publishing Ltd., 2018.

Kendi, Ibram X. *Stamped from the Beginning: The Definitive History of Racist Ideas in America*. New York: Nation Books, 2016.

Löwenthal, Leo. *The Unmastered Past*. Berkeley: University of California Press, 1987.

Marx, Karl, and Friedrich Engels, "Manifesto of the Communist Party." In *The Marx-Engels Reader*. Edited by Robert C. Tucker. New York: W.W. Norton & Co., Inc., 1978.

Mignolo, Walter. *Yes, We Can: Non-European Thinkers and Philosophers*. February 19, 2013. https://www.aljazeera.com/indepth/opinion/2013/02/20132672747320891 .html.

Sartre, Jean-Paul. "Preface." In *The Wretched of the Earth*, by Frantz Fanon. New York: Grove Press, 1963.

Siebert, Rudolf J. *From Critical Theory to Critical Political Theology: Personal Autonomy and Universal Solidarity*. New York: Peter Lang, 1994.

Tirman, John. *Dream Chasers: Immigration and the American Backlash.* Cambridge, MA: The MIT Press, 2015.

Ye'or, Bat (Gisele Littman) *Eurabia: The Euro-Arab Axis.* Cranbury, NY: Associated University Presses, 2005.

Žižek, Slavoj. "The Populist Temptation." In *The Great Regression.* Edited by Heinrich Geiselberger. Malden, MA: Polity Press, 2018.

Žižek, Slavoj. "Žižek responds to his Critics." http://www.critical-theory.com/zizek-responds-to-his-critics/.

CHAPTER 5

Fanon, Hegel and the Materialist Theory of History

Richard Curtis

> The Negro enslaved by his inferiority, the white man enslaved by his superiority alike behave in accordance with a neurotic orientation.
>
> – FRANTZ FANON, MD[1]

In considering the implications of Frantz Fanon's work, I am struck by the significance of the word, "diagnosis." We, non-physicians, often do not fully appreciate the significance attached to the word by physicians.[2] Fanon was, of course, a psychiatrist and one idea that he is especially famous for is the diagnosis of the conditions caused by colonialism, and indeed injustice generally. One early inkling of this idea was in the quote above from *Black Skin, White Masks*. The idea is that human beings, whether the oppressed or oppressor, are the sorts of creatures who respond to the injustice of colonialism with predictable diagnosable psychiatric conditions. This tells us something important about ourselves and our history. I submit that this important detail is the detail we needed in order to understand why Karl Marx could so confidently predict the coming of socialism, in fact to understand the mechanism behind his theory of history. It is important to Marx that his theory relied on economics to make this prediction, but when combined with newer insights from the 20th and 21st Centuries we can see that there are human reasons why history moves the way it does, not just economic ones. I will offer here a defense of Marx's theory of history using Fanon's diagnosis as the key concept for understanding the mechanism behind the history. I would like to add that while this is new to Marx the person, his reliance on science methodologically tells us that

---

1 Frantz Fanon, *Black Skin, White Masks* (London: Pluto Press, 1986), 60.
2 I first became aware of this point interviewing Dr. Warren Hern of the Boulder Abortion Clinic, for a radio show on KGNU in 1997. He is an epidemologist by training and wrote an article in 1993 called, "Has The Human Species Become A Cancer On The Planet?: A Theoretical View Of Population Growth As A Sign of Pathology." He went on to argue that there are five criteria for diagnosing cancer and a diagnosis is made when two or three of those criteria are met. Human beings meet all five relative to the earth. He was absolutely insistent that he was making a literal diagnosis and that this term has important meaning to physcians. It is like a scientist confirming a theory, once confirmed it has the status of fact. This was the inspriration for taking Fanon's diagnosis literally, as I assume he meant it as a physcian.

he would be among the first to value insights from new science like cognitive science.

Marcus Borg, the well-known scholar of the historical Jesus, famously said, "If you tell me your view of God, I will tell you your politics." What he meant by "God" was "view of ultimate reality," or what is "really real," or more commonly "worldview." "If you tell me your worldview, I will tell you your politics." Does that seem strange to claim? I submit that it is basic and even foundational to the whole project of philosophy. Thought, to be respectable, must be consistent. Plato, for example, is perfectly consistent in advocating a kind of monarchy because his view of ultimate reality is that only a select few can understand. From that perspective, totalitarian forms of politics and disdain for the masses follows in perfect logic.

It strikes me that it is important, then, that Fanon was an atheist. That sort of worldview has a natural affinity to democracy. This is especially true if one's worldview includes the idea of equality as basic to the material nature of reality. Not all atheists think that way, so not all atheists are egalitarians; but Fanon was. On the 50th anniversary of his death, one newspaper in the Caribbean carried a story about his life entitled, "Frantz Fanon: Echoes of Equality."[3] He was both an egalitarian and materialist. It also matters that he was a physician, and not just that but a psychiatrist as well. Although, he was not a philosopher, he was philosophical at times (and at other times seemed to reject philosophy, at least as we know it in Anglo-American philosophy, as an alien imposition).

The Internet Encyclopedia of Philosophy offers a fairly standard and well agreed upon understanding of what Fanon's work and life was about.

> Fanon situates his diagnosis within an unambiguous ethical commitment to the equal right of every human being to have his or her human dignity recognized by others. This assertion, that all of us are entitled to moral consideration and that no one is dispensable, is the principled core of his decolonization theory, which continues to inspire scholars and activists dedicated to human rights and social justice.[4]

Interestingly further along the writer of that entry makes this observation, one that I think has not received the attention it deserves.

---

3 http://www.thedailyherald.info/index.php?option=com_content&view=article&id=34049:
   frantz-fanon-echoes-of-equality&catid=24:weekender&Itemid=37.

4 https://www.iep.utm.edu/fanon/#H3.

Far more fruitful, in Fanon's view, were his studies in France of Hegel, Marx, and Husserl. From these sources he developed the view that dialectic could be the process through which the othered/alienated self can respond to racist trauma in a healthy way, a sensitivity to the social and economic forces that shape human beings, and an appreciation for the pre-conscious construction of self that phenomenology can reveal. He also found in Sartre's existentialism a helpful resource for theorizing the process of self-construction by which each of us chooses to become the persons we are.[5]

Both of these paragraphs include something vital about Fanon's thinking that deserves exploration. In the first case, Fanon the psychiatrist diagnoses the disorders of colonialization, and even more basically of inequality. Fanon the theorist read G.W.F. Hegel and Karl Marx and understood that society (and history) offer the parameters within which we all live and function, what Jean-Paul Sartre called, "facticity." In practical terms this meant he joined the resistance and devoted his life to the struggles of colonized people. Marx once said that people make history but not of their own accord; meaning, we do not choose the facticity of our lives and so can only make the sorts of changes that facticity allows.

Let me begin with the first point, the malady of inequality. Fanon was one of those people who believed that human nature has a significant cooperative element and tends towards being egalitarian. We do not always act this way, of course. So, to be clear, when anyone observes that we have an egalitarian tendency, they are not saying that this is all there is to the human experience or that this aspect of our nature is dominant. In fact, it seems rarely dominant thus far, but I am nonetheless using this occasion to argue from Fanon and others that humanity has a tendency towards being more egalitarian and that it is important to history. In terms of our motivations in this direction, the noted Marxist political theorist Bertell Ollman wrote:

> There is without any doubt the motivation to achieve a better, happier, more secure, and more fulfilling life in all of us, and our imagination has a role to play both in helping us clarify what this is and in stimulating us to act upon it. To this extent at least, the roots of the emancipatory project can be said to exist within human nature itself.[6]

---

5 Ibid.
6 Bertell Ollman, "The Utopian Vision of the Future (Then and Now): A Marxist Critique," *Monthly Review* 57, no. 3 (2005): 79.

The reference to "the emancipatory project" is to an egalitarian future. Now, to be sure, I am making a claim that is not universally accepted. There are a wide variety of opinions on the subject of human nature and some of them quite insistent that human beings are anything but egalitarian. Ironically, I think for Fanon and much of medical science a basic idea of equality is presumed. There is no argument to be had there. Medical science treats us all equally, we are just humans to science and especially medicine. The psychological sciences make this even more clear, even though history shows that this basic nature is not as obvious as the sciences might lead us to expect. Our "circle of morality," the etiologist Frans de Waal's term, has usually been small.[7] Egalitarians have always argued that the natural impulse is to expand it, even though other factors motivate it to contract. Science now assumes it. Much of society does not take science seriously and here we see a profound example of that. Science assumes we are all equal; yet society does not operate on that assumption, it uses much older and discredited assumptions. The facticity of life.

Daniel Siegel, a contemporary psychologist, sums up the relevant science: "Attachment research suggests that collaborative interpersonal interaction, not excessive sensory stimulation, can be seen as the key to healthy development."[8] The context for this comment was a discussion of brain development as he countered the suggestion that sensory "bombardment" would help young brains develop. What research in his field shows, he says, is that the quality of our relationships is what matters, not simply the quantity of sensory stimulation we receive. Above that he said, "The generally held belief in neural science is that the patterns of neuronal connections determine the ways in which the brain functions and the mind is created... Human connections create the neural connections from which the mind emerges."[9] This process, however, is not limited to childhood. According to Siegel, "The capacity for attachment classifications to change beyond the early years of life may be related to this ability of the brain to continue to grow in response to experiences across our lifetimes."[10] That collaborative relationships are ideal for mental health indicates that they are normal for the species. These relationships are what we tend towards under ordinary and healthy conditions. Fanon seemed to see this, to diagnose this, more clearly than most before him.

---

7   See especially, Frans de Waal, *Good Natured: The Origins of Right and Wrong in Humans and Other Animals.* Cambridge: Harvard University Press, 1997.

8   Daniel J. Siegel, "Toward an Interpersonal Neurobiology of the Developing Mind: Attachment Relationships, 'Mindsight,' and Neural Integration," *Infant Mental Health* 22, no. 1–2 (2001), 72.

9   Ibid.

10   Ibid., 70.

In a more scientific idiom, Allan Schore, a contemporary psychiatrist, made this observation: "Attachment behavior is thought to be the output of a neuro-biologically based biobehavioral system that regulates biological synchronicity between organisms."[11] It seems clear that we need each other, that the human self, as a "neurobiologically based biobehaviroral system," requires other selves. Albert Camus made this point clearly in claiming that we need to be "recognized."

> Therefore desire must be centered upon another form of desire; self-consciousness must be gratified by another form of self-consciousness. In simple words, man is not recognized – and does not recognize himself – as a man as long as he limits himself to subsisting like an animal. He must be acknowledged by other men. All consciousness is, basically, the desire to be recognized and proclaimed as such by other consciousnesses. It is others who beget us. Only in association do we receive a human value, as distinct from an animal one.[12]

This thought is similar to much existential thought. In this vein, the noted Psychoanalyst Erich Fromm suggested that mutual recognition in the context of equality is the goal towards which the world's major religions have all been striving. This claim is similar to that made by Hegel, as I will outline below, which is where Fanon would have gotten the idea. In a discussion of Karl Marx's view of socialism, Fromm explains:

> Marx's concept of socialism is a protest, as is all existentialist philosophy, against the alienation of man: if, as Aldous Huxley put it, "our present economic, social and international arrangement are based, in large measure, upon organized lovelessness," then Marx's socialism is a protest against this very lovelessness, against man's exploitation of man, and against his exploitativeness towards nature, the wasting of our natural resources at the expense of the majority of men today, and more so of the generations to come.... Does not all of this mean that Marx's socialism is the realization of the deepest religious impulses common to the great humanistic religions of the past? Indeed it does, provided we understand that Marx,

---

11   Allan N. Schore, *Affect Dysregulation and Disorders of the Self* (New York: W.W. Norton & Co., 2003), 64.

12   Albert Camus, *The Rebel: An Essay on Man in Revolt*, trans. Anthony Bower (New York: Vintage Books, 1956), 138.

like Hegel and like many others, expressed his concern for man's soul, not in theistic, but in philosophical language.[13]

The biology behind the claim appears well documented, but cultural history shows that other forms of organization have been dominant, generally. I submit that the science is clear. We flourish in egalitarian social systems. As cultures change over time, the obvious question to ask of the theorists is: Are we progressing towards that optimal arrangement?

The short answer is yes, but it is not an easy answer.[14] I would like to suggest a basic argument for seeing human history as slowly realizing a general state of mutual care and respect; that is, making social and moral progress. The mathematician and physicist turned philosopher Alfred North Whitehead wrote: "Slavery was the presupposition of political theorists then [in Plato's time]; freedom is the presupposition of political theorists now."[15] There is an important corollary to this observation that I would offer: Totalitarian forms of government were generally held to be necessary and were widely accepted then; democracy is generally held to be optimal and is widely accepted now. While it is true that totalitarian forms of government are widespread today (even growing), it is also true that even those governments seem forced to at least pretend to be democratically legitimated. Today, even the most undemocratic countries have elections. These elections may not mean much in terms of actual governance; that rulers feel it is necessary to pretend and carry out the exercise speaks volumes. I would argue that pretending to be democratic today demonstrates that democracy is, in fact, a widely held value among the world's peoples. That this value is now widespread and deeply held forces even undemocratic governments to pretend to be democratic, presumably because otherwise they would face resistance from their populations, if not the world population generally.

Also along these lines, it is clear that the words *empire* and *imperial* have gone out of favor, for much the same reasons. An empire is, by definition, an

---

13   Erich Fromm, *Marx's Concept of Man* (New York: Frederick Ungar Publishing, 1966), 63. Fromm attributes the quotation of Huxley to: Aldous Huxley, *The Perennial Philosophy* (New York: Harper and Brothers, 1944), 93.

14   Stephen Pinker has attracted a lot of attention with his book, *The Better Angles of our Nature: Why Violence Has Declined* from 2012. There seems to be serious criticism of his methodology so it seemed a distraction to rely on his book. But I think he makes a challenging point that we see the level of violence around us as unacceptable but fail to notice how this present is actually much better than a past when violenece appears to have been a daily way of life for much of humanity over our history. We seem to have made real progress in terms of how much violence humans rely on in daily life.

15   Alfred North Whitehead, *Adventures Of Ideas* (New York: Free Press, 1971), 13.

undemocratic arrangement. In the nineteenth century, the major powers used the word empire freely to describe themselves. Parts of America are referred to with the word empire. But those names or designations are legacies of the past. This also demonstrates that people have come to see the propriety of mutually respectful relationships, so much so that even the great empire of today does not refer to itself as such. Another example is racism. In the past, it was widely accepted that some races were superior. While these views have not disappeared completely, there are no serious scientists supporting them any longer; these views are generally held to be illegitimate – politically incorrect, and in the idiom of the day. A third example is the way we treat, raise and educate our children. Without belaboring this point, the change is obvious from striking women and children going from commonplace to being criminal. Also, we no longer view women and children as property, at least in most cultures.

While it is undeniable that humanity continues to do horrible things, it is arguable that there has been progress, not just change. Most of the horrible things we do are not widely accepted, whereas historically the violent domination of other peoples was celebrated not merely rationalized. One very unusual example of this is that modern archeology has discovered that what the Bible calls "the Conquest of Joshua," the Hebrew takeover of Canaanite lands, was actually an internal revolt.[16] Hebrews were not escaped Egyptian slaves, they were self-freed Canaanite serfs. Why did they tell the story as being one of conquest not rebellion? Values have changed. In the ancient world it was legitimate to conquer a land and take it over; but it was not legitimate to rebel and destroy a kingdom from within. That change speaks volumes. Four thousand years ago the legitimate story was of external theft, or what we today see as theft. Today, we call it wrong and criminal. I do not claim that what we see today is great progress over the last few thousand years, at least in terms that are meaningful to the poor and oppressed, but we have shown some progress. Does this progress over the last few millennia prove that the progress is ongoing? I would say yes. Progress can be seen in a number of ways that have changed and continue to change slowly over time. Does it prove that the progress is constant or even? No, it does not. Sometimes we regress, but the general trend is toward greater respect for human dignity and toward greater mutual recognition of our shared humanity. As I write, we are in another period of regression, but even this cannot last.[17]

---

16   For a basic overview see the PBS TV show NOVA, an episode called, "The Bibles Buried Secrets." http://www.pbs.org/wgbh/nova/ancient/bibles-buried-secrets.html.

17   Assuming humanity survives global warming.

Here it is worth noting that the capacity for human destruction has increased. While this might be put forth as a counterargument, especially in the face of the genocides of the last century, I believe this to be an unwarranted interpretation. My point concerns the general behavior and attitudes of humanity. The scale of destruction may have increased in some ways but this is a result of technological improvements not a result of destructive behaviors themselves becoming more widespread, let alone accepted. In fact, these acts of destruction are widely condemned, rather than tolerated and are certainly not celebrated. This is evidence of progress, even if that progress is slow and uneven.

What might Fanon have learned from Hegel? Hegel's philosophical accomplishments were wide-ranging and vast. It is most likely beyond the scope of any one lifetime to elaborate his whole system. Further, the most significant accomplishment of Hegel's philosophy is its power to inspire new analyses of the human condition, the nature of reality, and a whole host of other topics. According to Richard Schacht, "No concept is more central to Hegel's philosophy than his concept of freedom."[18] Hegel believed that all of reality was rooted in the activity of the divine, for which he used the word "Spirit" (*geist*). It is Spirit's developing consciousness of freedom that provides the engine of all history.[19] This freedom is manifest in human and religious history even though for Hegel it is Spirit's freedom that is really at issue. The overarching story of human history is rooted in Spirit's relationship with humanity and the evolution of consciousness. Charles Taylor said, "Hegel is suggesting that we should see the evolution of religion in human society as more than just the evolution of human consciousness."[20] The evolution, according to Hegel, is Spirit's, although it takes place in human history, in human communities. Michael Vater explains, "The wholly universal vocation of the community in which Spirit is present is to realize the freedom and rationality of the self-conscious subjects who make up the community."[21] This phrase, "realizing the freedom and rationality of the self-conscious subjects" is what I have in mind when I use terms like "mutual recognition of our humanity," or "egalitarian." Hegel thus offers the tools for understanding not just his Absolute Idealist version of this history, but very real and material human history as well. And this detail is critical: what Hegel claimed is that we evolve culturally because Spirit needs a

---

18   Richard L. Schacht, "Hegel on Freedom" in *Hegel: A Collection of Critical Essays*, ed. Alasdair MacIntyre (Notre Dame: University of Notre Dame Press, 1976), 289.

19   It is a variation on this specific idea that I will propose below.

20   Charles Taylor, *Hegel* (Cambridge: Cambridge University Press, 1997), 197.

21   Michael Vater, "Religion, Worldliness, and *Sittlichkeit*" in *New Perspectives on Hegel's Philosophy of Religion*, ed. David Kolb (Albany: State University of New York Press, 1992), 210.

partner, another consciousness to reflect its own. This other consciousness is the collective self-consciousness of humanity having developed culturally and historically into societies based on human freedom. So, it is not enough that human beings have consciousness; this consciousness must be cumulatively free. Dialectically, the sum of the parts is more than just the sum. It is in this case sufficient to recognize and be recognized (in Camus' sense) by Spirit. It is vital to keep in mind that all of what Hegel says comes back to Spirit acting in history. History being the vital concept here.

My suggestion is that Hegel is right in part. The self, qua consciousness, needs recognition; it needs another, but not just any other, it needs an equal. Hegel described a historical process by which humanity became competent to recognize Spirit's consciousness. This was a process precisely because human culture – for as long as we have had written history – has been highly strati-fied, but what all selves need is respectful recognition. The most efficient way for that to occur would be in an egalitarian structure, a free society of some sort. Hegel supported capitalist freedom where Marx saw a socialist version. Hegel called that development the development of freedom, but I suggest that the pattern we see in history is a *tendency* in the direction of care and mutual respect for all selves as individuals endowed with dignity, deserving of the hu-man rights we now generally recognize, as in the *Universal Declaration of Hu-man Rights* from the United Nations (which is itself more evidence that we have made at least limited progress).[22]

I don't expect that anyone takes Hegel's metaphysics literally these days, and mostly I am uninterested in what any Idealist thinks. If we take Hegel seriously we must translate his mystical idealism into a real scientifically supportable view. This was Marx's goal in developing a materialst theory of history. Agree-ing with that view, history, I suggest, is the concrete process of human beings working out systems of interaction through which human rights tend to be universalized, thereby actualizing our inherent equality through mutually re-spectful and caring relationships (de Waal, from above, would say through the expansion of our circle of morality). This history has the *appearance* of a tele-ology that leads to mutually supportive relationships, that is what we get from Hegel. Such a teleology is impossible in a materialist world. What seems like te-leology is only apparent in the same way natural evolution has what looks like, but is not really, a teleology towards complex organisms. This is because our history is one line of the development of biological evolution in natural history as we are products of nature. Biological evolution is known to be essentially

---

22   See: United Nations, *Universal Declaration of Human Rights,* http://www.un.org/Over-view/rights.html.

random in its actual operation. Genes randomly mutate and it happens that some mutations are more adaptive than others. Individuals with those adaptations tend to reproduce more and over time new traits emerge in a species and then with even more time new species emerge. This process has no real teleology, but it does tend to develop complexity because that complexity is successful. Our kind is highly adaptive and, from an evolutionary standpoint, widely successful. The complexity, which we see in particular in the evolution of higher primates and the more intelligent marine mammals, appears as if the development had some sort of intention. Some people argue this is evidence for divine intervention, although the science behind that claim is non-existent. But, the *appearance* of teleology is undeniable. Let me be clear, arguing that there is a tendency in nature, or in human history, is not an argument for a necessary future. The tendency arises because certain factors (i.e., genes for intelligence or cultural forms that emphasize collaborative social behaviors) are successful and so they perpetuate themselves. The tendency is strong, so strong that frustrations of it cause mental illness (Fanon's diagnosis), but it is not a guarantee as other factors limit or change the actual development.

Fanon the liberation warrior and theorists attracts a great deal of attention, but Fanon, MD, the psychiatrist, was telling us things that modern science has recently confirmed. What we need to notice is that in the language of a physician he offers us a diagnosis of a condition. The condition is caused by colonialism specifically and injustice generally. It doesn't have a name, he didn't name the condition, but he described it as "zone of nonbeing" and in offering the diagnosis comes up with a prescription as well. When confronted with injustice we suffer psychological disorders and the treatment is to struggle for justice. Others have used the term "Epidemiology of Oppression" to describe his ideas.

What matters for the diagnosis is that human beings have typical responses to the world, and the Zone of Nonbeing is a threat that demands a response, demands an existential response to affirm the Being (Sartre's existential freedom) of the person. We all want to be self-determining. The foundation comes from the inherent value of each and every human being. That foundational equality means unequal treatment is inherently inhuman. Fanon observed this using his training but it took a couple of decades for science to understand some of the mechanisms at play.

Now we realize that the tendency we see in history is one which is towards universalizing mutually caring and respectful relationships, or the universal recognition of human dignity. Like biological evolution, this cultural evolution works; it is adaptive given the basic needs described by Schore and diagnosed by Fanon and now others. So the tendency appears as if it were a teleology (tendency is a subtle push, teleology an overt pull). However, we seem to have a difficult time agreeing with each other across cultures about how best to live. So it seems this trend cannot be the result of a collective intention (which would be a pull not a push). Our natural evolution developed efficient problem solving capacities like intelligence, patience, persistence, etc. The most significant development is probably language.[23] The human self is a complex entity that develops this special relationship to culture, which provides language and what anthropologists call cultural materials. And from religion we get the notion that we store vital information about how to live in cultural sources and pass this along, thus we can accumulate wisdom that can be used for real social progress. My claim is that this is a natural outcome of the fact that there can be no self, as a human self, without culture (this was Clifford Geertz's claim as I discussed in the Introduction). As quoted before:

> Rather than culture acting only to supplement, develop, and extend organically based capacities logically and genetically prior to it, it would seem to be ingredient to those capacities themselves. A culture-less human being would probably turn out to be not an unfulfilled ape, but a wholly mindless and consequently unworkable monstrosity.[24]

For reasons I explain below, combined with high intelligence and a cultural existence, our history has the potential for progress, not just change. This relates to the point of what the anthropologists call Cultural Take-Off. We have started to evolve through culture, and culture, in this sense, evolves with us. We change because we develop new forms of culture and these forms change us. As culture becomes more egalitarian we become more egalitarian; we tend to actualize the latent potential of our innate nature, our inherent equality. To say we are egalitarian by nature is not to say that we are egalitarian in our actions now, but that something about us produces this tendency.

This something is that it is in the nature of consciousness to need one another, and in particular an "other" who is equal. This is what Hegel says about humanity's relationship to Spirit: our consciousness was becoming sufficient to be an equal for Spirit. Hegel, I say, recognized something very important in a sense but confused human history with divine history and inverted it. Still, he was making a claim that is more profound than that made by Camus. Camus,

---

23   See Lem Semenovich Vygotsky, *Thought and Language*, ed. and trans. Eugenia Hanfmann and Gertrude Vakar (Cambridge, MA: MIT Press, 1962).

24   Clifford Geertz, *The Interpretation of Cultures: Selected Essays* (New York: Basic Books, 1973), 68.

implicitly correcting this inversion, said human consciousness needs to be recognized, but he did not add "by an equal." This is my contention; we develop this equality socially for the sake of healthy development. This term "healthy" is vital and the reason Fanon is important to this discussion. And, I keep reiterating, this is the profound implication of what modern scientists like Siegel and Schore tell us (that Fanon was right for reasons they discuss). Our mental health demands specific sorts of relationships to be healthy, and I add that this then provides the basic motivation for human beings to act historically in a positive direction, giving each succeeding generation materials with which to improve.

Here is the most vital detail, the engine for this development if you will: it is not that any one person seeks out a society in which equals can recognize them; it is rather that the human self experiencing the world reacts to mistreatment. Thus, the history is not a real teleology but can appear as if it were. I believe this is an important insight Gandhi exploited in motivating the Indian people to act on their resentment of mistreatment at the hands of the British occupation. In history though, the process is depersonalized in the same way natural evolution is. We have an inherent sense of our human dignity and it is violations of this sense that drives us, however slowly and unevenly. Interestingly, in more recent research, de Waal has found that this capacity to recognize injustice and to manifest behaviors showing resentment of it is not limited to human beings. He and his colleagues found that some species of monkeys react to unjust treatment with indignation, or at least what seems to us to be indignation. "The response is similar to the response people display when they see others get a better deal."[25]

The important point that Hegel made is that human societies have been historically structured so as to legitimate unjust treatment, but those structures are precisely the ones that change in the direction of universal freedom, or what I call mutually respectful and caring relationships – equality. The recognition of human equality is an abstraction that people have made at different points in history, but recognition of a principle and organizing a society around it are completely different issues. We do not organize society around abstract ideas but around real needs and actual possibilities, the facticity of life Sartre explains. Thus it will always be survival issues that have the most power to motivate change, positively or negatively. This inherent need to be recognized by an equal as overtly manifest in reaction to injustice, I suggest, has a

25   Lee Bowman, "Even Monkeys Know That Life Is Unfair," *Seattle Post-Intelligencer*, 18 September 2003, A2. The story concerned research de Waal co-directed at the Yerkes National Primate Research Center and the Living Links Center (both in Atlanta).

small but steady influence resulting in an uncertain tendency in the direction of an egalitarian future.

To be clear, I am defending Karl Marx's "materialist theory of history," and do not intend to say that a latent drive for dignity is the motive force in history. Rather, we tend to react to injustice and this contributes to historical transformations. I do agree with him and Frederick Engels, for example, that, "The history of all hitherto existing society is the history of class struggles."[26] I suggest that our history is one of class struggle due to resentments that motivate people to challenge unjust or inhumane treatment, combined with cultural knowledge of our past and significant ideas about a better future. Put another way, history is pushed in such a way that the pattern appears to have a general direction (Marx's materialist theory); history is not pulled toward a goal (Hegel's idealist theory). The push comes from actual human beings, with the biological needs and the capacities I discuss, reacting to their real life experiences. To be sure, the efficiencies of hierarchical and exploitative arrangements are compelling and motivational as well, and so exert a counter-tendency. But the overall trend, I maintain, and as suggested differently in the work of Hegel and Marx, is one of slowly moving towards democratic structures, towards more egalitarian arrangements.

The illustration Hegel offered was that in ancient China the only person who was free was the emperor. In feudal societies the King and the feudal aristocracy generally were free. And, in capitalist society the capitalist class is free (this is all in Hegel's sense of free). For Hegel, what he took to be the advanced capitalism of his day offered the possibility for all to be free. Marx criticized this claim and suggested that real freedom requires a classless society. Thus, socialism is the possibility of universal freedom because no class of people is subjected to exploitation by another. The material conditions for change must be met for there to be change, but it is the actions of people – indignant at their treatment empowered with cultural knowledge of the past and ideas about how to live – that make history. This is not an act of the will, but a basic response by the organism. We naturally reject injustice and this seems to us to be a moral choice. As in biological evolution, the cumulative activity and adaptation eventually produces a qualitative change. Certainly at times people tolerate and promote injustice, but that is not because of a will towards injustice but rather due to other benefits that derive from injustice (like wealth and power for some at the expense of others) or as a result of some pathology

---

26   Karl Marx and Frederick Engels, "Manifesto of the Communist Party," in Karl Marx and Frederick Engels, *Collected Works, Volume 6* (New York: International Publishers, 1976), 482.

(in day to day life). Given the opportunity, the material conditions necessary for change, we do act to make progress. We may not will the change or even will the direct actions that make the change; the narrative self just acts naturally. But that action is having a predisposition towards egalitarian arrangements that develop as a result of a predisposition to resist non-egalitarian arrangements. Since some ideas stored culturally are better for this purpose than others, the struggle between science and superstition is of historic significance and therefore part of this trend – even though the actors in this drama generally have no sense of its scale. Injustice is not just unjust it causes disease, and so from Fanon we see that a drive to equality is not just an abstract ethical point or an accident of history, but rather a concrete medical need that helps drive history.

This raises one significant philosophical issue. In the Foreword to the 2004 Grove Press edition of *The Wretched of the Earth*, we find this claim:

> Fanon's singular contribution to the theoretical understanding of the black consciousness movement lay in his extension of the economistic theories of Marxism toward a greater emphasis on the importance of psychological and cultural liberation – the psycho-affective realm of revolutionary activism and emancipation.[27]

What some people think this means is that Fanon moved away from the strict materialism of Marx to embrace some form of idealist confusion. The materialist side is quite insistent that appeals to ideas is a reactionary move that misunderstands history. I do not think this is what Fanon was doing, and that this criticism of his thinking is unfounded. To notice the medical implications of a situation is to bring the sophistication of medicine into a materialist analysis of history. Yes, the problems he is calling attention to are in our ideas, in our understanding, but what makes it a materialist analysis is that it is the material creature reacting to material conditions that creates a medical (psychiatric) condition. He is not moving into any sort of idealism by bringing medicince into the conversation. Rather, he showed us long before many others had the notion that medicine is a part of the materialist theory of history.

To conclude, it is worth noting that Fanon was critical of the way European Enlightenment writers talked about equality. He had no resepect for their liberal notions of equality, which devolve into mere libertarian aggrandizing of economic power. Liberalism gives us a negative sort of equality. People

---

27   Homi K. Bhabha, Foreword to Frantz Fanon, *The Wretched of the Earth* (New York: Grove Press, 2004), xxix.

are equal in that they should equally not be interfered with. Socialist thought gives us positive equality. Because people are equal they deserve equal treatment, resources and opportunity. Fanon, MD, the psychiatrist diagnosed the consequences of injustice before the neuroscience I discuss was established. Inequality produces mental illness, just as colonialism causes mental illness. Near the end of *The Wretched of the Earth*, Fanon wrote, "Since 1954 we have drawn the attention of French and international psychiatrists in scientific works to the difficulty of 'curing' a colonized subject correctly, in other words making him thoroughly fit into a social environmnet of the colonial type."[28] Difficult because the cure is justice and equality.

Bibliography

Bhabha, Homi K. Foreword to Frantz Fanon, *The Wretched of the Earth*. New York: Grove Press, 2004.

Bowman, Lee. "Even Monkeys Know That Life Is Unfair," *Seattle Post-Intelligencer*, 18 September 2003, A2.

Camus, Albert. *The Rebel: An Essay on Man in Revolt*. Translated by Anthony Bower. New York: Vintage Books, 1956.

Daily Herald, The. "Frantz Fanon: Echoes of Equality" December 7, 2012. http://www .thedailyherald.info/index.php?option=com_content&view=article&id=34049: frantz-fanon-echoes-of-equality&catid=24:weekender&Itemid=37.

De Waal, Frans. *Good Natured: The Origins of Right and Wrong in Humans and Other Animals*. Cambridge: Harvard University Press, 1997.

Fanon, Frantz. *Black Skin, White Masks*. London: Pluto Press, 1986.

Fromm, Erich. *Marx's Concept of Man*. New York: Frederick Ungar Publishing, 1966.

Geertz, Clifford. *The Interpretation of Cultures: Selected Essays*. New York: Basic Books, 1973.

Huxley, Aldous. *The Perennial Philosophy*. New York: Harper and Brothers, 1944.

Internet Encyclopedia of Philosophy. "Frantz Fanon (1925–1961)".

Marx, Karl and Frederick Engels. "Manifesto of the Communist Party," in Karl Marx and Frederick Engels, *Collected Works, Volume 6*. New York: International Publishers, 1976.

Ollman, Bertell. "The Utopian Vision of the Future (Then and Now): A Marxist Critique," *Monthly Review* 57, no. 3 (2005).

Pinker, Stephen. *The Better Angles of our Nature: Why Violence Has Declined*. New York: Penguin Books, 2012.

---

28   Frantz Fanon, *The Wretched of the Earth*, 183.

Schact, Richard L. "Hegel on Freedom" in *Hegel: A Collection of Critical Essays*. Edited by Alasdair MacIntyre. Notre Dame: University of Notre Dame Press, 1976.

Schore, Allan N. *Affect Dysregulation and Disorders of the Self.* New York: W.W. Norton & Co., 2003.

Siegel, Daniel J. "Toward an Interpersonal Neurobiology of the Developing Mind: Attachment Relationships, 'Mindsight,' and Neural Integration," *Infant Mental Health* 22, no. 1–2 (2001).

Taylor, Charles. *Hegel.* Cambridge: Cambridge University Press, 1997.

United Nations, *Universal Declaration of Human Rights.* http://www.un.org/Overview/rights.html.

Vater, Michael. "Religion, Worldliness, and *Sittlichkeit*" in *New Perspectives on Hegel's Philosophy of Religion*. Edited by David Kolb. Albany: State University of New York Press, 1992.

Vygotsky, Lem Semenovich. *Thought and Language.* Edited and Translated by Eugenia Hanfmann and Gertrude Vakar. Cambridge, MA: MIT Press, 1962.

Whitehead, Alfred North. *Adventures Of Ideas.* New York: Free Press, 1971.

CHAPTER 6

Connecting with Fanon: Postcolonial Problematics, Irish Connections, and the Shack Dwellers Rising in South Africa

Nigel C. Gibson

1 Theory Is always Travelling[1]

Fanon argued that his work was a product of a definite time and place, famously stating that "each generation must discover its mission, fulfill it or betray it" and yet each of Fanon's books continue to have important and significant afterlives.

My initial interest in Fanon was far from academic, reflecting a movement represented by people in freedom struggles who discover Fanon in different situations and take what they need in the encounter. I first came across Fanon in 1980 in London through a book by the African American Marxist Humanists Lou Turner and John Alan, *Frantz Fanon, Soweto and American Black Thought* (1978). It was also then that I met Black Consciousness Movement exiles from South Africa, who in contrast to the official anti-apartheid movement, were quite open to discussing revolutionary ideas.

Fanon argued that his work was very much of his time and yet importantly his work continues to be read and translated into new times and spaces. This chapter considers some of these translations of Fanon, namely how theory travels and becomes alive, redeveloped, translated and mistranslated, and sometimes distorted in new situations. By theory I do not mean academic canons but radical theory that challenges the status quo. What Edward Said called "travelling theory" included the idea of ideas carrying across geographical and cultural spaces.[2]

---

1 This is an expanded and revised version of a paper I presented at the *Féile an Phobail* [Festival of the People] on August 10, 2017, in Belfast, under the title "the Failures of Post-Apartheid South Africa: Frantz Fanon and the shack dwellers' revolt." Post-Apartheid South Africa has many resonances with post-good Friday agreement in the North of Ireland especially in the present (2017) interregnum when Stormont has fallen apart.
2 Edward W. Said, "Travelling Theory," in *Rethinking Fanon*, ed. Nigel C. Gibson. Amherst NY: Humanity Books, 1999.

Under consideration in this chapter will be two types of translation: Fanon's travel to and continued relevance to South Africa, and the original English translation of Fanon's *Les damnés*, which will take us to Ireland.

There is at first an applied element to travelling theory, or in other words, travelling theory has to be applicable to a new context and applied to a new situation. I was reading Fanon in early 1981 as the hunger strike led by Bobby Sands was underway in the H-blocks. Little did I know that Fanon was being read and had been part of the prisoners' library a few years earlier when prisoners in Long Kesh had had political status. As well as applying theory to new situations, there is also the creative element of thinking through and employing Fanon's dialectic of liberation to a new situation. How can the revolutionary thinker enliven our present and also how does our period and our questions enliven the revolutionary thinker? This creativity can be expressed in new theoretical insights (such as Homi Bhabha's reading of Fanon in the 1980s) or out of a movement from practice, from below (such as through the work of the shack dwellers movement, Abahlali baseMjondolo, which I will discuss later). Both are acts of translation. And at the same time, I am aware that these acts of translation (in the literal sense of the Latin *translatus* "carried over," transfer—movement / carrying) as well as interpretation, includes some kind of treachery—contained in the Italian saying "traduttore, traditore" (literally "translator, traitor")—even if one is consciously attempting a "fidelity to Fanon."[3] The important point, I believe, is fidelity to Fanon's "untidy" dialectic.[4]

Fanon's legacy, in other words, is contested and continues to be contestable. If for example, the still dominant view of Fanon as an advocate or "prophet of violence" can be traced to an interpretation of Fanon in the United States in 1970s, one also needs to note the importance of Steve Biko's engagement with Fanon in the early 1970s, for whom violence was not an essential category.[5] Indeed, while the Black Power movement in the US mediated Biko's engagement with Fanon and whose readings of Fanon were more nuanced than often thought, the African context also remains important. Across the African continent of the 1970s,[6] it was Fanon's chapter on the "Misadventure [Pitfalls]

---

3 Richard Pithouse, "Thought Amidst Waste," *Journal of Asian and African Studies* 47, no. 5 (2012): 482–497.

4 See Nigel Gibson, *Fanon: The Postcolonial Imagination*. Cambridge, UK: Polity Press, 2003.

5 See Nigel Gibson, *Fanonian Practices in South Africa: From Steve Biko to Abahlali baseMjondolo*. Pietermaritzburg: UKZN Press, 2011; Mabogo Percy More. *Biko: Philosophy, Identity and Liberation*. Pretoria: HSRC Press, 2017.

6 See for example the book-length treatments by Emmanuel Hansen, *Frantz Fanon: Social and Political Thought*. Oxford: Oxford UP, 1978; Adele Jinadu, *Fanon: In Search of the African*

of National Consciousness" that had an important resonance.[7] While Ngũgĩ wa Th'iongo, who came across Fanon in the mid-1960s, later characterized the literature about postcolonial Africa as a "series of imaginative footnotes" to Fanon's chapter Misadventures of National Consciousness,[8] fellow Kenyan, Alamin Mazrui, recalls that no other chapter, and to a lesser extent the chapter on National Culture from *The Wretched of the Earth*, was "discussed with greater passion among East Africans" because "these two were seen to be particularly prophetic analyses of the postcolonial condition." In Kenya, Fanon was linked to a critique of the increasingly kleptocratic and authoritarian Kenyatta government, while in Tanzania, Fanon's reception "went hand in hand with the country's revolutionary move toward *ujaama*."[9] His work was essential to radical students and faculty at the University of Dar es Salaam, including Walter Rodney, Issa Shivji and others, which lead to two Swahili translations (in 1977 and 1978).[10] In addition, it is worth remembering that Biko's engagement with Fanon should also be seen in its African context with Black consciousness resonating with the dialectic of national consciousness that Fanon articulated. As Biko approvingly quotes Fanon in *I Write What I Like*: "The consciousness of the self is not the closing of a door to communication... National consciousness, which is not nationalism, is the only thing that will give us an international dimension."[11]

But just as translations are neither neutral nor equal, neither are interpretations. By the 1970s, Fanon's contribution was generally reduced to the question

---

  Revolution. London: Kegan Paul International, 1986 [1980]; Nigel C. Gibson, Introduction to *Rethinking Fanon: The Continuing Dialogue.* Amherst NY: Humanity Books, 1999.

7 We should note that the *mésaventure* in the title "Mésaventure de la conscience nationale" which is translated by Constance Farrington as "Pitfalls" becomes in the Philcox translation "trials and tribulations." I prefer the more literal translation *mésaventure*, which in part speaks to Merleau-Ponty's essay "adventures in the dialectic" where he coins the term "Western Marxism." Fanon's chapter could be seen as an engagement with this in terms of the misadventures in the dialectic. Here there is also a connection to Said's claim of Fanon's reading of Western Marxism's foundational text, Lukács' *History and Class Consciousness*. At the same time the misadventure Fanon is talking about is directly connected to national consciousness. Philcox's unwillingness to translate *mésaventure* as misadventure is strange given that he literally translated "Grandeur" as Grandeur in the title of the second chapter.

8 Ngũgĩ wa Th'iongo. "The Writer in the Neo-colonial State," in *Moving the Centre* (Portsmouth, N.H: Heinemann, 1993), 66.

9 Mazrui in Kathryn Batchelor and Sue-Ann Harding, *Translating Frantz Fanon Across Continents and Languages.* New York: Routledge, 2017.

10 The 1977 translation, *Mafukara wa Ulimwengu* (*The Wretched of the Earth*) and the 1978 translation *Viumbe Waliolaaniwa* (*The Damned*). On these translations see Mazrui (2017).

11 Steve Biko, *I Write What I Like* (London: Heinemann, 1978), 72.

of violence, reflecting American dominance. Of course, this was buttressed by the authority of Sartre's introduction to *The Wretched* and Hannah Arendt's critique and indeed caricature of Fanon in her book *On Violence*, but it also reflected powerful opinion-makers such as *Time* magazine, which reduced Fanon's thought to the idea that violence equaled liberation.[12] The power of this reduction has continued to be reinscribed. When Homi Bhabha writes of Fanon being read in the H-blocks in his important 2004 foreword to *The Wretched of the Earth*, he emphasizes the historian Richard English's speculative suggestion that "Fanon's incendiary spirit may have set alight IRA [Irish Republican Army] passions."[13] And yet, when one speaks to some of those same prisoners from the H-blocks, one gets a different story; they remember looking to Fanon as part of an anti-colonial curriculum having little to do with claiming him to justify their actions. Their reading was more in line with what Ngũgĩ wa Th'iongo would later call "decolonizing the mind."[14]

In Durban, South Africa, the shack dweller movement, Abahlali baseMjondolo (a grassroots movement of over 50,000 members founded in 2005) is an implicit interlocutor with Fanon's revolutionary humanism in the context of the increasingly open repressive actions of the police and the political violence especially marked by the ruling provincial African Nationalist Congress (ANC) which acts in exactly the ways Fanon describes in the "Misadventures of National Consciousness," namely as a kleptocratic and predatory party/state which continues to murder impoverished black activists. As Abahlali argues in an emergency press release written as shacks were being destroyed and shack dwellers beaten up by in Cato Manor, Durban in 2017: "The ANC tells us that we must support them as they will bring land to the people. Yet when we occupy land they repress us with violent criminality. We are confronting a gangster state."[15]

At the local level, the threat of violence and indeed the atmosphere of political violence, including murder in KwaZulu-Natal, has become part of the apocalyptic climate. While political murders of councilors and political activists (often within the ANC) are taking place in KwaZulu-Natal at an increasing rate, the murders of Abahlali activists are often barely reported and the daily violence Abahlali experience is ignored. The class character of this is profound,

---

12   On a nuanced reading of Fanon and Arendt that indicates their compatibility rather than incompatibility see Richard J. Bernstein, *On Violence*. Cambridge: Polity Books, 2013.

13   Frantz Fanon, *The Wretched of the Earth,* trans. by Richard Philcox (New York: Grove Press, 2004), xxix.

14   Ngũgĩ wa Th'iongo, *Decolonising the Mind: The Politics of Language in African Literature* Portsmouth, N.H.: Heinemann, 1986.

15   Abahlali baseMjondolo. Emergency Press Statement "Brutal Attacks on the new Cato Manor Land Occupation," October 2, 2017b. http://abahlali.org/node/16277/.

and thus our turn to Fanon should take seriously his critique of the limitations of the politics of nationalization and Africanization, which he argues are "increasingly tinged with racism."[16] While politicians accumulate massive wealth, popular anger is channeled toward foreigners. He maintained that this xenophobia and racism "neatly defer[s] attention from local politicians and their business interests to 'foreigners.'"[17]

To equate Fanon's thought with violence however fixes it in terms of the Manicheanism and abstraction that Fanon criticizes in *Black Skin Whites Masks* and *The Wretched of the Earth*. Fanon understands the "orgy of violence without reason" as a legitimate reaction to colonial domination built on violence.[18] But *The Wretched of the Earth* is less a book that justifies violence as an end in itself, as one that demands thought: "Antiracist racism, and the determination to defend one's skin," he argues, with an implicit reference to Sartre's critique of Negritude in *Orphée Noir*,

> which is characteristic of the colonized's response to colonial oppression, clearly represent sufficient reasons to join the struggle. But one does not sustain a war, one does not endure massive repression or witness the disappearance of one's entire family in order for hatred or racism to triumph. Racism, hatred, resentment, and 'the legitimate desire for revenge' alone cannot nurture a war of liberation.[19]

Thus we arrive at the heart of a Fanonian dialectics and Fanonian politics. What I mean by dialectics is, in a word, movement. For example, Fanon did not advocate a politics of race, but that did not mean he dismissed black consciousness as false consciousness. Writing about the veil in *A Dying Colonialism*, Fanon's sentences, "It is the white man who creates the black. But it is the black who creates negritude"[20] are foundational, returning us to his double critique of Sartre's conception of negritude that Fanon articulates in *Black*

---

16   Fanon, *The Wretched of the Earth*, 103.
17   Ibid.
18   The idea that Fanon's "first rule of decolonization" is disorder Andile Mngxitama maintains, equating what Fanon describes "an orgy of violence for no reason" is Fanon's politics. This position aligns well with the caricatures of Fanon promoted by the reactionary Robert Fulford in the *National Post*. The source for Fulford is Adam Schatz's review in *The New York Times* of David Macey's biography of Fanon, titled "The Doctor Prescribed Violence." Macey, himself, is another source for this caricature. See David Macey, David. *Fanon* (London: Granta, 2000), 503.
19   Fanon, *The Wretched of the Earth*, 89.
20   Frantz Fanon, *A Dying Colonialism*. (New York: Grove Press, 1965), 25.

Skin White Masks.[21] First, Fanon responds to Sartre that the phenomenology of black's corporal experience is quite different to the white's, and thus the dialectic of self-consciousness is quite different from the one that Hegel had articulated as universal in "Lordship and Bondage."[22] While it is possible to read Fanon's critique of Sartre and Hegel as dismissive, Fanon remains committed to the dialectic. In his critique of Hegel, the black is forced back, as he writes in his critique of Sartre, who he ironically calls a "born Hegelian." In place of a dialectic of absolute negativity, Sartre had posited an external, synthetic and formulaic framework. Instead of the necessity of experiencing black self-consciousness, we are told by Sartre that it is a passing stage. For Fanon, this was shocking coming from "a friend of the colored people" and it was a shock that created a collapse of the sense of self which "robbed me of my last chance."[23] And yet, Fanon's engagement with Sartre is nuanced. After stating that it is no coincidence that the "most ardent of apostles of Negritude are at the same time militant Marxists,"[24] in the next chapter of *Black Skin* Fanon returns to Sartre's *Orphée Noir*: "*We can understand why* Sartre sees in the black poets' Marxist stand the logical end to negritude."[25]

Defining Black consciousness, the Fanonian Steve Biko insisted that for blacks it was not about pigmentation but an "attitude of mind."[26] Similarly, Fanon argues that it is necessary to "skim over this absurd drama that others have staged around me; rule out these two elements that are equally unacceptable; and *through the particular, reach out for the universal.*"[27] This particularization necessitates, says Fanon, following Césaire, killing the white man within: Mental liberation. In short, we must, with Fanon, hold onto this apparent contradiction. In other words, while we might agree with Gayatri Spivak that the recovery of "lost origins are suspect... as grounds for counter-hegemonic ideological production," we cannot dismiss the work of recovering history and

---

21   We should not forget that these short sentences appear in "Algeria unveils itself" and follows the hypothesis that "In an initial phase, it is the actions, the plans of the occupier that determine the centers of resistance around which a people's will to survive becomes organized." Ibid.

22   In other words, what Fanon said of Freud, Adler, and "even the cosmic Jung," that neither "took the black into consideration in the course of their research. And each was perfectly right" (2008: 130), could be applied to Hegel, despite Susan Buck-Morss' claim to the contrary in *Hegel, Haiti and Universal History*. Pittsburgh: University of Pittsburgh Press, 2009.

23   Frantz Fanon, *Black Skin White Masks* (New York: Grove Press, 2008), 112.

24   Ibid.

25   My emphasis. Fanon, *Black Skin White Masks*, 160. Translation altered.

26   Biko, *I Write What I Like*, 48.

27   Fanon, *Black Skin White Masks*, 160. My emphasis.

culture in the context of struggle.[28] For Fanon, the colonized intellectuals express this ambivalence. Their "secret hope of discovering beyond the misery of today, beyond self-contempt, resignation, and abjuration, some very beautiful and splendid era whose existence rehabilitates us both in regard to ourselves and in regard to others," is problematically idealistic as an end in itself especially when it becomes divorced from the real experiences of the oppressed, exploited and marginalized.[29] This is not only the case of his political critique of Negritude in *The Wretched,* but also seen in *Black Skin* where he virtually dismisses Diop's Bantu Philosophy, wondering what this mediation has to do with reality—the reality of black miners forced back to work at gunpoint in South Africa: "Bantu society no longer exists," he reminds Diop in terms similar to his critique of Mannoni's "Dependency Complex" in *Black Skin White Masks*, adding that "there is nothing ontological about segregation. Enough of this outrage."[30] The point is underscored in *The Wretched* when he argues that reality includes "emptying the colonized's brain of all form and content [and] by a kind of perverted logic, it turns to the past of the oppressed people, and distorts, disfigures, and destroys it."[31]

Fanon, the phenomenologist, is critical of Sartre, while also appreciating that the black soul is a white artifice.[32] There is nevertheless a particular concreteness to fully experiencing the "moment" of self-consciousness, which is why later in *The Wretched*, Fanon insists that national consciousness is absolutely essential to any international perspective. And yet, again we should consider this contextually and historically. National consciousness is also a new moment. Fanon explicates this in *L'an V de la révolution algérienne* (the English title, *A Dying Colonialism*, loses the historical context of the work). In *L'an cinq* the new moment, in regard to Algeria, is the line demarcated by the struggle for liberation declared by the Front Libération Nationale (FLN) on November 1, 1954, and carried out in a series of coordinated attacks on what became known as Toussaint Rouge or Toussaint Sanglante (Bloody All-Saints' Day). For Fanon, this political/military action marked the beginning of the end of

---

28 Gayatri C. Spivak, *A Critique of Postcolonial* Reason: *Toward a History of the Vanishing Present* (Cambridge, MA: Harvard University Press, 1999), 306.

29 Fanon, *The Wretched of the Earth* (1968), 209; Fanon, *The Wretched of the Earth* (2004), 148.

30 Fanon, *Black Skin White Masks*, 163.

31 Fanon, *The Wretched of the Earth* (1968), 209; Fanon, *The Wretched of the Earth* (2004), 149.

32 We should also note Fanon's influence on Sartre who took note of this critique (see for example George Ciccariello-Maher, "European Intellectuals and Colonial Difference: Césaire and Fanon beyond Sartre and Foucault"), in *Race after Sartre: Antiracism, Africana Existentialism, Postcolonialism*, ed. Jonathan Judaken. (Albany: State University of New York, 2009), pp. 141–143).

colonial Manicheanism that characterized pre-1954 resistance and defensive positions that opposed anything associated with colonialism (even when, he suggestively says it was not *objectively valid*) and the beginning of a new moment (socially and philosophically).[33] In Algeria there is, he argues, a radical mutation of social relations and culture including new attitudes toward medicine, the radio, and even the French language.[34]

In short, Fanon is critical of *a priori* universals. Freedom remains an important category for him given a situational analysis that begins from the ground up; a universal rich with concrete particulars. Rather than simply laying hold of the past, it is the struggle against colonialism that gives it new meaning and enlivens it. Culture becomes newly alive, and an element of praxis, including violence in the broad sense, which Fanon includes, as examples, the renaming roads and buildings, pulling down statues, and changing the physical structure.[35] Fanon's concept of dialectic, as lived, aware of internal contradictions, and the need to work through them, is certainly helpful to understanding the centrality of violence and the importance of violence in the fight for liberation, and also the limitations of violence, not simply as a strategy but as a stand in for strategy. Philosophically and psychically a new society cannot simply emerge from violence. Yet at the same time, that is exactly the political problem that has to be faced.

2   Fanon: World Revolutionary Outside Civil Society

In a chapter of *Translating Frantz Fanon Across Continents and Languages*, subtitled "Irish connections," Kathryn Batchelor takes issue with Homi Bhabha's speculation in his introduction to the 2004 English translation of Fanon's *The Wretched of the Earth*, about the importance of *The Wretched* to the provisional IRA. Bhabha's writes that on the shelves of the H-blocks *The Wretched* was "in some sense a contributor to, or even catalyst for, IRA violence."[36] While Batchelor is critical of the reduction of Fanon to violence, she argues that there is "no evidence that [Fanon's] ideas circulated with any intensitivity" in Long

---

33   Fanon, *A Dying Colonialism*, 121.

34   Fanon, *A Dying Colonialism*.

35   See Fanon, *The Wretched of the Earth* (2004), 1.

36   Kathryn Batchelor, "The Translation of Les damnés de la terre into English: Exploring Irish Connections" in *Translating Frantz Fanon Across Continents and Languages,* ed. Batchelor, Kathryn and Sue-Ann Harding. (New York: Routledge, 2017), 55. Here Bhabha finds support from Richard English, "A historian of the IRA suggests that Fanon's incendiary spirit may have set alight IRA passions." See Fanon, *The Wretched of the Earth* (2004), xxix.

Kesh.[37] Fanon was being studied at Long Kesh, and Batchelor quotes Jake Mac Siascis, one of the interviewee's in Feargal Mac Ionnrachtaigh's essential book, *Language, Resistance and Revival*, who draws attention to the importance of Fanon in thinking about culture, language and decolonization: "in the cages *we were reading in depth...* about the central role of culture in the reconquest of the country... about the mentality of colonization and the role that... [language has] in the fight back against the colonizer."[38] In the Long Kesh cages, in other words, Fanon was read as part of a curriculum decided by the prisoners that included such work as Paulo Freire's *Pedagogy of the Oppressed*, and James Connolly's writings on Irish history.[39] Freire's work became important to the teaching of Irish language in the prison, and it is interesting to note that in the same period Steve Biko and his colleagues were emphasizing the importance of Freire to their thinking and practice.[40] There was, of course, no access to books in the H-Blocks during the blanket campaign, which came in response to the British government's criminalization policy putting an end to political status.[41]

In 2017, I was contacted by a group from MuckRock in the United States, who were undertaking a project focusing on books banned in prisons around the country. Among the books banned in Michigan's Prisons is Fanon's *Black*

---

37   Batchelor, "The Translation of Les damnés de la terre," 63. Homi Bhabha writes, "In a prison cell in the notorious H-Block of Belfast prison, sometime after 1973, a young apprentice coach builder and member of the Irish Republican Army, Bobby Sands, first read Fanon's *The Wretched of the Earth*, of which there were multiple copies on the H-Block shelves" (2004: 29). While Batchelor is right to question the veracity of Bhabha's claims since the H-Blocks did not exist in 1973, it is likely that Sands could have read Fanon during his first imprisonment from April 1973 to April 1976, since Fanon and other works were being read by many of the republican prisoners but could not true of Sands's second imprisonment since books were banned. The British Government's "phasing out" of special category status did not begin until March 1976 and Kieran Nugent, sentenced on September 16, 1976 and placed in the H-Blocks, was the first republican prisoner to be refused political status. He began the blanket protest soon after.

38   Mac Ionnrachtaigh quoted in Batchelor, "The Translation of Les damnés de la terre," 66. My emphasis.

39   And over 40 years later participants still vividly remember the discussion and reading of these books, including Fanon's *The Wretched*.

40   See Leslie A. Hadfield, Liberation *and Development: Black Consciousness Community Programs in South Africa* (East Lansing: Michigan State University Press, 2016), 40–47.

41   In 1972, as part of discussions about negotiations between the British government and the IRA, any prisoner convicted of "troubles" related offences was given a "special status" akin to being considered prisoners of war (but avoiding that language). The privileges of this special status included the right to wear their own clothes and not do prisoner work, and to receive additional food and tobacco parcels. Special status was abolished in March 1976.

Skin, White Masks, on the grounds that it "advocates racial supremacy."[42] I was asked for my response and stated that the authorities had clearly not read the book.[43] The 65-year-old book's first title, we should remember was the *Disalienation of the Black*. In other words, the book is not only a critique of racism but also about black people's liberation from the internalization of the "historico-racial schema." The goal of Fanon's book is enlightenment about the multiple ways this objectification is created and recreated by ourselves, and as such can be undermined. The racial gaze is mediated by the brain, he argues, and eye is a correcting mirror.[44] "As a psychoanalyst," he adds, 'I must help my patient to "consciousnessize" their unconscious, to no longer be tempted by a *hallucinatory lactification*, but also to act along the lines of a change in social structure.'[45] In other words, the black person "must become aware of *the possibility of existence*" (my emphasis).[46]

Black Skin White Masks, then, is about the possibility of existence framed by a critique of racial supremacy in terms of helping the self-conscientizing and disalienation of the racialized object. In other words, consciousnessizing the unconscious internalization of the image of the racialized other (and all that means) and the temptation of hallucinatory lactification (including self-hatred and negrophobia). Becoming conscious of this internalization, Fanon argues, begins the necessary work to change the social structure that produces this alienation and dehumanization. The possibility of existence is therefore intimately connected to liberation and becoming a historical subject is thus intimately connected with thoughtful action.

The interviewer then asked me about what I thought about the banning of the book. I responded that it sounded like the banning of books in apartheid South Africa. Of course, in the United States, the ideology of prison reform might include notions of rehabilitation and self-reflection, but the reality is quite different and such notions are considered a threat to the carceral system. The prison system understands racial supremacy just as it understands

---

42   On the same page of the 60-page document of banned books is *Blood in My Eye* by George Jackson. The reason given for banning it is that it is a threat to order/security of the institution. Another coincidence, Jake Mac Saisas informed me (pers comm) that Jackson's *Soledad Brother* was on the Republican prisoner curriculum. While Fanon's work might not always be available in prison libraries Fanon is discussed in US prisons and I've had the pleasure of engaging in serious discussions of Fanon and Fanonian practices in the system.

43   Perhaps they had not understood it!

44   Fanon, *Black Skin White Masks*, 178.

45   Ibid., 80.

46   Ibid.

violence because it is its daily reality, but the idea of prisoners becoming con-
scientized and self-reflective and thereby acting to change the social structure
is quite another thing.

In these almost subterranean situations, Fanon is read in a practical and often a fragmented way, and yet read also as part of thinking about the specifics
of liberation involving all areas of life.[47]

Mental liberation, the positive answer to the question, "who am I?" is the
beginning of the liberation from colonization's zombification, or what Fanon
calls "living death" in his 1952 essay "The North African Syndrome." Additionally, Fanon speaks about the process of this liberation at the same time as *becoming historical* in the chapter on the strengths and weaknesses of spontaneity in
The Wretched of the Earth. The lucidity of this praxis, Fanon argues, "must remain deeply dialectical."[48] Liberation will not come like a shot from a gun but
is a fragmented and often precarious process that is constantly challenged. In
this context, praxis is often like "thought on the ground running," as the South
African shack dweller movement, Abahlali baseMjondolo, put it.

Shack dwellers in South Africa are often considered detritus, society's surplus; the uncivil and fragmented lumpen-proletariat, the reactive, voiceless,
criminal and lazy, and those against "development." As Fanon describes colonialization's idea of "the native" "impermeable to logic and science ... [an]
indolence sprawling under the sun ... [a] vegetating existence."[49] As it emerged
with neoliberalism the racist apartheid discourse about the ontology of blackness was recoded not replaced in post-apartheid South Africa. The poor are
poor because of their lazy essence. Rather than the hard work of addressing
the structural poverty created by colonialism and apartheid, the poor are simply blamed for their poverty. Neoliberal orthodoxy encourages the poor to become entrepreneurs of themselves, and while there certainly are many people
who try to scrape by doing all kinds of precarious work, from serving as maids
and gardeners, to selling food on the street and collecting scrap for recycling,
official unemployment at nearly 30% means that such prospects are limited.
By organizing themselves since 2005, Abahlali baseMjondolo, which means
residents of the shacks, seeks to undermine the silencing of the shack dwellers, giving voice to their common situation in a demand not only for housing,
land and security but also for dignity, while asking political questions—such
as, why are we, human beings, considered detritus in this society? Why are

---

47   See, for example, James Yaki Sayles, *Meditations on Frantz Fanon's Wretched of the Earth*.
      Montreal: Kersplebedeb, 2010.
48   Fanon, *The Wretched of the Earth* (2004), 135.
49   Ibid., 108.

we not listened to? —while consciously insisting on autonomy and grassroots democratic organization. Organized horizontally, decision making rests in the local shack settlement meetings. This is a principle. Echoing Fanon's demand that everything should be explained in a language the people understand,[50] Abahlali says "our politics is understood very well by all the old mamas and go-gos [grandmothers]."[51] Abahlali's politics intentionally seek a situation which is collective and inclusive in a language which all can participate. Rejecting political doubletalk of governance and the technical language of neoliberal civil society, they begin with what Fanon called a "situational diagnosis," taking seriously the lived experiences, struggles and thinking of the shack dwellers.[52] In other words, thinking, solidarity, and action emerge out of these fragmented and impoverished spaces, spaces that are considered impervious to thinking.[53]

In 2005, shack dwellers in Durban revolted because they felt betrayed. They had waited patiently for change, but the promises of 1994 had not reached them. They saw bulldozers on land that had been promised to them and start-ed to organize a protest by word of mouth. Their demand for recognition goes beyond the idea of "inclusion" in a political or legal system. They didn't close down the N2 ring road in Durban because they had read Fanon. They did it because they had tried all other methods and had simply been ignored. Seen as a vote bank for the ANC during election campaigns, when councilors would come around to the settlements with Biryani in an exchange for votes, their re-sponse was "No House, No Land, No Vote." They did not plan on a long struggle but today their struggle continues. Over these years they have grown into a formidable local movement, one that continues to occupy land and fight for the shack dwellers' right to the city. As they developed their own philosophy *in the struggle*, they were continuously subject to state repression, police vio-lence, and assassinations. While they have learned that no condition is per-manent, agreements with the provincial government and with the local police are negotiated, and promises about being consulted are constantly made and constantly broken, theirs is a constant struggle to live. Thus, there is no choice but to struggle. A rich archive has thereby developed based on their experi-ence and thinking. In 2009, after careful reading and discussions across the communities, they took the provincial government to the constitutional court

---

50   Ibid., 131.
51   Quoted in Nigel Gibson, *Fanonian Practices in South Africa*, 160.
52   Fanon, *Toward the African Revolution*. (New York: Grove Press, 1967), 10.
53   Richard Pithouse, "Thought Amidst Waste," *Journal of Asian and African Studies*, 47:5 (2012): 482–497.

against the "slums act"[54] and won; only days after this victory there was a massive backlash. Armed men organized by the local ANC violently removed Abahlali from the Kennedy Road shack settlement, which had been the movement's center. Their office was destroyed along with many members' homes. In context of this violence and death threats, up to one thousand people left the settlement and the organization was forced underground. At the time they had to rely on their wits and principles, keeping their organization alive under severe repression. Today, these events, as well as other sacrifices and victories, have become part of the movement's collective memory.

Demanding electricity and sanitation, they are accused of being against "development," because they refuse to move to temporary relocation centers (Government shacks), so-called transit camps, or housing on the urban peripheries. And thus, they discuss the notion of development from a different perspective connected to land and dignity. Critical of political corruption that controls the allocation of houses by patronage they are also critical of the small poorly constructed buildings called "houses" (built as cheaply as possible, often without foundations). They refuse this so-called "development," which means removal to often-desolate areas, miles from schools, hospitals, and work opportunities. Instead they demand full rights to the city and thus challenge the warehousing of the "surplus population," in the same way that the so-called homelands during the late-apartheid period were challenged as "puppet regimes" dressed up in ethno-politics.

After the attacks of 2009, there was debate about the direction of the movement with some saying it should become more security conscious and hierarchical. This was discussed carefully, and in the end, the movement decided to remain true to its principle of openness. Celebrating its tenth year of existence in 2015, the crisis in South Africa has continued to deepen with Abahlali facing increasing repression. Yet, the weekly meetings of 30 people, representing the communities that had once gathered in their Durban office, have grown to monthly meetings of 800 to 1000 people, now meeting on football grounds. Their commitment to the principle of inclusivity has paid off.

---

54 The KwaZulu-Natal Elimination and Prevention of Re-emergence of Slums Act, was passed in 2007. In the name of upgrades and housing development, it included forced and compulsory evictions even where municipalities and private landowners were unwilling. Beginning in KwaZulu-Natal it was set to become law across all of South Africa's provinces. The Constitutional Court found that the act violated the Prevention of Illegal Evictions Act (PIE Act).

3   The Rising of the Damned of the Earth

I believe I am but another of those wretched Irishmen born of a risen gen-
eration with a deeply rooted and unquenchable desire for freedom.
~ BOBBY SANDS, Writings from Prison

In the conclusion to *Black Skin White Masks*, which begins with a quote from
Marx's *18th Brumaire*, Fanon writes that,

> For the Antillean working in the sugarcane plantations in Le Robert, to
> fight is the only solution. And [they] will undertake and carry out this
> struggle not as the result of a Marxist or idealistic analysis but because
> quite simply [they] cannot conceive life otherwise than as a kind of com-
> bat against exploitation, poverty, and hunger.[55]

Fanon's reflection speaks to the spontaneous birth of the shack dweller movement when they decided to block the ring road. Like any movement, it has a
pre-history: Many who became involved came out the anti-apartheid struggle,
and with others, they had been discussing what to do for a while. Yet, they
understood from the beginning that they would not be allied to any particular
organization. Their commonality instead was their lived experience of being
in the shacks. Five years later, S'bu Zikode, the elected President of Abahlali,
wrote the preface to my *Fanonian Practices in South Africa*, highlighting Fanon's
comment that "each generation must discover its mission, fulfill it or betray
it." Zikode argued that Fanon was one of the ancestors of the struggle who
could be brought into conversation with the thinking of the shack dwellers. In
other words, by taking thought seriously they developed what they called "living learning" as one expression of their truth in post-apartheid South Africa.
I was thrilled that Zikode wrote what in my mind is a most important forward
to a book which was never intended to be about debates between academics
and intellectuals even though there is plenty of discussion, philosophy, and
history and not only engaged Fanon but challenged activist intellectuals to
shift the ground of reason and open their ears to these new struggles of *les
damnés*.

Abahlali did not read Fanon, said critics of *Fanonian Practices in South Africa*. I was at a book launch in Durban in 2011 when one person made it clear that
he thought I'd made Abahlali up, romanticizing the shack dwellers (this was
from an academic, who although from Durban, had never bothered to meet

---

55   Fanon, *Black Skin White Masks*, 199.

any of the local members of Abahlali). Fortunately, I had been speaking and meeting with Abahlali and also had the privilege to take part in a seminar on Fanon with Abahlali as part of the "living learning" seminar organized by the radical (and radically anti-NGO) NGO Churchland Programme in Pietermaritz-burg. At the meeting, Ntombifuthi Shandu, an activist from the Rural Network, which was working with Abahlali at the time, remarked that life had gotten more difficult since the end of apartheid. Reflecting on the brutality of some of those who rule, she wondered whether "we are led by people who *were damaged by the struggle* during apartheid." The remark immediately reminded me of Fanon who counseled (Algerian) FLN militants insisting that it was essential that each continue to "harry the insult to humanity that exists in themselves."[56] Fanon understood that the extreme conditions experienced under coloniza-tion and the struggle against it also bred new pathologies, psychological dis-orders, traumas, and stresses. The question of psychological liberation is part of Fanon's conception of "humanism" and reflection on "human things," which would have to be continually addressed not only during the liberation struggle but also long after it, alongside building the new society and the necessary socio-economic and political decolonial transformation.[57]

Fanon also frequently points out that the people quickly get the feeling that they have been betrayed by their leaders who have begun to use the old sys-tems of repression against them. The betrayal, he says, is not individual but social. On this point, Shandu's comment that the poor were now subject to the brutality of the leaders insightfully expresses two of Fanon's concerns. First, that hatred, resentment, and revenge, feelings often encouraged during the struggle for short-term ends, cannot sustain liberation nor create liberated beings.[58] Second, that actions based on taking the place of the colonizer also recapitulate colonial pathologies, which become the foundation for new forms of chauvinism.[59] Intimately aware of the need for unity, he argues that this of-ten becomes a justification for a politics of subservience, which often takes the place of a culture of discussion and democracy. He called this the "sclerotiza-tion of politics"[60] (Fanon often likes to make use of medical terms to describe politics), arguing that it leads to a brutality and contempt of thought.[61] In ad-dition, there is an implicit elitism in the militant's will to get things done. He calls this pathology of activism without thought, "atrocious," "inhuman" and

---

56   Fanon, *The Wretched of the Earth* (1968), 304.
57   Fanon, *The Wretched of the Earth* (2004), 144.
58   Ibid., 89.
59   Ibid., 105.
60   Fanon, *A Dying Colonialism*, 67.
61   Fanon, *The Wretched of the Earth* (2004), 95.

"sterile" and insists instead that the search for truth is the "responsibility of the community."[62] In contrast to the vanguardist party structure or foco-ist guerilla organization that characterized the anticolonial period, he was particularly critical of intellectuals and militants who used the dire repressive situation, whatever it might be, as a justification to suppress thinking.

4   Irish Connections

What is really fantastic about Kathryn Batchelor's essay, "Fanon in English: Irish Connections," is her discussion of an earlier Irish connection other than the one mentioned by Homi Bhabha. The fact that the first English translation of *The Wretched of the Earth* that we've been reading since the early 1960s was by an Irish woman, Constance Farrington, who according to a report in the *Irish Times* on the publication of *The Damned* (the first English title of *The Wretched of the Earth*) in 1963, "will be remembered by old members of the Irish Association."[63]

I did not know of this connection, mistakenly thinking (perhaps because of the dominance of the American English edition) that Constance Farrington was American. In other words, while *The Wretched of the Earth* had become "famous" in the United States, and only then published by Penguin in England (the edition that is still being read in South Africa and indeed in Ireland), it was forgotten that it had been translated by an Irish woman living in France. Farrington had in fact translated *The Damned* for *Présence Africaine*. She was a socialist who saw connections between the Irish struggle and the Algerian struggle against the French, and while in France she became "caught up" with the Algerian struggle through her friend Micheline Pouteau. Pouteau was a humanist who was completely opposed to the French government torture regime in Algeria and also disillusioned with the French Communist Party's attitude towards the Algerian war. Wanting to take a stand, she became a member of the underground Jeanson Network, supporting the FLN. In 1960, eighty members of the network, including Pouteau were arrested and "she and nine others were given the maximum sentence of 10 years."[64] Constance Farrington visited her frequently and apparently helped Micheline and her comrades escape from prison by giving her numerous pairs of nylon stockings, which were

---

62   Ibid., 139.
63   Quoted in Batchelor, "The Translation of Les damnés de la terre," 42.
64   Brian Farrington, *A Rich Soup: A Memoir* (Dublin: Linden Publishing, 2010), 177.

knotted together and used as a rope.[65] So Constance Farrington was not simply a translator of Fanon but an activist indirectly connected to FLN circles.[66] Interestingly, Batchelor draws attention to Farrington's wish that the title of *Les damnés de la terre* (*The Wretched of the Earth*) (with its echoes of the Internationale) be translated as *The Rising of the Damned*.[67] Farrington wrote to *Présence Africaine* and then to Grove Press arguing that "anyone with even a knowledge of the history of imperialism" would see a resonance with the risings of the 19th the 20th century.[68] In the event, neither *Présence Africaine* nor Grove Press took any notice.

In addition, it is significant that her husband, Brian, was at the same time writing about the Algerian war. An article in the *Irish Times* in 1958 titled "Algerian Atrocities: The psychosis of Fear," focused on the on-going torture in Algeria—constantly denied by the French—but described in Henri Alleg's book *La Question* that had just been published.[69] The phrase "psychosis of fear" brings us right back to thinking about Fanon's work in Algeria as a psychiatrist and as a revolutionary, and at the same time the purposeful instillation of fear by police, military raids, and systematic torture. Writing of contemporary South Africa, one sees an echo in what the South African theorist Michael Neocosmos considers the intention of the police raid: "to instill fear into communities." Neocosmos writes, "the emphasis on the militarization of the police and on 'shoot to kill' polices introduced by the Zuma government ostensibly to combat crime... [conceive] poor communities as enemy territory, a familiar notion under colonial forms of state."[70]

Fanon was by training and profession a psychiatrist and his concern about mental health is reflected in all his books, *Black Skin White Masks*, *A Dying*

---

65   Ibid.
66   See Batchelor, "The Translation of Les damnés de la terre," 48–49. Brian Farrington points out that Constance never made much money from the book because "she failed to sign a regular contract with the first publisher." He remembers that it was Charles-André-Jullien who "got her the job translating into English a book that was very important at the time: Frantz Fanon's *Les Damnés de la Terre*." See Farrington, *A Rich Soup*, 196.
67   It is worth noting that the opening lines of Fanon's *Les damnés de la terre* echo the opening lines of Eugéne Pottier Internationale, "Debout! Les damnés de la terre, Debout! Les forçats de la faim" (Arise wretched of the earth. Arise prisoners of hunger), and also resonates with the Haitian Marxist, Jacques Roumain, whose poem about black revolt "Nouveau sermon négre," concludes with the same lines, "Debout les damnés de la terre, Debout les forçats de la faim." Written in 1945, the poem was included in Senghor's *Anthologie de la nouvelle poésie négre et malgache de langue française*.
68   Quoted in Batchelor, "The Translation of Les damnés de la terre," 49.
69   Ibid., 43.
70   Michael Neocosmos, Thinking *Freedom in Africa*. (Johannesburg: Wits University Press, 2017), 179.

Colonialism, and *The Wretched of the Earth*. The latter, of course, ends with the mostly under-read chapter, "Colonial Wars and Mental Disorders" and he wonders whether the chapter might seem "out of place ... in a book like this."

What is a book like this? In the 1960s and 1970s, *The Wretched* was called the bible of black and anti-colonial revolutions but with little regard to the final chapter on mental disorders. Perhaps today, the question of mental health is at the heart of the problems we face across the postcolonial world, seen for example in the epidemic of suicides among men in poor areas of Belfast, which in the years since 1998 outnumber the number killed in the period of "the troubles" from 1969 to 1997 (with over 30% of all deaths of those in the 25 to 34 age bracket attributable to suicide in the years 2005 to 2009).[71]

Fanon argues that the trauma, pain, and destruction of the human as well as the legacy of acts taken in the context of war and colonial terror remain part of the continuing and necessary *work* of building the new society and are intimately connected with his political critique. "For many years to come," he writes, "we *shall be bandaging* the countless and *sometimes indelible wounds* inflicted on our people by the colonialist onslaught."[72] The more Fanon, the "political revolutionary," advanced in imagining the new society, the more Fanon, the psychiatrist, could not forget the wounded society on which the new nation would be built.[73]

The new society, Fanon argues in the chapter "Misadventures of National Consciousness," would be built on the subversion of colonial Manicheanism and its spatial division. This Manicheanism is powerfully expressed in an important opening paragraph of *The Wretched of the Earth* and remains fundamental:

> The 'colonized' sector is not complementary to the 'colonial' sector. Two confront each other, but not the service of a higher unity... [but] mutual exclusion: There is no conciliation possible, one of them is superfluous. The colonist's sector is a sector built to last, all stone and steel. It's a sector of lights and paved roads, where the trash cans constantly overflow with strange and wonderful garbage, undreamed-of leftovers. The colonist's feet can never be glimpsed, except perhaps in the sea, but then you can never get close enough. Solid shoes protect them in a sector where the streets are clean and smooth, without a pothole, without a

---

71   See www.detail.tv/articles/suicide-deaths-in-northern-Ireland-highest-on-record.

72   Fanon, *The Wretched of the Earth* (2004), 181.

73   See Gibson and Roberto Beneduce, *Frantz Fanon, Psychiatry and Politics*. Lanham MD: Rowman and Littlefield, 2017.

stone. The colonist's sector is a sated, sluggish its belly is permanently full good things... The colonized's sector, or at least the quarters, the shanty town, the Medina, the reservation, is a disreputable place inhabited by disreputable people... It's a world with no space, people are piled one on top of the other, the shacks squeezed tightly together. The colonized's sector is a famished sector, hungry for bread, meat, shoes, coal, and light. The colonized's sector is a sector that crouches and cowers, a sector on its knees.[74]

"Out of place" is an important and interesting metaphor. Considered socially, those out of place are the migrants and the marginalized, literally people who are objectified, denied subjectivity and history. The subjects of *The Wretched of the Earth,* the majority of the world's population are those who are out of place, ordered to stay in place by the police, the military, the state, and its institutions, and told to "not overstep its limits"[75] These are the people who have no space, and are hemmed in "by lines of force"—including walls and security cameras to keep them out and to "keep the peace" (as in the peace walls of Belfast). But almost as a "biological" necessity, Fanon argues, the colonized subvert these barriers, continually threatening to break across the interstices of colonial and postcolonial spaces.[76] In South Africa, as in many postcolonial spaces, the shack settlements exist right next to the gated communities. The two worlds—the securitized global cities of the rich and the precarious life of the poor—is the world of "reciprocal exclusivity" not in service of a higher unity. "One is superfluous," Fanon argues.[77] Today, this Manicheanism is absolutely clear.

The notion of place and space remains essential to Fanon's thought: From *Black Skin, White Masks,* and the idea of blacks' "illicit appearance," as Lewis Gordon puts it, where every time a black person appears reason walks out (in other words the black is not only unreasonable but the appearance of the black also subverts the reasonable), to the articles in *A Dying Colonialism,* where Fanon writes of Algeria unveiling itself with women's actions in the Algerian revolution subverting the Manichean divisions of the colonial city and the cloistered Arab woman's passivity (so brilliantly recognized in

---

74 Fanon, *The Wretched of the Earth* (2004), 4.

75 Ibid., 15.

76 We should remember that Fanon gestures to the political-organizational importance of the shack dwellers, the people who live in the bidonvilles, the tin-towns of Algiers, in chapter two of *The Wretched,* as an important connection between the rural and the urban.

77 Ibid.

Gillo Pontecorvo's film "The Battle of Algiers"), to the battle over space as an expression of the timeless Manicheanism of colonial society and the place of a new humanism in *The Wretched*.[78] A politics of space—the hemming in of people—is essential to understanding Fanon's thought and practice, from the ordering of the psychiatric hospital to the lines of force in colonial society. Such a politics, because it must become radically humanist, therefore must include the necessary of reordering, questioning and transgressing the spatial order.

5 Unfreedom in South Africa

The apogee of this spatial Manicheanism is apartheid, including its "pass" laws, forced removals in order to whiten cities, its so-called "homelands," and the racial division of urban space. Built on the architecture of colonial segregation, it continued and developed its structural and violent brutalization, exploitation, and pauperization, but also saw the development of new forms of resistance, from the defiance campaign of the early 1950s to the Black Consciousness Movement and the trade union movements of the 1970s, which foregrounded the mass opposition of the 1980s. Thus it is not surprising that resistance to the Manichean structure of apartheid was expressed in a spatial context. The same can be said of post-apartheid South Africa, where an important critique of lived experience is based in the politics of space and exclusion.

Apart from the neoliberal de-racialization of some urban spaces like shopping malls, the first thing one sees arriving in South Africa and driving from the airport to the city is the miles and miles of shack settlements. The settlements are still growing and the urban struggle over space continues despite constant eviction and the illegal destruction of shacks. It is from these spaces of struggle that one of the clearest critiques of unfreedom in South Africa would be made and since 2006, Abahlali baseMjondolo has held an annual Unfreedom Day to mark the freedom that they do not have. As they said in 2013:

> Who can say that they are really free when they do not have the right to organize freely and safely?
> Who can say they are really free when they are forced out of the city and taken to dumping grounds in the middle of nowhere?
> We cannot pretend [that] we are free.

---

78   Lewis R. Gordon, "Of Illicit Appearance: The L.A. Riots/Rebellion as a Portent of Things to Come," http://www.truth-out.org/news/item/9008-of-illicit-appearance-the-la-riots-rebellion-as-a-portent-of-things-to-come.

We would be bluffing the nation if we agreed to go to the stadiums [where the official freedom day celebrations take place] and say we are free while we suffer police politician brutality.

Why are we told and even educated about freedom? There are campaigns and expensive adverts on television and radios about how free we are. Real freedom would not come only once a year and we will not have to be told about it. Real freedom will be something we feel from inside our hearts each second, each minute, each hour and each day.[79]

This critique of freedom, which is what they call unfreedom, represents a significant thinking about politics fully grounded in contemporary material realities.[80] It is a contemporary Freedom Charter for South Africa with a Fanonian resonance: "Real freedom is something felt "inside our hearts" all the time."

Fanon has a long relationship with South Africa that goes back to the founding of the Black Consciousness Movement in the early 1970s. The relationship seems almost arbitrary and at least fantastic in its beginnings since his writings were hardly available, banned by the South African censors on their publication. Interestingly, when *The Wretched of the Earth* was first banned in South Africa in 1965 (the 1965 Penguin edition) there was not a word in the censor's report about violence. Rather they found the final chapter on the colonial war and mental disorders "far-fetched." The report marked only one page from the chapter on violence and this referred to conditions of work, which were perhaps too Marxian for the censors. Fanon's sentence, "if conditions of work are not modified, centuries will be needed to humanize this world which has been forced down to animal level by imperial powers" was deemed particularly threatening to the apartheid system built on the super-exploitation of African labor.

When *The Wretched of the Earth* was re-banned in 1977, things were different and the new 1974 publications act now included possession as a punishable act.[81] The 1976 Soweto revolt—which Biko had considered synonymous with Black consciousness—had shaken the country, and Fanon's influence on Black consciousness was known (at least among BC militants and students). Yet, the author of the much more extensive but superficial censor report (a Professor J.P. Jansen) focused entirely on writings from the USA, particularly an article in the then quite influential *TIME* magazine about Fanon as the philosopher of violence. Fanon "was one of the most important black activists that has ever

---

79   Quoted in Neocosmos, *Thinking Freedom in Africa*, 364–366.
80   Ibid., 366–372.
81   See Peter McDonald, *The Literature Police: Apartheid Censorship and Its Cultural Consequences* (Oxford: Oxford University Press), 61–65.

lived," believing, he quotes, "that the oppressed can heal their souls through the cathartic effect of revolutionary violence."[82]

Banned in South Africa, Fanon traveled across the Limpopo through the American Black power movement, Black theology and the writings of James Cone in particular. Cone directly engaged with Fanon in his 1969 book *Black Theology and Black Power,* the same year Biko became the first President of the Black Consciousness South African Students' Organization (SASO), and Rubin Phillip (who later became the Bishop of Durban and important supporter of Abahlali) its Vice President. One thing that Biko and Cone shared with Fanon was a critique of white liberalism emphasizing notions of autonomy and self-standing (of recognizing that they were "on their own"), self-consciousness, and cultural revival as ongoing projects; that is to say as Biko defined Black consciousness "as a reflection of a mental attitude."[83] So while Fanon was being dismissed in the mainstream media in the United States as a prophet of violence, in South Africa he became essential to a rethinking and revolutionary shift in consciousness.

6   The South Africa Retrogression: a Fanonian Balance Sheet

Fanon cannot be simply applied to new situations. While his dialectic arose out of specific events, actions and choices, each situation might demand that we ask the question: what might a revolutionary like Fanon think? The degeneration of national liberation struggles, about which Fanon warned so presciently in *The Wretched of the Earth,* was not an inevitability, but a product of the will of the national (petit) bourgeoisie who in place of solidarity and the principle of equality, mimic the European bourgeoisie in its quest to accumulate. But he adds that it is accumulation without productivity, a re-inscribing of racism, nativism and ethno-nationalism in a neocolonial set-up:

> The national bourgeoisie... who have assimilated to the core the most despicable aspects of the colonial mentality, take over from the Europeans and lay the foundations for a racist philosophy that is terribly prejudicial to the future of Africa. Through its apathy and mimicry it encourages the growth and development of racism that was typical of the colonial period... In certain regions of Africa, bleating paternalism toward blacks and the obscene idea drawn from Western culture that the black race is impermeable to logic and science reign in all their nakedness.[84]

---

82   J.P. Jansen. P77/2/16, IDP, National Archives, 72 Roeland Street, Cape Town.
83   Biko, *I Write What I Like,* 48.
84   Fanon, *The Wretched of the Earth* (2004), 108.

Fanonian Practices in South Africa develops a critique of post-apartheid South Africa employing Fanonian concepts. A balance sheet—mediated by the promises of the Freedom Charter—of post-apartheid South Africa, which today, in the current period of retrogression seem almost utopian, as incredible corruption in all areas of life becomes the everyday norm.[85] The corruption is however not incidental but fulfills a logic of Fanon's dialectic. Patronage through the ANC—the filling of individual pockets at the expense of the community— has almost completely replaced notions of solidarity as the norm. In practice, Fanon's pithy remark, "my brother is my wallet and my comrade, my scheming" has become the daily activity of the old party of liberation.[86]

The degeneration has been constant: Biko's prediction in the early 1970s that it was possible to create a "capitalist black society, [a] black middle class," in South Africa, and "succeed in putting across to the world a pretty convincing, integrated picture, with still 70 percent of the population being underdogs," seemed to come true after 1994. By the end of the decade it was becoming clear that the principles set forth in the Freedom Charter and promises made by Nelson Mandela were not going to be realized. While the xenophobic attacks of 2008, which left over 60 dead, "denoted the ultimate failure of human rights discourse in South Africa,"[87] Abahlali—a voice from shacks irrespective of assumptions of indigeneity and nativism – played an active role against the violence in the settlements and also used all the means at their disposal, including the constitutional court to defend themselves. The Marikana massacre in 2012 represented a real nodal point which illuminated not only the violence of the party/state but the hollowing out of liberal institutions, laws and rights, including the Constitutional Court and the public protector's office, that were products of the unfinished struggle against apartheid. The ANC's attempt to regain legitimacy by making bold statements about land redistribution, often mobilized by nativism, xenophobia, and rhetoric functioned as a veneer over systemic corruption. With a Fanonian resonance Richard Pithouse predicts that it seems likely that any land redistribution by the ANC would be carried out in an "authoritarian manner that strengthens its repressive capacities and primarily benefits people in and around the party through an expansion of the

---

85   Adopted in June 1955 at the "Congress of the People," in Kliptown, South Africa, the Free-
       dom Charter was a key document of the anti-apartheid struggle. Its demand for human
       rights and equality (housing, education and land), and the nationalization of the banks,
       mines and industry under popular control was considered the basis of a post-apartheid
       society.
86   Ibid., 11.
87   Neocosmos, *Thinking Freedom in Africa*, 134.

patronage machine. There is very little chance that land will be allocated on the basis of a democratic and social logic."[88]

Here the impulse towards authoritarianism and nativism includes, as Fanon suggests, a rhetoric opposing some aspects of historical injustice. Propaganda organized in support of Jacob Zuma, especially in his last days as President, relentlessly conflated the often-predatory interests of the political elite with those of the oppressed majority. Even if the election of Cyril Ramaphosa as President of the ANC in 2017 means that corruption is seriously addressed it lacks real capacity, the best that could be expected is a technicist neoliberal approach. Opposition within the political party has often been hamstrung by its lack of real connections with the mass of the people. The violence of authoritarian populism is, as I have argued, experienced quite directly in the shack settlements where opposition is seen as disloyalty, as local political figures and gangsters seek the benefits of an ANC patronage system. Born out of a politics of broken promises and educated by experience, Abahlali listened to the new promises made by Durban mayor Zandile Gumede, who was elected in August 2016. She promised the end of evictions and repression and that Abahlali would have a voice in the city's plans for housing. None of this happened. Rather, 2017 saw an increase of violent repression with shack leaders assassinated in the context of a politics of war, bribery, corruption, and divide and rule.

Land redistribution has not occurred in post-apartheid South Africa where black South Africans own only 7% of the land. The popular demand for land reform has forced the ANC and other parties such as the Economic Freedom Fighters into raising the issue of appropriating land without compensation. Though this appears radical, Abahlali has been quick to point out its latent class character. Appropriation without compensation was already happening, they argued, to poor people who were being forcefully evicted from unused land. Echoing Fanon, they posed the creative potential and social organization of land occupations as a "development from below"—the democratic participation of the landless in urban planning—in opposition to the regressive "development from above" that often justified violent expulsion. The question of land, in other words, is not simply a question of addressing the expropriation of the rural land stolen by settler colonialism but addressing the land needs of urban dwellers since it is in the towns and cities where most of South Africa's population live and where the housing backlog of over two million makes the daily situation desperate. The state's response? A politics of blood. In June 2017, Samuel Hloele was shot dead by the Anti Land Invasion Unit. In November 2017, Sibonelo Patrick Mpeku, the chairperson of the Sisonke

---

88   Richard Pithouse, "The ANC is misusing *the* land question" https://mg.co.za/article/2017-07-13-the-anc-is-misusing-the-land-question.

Village branch was kidnapped and murdered. Just a few days later Soyiso Nkqa-yini, one of the leading militants in the eNkanini land occupation in Cato Man-or, and the Abahlali Youth League, was murdered. Just as the ANC was mov-ing to endorse the multi-millionaire businessman Cyril Ramaphosa (who as a Lonmin director was intimately connected with the Marikana massacre) as its new leader, the movement pointedly spoke of the young shack dweller Soyiso Nkqayini as the "honorable and brave leader that our country so lacks."[89] The price for land and dignity is paid in blood.

The speed of degeneration into kleptocracy first analyzed by Fanon and novelized 50 years ago in Ayi Kwei Armah's *The Beautyful Ones Are Not Yet Born*, has been so astounding that new revelations are quickly forgotten just as state violence goes unreported. In a press statement, "Why we marched on Durban City Hall on June 26, 2017," Abahlali echoed Fanon's *The Wretched of the Earth* bluntly stating, "Now we face the politics of lies and the rule of the gun. We face a gangster state that only sees development as a way for politicians and their friend to get rich [with]... the City is being run on a violent and criminal basis yet the police do not act against this criminality, or even open cases. It is a Mafia politic[s]."[90] Across Durban, the Anti Land Invasion Unit continues to use live ammunition as homes are demolished despite court interdicts.

But in the face of "lies, evictions, life threatening living conditions and se-rious repression," the movement continues to grow articulating a politics of space that challenges post-apartheid urban planning:

> No politician or political party has taken the urban crisis seriously or tak-en real steps to allocate urban land on the basis of social need, address the life threatening conditions in the settlements with urgency and begin a program of real action to ensure decent housing for all. When impover-ished people have occupied land, which is a form of urban planning from below that can help to democratize our cities, we continue to face armed evictions, which are often illegal.[91]

The violence does not derive from a lack of capacity to enforce the law, but rather is systematic, organized, and politically sanctioned from above. It ex-poses the reappearance of the Manicheanism of the apartheid period in a new

89   Abahlali baseMjondolo. "eNkanini to honour Comrade Soyiso Nkqayini," Friday, 22 De-cember 2017. Abahlali baseMjondolo Press Statement, http://abahlali.org/node/16358/.

90   Abahlali baseMjondolo. Press statement, "We March on the Durban City Hall on 26 June 2017," June 14, 2017. www.Abahlali.org.

91   Abahlali baseMjondolo. "Year-end statement: Building Democratic Popular Power in the Struggle for Land & Dignity." http://abahlali.org/node/16347/.

guise. It is not simply that notions of civil society and law are paper-thin, and that we have moved from the politics of reconciliation and rainbowism, but that the shack dwellers were never considered part of civil society in the first place.

Fanon concludes his "Misadventures of National Consciousness" arguing against any state/ party/ leadership-centric notion of liberation: The idea that some magical force, dressed up in the language of technicism and professionalism, or in the language of populism and militarism, will save us. Instead, Fanon insists in *The Wretched of the Earth* that you can easily prove that the masses have to be managed from above. "But if you speak the language of the everyday... then you will realize that the masses are quick to seize every shade of meaning ... Everything can be explained to the people, on the single condition that you really want them to understand... The more people understand, the more watchful they become and the more they come to realize that everything depends on them."[92] This is the standpoint from which Fanon's notion of developing "new concepts" can emerge.

Bibliography

Abahlali baseMjondolo. 2017a. Press statement, "We March on the Durban City Hall on 26 June 2017," June 14, www.Abahlali.org.

Abahlali baseMjondolo. 2017b. Emergency Press Statement "Brutal Attacks on the new Cato Manor Land Occupation," October 2 http://abahlali.org/node/16277/.

Abahlali baseMjondolo. 2017c. "Abahlali Women's Choral Society to Launch its First Album," October 6 http://abahlali.org/node/16287/.

Abahlali baseMjondolo. 2017d. "Year end statement: Building Democratic Popular Power in the Struggle for Land & Dignity," http://abahlali.org/node/16347/.

Abahlali baseMjondolo. 2017e. "eNkanini to honour Comrade Soyiso Nkqayini," Friday, 22 December 2017 Abahlali baseMjondolo Press Statement, http://abahlali.org/node/16358/.

Alan, John and Lou Turner. *Frantz Fanon, Soweto, and American Black Thought*. Detroit: News and Letters, 1978.

Batchelor, Kathryn. "The Translation of Les damnés de la terre into English: Exploring Irish Connections." In *Translating Frantz Fanon Across Continents and Languages*, edited by Kathryn Batchelor and Sue-Ann Harding, 40–75. New York: Routledge, 2017.

---

92   Fanon, *The Wretched of the Earth* (1968), 188–189, 191.

Batchelor, Kathryn and Sue-Ann Harding, eds. *Translating Frantz Fanon Across Continents and Languages.* New York: Routledge, 2017.

Bernstein, Richard J. *On Violence.* Cambridge: Polity Books, 2013.

Biko, Steve. *I Write What I Like.* London: Heinemann, 1978.

Buck-Morss, Susan. *Hegel, Haiti and Universal History.* Pittsburgh, University Press of Pittsburgh, 2009.

Ciccariello-Maher, George. "European Intellectuals and Colonial Difference: Césaire and Fanon beyond Sartre and Foucault." In *Race after Sartre: Antiracism, Africana Existentialism, Postcolonialism,* edited by Jonathan Judaken, 129–156. Albany: State University of New York, 2009.

Fanon, Frantz. *A Dying Colonialism.* New York: Grove Press, 1965.

Fanon, Frantz. *Toward the African Revolution* New York: Grove Press, 1967.

Fanon, Frantz. *The Wretched of the Earth.* Translated by Richard Philcox. New York: Grove Press, 2004.

Fanon, Frantz. *The Wretched of the Earth.* Translated by Constance Farrington. New York: Grove Press, 1968.

Fanon, Frantz. *Black Skin White Masks.* New York: Grove Press, 2008.

Farrington, Brian. *A Rich Soup: A Memoir.* Dublin: Linden Publishing, 2010.

Gibson, Nigel C. Introduction to *Rethinking Fanon: The Continuing Dialogue.* Amherst NY: Humanity Books, 1999.

Gibson, Nigel C. *Fanon: The Postcolonial Imagination.* Cambridge, UK: Polity Press, 2003.

Gibson, Nigel C. *Fanonian Practices in South Africa: From Steve Biko to Abahlali baseMjondolo,* Pietermaritzburg: UKZN Press, 2011.

Gibson, Nigel C. and Roberto Beneduce. *Frantz Fanon, Psychiatry and Politics.* Lanham MD: Rowman and Littlefield, 2017.

Gordon, Lewis R. "Of Illicit Appearance: The L.A. Riots/Rebellion as a Portent of Things to Come," May 12, 2012. https://truthout.org/articles/of-illicit-appearance-the-la-riots-rebellion-as-a-portent-of-things-to-come/.

Hadfield, Leslie A. *Liberation and Development: Black Consciousness Community Programs in South Africa.* East Lansing: Michigan State UP, 2016.

Hansen, Emmanuel. *Frantz Fanon: Social and Political Thought.* Oxford: Oxford University Press, 1978.

Jinadu, Adele. *Fanon: In Search of the African Revolution.* London: Kegan Paul International, 1986 [1980].

Mac Ionnrachtaigh, Feargal and Philip Scraton. *Language, Resistance and Revival: Republican Prisoners and the Irish Language in the North of Ireland.* London: Pluto, 2013.

Macey, David. *Fanon* London: Granta, 2000.

Mazrui, Alamin. "Fanon in the East African Experience: Between English and Swahili Translations." In *Translating Frantz Fanon Across Continents and Languages*, edited by Kathryn Batchelor Kathryn and Sue-Ann Harding, 76–97. New York: Routledge, 2017.

McDonald, Peter D. *The Literature Police: Apartheid Censorship and Its Cultural Consequences*. Oxford: Oxford University Press, 2009.

More, Mabogo Percy. *Biko: Philosophy, Identity and Liberation*. Pretoria: HSRC Press, 2017.

Neocosmos, Michael. *Thinking Freedom in Africa*. Johannesburg: Wits University Press, 2017.

Pithouse, Richard. "Thought Amidst Waste." *Journal of Asian and African Studies* 47: 5 (2012): 482–497.

Pithouse, Richard. The ANC is misusing the land question. July 13, 2017. https://mg.co .za/article/2017-07-13-the-anc-is-misusing-the-land-question.

Said, Edward W. "Travelling Theory," In *Rethinking Fanon*, edited by Nigel C. Gibson. Amherst NY: Humanity Books, 1999.

Sands, Bobby. "Prison Diary." http://www.bobbysandstrust.com/writings/prison-diary.

Sayles, James Yaki. *Meditations on Frantz Fanon's Wretched of the Earth*. Montreal: Kersplebedeb, 2010.

Spivak, Gayatri C. *A Critique of Postcolonial Reason: Toward a History of the Vanishing Present*. Cambridge MA: Harvard University Press, 1999.

wa Th'iongo, Ngũgĩ. *Decolonising the mind: the politics of language in African literature*. Portsmouth, N.H.: Heinemann, 1986.

wa Th'iongo, Ngũgĩ. "The Writer in the Neo-colonial State." In *Moving the Centre: The Struggle for Cultural Freedoms*. Portsmouth, N.H: Heinemann, 1993.

CHAPTER 7

Hegel, Fanon, and the Problem of Recognition

Ali S. Harfouch

It is no longer tenable to critique Georg W.F. Hegel on the basis that he was a "philosopher of imperialism" or on the grounds that his philosophical works are "Eurocentric," or grounded in "racism." These critiques amount to nothing short of inverted racism, a reification of the same colonial relations one wishes to transcend and an essentialization of the mythos called "Europe." Accordingly, in this response I want to take Hegel seriously and in doing so put him in conversation with Frantz Fanon and Paulo Freire. The aim is to show that, although Fanon is unique in that he does indeed critically engage with the Hegelian Master-Slave dialectic, his engagement is marred by contradictions that circumvent both his political imagination and praxis of "liberation." Ultimately, this results in a reductionist approach on the part of Fanon and an impediment to the articulation of a truly emancipatory and radical politics. This chapter is split into four sections. In the introductory section, we will look at why we must return to philosophy, more specifically, by abandoning post-colonial responses to "Eurocentric" thinkers and re-engaging with ideals posited by the likes of Hegel. Section two will provide a cursory overview of Fanon's response to Hegel. Section three will introduce an important problem: the inescapable ontological-grounding of the master-slave dialectic. Section four will then return to the Fanonian critique of the master-slave dialectic in light of the problem introduced in section three.

1 Why Hegel? Beyond Post-colonialism

To dismiss Hegelian philosophy on the basis that it is Eurocentric is to invert the supposedly "racist" knowledge-hierarchy of modernity. Post-colonial discourse ostensibly displaces philosophy by *negating* Eurocentric philosophy and in turn paradoxically sublimates their critique from a critique of *a* philosophy to a universal critique *of* philosophy. It is, perhaps, a post-colonial anxiety – for while the post-colonial ideologue will bemoan the long-standing inability of the subaltern to speak, this capacity is also stripped from those in the center. While the ideologue works to deconstruct "Europe," they essentialize the *mythos* of Europe by making explicit claims as to what *it is* and what it *is not*.

Furthermore, they negate their own autonomy when they equivocate ideas *appropriated* by modernity with ideas that are fundamentally *part-and-parcel* of modernity. To speak of "reason" is to be Eurocentric. To speak of identity-based politics is to be Eurocentric. This has created a quandary for the post-colonial ideologue, who cannot do away with humanistic ideals like freedom, equality, and self-dignity, all of which are constitutive elements in modern discourse, but must also remain critical of the epistemic foundations of these ideals. The late Lebanese-Marxist, Mehdi 'Amil, aptly notes:

> It is not strange then that cultural structuralism, that characterizes the thought of Michel Foucault, would meet Nietzschean Nihilism, on a common ground... Rationalistic imperialism would reconcile itself with the anti-rational nihilism in asserting the oneness of reason, and hence, the refusal of revolutionary reason, the only opposition to the dominant reason.[1]

There are several reasons why we must take the Hegelian dialectic seriously. First and foremost, the dialectic provides the basis for a *general* theory of oppression as opposed to the post-colonial theorization of one mode-of-oppression (colonization). That is to say, we can conceptualize the origins and modalities of oppression reducing oppression to colonial oppression. Paradoxically, this reduction of oppression to a singular moment (the colonial trauma) – this inter-subjective relationship (the colonized and the colonizer) becomes the constitutive element in the colonized's self-recognition, one in which the very identity of the colonized is based on a *negation* (that is to say, a negation of the colonizers' negation).[2] Thus, the slave/colonized attains self-recognition vis-à-vis a negation of the master/the colonizer. Otherwise, the "new" man who emerges from the colonial trauma could not have been without the colonizer. To be is to negate, and to negate is to recognize (the colonizer); the "Other" remains "the theme of his action [the colonized]." As McClintock explains: "post-colonial," despite its critical deconstruction of post-Enlightenment binaries, "re-orients the globe once more around a single, binary opposition: colonial/post-colonial."[3] This new colonial/post-colonial and/or colonizer/colonized

---

1   Mehdi 'Amil, *Hal al-Qalb li-l-Sharq wa-l-'Aql li-l-Gharb? Marx fī Istishrāq Idwar Sa'īd* [Is the Heart for the East and the Mind for the West? Marx in Edward Said's Orientalism] (2nd edition) (Beirut: Dār al-Fārābī, 2006), 72.

2   More will be said about this later.

3   Anne McClintock, "The Angel of Progress: Pitfalls of the Term Post-Colonialism," in *Colonial Discourse and Post-Colonial Theory: A Reader*, eds. Patrick Williams and Laura Chrisman. (New York: Columbia University Press, 1994), 292.

binary becomes, paradoxically, universalized and comes to serve as the new "master-narrative."

At the level of praxis, the colonized/slave is left in a quandary; Post-colonial discourse tells us little of what those occupying Tahrir Square or Wall Street *ought* to do, or how to proceed? To speak of "strategic essentialism" is to oscillate a thin line between liberational-emancipatory politics on one hand, and pragmatic self-essentialization on another; between liberating the colonized from the confines of identity-politics to recreating an equally problematic identity-politics based fundamentally on a negation. If, as the post-colonialist bemoans; the hegemonic colonial matrices of power are rooted in an exclusionary and racist logic of exploitative capitalism, and that this logic is sustained through the State's omnipresent and all-pervading machinations of power, what is to be done vis-à-vis the State? Perhaps, this is why the reception of the work of Edward Said in the Arab-Muslim world was less prophetic than its reception in Western academia.

Furthermore, the post-colonial reading of the Master-Slave dialectic reduces reality to that which is created through the *reified* inter-subjective relations between the Master and the Slave. It does not, however, tell us about the world *outside* of this dialectic. It displaces ontology through an elusive latent ontology (the ontology of no ontologies), which replaces questions of metaphysics and ontology with questions relating to power. This is fallacious in that (1) it is blind to its own metaphysics and ontology assumptions; (2) it negates the very same epistemic grounds according to which it can make such assumptions, and (3) it displaces any form of emancipatory praxis-politics by failing to recognize that power, "as a quantum in which less of it is good and more of it is bad: the issue is not the concentration of power, but its accountability."[4] As Jason Schulman aptly notes, "a movement that rejects seeking power is ultimately rejecting the possibility of lasting radical change."[5] Power *can* corrupt, it is *not intrinsically* corrupt – it is merely a capacity that can be used to mediate between the oppressed and the emergence of a "new order," or a capacity that can sustain a subversive order. Power, from this perspective, becomes an instrument for liberation rather than a philosophy of fatalism (*à la* Foucault).

To return to the first two points made above; any normative proposition on what ought-to be is predicated on a consciousness of *what-is,* i.e. the "natural" order of things, and the extent to which an oppressive reality is not in

---

4   Stephen Eric Bronner, *Socialism Unbound: Principles, Practices, and Prospects.* (New York: Columbia University Press, 2001), 168.

5   Jason Schulman, "In Defense of Grand Narratives," *Jacobin,* March 26, 2011. https://www .jacobinmag.com/2011/03/in-defense-of-grand-narratives/.

accordance with *what-is*.[6] To speak of oppression is to speak of the transgression of certain boundaries, and such boundaries cannot escape ontological considerations. In other words, how is it possible for the slave to attain self-recognition, or as Paulo Freire would put it, a critical consciousness, when the consciousness of the slave is determined positively or negatively by the ontological consciousness of the Master? To what extent can the slave *step out* of the Master-Slave dialectic in his engagement with nature and objects? Otherwise, we must claim that beyond the ontology of the colonizer-master (that is, the imputation of an epistemic perspective onto the world and conflating it with ontology) there is *nothingness*. The Arabs have a name for such blindness: *al-Jahl* (ignorance). For the Arabs, *Jahl* is not only the absence of knowledge, but rather knowledge which is not in accord with reality. But they went a step further: to be ignorant of one's ignorance is *Jahl Murakab* (compound ignorance/double-ignorance). However, I am not sure the Arabs have a word for a "philosophy" that makes truth-claims on the basis of professed ignorance (the "incredulity with meta-narratives"). We will have more to say about this later on.

Lastly, a note should be made as to why Fanon was chosen in reading Hegel. Frantz Fanon, unlike many of his contemporaries, took Hegel seriously, albeit not seriously enough: "rather than simply dismissing Hegel as a philosopher of imperialism, [Fanon] engages the methodological core of this key thinker of European modernity – the dialectic."[7] It is, to use Hegel's own words, an "immanent critique."

2   Fanon on Hegel and Colonial Dialectics

For Fanon, Colonial Dialectics differ from the Hegelian Master-Slave dialectic because of the way in which racism, in the colonial context, obstructs a "fully reciprocal recognition." From the onset, it is pertinent to note that for both Fanon and Hegel, there is a fundamental difference between "merely living"/ simple consciousness, and a living self-consciousness. The latter can only be attained through recognition: self-consciousness exists for a self-consciousness, as Hegel argued. Fanon similarly explains that:

---

6   By "what-is," we refer not to the concrete constellations of power that constitutes and constructs "reality," but the reality that precedes those constellations and onto which such constellations are imposed.

7   Nigel C. Gibson, *Fanon: The Postcolonial Imagination*. (Polity Press: Cambridge, UK, 2003), 30.

Man is only human to the extent to which he tries to impose his existence on another man in order to be recognized by him. As long as he has not been effectively recognized by the other, it is this other that will remain the theme of his action. It is on this other, it is on the recognition of this other, that his human value and reality depend. It is this other, in which the meaning of his life is condensed.[8]

This recognition is critical when we note that reciprocal recognition is a phase in a more grandiose "progressive sequence," which manifests in one of these three possibilities: (1) non-recognition, in which the consciousness of the Master and that of the Slave perceive the other as an object; (2) a fight to the death which results from a realization that the other, be it the Master or the Slave, poses an existential threat to one's autonomy, and (3) the subordination of one consciousness to the other. This last phase is formative in the constitution of the Master-Slave dialectic for it is only through the Slave's recognition of the Master, that the Master attains certitude of his [false] autonomy and the subsequent progressive move in which the Slave, through his engagement with the natural world, comes to realize their own individual consciousness. The Slave's consciousness of their own self-consciousness is thus independent in that it was not realized vis-à-vis the Master, but rather the natural world. On the other hand, the Master's self-consciousness is dependent on the Slave. Fanon, at this critical point, intervenes to argue that the Slave's self-recognition and independence is untenable, because the Slave (in the colonial context) has not engaged in a true struggle. The Slave was recognized without conflict. This, for Fanon, means that the Slave cannot prove to either himself or the Master that he is fully human and/or independent. As Fanon goes on to point out, the Slave cannot even attain certitude of his own autonomy for he has no memory of a "fight to death," i.e. an autonomous struggle for self-recognition. The Slave reaffirms the Master's exclusive right to give rights. This is, in its crux, the paradox facing anti-colonial national movements who seek recognition from colonial hegemons. In a self-subverting move, the anti-colonial nationalist subject(s), who bemoan the hegemony of the "Colonial West," reaffirms the hegemony of the Colonial center by seeking their recognition. To be, for the Turkish Muslim Subject, is to be recognized by the European Union. To be, for the Muslim Brotherhood, is to have their political legitimacy recognized by the international community. To seek recognition is to seek the impossible. The colonial hegemon is only a hegemon insofar as there is a distinct "Other."

---

8   Fanon, quoted in Gibson, *Fanon: The Postcolonial Imagination*, 216.

Furthermore, the Colonial Master does not seek the Slave's recognition and does not perceive such recognition to be essential to his own autonomy. This can only be understood, according to Fanon, by understanding the ways in which racism creates a colonized "Other" who is essentially inferior – not fully human. And thus, what the Colonial Master wants from the Slave, is not recognition but rather labor. However, this need not mean, for Fanon, the *absolute* exclusion of the Slave.

3   The Fight to Death and the Politics of Becoming

To further problematize the situation, the Master does indeed recognize the Slave but only does so out of his own independent will, out of a bellicose commitment to the "white man's burden." The recognition of the Slave by the Master, without a "fight to death" as we have explained is, according to Fanon, the reason why the Hegelian dialectic cannot fully progress into *true* independence for the Slave. The "fight to death" is similar to childbirth, as Paulo Freire explains, without the pains of childbirth i.e. the "fight to death" – one is not "born" and there is no liberation. More so, for Freire the "fight to death" should not be a Hobbesian struggle or one in which the oppressed/colonized strikes in vengeance against the oppressor/colonizer – it is a process which restores humanity to *both* the Master and the Slave, a process which Freire goes so far as to state is the "ontological vocation" of man:

> Liberation is thus a childbirth, and a painful one. The man or woman who emerges is a new person, viable only as the oppressor-oppressed contradiction is superseded by the humanization of all people. Or to put it another way, the solution of this contradiction is born in the labor which brings into the world this new being: no longer oppressor nor longer oppressed, but human in the process of achieving freedom.[9]

Without struggle, the newly "freed" slave is thus set out into a world which has been created in the image of the Master, or what we will refer to as the "second-creator" (Jackson). It is a world constituted by the reification of paternalistic colonial relations. In speaking of a "second-creator," we refer to the ways in which the colonizers *ontological consciousness/weltanschaaung*, is imputed onto the world. The process of naming, or even the study of semantics,

---

9   Paulo Freire, *Pedagogy of the Oppressed.* (New York: Continuum, 2000), 49.

is extricable from the study of a semantic structure underlying ontology and metaphysics: Toshihoko Izutzu aptly recognizes that:

> Semantics as I understand it is an analytical study of the key-terms of a language with a view to arriving eventually at a conceptual grasp of the *weltanschaaungs* or worldview of the people who use that language as a tool not only of speaking and thinking, but, more important, still, of conceptualizing and interpreting the world that surrounds them. Semantics, thus understood, is a kind of *weltanschauungslehre*, a study of the nature and structure of the world-view of a nation at this or that significant period if its history, conducted by means of a methodological analysis of the major cultural concepts the nation has produced for itself and crystallized into the key-words of its language.[10]

That is to say, the colonizers political imagination – or any political imagination – which makes truth-claims as to what *ought-to-be* is predicated on an "invisible signifier" grounded in a distinct ontology and metaphysics which makes truth-claims on *what is*. It is a world, or a "totality," which "tends to totalize itself, to center on itself, and to attempt – temporally – to eternalize its present structure. Spatially, it attempts to include within itself all possible exteriority."[11] This totalization takes place when the colonial-master re names the slave and thereby granting the slave "recognition" and "liberation." There is, be it by the colonial-master or the colonial-slave, no breach of the colonial-master's ontological horizon or the material expressions of that horizon. After all, Fanon says: "the white man is a master who allowed his slaves to eat at his table" and that the "the black man is a slave who was *allowed* to assume a master's attitude."[12] This brings us to the following problem: The precarious relationship between the invisible ontological consciousness of the colonizer and the slave's "fight to death" becomes one in which the colonial-slave must penetrate, not only the concrete [sub-] systems of the colonial-master (e.g. the political, economic, and social constellations of power), but such a break cannot but be predicated on an ontological penetration; it must emerge from both ontological and political exteriorities. For to "fight" does not mean that one emerges from the womb of the colonial trauma, in which the colonizer becomes the "theme of one's action." On the contrary, it refers to a struggle

---

10   Toshihoko Isutzu, *God and Man in the Qu'ran*, (Islamic Book Trust), 11.

11   Enrique D. Dussel, *Philosophy of Liberation*. (Maryknoll, NY: Orbis, 1990), 49.

12   Frantz Fanon, *The Wretched of the Earth*, trans. Constance Farrington. (New York: Grove, 1965), 194.

which takes place *only* when one attains self-consciousness through thinking and praxis that is *anterior* to the Master-Slave relations. It is for this reason that Hegel explains that the Slave's independent self-consciousness is independent insofar as it is not constituted by the Slave's relationship with the Master but rather that which is anterior to both the Slave and the Master: the natural-world. There remains, however, a problematic, which Marxists have stressed: to what extent do the inter-subjective relations between the Master and Slave permeate into other relations, i.e. the Slave-Nature relationship? That is to say, when the Slave turns to the natural world, to what extent is the Slave's gaze onto that world not shaped by the reified relations of the hegemonic Colonial-Bourgeoisie order? It is insufficient to merely state that the reification of capitalist relations is limited to those between men, for history has taught us that these reifications have even shaped the ways in which man relates to that Being which, theoretically, is transcendent to man: God. Therefore, the only way to step outside of the Master-Slave dialectic is to become conscious of the colonizers' ontological consciousness and the ways in which it shapes the slaves' perceived reality. The slave's inability to transcend the ontological horizons (the "world") of the colonial-master becomes a form of "routine praxis" (as opposed to radical praxis), which Enrique Dussel describes as "dominating because it consolidates the existing totality; it is an ontic activity or a mere mediation internal to the world, founded in its *proteycto*. It is the praxis of consolidating the old and the unjust."[13] In contrast, a radical praxis is one which "opens a world from itself, its own road from within itself."[14]

The Slave who works within the totality of the Master and has been recognized without a "fight to death" does not seek his autonomy and/or attain self-consciousness through his labor and his engagement with the natural world, but rather he sets his gaze onto the Master, for to become "free" is to be like the Master. Having spoken of the inextricable link between the colonizers' political imagination and the ontology which informs it, we will now critically examine Fanon's resistance-based political imagination, and the extent to which that political imagination, in itself, was able to transcend the Hegelian dialectic.

4   Fanon and the Illusion of Independence

Thus far, we have seen the ways in which Fanon problematizes the Hegelian dialectic. More specifically, the ways in which the colonized/slave seeks to

---

13   Dussel, *Philosophy of Liberation*, 63.
14   Ibid.

imitate the colonial/master. Fanon, however, was not only an anti-colonial thinker but also very much involved in the Algerian war for independence. This, in turn, brings into question the extent to which Fanon himself was able to transcend the very same colonial mimicry that he so vehemently opposed. It will be argued below that, whilst Fanon held that the colonized/slave must emerge as a "new man," his political project was very much informed by the "political imagination" of the colonizer, primarily the nation-state and the mythical image of the "national-self." In speaking of "political imagination," we refer to what Barnor Hesse explains is "a situation in which dominant forms of representation and contestability frame and limit the terms in which the meaning of any social or cultural phenomena can be understood."[15] In her penetrative critique of post-colonialism, Leela Gandhi explains:

> While the logic of power... is fundamentally coercive, its campaign is frequently seductive. We could say that power traverses the imponderable chasm between coercion and seduction through a variety of baffling self-representations. While it may manifest itself in a show and application of force, it is equally likely to appear as the disinterested purveyor of cultural enlightenment and reform. *Through this double representation, power offers itself both as a political limit and as a cultural possibility. If power is at once the qualitative gap between those who have it and those who must suffer it, it also designates an imaginative space that can be occupied, a cultural model that might be imitated and replicated.*[16]

To what extent was Fanon able to transcend the "imaginative space" created by the colonizer? For Fanon, there are two ways in which resistance against the colonizer can take place. The first involves a return to a primordial pre-colonial culture and identity, whereas the second response emerges out of a post-colonial identity shaped by resistance. Fanon asserts that a pre-colonial "culture" merely signifies a set of "mummified fragments" – customs – it is static and the ambivalence of which becomes a medium through which the native-elites can pursue and legitimize self-colonization. On the other hand, culture, emerging from resistance, is an ideal expression of the present, and is a "fluctuating movement which they [the masses] are just giving a shape and to which as soon as it has started, will be the signal for everything to be

---

15   Barnor Hesse, "Self-Fulfilling Prophecy: The Postracial Horizon," *The South Atlantic Quarterly* 110, no. 1 (2011): 155.

16   Leela Gandhi, *Postcolonial Theory: A Critical Introduction.* (New York: Columbia University Press, 1998), 14. Italics added.

called into question."[17] In other words, a post-colonial culture is one driven by the creative powers of resistance, rejecting mythical representations and pre-conceived significations. This move, on Fanon's part, is grounded in a desire to shift from the tyranny of abstract universals and the hubris of ontology, towards the concrete, the real: the whipping of the black skin. In *Black Skin, White Masks*, Fanon states:

> Ontology does not allow us to understand the being of the black man, since it ignores lived experience. For not only must the black man be black; he must be black in relation to the white man. Some people will argue that the situation has a double meaning. Not at all. The black man has no ontological resistance in the eyes of the white man.[18]

However, this brings into question: (1) to what extent can the concrete, the particular be divorced from the ontology – the totality – that informs those particulars? And concomitantly, (2) to what extent does the "post-colonial culture" espoused by Fanon allow for a situation in which "everything" is to "be called into question"? Fanon asserts,

> There is no fight for culture which can develop apart from popular struggle. To take an example, all those men and women who are fighting with their bare hands against French colonialism in *Algeria are not by any means strangers to the national culture of Algeria*. The national Algerian culture is taking on form and content as the battles are being fought out, in prison, under the guillotine and in every French outpost which is captured or destroyed.[19]

In the above passage, Fanon speaks of an "Algerian National Culture," which is in itself a colonial construct. To contextualize this problem and put it in concrete historical terms; the colonized are "independent" insofar as they seek to assert "national independence" in a world in which nation-states are the primary markers of identity and political-cultural sovereignty. Yet, the very "we" (the national-self) and entity that they seek to liberate is in itself a colonial construct, an appellation given to the colonized by the colonial master. In turn, the colonized paradoxically accept the name given to them and the boundaries of resistance become defined by the boundaries drawn by the colonizer:

---

17   Fanon, *Black Skin, White Masks*, 168.
18   Frantz Fanon, *Black Skin, White Masks*. (London: Pluto Press, 1986), 90.
19   Ibid., 42. Italics mine.

"it is a moment of celebrating the chains, winding them over one's head and calling them a crown."[20]

However, as we have noted in section three, it is only within a system-of-meanings that a "name" can be imputed onto the world, and this naming is part of an "intentional constitution of meaning" grounded, inextricably, in an ontological horizon i.e. the world as it *appears* predicated on a conception of the world *as-it-is* and *in-itself.* To impute "meaning" is not to create, in the primordial sense, *ex nihilo*, for the being that is being named already exists, existentially, in the world. The "slave," before being a Slave, is a real and concrete being; he is *named* a slave and thus re-created. That is to say, the African man is *discovered* and *then* created. For example, water is, a priori, H_2o, and it exists in-itself, and *a priori* to our comprehension of the world. However, water becomes a *drink* that can satisfy my thirst only when I *interpret* the world *as it relates to me* (when I am thirsty).[21]

The "naming" of the colonized "we" (e.g. Algerians) amounts to a speech-act: "it is in speaking of their world that people, by naming the world, transform it" – what is at stake for the slave is: "the way which [through naming] they achieve significance as human beings."[22] For Freire, the act of "naming" is an essential step in the process of liberation: "dialogue is the encounter between men, mediated by the world, in order to name the world: hence, dialogue cannot occur between those who want to name the world and those who do not wish this naming."[23] In his *Pedagogy of the Oppressed*, Paulo Freire explains that *naming, if it is to be emancipatory,* must possesses two dimensions: (1) reflection and, (2) action. The former is predicated on a critical consciousness that recognizes the ways in which the prevailing "words" (names) transform and shape the world, and the ways in which new "words" can change the existing world. If such a word is inauthentic, it will be unable to transform reality. Without reflection, there can be no action. And without authentic words/names, there can be no "fight to death." Fanon is left unable to escape the spectre of Hegel, for Hegel would claim that any "*exteriority*" cannot but be *interior* to the totality of the idea, and Fanon's reductionist approach only seems to add empirical credibility to such a claim. To posit the problem differently, in a manner similar to other post-colonial thinkers, Fanon's political trajectory (and elusive ontology) is based on a *negation* (of the colonial "order of things")

20   Tamim al-Barghouti, *The Umma and the Dawla: The Nation State and the Arab Middle East.* (London, Pluto Press, 2008), 78.
21   Example adopted from Enrique Dussel.
22   Paolo Freire, *Pedagogy of the Oppressed*, 69.
23   Ibid.

with no *affirmation* (an ontological statement on what is beyond the colonial-order). This negation, represented by resistance, creates a consciousness in which the "we" – the oppressed – is reified, and the "we" makes sense only in relation to a pre-existing colonizer-colonized relationship and not the "order of things" that preceded it. The "new man" is, after all, hardly "new" but rather an extension and prolongation of the present. What is left, as Saidiya Hartman puts it, is an "afterlife of slavery," but one which is hardly a paradise.[24]

This "internalization of servitude" creates a situation in which the colonized seeks to both (1) imitate the colonizer and (2) demand recognition from the colonizer, i.e. recognition of national independence and sovereignty. And thus, in acquiescing to the "political imagination" of the colonizer, the world named by the Master, the political horizons of the colonized-slave are circumvented. It is pertinent to note that the very concept of the "nation" is inextricable from Hegel's political philosophy, the very same philosophy that Fanon critiques. In Hegel's discourse on civilization, the nation serves as an expression of consciousness in an evolutionary process of development amounting to a form of secularized religion, in which state-consciousness becomes the ultimate arbiter of temporal affairs replacing the native god. And as such, the very idea of the "nation" and the nation-state emanates from a distinct ontological and epistemological framework.

In conclusion, the political project of Frantz Fanon is a reflection of a reductive "philosophy," one which fails to transcend the ontological consciousness and "names" of the Master. The implications of this reductionism is not merely theoretical, as it bears directly on the question of emancipation and liberation in an age that is far from "post-colonial," and one in which the political horizons of the oppressed, around the world, remain circumvented by the hubristic posture of the global-bourgeoisie. If we are to think beyond capitalism, that is to say a *world* beyond capitalism, we must return to philosophy in a manner that creates a progressive dialectic relationship between the abstract (questions of ontology and metaphysics) and the concrete (machinations of power and praxis).

Bibliography

al-Barghouti, Tamim. *The Umma and the Dawla: The Nation State and the Arab Middle East*. London, Pluto Press, 2008.

---

24   Saidiya Hartman, *Lose Your Mother: A Journey Along the Atlantic Slave Route*. New York: Farrar, Straus and Giroux, 2008.

'Amil, Mahdi. *Hal al-Qalb li-l-Sharq wa-l-'Aql li-l-Gharb? Marx fī Istishrāq Idwar Saʿīd* [Is the Heart for the East and the Mind for the West? Marx in Edward Said's Orientalism] (2nd edition) Beirut: Dār al-Fārābī, 2006.

Bronner, Stephen Eric. *Socialism Unbound: Principles, Practices, and Prospects.* New York: Columbia University Press, 2001.

Davutoglu, Ahmet. "Islamic Paradigm: Tawḥīd and Ontological Differentiation." In *Alternative Paradigms: The Impact of Islamic and Western Weltanschauungs on Political Theory.* Lanham, MD: University Press of America, 1994.

Dussel, Enrique D. *Philosophy of Liberation.* Maryknoll, NY: Orbis, 1990.

Fanon, Frantz. *Black Skin, White Masks.* London: Pluto, 1986.

Fanon, Frantz. *The Wretched of the Earth.* Translated by Constance Farrington. New York: Grove, 1965.

Frangie, Samer. "On the Broken Conversation between Postcolonialism and Intellectuals in the Periphery." *Studies in Social & Political Thought* 19 (Summer 2011): 41–54.

Freire, Paulo. *Pedagogy of the Oppressed.* New York: Continuum, 2000.

Gandhi, Leela. *Postcolonial Theory: A Critical Introduction.* New York: Columbia University Press, 1998.

Gibson, Nigel C. *Fanon: The Postcolonial Imagination.* Cambridge, UK: Polity Press, 2003.

Hartman, Saidiya. Lose Your Mother: A Journey Along the Atlantic Slave Route. New York: Farrar, Straus and Giroux: 2008.

Hegel, Georg Wilhelm Friedrich. *Phenomenology of Spirit.* Translated by Arnold V. Miller. Oxford: Clarendon, 1977.

Hesse, Barnor. "Self-Fulfilling Prophecy: The Postracial Horizon." *The South Atlantic Quarterly* 110, no. 1 (2011): 155–178.

Honenberger, Phillip. "'Le Nègre et Hegel': Fanon on Hegel, Colonialism, and the Dialectics of Recognition." *Human Architecture: Journal of the Sociology of Self-Knowledge* Vol. 5: Issue 3, (2007): Article 15.

Izutsu, Toshihiko. *God and Man in the Qur'an; Semantics of the Qur'anic Weltanschauung.* Tokyo: Keio Institute of Cultural and Linguistics Studies, 1964.

McClintock, Anne. "The Angel of Progress: Pitfalls of the Term Post-Colonialism," in *Colonial Discourse and Post-Colonial Theory: A Reader,* eds. Patrick Williams and Laura Chrisman, 291–304. New York: Columbia University Press, 1994.

Schulman, Jason. "In Defense of Grand Narratives." *Jacobin,* March 26, 2011. https://www.jacobinmag.com/2011/03/in-defense-of-grand-narratives/.

CHAPTER 8

Frantz Fanon and the Peasantry as the Centre of Revolution

Timothy Kerswell

Frantz Fanon is probably better known for his work on decolonization and race, but it would be remiss to ignore his contribution to the debate about social classes and their roles as revolutionary subjects. In this respect, Fanon argued for a position that was part of an influential thought current which saw the peasant at the center of world revolutionary struggles.

In *The Wretched of the Earth,* Fanon argued that "It is clear that in the co-lonial countries the peasants alone are revolutionary, for they have nothing to lose and everything to gain. The starving peasant, outside the class system, is the first among the exploited to discover that only violence pays."[1] This statement suggests not only that the peasant would play an important part in liberation and revolutionary struggles, but that they would be the sole revolutionary subjects in forthcoming change.

Fanon's attempt to place the peasant at the center was part of a wider current of thought. This can be seen in the statement of Lin Biao, one of the foremost thinkers of Maoism who argued, "It must be emphasized that Comrade Mao Tse-tung's theory of the establishment of rural revolutionary base areas and the encirclement of the cities from the countryside is of outstanding and universal practical importance for the present revolutionary struggles of all the oppressed nations and peoples, and particularly for the revolutionary struggles of the oppressed nations and peoples in Asia, Africa and Latin America against imperialism and its lackeys."[2]

It was this theorization that "turn[ed] the image of the peasantry upside down,"[3] especially from Marx's previous assessment that peasants constituted a "sack of potatoes"[4] in terms of their revolutionary class-consciousness. The

---

1 Frantz Fanon, *The Wretched of the Earth* (New York: Grove Press, 1965), 48.
2 Lin Biao, *Long Live the Victory of People's War,* (1965). https://www.marxists.org/reference/archive/lin-biao/1965/09/peoples_war/cho7.htm.
3 B Perinbam, "Fanon and the Revolutionary Peasantry – The Algerian Case," *The Journal of Modern African Studies* 11, no 3 (1973): 432.
4 Karl Marx, *The Eighteenth Brumaire of Louis Napoleon* (1937). https://www.marxists.org/archive/marx/works/subject/hist-mat/18-brum/cho7.htm.

peasant had seemingly traversed from a sack of potatoes, to temporary allies, to the central driver of the revolutionary movement.[5] Che Guevara placed the peasant at the center of his theory of guerrilla warfare suggesting that, "The guerrilla is supported by the peasant and worker masses of the region and of the whole territory in which it acts. Without these prerequisites, guerrilla warfare is not possible."[6] It is this very possibility that will be considered by this chapter; to what extent is it true that the peasant, Fanon's revolutionary subject and the focus of many other political perspectives, constitutes a viable revolutionary force in an urbanizing world?

Peasant guerilla strategies reached their zenith in the mid-twentieth century. There are a number of successful examples: China 1949, Vietnam 1954 and 1973, Cuba 1959, and Algeria 1962. However, there were also a number of unsuccessful examples: Colombia 2018, India 1967, Philippines 1969, Peru 1980, Turkey 1972, Iran 1982, Nepal 1998. While it is possible to argue that subjective decisions contributed to the success of the former and the failure of the latter, the central argument presented in this paper is that changing material conditions offer a better explanation.

Since the defeat of US imperialism in Vietnam, those leftist movements that have achieved success have deployed a combination of urban insurrections and popular front politics (e.g. Sandinistas in Nicaragua, United Socialist Party of Venezuela (PSUV), Movement for Socialism (MAS) in Bolivia). By contrast, movements which remained committed to a peasant guerilla focus have experienced marginalization and defeat or decline. In this chapter, I argue the root of this decline is in a failure to understand key interrelated demographic changes in the global South (Urbanization), in terms of developments in the Productive Forces (the end of semi-feudalism and the rise of capitalist agriculture), and in terms of Depeasantization through rural-urban migration.

Marks and Rich note that "There are few classic peasantries left in the modern global system as were present in China and Vietnam," which suggest these examples are far from representative and should instead be considered as exceptions.[7] Research on the role of previously rural peoples who have migrated to urban space is significant, and this appears as a global trend.[8] In addition to

5   Vladimir Lenin, *Collected Works, vol. 24* (Moscow: Progress Publishers, 1973), 21–26.

6   Che Guevara, *Guerrilla Warfare* (Lincoln: University of Nebraska Press, 1998), 143.

7   Thomas Marks and Paul Rich, "Back to the Future–People's War in the 21st Century," in *Small Wars & Insurgencies*, 28:3, 409–425. (2017), 422.

8   See for example: Franz Fahri, *States and Urban-Based Revolutions: Iran and Nicaragua.* Champaign, IL: University of Illinois Press, 1990.

this, modern counter-insurgency techniques, satellite technology and drones, have limited the effectiveness of rural "base areas" as a strategy.[9]

The concept of the peasantry is a sprawling one, covering a wide range of actors with extremely varied socio-economic status. The concept of the peasantry also carries a connotation of the persistence of feudalism in the countryside, a claim which, even if previously debatable, is no longer sustainable. Bill Warren noted that a key impact of imperialism involved the worldwide introduction of capitalist production relations and the associated commodification of labor.[10] This has led to the "developing [of] the forces of production and establishing... capitalist agriculture" in the global South.[11]

Defining the peasantry is notoriously difficult due to the vast differentiation in economic status and the constantly changing conditions of its existence. In Mao's *Analysis of Classes in Chinese Society*, for example, peasants are located both in the petty bourgeoisie and the semi-proletariat.[12] Carlos Barros, Ari de Araujo, and Joao Faria, in their study of *Movimento dos Trabalhadores Rurais Sem Terra* (MST) in Brazil, also include "landless" peasants in their understanding of the peasantry, and in the opposite sense, Nigel Harris includes landlords who do not perform farm work in this category as well.[13]

In the famous mode of production debate, Utsa Patnaik noted that the size of landholdings does not strictly translate into class status, as various relations of production are possible on various sizes of property.[14] Nonetheless, as Amit Basole and Dipankar Basu have shown, the size of landholdings can be used as a proxy for class position, as empirically

> (a) there is a very strong positive correlation between the size of land possessed and the ownership of animals, minor tools and implements (like sickles, chaff-cutters, axes, spades and choppers) and tractors; and
> (b) if we define, following Patnaik, the rural classes as full-time laborer, poor peasant, middle peasant, rich peasant, capitalist and landlord, then

9   A Joes, *Urban Guerrilla Warfare* (Lexington: University of Kentucky Press, 2013), 5.

10   Bill Warren, *Imperialism: pioneer of capitalism,* (London: Verso, 1980).

11   Haroon Akram-Lodhi and Cristóbal Kay, "Surveying the Agrarian Question (Part 2): Current Debates and Beyond," *The Journal of Peasant Studies* 37, no. 2 (2010).

12   Mao, *Analysis of Classes in Chinese Society* (1926). https://www.marxists.org/reference/archive/mao/selected-works/volume-1/mswv1_1.htm.

13   Carlos Barros, Ari de Araujo, Jr., and Joao Faria, "Brazilian Land Tenure and Conflicts: The Landless Peasants Movement," *Cato Journal* 33, no. 1 (2013); Nigel Harris, "The Revolutionary Role of the Peasants," *International Socialism* no. 41 (1970).

14   Utsa Patnaik, "Class Differentiation within the Peasantry: An Approach to Analysis of Indian Agriculture," *Economic and Political Weekly* 11, no. 39 (1976).

the proportion of the 'upper classes' tend to increase as we move from smaller to larger sizes of ownership holdings.[15]

Having said this, we can perhaps approach some definitions and make a meaningful distinction between (1) the peasantry, (2) the rural semi-proletariat, and (3) the rural proletariat. The rural proletariat is the simplest class to define and includes all landless or "effectively landless" rural workers.[16] The rural semi-proletariat includes sharecroppers, tenant farmers, and, generally speaking, anyone whose income is primarily derived from wages or other activities that involve surplus extraction, but who retain some land ownership and supplement their incomes through the ownership and use of this land. Finally, the peasantry represents the other side of this coin, whereby the majority of income comes through the ownership and use of land and not wage labor, or the exploitation of wage labor.

In this chapter, I will consider some of the main political and economic trends impacting the peasantry and the rural semi-proletariat. The overall argument presented here is that the development of world productive forces, as well as certain forms of government policy, has created a seemingly irreversible trend towards world urbanization. For most of the twentieth century, a division existed between the majority urban and industrialized global North and the majority rural and agricultural global South, a picture which no longer accurately reflects the realities of the global political economy.

An important implication of the foregoing analysis is demonstration of the continuing relevance of Paul Baran's concept of economic surplus. While imperialism has been able to appropriate a significant part of the economic surplus produced in the global South, it has not locked the global South in a state of semi-feudalism. The level of surplus retained within these countries is lower than both the "potential economic surplus,"[17] representing the limits of a society's potential, and what would be achieved in a rationally ordered socialist society, without the anarchy and waste of capitalism – or, what Baran called, the "planned economic surplus."[18] Nonetheless, agricultural transformation has occurred, allowing the development of a capitalist agriculture, based on the ability of indigenous capitalist formations to retain a portion of the actual

---

15   Amit Basole and Dipankar Basu, "Relations of Production and Modes of Surplus Extraction in India: An Aggregate Study," *Sanhati,* http://sanhati.com/wp-content/uploads/2009/05/india_surplus_may_11.pdf.

16   Basole and Dipankar, "Relations of Production," 13.

17   Paul Baran, *The Political Economy of Growth* (New York: Monthly Review Press, 1957).

18   Ibid., 155.

economic surplus.[19] As a result, enormous changes have occurred in the economic and demographic structures of the global South in the twentieth century, a process which is ongoing.

These developments spell a declining role for the peasantry, in terms of global class politics, and simultaneously, an increasingly important role for the semi-proletariat and the proletariat. It is important to stress here that this argument does not represent an assertion that the peasantry will disappear, rather that the relative importance of different classes is being reconfigured by developments in the global political economy. To substantiate these arguments, the chapter will analyze some key emerging trends in different countries and some theoretical questions in terms of the changing nature of the "agrarian question." India and China have been selected as case studies due to their population size and relative influence on the global political economy; additionally, Latin America was included in the discussion to highlight the situation in a highly urbanized region of the global South. The implications of this section are important, as these trends will have a significant impact on the strategy and tactics of future progressive struggles.

1   Urbanization Is Reducing the Size and Importance of the Peasantry
          Even in the Global South

The overarching narrative, when considering agriculture and its place in the global political economy, is the trend toward urbanization. While countries in the global North are more likely to have higher levels of urbanization, evidence demonstrates that even the majority of Latin America is now urban, and the remaining regions of the South will become urbanized in the near future. In 2014, the *United Nations World Urbanization Prospects* report noted that:

> Today, the most urbanized regions include Northern America (82 percent living in urban areas in 2014), Latin America and the Caribbean (80 percent), and Europe (73 percent). In contrast, Africa and Asia remain mostly rural, with 40 and 48 percent of their respective populations living in urban areas. All regions are expected to urbanize further over the coming decades. Africa and Asia are urbanizing faster than the other regions and are projected to become 56 and 64 percent urban, respectively, by 2050.[20]

---

19   Ibid., 132–133.
20   *World Urbanization Prospects,* United Nations (2014), https://esa.un.org/unpd/wup/Publications/Files/WUP2014-Highlights.pdf.

As urbanization progresses, the political importance of the countryside and the peasantry, both as historical actors and as concepts, declines. The result of this is that revolutionary strategies and tactics will need to be realigned with global conditions. Concepts such as "People's War" and related strategies of peasant guerrilla movements that "surrounding the cities from the country-side" are becoming less relevant over time. That said, it is worthwhile to consider the current status of the "peasantry" as an agent in transition in order to understand its likely impact on global class politics.

While noting that it may be possible to cite small examples of ongoing feudal property relations, characterization of agricultural societies in the global South as feudal is indefensible in light of general trends. The case studies selected demonstrate how important changes in the world economy point to the polarization of landholders and the migration of "peasants" from rural areas to join the ranks of wage laborers. At this intermediate stage in their transition from rural to urban, Immanuel Wallerstein refers to them as a "rural semi-proletariat," not yet fully proletarianized but, by circumstance, forced to join the labor market.[21] Akram-Lodhi and Kay note that a key trend in the global class structure concerns the "stark growth in semi-proletarianisation throughout the developing capitalist countries."[22] Due to the significance of the impact of these countries on the global political economy, these trends provide a major indication of the decline of the peasantry as a significant social force relative to other social classes.

2   Changes in Indian Agriculture – Polarization and Urbanization

The average size of operational land holdings in India has been reduced to an unsustainable level. From 1970–71 to 2010–11, the average size of operational holdings decreased from 2.28 hectares (ha) to 1.16 ha. The total number of operational holdings increased from 71 million in 1970–71 to 138 million in 2010–11, swelling the number of marginal (<1 ha) and small (1–2 ha) land holdings by 56 million and 11 million, respectively. The average size of marginal holdings is only 0.38 ha, and they currently constitute 67 percent of operational holdings, but only 22 percent of operated areas in 2010–11. The operated areas under small land holdings also increased from 12 percent to 22 percent during the same period. Marginal and small land holdings together constitute about 85

21   Immanuel Wallerstein, *The Capitalist World Economy* (Cambridge: Cambridge University Press, 1979), 10.

22   Akram-Lodhi and Kay, "Surveying the Agrarian Question," 278.

percent of operational holdings and 44 percent of the operated areas in the country. The shift from subsistence agriculture to a commercial agriculture system, combined with alarmingly rising input costs, has made cultivation on small farms largely unsustainable.[23]

Regarding marginal farmers, for example, Jens Lerche has demonstrated that "more than 70 percent of all landowners fall into the category of 'marginal farmers' owning less than one hectare of land, up from 39 percent in 1960–61, while less than 1 percent own more than 10 hectares, down from 5 percent in 1960–61. More than half of the income of marginal farmers is from wages, so this group is best understood as wage workers who receive a subsidiary income from the plots of land that they own."[24] This analysis suggests a polarization of ownership patterns, and a transformation of small and marginal farmers into a proletariat or a semi-proletariat. V.K. Ramachandran even argues that it is no longer relevant to distinguish between agricultural and non-agricultural workers in village settings.[25]

It was considered a great paradox of the Indian economy that capitalist development was not leading to the disappearance of small farms and small economies in general and to the consolidation of land holdings. The assumption behind this has been discussed by C.P. Chandrasekhar, who argues that, in a relatively closed economy, agricultural productivity acts as a strong constraint, limiting the possibilities of economic transformation.[26] Chandrasekhar observes that a key change occurred in the late 1980s and early 1990s, as India began to liberalize its economy, and as the world of global finance began to penetrate India after a long period of national bourgeois resistance.[27] As a result of this, it became possible for the non-agricultural sector to grow significantly faster than the agricultural sector, in such a way that agriculture was no longer a constraint on India's overall growth. In addition to this, the fact that it was India's service sector (less dependent on agricultural inputs than industry)

23   National Bank for Agriculture and Rural Development, "Agricultural Land Holdings Pattern in India," NABARD Rural Pulse I (January-February, 2014). https://www.nabard.org/Publication/Rural_Pulse_final142014.pdf.

24   Jens Lerche, "Agrarian Crisis and Agrarian Questions in India," Journal of Agrarian Change 11, no 1 (2014): 106.

25   V.K. Ramachandran, "Classes and Class Differentiation in India's Countryside," World Review of Political Economy 2, no 4 (2011): 62.

26   C.P. Chandrasekhar and Jayati Ghosh, "Recent Employment Trends in India and China: An Unfortunate Convergence," paper presented at JNU-IIAS conference "Making Growth Inclusive with Reference to Employment Generation," Jawaharlal Nehru University, New Delhi, 28–29 June, 62.

27   Chandrasekhar and Ghosh, "Recent Employment Trends," 66.

that grew is a further reason that agricultural growth became decoupled from non-agricultural growth.[28]

Another major feature of Indian agriculture is that capitalism has been firmly established as the mode of production in the Indian countryside. Despite the overwhelming empirical evidence in favor of this position, arguments in favor of Indian agriculture being semi-feudal die hard and there is a willingness in some sections of the Indian-left to look at agriculture as an unchanging sector. This can be observed in the statement of Guruprasad Kar, that "those who constructively want to understand the Indian economy and want a healthy debate, agree that no important measures had been taken by the post-1947 rulers to ensure the process through which Indian agriculture could move to a capitalist mode of production."[29]

Important developments in productive forces stemming from both technological development and from various changes resulting from government initiatives refute this analysis. Gail Omvedt, in 1981, noted that "there is clear evidence for a substantial growth in the use of capital in agriculture, such as fertilisers, tractors, oil engines, [and] irrigation pumpsets."[30] While the government of India began to withdraw various subsidies or capital goods as a result of the implementation of the liberalization policy framework, agricultural policy had an impact on the development of the productive forces of agriculture during this time, and even now, subsidies have not been totally removed.

In addition to this, Indira Gandhi's bank nationalization and subsequent lending policy enabled an increase in access to credit for farmers and the development of various cooperative lending societies giving wide access to credit, which broke the power of the rural money lenders who were traditionally associated with feudal and semi-feudal relations of production.[31] Again, this system would end during the liberalization period, but it would be incorrect to say that it had no impact in the development and modernization of Indian agriculture, which led to rates of post-independence agricultural growth that were at or above world averages (albeit below the growth levels achieved by socialist China).[32]

---

28   Ibid., 67.

29   Guruprasad Kar, "The Semi-Feudal Character of Indian Agriculture" *Sanhati*, trans. Ipsita Samanta (Aneek, 2012), http://sanhati.com/excerpted/8197/.

30   Gail Omvedt, "Capitalist Agriculture and Rural Classes in India," *Economic and Political Weekly* 16, no. 52 (1981): 143.

31   Omvedt, "Capitalist Agriculture and Rural Classes," 145; Basole and Basu, "Relations of Production...an Aggregate Study," 52.

32   Omvedt, "Capitalist Agriculture and Rural Classes," 145.

It is also notable that when formal sources of credit dried up as a result of the liberalization reforms, this did not spell the return of the traditional money lending castes to village life, but rather this created space for private informal lending dominated by a new group of petty bourgeois credit providers such as "traders, schoolteachers, government servants, lawyers, rich farmers, and other members of the petty bourgeois class."[33] The withdrawal of the developmental state from the provision of credit led to the entrance of capitalist lending.

Omvedt, as well as Basole and Basu, have noted the declining importance of tenancy in India's agriculture, which is a key indicator of semi-feudal relations of production, and an increase in non-farm employment and wage.[34] According to Basole and Basu, this has had an important impact on India's rural poor, in ways that have further weakened traditional social structures:

> First, it directly augments their income by offering employment during off-peak seasons of agricultural production. Second, it increases the bargaining position of the rural poor vis-à-vis their employers within the village; this is one of the most important factors contributing to higher real wages and better conditions of work in agriculture. Third, by offering escape routes from the closed village milieu, it helps in countering the worst aspects of caste-based oppression. Thus, non-farm employment opportunities have not only economic but also social and political implications for the rural poor.[35]

It is important to note that during the time the Indian state provided various forms of assistance to agriculture, the rate of capital formation in Indian agriculture was high by international standards, and was accomplished primarily by "tractorisation and the development of irrigation facilities."[36] After the adoption of liberalization policies, growth in agriculture slowed as a result of government neglect and the significance of agriculture relative to other aspects of the economy declined.[37]

All of this occurred despite the ability of the imperialist world market to siphon off some of India's agricultural surplus. The development of Indian agriculture, and its transition into capitalist agriculture, was not prevented

---

33   Basole and Basu, "Relations of Production...an Aggregate Study," 53.
34   Omvedt, "Capitalist Agriculture and Rural Classes," 147; Amit Basole and Dipankar Basu, "Relations of Production and Modes of Surplus Extraction in India: Part 1 – Agriculture," *Economic and Political Weekly*, 46, no 14, 47–48, 49–50.
35   Basole and Basu, "Relations of Production...Agriculture," 52.
36   Ibid., 53.
37   Ibid.

by imperialism or "semi-feudalism," and the mode of production in contemporary Indian agriculture is undoubtedly capitalist. The Indian state played a leading role in India's agricultural transition and growth in the same way that the Indian state is currently playing a key role in generating processes of urbanization and semi-proletarianization through its neglect of the agricultural sector.

3   China's Capitalist Agriculture Generates Urbanization

In the case of China, the current land regime is profoundly capitalist, despite its constitutional declaration of public/state ownership. While officially there is no private ownership of land, this does not prevent land from becoming a commodity in China. The land-ownership system has been defined by rural-urban dualism throughout most of modern times in China. In the post-socialist era, rural lands are "collectively owned" while urban lands are "state-owned." However, in urban China, citizens have had *de facto* rights to own property since market reforms began. After multiple failures between 2002 and 2006, the Property Law was finally passed at its 6th reading in 2007. It officially recognized that urban citizens could freely trade, circulate, mortgage or sublease real estate properties. Despite this, it claims the system of land tenure, where the state owns all land, is still intact. Many in the Chinese legal community feared that the controversial law would facilitate privatization and asset stripping of state-owned enterprises. Legal scholars, notably Gong Xiantian of Peking University, argued that it violated the constitutional characterization of the People's Republic of China (PRC) as a socialist state. Irrespective of their formal legal status, we can conclude that urban properties are effectively privately owned.[38]

Rural land and property rights, however, remain much more problematic since the creation of PRC. The land regime evolved over three major stages: (1) the land reform from 1949 to the mid-1950s, when "peasant associations" were established to ensure peasants' full rights to their land; (2) the collectivization period from the mid-1950s to 1978; and (3) the "household contract responsibility system" in 1980. The "contract" between the "contracting household" and the "collective economic organization" served to privatize rural production without changing the constitutional definition of ownership. By 1984,

---

38   Ma Licheng, *Leading Schools of Thought in Contemporary China* (Singapore: World Scientific, 2013), 47.

99 percent of production teams (of the communes) had dismantled and switched to the new system.[39]

The Communist Party of China claims that the household contract system is socialism with Chinese characteristics because the land remains collectively owned and is supposedly more efficiently utilized than under the people's communes. A closer look proves this is not true. Historically speaking, the system is many steps backward and a complete negation of the socialist experiment, resembling what existed in the 1950s. Under this system, work is contracted to families who produce on the collectively owned land, and who then keep a portion of the profit for themselves. This is undisputedly market-oriented and based on a capitalist contract system.

Since the 1990s, the process of rural land commodification has accelerated. Urbanization has turned more and more rural land into urban usage, such as residential property or industrial production. The rural cadre effectively has the control of use and disposal of the rural land. Consequently, more and more rural collectively owned lands have become commodities and therefore "circulate" in the market. For example, 35 percent of rural land management rights administered through the "household contract system" in Chongqing had been circulated through the market by 2010.[40]

Just as China tested its earlier market based economic reforms in Anhui province, most recently Anhui province was used once again to test the recommodification of land. Whereas rural land was once collectively owned by the people, the experiment allows land designated for construction purposes to be sold.[41] The Third Plenum, held in 2013, more broadly adopted the decision to marketize rural construction land.[42] We can see, therefore, that the trade in land through an informal title system is slowly being complemented by the introduction of formal systems of title.

China's ambiguous rural land-property rights are severely at odds with market-oriented reform, as the Communist Party of China failed to clearly define who the rural "collective" are and who "owns the land" in rural China. This is illustrated by the "17 Provinces Land Rights Survey" conducted by Renmin University in 2008. When they asked a relatively simple question of rural households about "rural housing land" 22.8 percent of respondents believed

---

39   J Lin, "Rural Reforms and Agricultural Growth in China," *The American Economic Review* (1992).

40   Jason Young, *Markets, Migrants and Institutional Change* (Basingstoke: Palgrave MacMillan, 2013), 252.

41   Zhou Tian, *Anhui Experiments with Sales of Rural Land in 20 Counties*, 2013, http://english. caixin.com/2013-11-15/100605583.html [Online].

42   Samson Yuen, "China's New Rural Land Reform? Assessment and Prospects," *China Perspectives* no. 1 (2014): 61.

the land was "state land," 4.2 percent the "rural town collective," 18.6 percent the "rural collective," and 52.4 percent believed it was their own land.[43]

Unclear rural land ownership leads to growing land-grab problems. In many respects, urbanization in China can be understood as "the process of local government driving farmers into buildings while grabbing their land."[44] The pseudo-collective-ownership of rural land has also increasingly become a front for "rural cadres" rampant corruption and cronyism in pursuit of personal interest through the process of transferring land-use rights. Since 2005, surveys have indicated a steady increase in the number of forced land requisitions, and about four million farmers are losing their land annually. Whereas the mean compensation to farmers for the transfer of contractual rights to land was $17,850 an acre, the mean selling price to commercial developers was $740,000 an acre.[45] An estimated 65 percent of the 180,000 "mass incidents" in China in 2010 stemmed from grievances over forced land requisitions.[46] Mingi Li notes that China's peasant workforce has been in decline since 1990 (from 389 million in 2010 to 219 million in 2014), and that the declining rural population has been due to the migration of peasants into the cities.[47]

China's transition away from collectivized forms of agriculture, beginning in the late 1970s, re-embedded China's economy within the world imperialist system. Despite this, and the ability of imperialism to extract surplus from China, it is notable that China's agricultural sector is capitalist. While imperialism certainly limits the development of China, causing it to fall short of its potential, it is simply not the case that it prevents development from occurring in China, whether in agriculture or in any other sector.

4   The Proletarianization and Semi-proletarianization of Latin America

Writing on agricultural developments in Latin America, Vergara-Camus and Kay note that,

---

43   Timothy Kerswell and Jake Lin, "Capitalism Denied with Chinese Characteristics," *Socialism and Democracy*, 31, no 2 (2017): 39.

44   James Pomfret, *Freedom Fizzles in China's Rebel Town* (Reuters, February 28, 2013). http://reuters.com.

45   Pomfret, *Freedom Fizzles in China's Rebel Town.*

46   Alan Taylor, *Rising Protests in China* (2012)., http://www.theatlantic.com/photo/2012/02/rising-protests-in-china/100247/.

47   Minqi Li, "China's Changing Class Structure and National Income Distribution 1952–2015," *Journal of Labor and Society,* 20, no 1 (2017): 68.

Although peasant producers continued to play an important role in the production of food crops nationally, agriculture became more and more dominated by agribusiness and corporate capital. The old land-lord class was swept away or transformed itself into capitalist producers. Tenant labour, which was the main source of labour on the *latifundia* and largely resident within the estate, was eliminated by mechanization and/or legal measures and gave way to fully proletarianized wage labour predominantly of a temporary kind and no longer resident within the *latifundia* – now better described as a large capitalist farm.[48]

The end result of this process has been the migration of formerly rural to either urban areas or wealthier countries, despite the existence of movements of resistance, which will be discussed later in this section.[49]

Of all the regions of the global South, Latin America is the one where the most urbanization has taken place, with Fay noting already in 2005, that "with three-quarters of its population living in cities, Latin America and the Caribbean is now essentially an urban region."[50] These developments in the social structure have important implications for transformative politics.

In 2001, James Petras and Henry Veltmeyer argued that "peasant-based guerrilla movements" continued to be an effective force, pointing to examples such as the *Fuerzas Armadas Revolucionarias de Colombia* (FARC) in Colombia as "the most potent peasant-based insurgency in its history."[51] And yet in 2018, FARC is in the process of disarmament. At the time Petras and Veltmeyer penned their article, it is notable that Colombia already had 72 percent of its population in urban areas, and that figure has grown to 76 percent, according to the latest calculations.[52] How a peasant-based guerrilla movement is supposed to succeed in capturing state power under these conditions is not explained by Petras and Veltmeyer, who instead chastise what they call "structuralist arguments" for apparently superimposing European and US development

---

48   Leandro Vergara-Camus and Cristóbal Kay, "Agribusiness, Peasants, Left-Wing Governments, and the State in Latin America: An Overview and Theoretical Reflections," *Journal of Agrarian Change*, 17 (2017): 250.

49   Vergara-Camus and Kay, "Agribusiness, Peasants, Left-Wing Governments," 250; Sutti Ortiz, Susana Aparicio, and Nidia Tadeo, "Dynamics of Harvest Subcontracting: The Roles Played by Labour Contractors," *Journal of Agrarian Change* 13, no 4 (2013).

50   Marianne Fay, *The Urban Poor in Latin America* (Washington DC: The World Bank, 2005), 1.

51   James Petras and Henry Veltmeyer, "Are Latin American Peasant Movements Still a Force for Change? Some New Paradigms Revisited," *The Journal of Peasant Studies*, 28, no. 2, 92.

52   *World Urbanization Prospects*, United Nations.

histories, and their associated decline of rural movements, onto the history of Latin America.[53]

In what is a clear dismissal of the actually existing social forces both in Latin America, and, indeed, in most of the global South, they conclude that "the only class which might be considered majoritarian is that composed of low paid service workers in the so-called informal economy, and few scholars identified this group as the spearhead of any process of change."[54] Instead of centering strategies around the actually existing developments and dynamics of the capitalist social structure, Petras and Veltmeyer prefer to superimpose old theory onto the concrete situation. Their criticism of Kay, and his argument of the semi-proletarianization of the Latin American peasantry can also be seen as an example of a willful negation of empirical evidence.[55] Indeed their statement that "capitalist transformation and wage formation under current 'free market' conditions in many parts of Latin America does not offer as attractive an option as staying in the countryside and fighting to create an alternative, modern rural-based settlement, an objective to be realized through class struggle and agrarian reform" stands in diametric opposition to the actual situation.[56]

Petras and Veltmeyer rightly note that MST's success is the result of "coalitions with urban trade unions, urban shantytown organizations, and church and human rights groups."[57] In other words, MST has achieved whatever success it has as a result of alliances with the urban proletariat and semi-proletariat, including the informal sector workers, which Petras and Veltmeyer discuss in such disparaging terms.

What the Latin American experience demonstrates is consistent with the analysis that has been presented regarding India and China. Imperialism is able to extract significant surplus from the agricultural sector in Latin America, hindering its potential development. This has not, however, prevented the development of capitalist agriculture in Latin America and the demise of feudal and semi-feudal property relations.

---

53   Petras and Veltmeyer, "Are Latin American Peasant Movements Still a Force for Change," 93.
54   Ibid.
55   Cristóbal Kay, "Latin America's Agrarian Transformation: Peasantization and Proletarianization," in *Disappearing peasantries? Rural labour in Africa, Asia and Latin America*, ed. Deborah Fahy Bryceson, Cristóbal Kay, and Jos Mooij (London: ITDG Publishing, 2000); James Petras and Henry Veltmeyer, "Are Latin American Peasant Movements Still a Force for Change?" 88.
56   Petras and Veltmeyer, "Are Latin American Peasant Movements," 102.
57   Ibid., 98.

5   "Peasant" Revolutions in Africa Are Limited to Settler Questions

In considering the regions of the Global South, it is necessary to carefully consider the nature and significance of peasant struggles in Africa for a number of
reasons. Firstly, of all the regions of the world, Africa is the least urbanized and
should therefore, in theory, find itself the most amenable to Fanon's observations regarding the revolutionary peasantry, if indeed those are correct.

Secondly, a possible objection to the theory proposed in this chapter is that
various land/farmers movements exist and have achieved relative success in
decolonization efforts. The question, then, is whether these movements represent a general trend across the African continent or a series of historical
exceptions.

Archie Mafeje observes that "African researchers have not found any relevance of the concept of land reform outside the Southern African settler
societies."[58] The reason for this is that "sub-Saharan Africa had endured no
landlordship, had an abundant supply of land, and producers, including mar-
ried women, had guaranteed access to land for cultivation."[59] This again calls
into question Fanonist narratives about a revolutionary peasantry, as well as
Maoist narratives about feudalism and semi-feudalism. Malumbu-Mvuluya,
for example, directly attacked the notion that a revolutionary peasantry even
existed in Africa in the 1970s.[60]

The exception, of course, comes in the form of land reform movements
in current or former settler societies. Part of Fanon's life and work centered
around the successful expulsion of the settler population from Algeria, and in
the settler societies of southern Africa can be observed genuine land questions
that resulted from minority rule. Basil Davidson documented important cases
of peasant uprisings in the former Portuguese colonies of Angola, Mozambique, and Guinea-Bissau, and his emphasis on the role of vanguardist organizations such as the *Movimento Popular de Libertação de Angola* in furthering
these struggles were central to his argument.[61] These examples closely correspond to Fanon's idea of a revolutionary peasantry being steered by radical
intellectual leadership.

---

58   Archie Mafeje, "The Agrarian Question, Access to Land, and Peasant Responses in Sub-
     Saharan Africa," (Geneva: UNRISD, 2003), 1.
59   Ibid.
60   F Mulumbu-Mvuluya, "Introduction a l'etude du role des payans dans les changements
     politiques," in *Cahiers Economiques et Sociaux* 8, no. 3 (1970): 439–442.
61   Basil Davidson, "African Peasants and Revolution," *The Journal of Peasant Studies* 1, no. 3
     (1974): 269.

More recently, Zimbabwe's land occupation movement and the subsequent land reforms captured a great deal of attention. Sam Moyo argued that this was part of a broader wave of land occupations across the global South.[62] While this is incorrect, the drive for land reform and its accomplishment in Zimbabwe certainly had an impact on other settler societies in southern Africa, as can be seen in South Africa's recent legislation to allow the nationalization of land without compensation.[63] Similar struggles existed in other countries such as Namibia.[64]

What is notable, however, is that in settler societies, even non-peasant political formations are closely involved in the arguments for land reform. Martin Adams, Sipho Sibanda, and Stephen Turner note that "Since the settlement following the Anglo-Boer war, a central objective of the Swazi monarchy has been the return of land lost through alienation to settlers," and that Lesotho's constitutional monarchy has pursued land reform as well, albeit complicated by the existence of ancestral lands in what is the modern republic of South Africa.

These examples demonstrate two key points: "peasant" uprisings and movements for land reform in Africa are limited to questions of settler colonialism, which, while significant, do not constitute the typical case for the African continent and are being progressively resolved through government action in the post-colonial context; and even within these settler-colonial contexts, peasant uprisings do not constitute the only motivating force behind land reform – governments, even highly conservative governments such as the Swazi monarchy, are actively pushing for land reform. Thus, Moyo's assertion that there is a widespread movement of land occupation does not hold even for Africa, let alone for the global South in general.

In terms of a possible explanation for this, it is necessary to look into the Eurocentric bias of much of the analysis, whether Marxist or otherwise. Mafeje argues that in the capitalist analysis of Africa "The underlying Eurocentric supposition was and still is that lack of exclusive rights to land gives rise to insecurity of tenure and, therefore, inhibits permanent investment in land. This is based on the mistaken idea that African land tenure systems are communal and as such any and every individual can lay claim on any piece of land or be

---

62   Sam Moyo, "The Land Occupation Movement and Democratization in Zimbabwe: Contradictions of Neoliberalism," *Millenium: Journal of International Studies* 30, no. 2 (2110): 311.

63   N Mathibela, "South Africa: Unpacking Expropriation without Compensation," *Pambazuka News* (Retrieved August 10, 2018), http://www.eurasiareview.com/05082018-south-africa-unpacking-expropriation-without-compensation-oped/.

64   Martin Adams, Sipho Sibanda, and Stephen Turner, "Land Tenure Reform and Rural Livelihoods in Southern Africa," *Natural Resource Perspectives* no. 39 (1999).

granted access at will. This is a basic misconception."[65] While it is outside the scope of this chapter to discuss in depth the variety of African land tenure systems, a very simple summary would be that the lineage system is based on "persistent customary tenure whereby chiefs or heads of lineages are responsible for distribution of land for use among members of the local community, who are invariably bound together by agnatic ties."[66] Land ownership is thus neither communal, nor individual.

Equally flawed are arguments that suggest that the typical land tenure system is an example of feudal or semi-feudal modes of production.[67] As early as 1962, Soviet theorists Avakov and Mirskii noted that "in most of the African countries, the peasantry lives under patriarchal-communal conditions, knowing neither feudal nor capitalist forms of land ownership. In the African countries, in contrast to many other underdeveloped countries, feudalists and rural bourgeoisie are, with rare exceptions, absent as a class."[68] Other theorists developed an analysis of what is referred to as a "lineage mode of production" to describe the African specificities of land tenure.[69] This analysis is similar to that of Samir Amin's critique of much of Marxism after Marx for its steadfast adherence to the idea of five strict modes of production, of which feudalism was necessarily a part.[70] Instead, Amin proposed a tributary mode of production as the most common pre-capitalist mode, whereby a political apparatus extracted value in some form from the village communities.[71] The benefit of Amin's theorization is that it allows for a wide variety of pre-capitalist modes of production, which are not limited by European or East Asian conceptions of feudalism and their peasantries.

65   Mafeje, "The Agrarian Question," 5–6.
66   Ibid.
67   Sam Moyo, "Land in the Political Economy of African Development: Alternative Strategies for Reform," *Africa Development* 32, no. 4 (2007): 7.
68   R. Avakov and G. Mirskii, "Class Structure in the Underdeveloped Countries," *Mirovaia Ekonomika I Mezhdunarodnye Otnosheniia* no. 4 (1962).
69   Catherine Coquery-Vidrovitch, "Research on an African Mode of Production," in *Gutkind*, ed. Peter Gutkind and Peter Waterman, *African Social Studies* (London: Heinemann, 1977); P. Ray, "The Lineage Mode of Production," *Critique of Anthropology* 2, no. 2 (1975); and Claude Meillassoux, *L'Anthropologie Economique des Gouro de Cote D'Ivoire* (Paris: Mouton and Cie, 1964).
70   Timothy Kerswell, "Samir Amin," in *The Palgrave Encyclopedia of Imperialism and Anti-Imperialism*, ed. Immanuel Ness and Zak Cope (Basingstoke: Palgrave MacMillan, 2016), 2.
71   Samir Amin, "Modes of Production and Social Formations," *Ufahamu: A Journal of African Studies* 4, no. 3 (1972): 57–58.

6   Development of Industrial/Services Capitalism No Longer Depends
       on Resolving the Agrarian Question

From the perspective of capital, the foregoing analysis leads to the overall conclusion that agriculture is less a significant sector than it was previously. This
raises discussions about whether the "agrarian question" has been bypassed,
at least from the perspective of capital. Byres defines the agrarian question as,

> the continuing existence in the countryside of poor countries of substan-
> tive obstacles to an unleashing of the forces capable of generating eco-
> nomic development, both inside and outside agriculture. It represents
> a failure of accumulation to proceed adequately in the countryside –
> that impinging powerfully upon the town; an intimately related failure
> of class formation in the countryside, appropriate to that accumulation;
> and a failure of the state to mediate successfully those transitions which
> we may encapsulate as the agrarian transition.[72]

Jens Lerche observes that there are two major explanations concerning
changes to this "agrarian question" reflected by McMichael and Bernstein.[73]
Briefly summarized, McMichael argues that as a result of neoliberalism and
exposure to the world market, the peasantry now confronts an international
corporate food-producing regime. The implication of this is that the peasantry,
as a political agent, is more significant than ever, becoming a "radical world-
historical subject."[74]

There are both normative and quasi-empirical arguments in a theoretical
current that can be seen in the arguments of MST and also the Zapatistas as
demonstrated by the work of Vergara-Camus, as well as Moyo, Jha, and Yeros.
In Vergara-Camus' field study of these political movements, the "valorization
of village life" is seen as a centrally important strategy within their political
discourse.[75] According to this logic, small-scale and subsistence farming is to
be held up as a viable alternative to capitalism and as a viable method of resisting monopoly capital. This type of thinking has a long theoretical legacy,

---

72   Terence J. Byres, "Political Economy, the Agrarian Question and the Comparative Meth-
     od," *The Journal of Peasant Studies*, 22, no 4 (1995): 509.

73   Jens Lerche, "The Agrarian Question in Neo-liberal India: Agrarian Transition Bypassed?"
     Journal of Agrarian Change, 13, no 3 (2013): 384.

74   Philip McMichael, "Peasants Make Their Own History, but not as They Please," *Journal of
     Agrarian Change*, 8, no. 2- (2008): 210–211.

75   Leandro Vergara-Camus, "The MST and the EZLN Struggle for Land: New Forms of Peas-
     ant Rebellions," *Journal of Agrarian Change* 9, no. 3 (2013): 385.

dating back to the *Narodnik* (people) movement in Russia and should not be seen as a new or innovative understanding of peasant politics. The difference, in this case, is that the Narodniks developed their theory in a time when Russia was overwhelmingly a peasant society, and with no substantial evidence that it would change its character anytime soon. Contemporary neo-Narodnik theorists cannot deploy an ignorance-based defense in support of their theories.

Moyo, Jha, and Yeros argue that a "peasant path" to socialism is more relevant than ever in the twenty-first century, and particularly in the global South.[76] There are numerous weaknesses with this argument. Firstly, there is an attempt to malign as "Eurocentric" any type of argument that stresses any decline in the significance of peasant agriculture.[77] As has been demonstrated in this section, this argument is empirically weak considering that the global South is now rapidly urbanizing, and large parts of the global South are already majority urban, and there are no signs of a reversal of this trend. There is also a general trend within the world economy toward the industrialization of the global South and the deindustrialization of the global North as part of the current global division of labor. Moyo, Jha, and Yeros attempt to sidestep this reality, tarnishing any admission of the industrialization of the global South and its consequences for transformative politics with the accusation of Eurocentrism.

This line of reasoning ignores the significant impact of the agricultural productive forces in the development of the world and on the peasantry in general. Marcel Mazoyer and Laurence Roudart have noted that at the beginning of the twentieth century, the output gap between the least productive and most productive forms of agriculture worldwide was a ratio of 1:10, while by the end of the century, that ratio had expanded to 1:1000 due to motorization and various other technical developments.[78] This feature, coupled with revolutionary developments in transportation, led to a fall in world prices of agricultural commodities and is one of the key forces in world urbanization.

As a direct result of the fall in the price of agricultural commodities, the peasantry must dedicate a greater share of their productive power to the production of commodities for sale, with an associated fall in production for themselves and reduction in maintenance of their land, which in turn causes a fall in production and incomes.[79] Then, "the moment soon comes when the already undernourished peasantry can no longer even renew its seeds and

---

76   Sam Moyo, Praveen Jha, and Paris Yeros, "The Classical Agrarian Question: Myth, Reality and Relevance Today," *Agrarian South: Journal of Political Economy* 2, no. 1 (2013): 104.

77   Moyo, Jha, and Yeros, "The Classical Agrarian Question," 94.

78   Marcel Mazoyer and Laurence Roudart, *A History of World Agriculture: From the Neolithic Age to the Current Crisis* (New York: Monthly Review Press, 2006), 441.

79   Ibid. 443.

tools. The peasant population falls below the threshold of survival and has no other option than to leave for the shantytowns..."[80] It is in this context that arguments for small-scale or subsistence agriculture as a solution to the overall crisis of world agriculture seem scarcely credible.

Moyo, Jha, and Yeros also conflate stocks and flows in their perspective that "neither imperialism nor sovereignty has become relevant enough a category to the mainstream of agrarian studies to organize the discussion on the agrarian question. Indeed, how can one defend the national question after having wished away the inhabitants of whole nations?"[81] Analyses that stress the empirical significance of urbanization are not necessarily an ideologically postpeasant "wishing away" of people as they have claimed. Similarly, none of the authors they cite (Bernstein, Byres, et al.) suggest that the death or the disappearance of the peasantry has occurred. Instead, such perspectives encourage us to understand the vast changes that are happening in the global political economy and their impact on future transformative struggles, which involve a shifting of the center of gravity to the urban centers of the global South.

Harry Bernstein's argument is that from the perspective of capital, the agrarian question has been bypassed as capitalists no longer require the transformation of agriculture within a national context in order to pursue capital accumulation.[82] There is overwhelming evidence for this position. The rapid global expansion of services and industry, in terms of their world value share, and the peripheralization of agriculture, correspond to a generalized trend, even in the global South.[83] On a country-specific level, China's massive economic expansion has coincided with a declining agricultural sector and even a fall in per capita grain output.[84] China has resolved this issue by sourcing food supplies from the global market, further demonstrating how national agriculture no longer acts as a constraint. The enormous expansion of value-added output in services (and to a lesser extent in manufacturing) against the sluggish growth of agriculture in post-liberalization India is further evidence to support this claim.[85]

---

80   Ibid.
81   Ibid., 112.
82   Harry Bernstein, "Is There an Agrarian Question in the 21st Century?" *Canadian Journal of Development Studies/Revue canadienne d'études du* développement 27, no. 4 (2006): 450–451.
83   Akram-Lodhi and Kay, "Surveying the Agrarian Question," 264.
84   Zhun Xu, Wei Zhang, and Mingi Li, "China's Grain Production: A Decade of Growth or Stagnation?" *Monthly Review* 66, no. 1 (2014).
85   Chandrasekhar and Ghosh "Recent Employment Trends," 62.

On the other hand, there remains the fact that agriculture "is struggling to construct a livelihood in the face of the development of the productive forces of capital."[86] Moyo, Jha, and Yeros incorrectly state that the framing of this question is intrinsically linked to "a new set of reformist and welfarist policies to be undertaken by the development industry."[87] The agricultural question of labor is significant, as the exodus of poor peasants has led to a rise in urban poverty. This, in turn, has contributed to the "lowering of basic wages in all branches of employment" in the global South, and it "drags down the prices of all goods and services supplied by these countries as well."[88] In other words, the agrarian question of labor, as Bernstein frames it, can be seen as strongly connected to any contemporary understanding of imperialism and unequal exchange.

According to Bernstein's position, the key faulty assumption in those who maintain the existence of an "agrarian question" is the assumed existence of a pre-capitalist agricultural sector.[89] Bernstein argues that pre-capitalist social classes have been subsumed into either the broader capitalist class by becoming capitalist farmers, by diversifying into other sectors, or are slowly being shifted into the broader working class within a capitalist mode of production.[90] This brings us to the question of whether imperialism relies on the existence of semi-feudalism in agriculture within the contemporary agrarian context, and indeed the question of whether semi-feudal arrangements exist at all.

7   Imperialism Helps to Generate Processes of Urbanization and a Semi-proletariat but not through Semi-feudalism

Farshad Araghi has noted that imperialism has created an "enclosure food regime," which "established the subsidised consumption and overconsumption of classes in the global North" while having a significant impact on the agricultural sectors in the third world, where competition with heavily subsidized agriculture is leading to rural displacement.[91] The resulting impact is the rapid

86   Akram-Lodhi and Kay, "Surveying the Agrarian Question," 267.
87   Moyo, Jha, and Yeros, "The Classical Agrarian Question," 112.
88   Mazoyer and Roudart, A History of World Agriculture, 443.
89   Lerche, "Agrarian Crisis and Agrarian Questions in India," 385.
90   Harry Bernstein, "Agrarian Questions Then and Now," The Journal of Peasant Studies 43, no. 3 (1996): 42–43.
91   Farshad Araghi, "The Invisible Hand and the Visible Foot: Peasants, Dispossession and Globalization," in Peasants and globalization: Political economy, rural transformation and the agrarian question, ed. A. Akram-Lodhi and C. Kay (London: Routledge, 2009a).

urbanization of the global South with surplus labor migrating from the countryside to cities which are unable to fully absorb them into the labor market in what Mike Davis calls the "planet of the slums."[92] The end result of this process is "both lowering the value of labor-power and... raising the rate of relative surplus value for capital."[93]

It is a significant error to consider the agricultural sectors in Africa, Asia, and Latin America pre-capitalist when the lives of farmers worldwide are now profoundly shaped by global market forces. Writing in relation to both the Zapatista movement of Mexico and the Landless Workers Movement in Brazil, Vergara-Camus notes that the

> contemporary crises of peasant agriculture can no longer be seen in terms of encroachment upon the non-capitalist logic of isolated peasant villages by the logic of capitalist market relations. Members of the MST and the Ejército Zapatista de Liberación Nacional (EZLN), although they partly rely on non-capitalist social relations for their survival, have engaged in capitalist exchanges for a long time, either through the sale of the crops they produce or for a wage.[94]

A conceptualization of the global South as being feudal or semi-feudal is not correct in the current landscape. This is because the traditional landlord class, typified by rent extraction from a subject population in exchange for certain protections, no longer has political or economic power having been converted into capitalist farmers or have diversified into other economic activities responding to the logic of market capitalism.[95]

These same market forces have an impact in the class polarization that is occurring in the countryside of the global South and have played a large role

---

92   Mike Davis, *Planet of Slums.* New York: Verso, 2000.

93   Farshad Araghi, "The Great Global Enclosure of our Times: Peasants and the Agrarian Question at the end of the Twentieth Century," in *Hungry for Profit: the Agribusiness Threat to Farmers, Food, and the Environment,* ed. Fred Magdoff, Frederick H. Buttel and John Bellamy Foster (New York: Monthly Review Press, 2000).

94   Vergara-Camus, "The MST and the EZLN," 368.

95   Cristóbal Kay, "Rural Latin America: Exclusionary and Uneven Agricultural Development," in *Capital, Power and Inequality in Latin America,* eds Sandor Halebsky and Richard Harris, 21–51 (Boulder, CO: Westview Press, 1995); Kay, "Latin America's Agrarian Transformation"; Moacir Palmeira and Sérgio Leite, "Debates econômicos, procesos sociais e lutas políticas," in *Política e reforma agrária,* ed. Raimundo Santos and Luiz Flávio Carvalho Costa (Rio de Janeiro: MAUAD Consultoria e Planejamento Editorial, 1998), 122–125; Vergara-Camus, "The MST and the EZLN," 375; and Basole and Basu. "Relations of Production... an Aggregate Study."

in expanding the rural semi-proletariat. The rural semi-proletariat occupies a transitory position between the emergence of capitalist farming and the fully proletarianized urban workforce. Kay has argued that this trend is caused by the development of productive forces in agriculture, with agricultural modernization being strongly related to the rise of seasonal patterns of labor demand, causing semi-proletarianization.[96] This begins when farmers start to participate in wage labor during the lean times of the year, and in agriculture during harvest times. In many countries in the global South, this also involves the trend of seasonal migration to urban centers whereby the economic circumstances of the rural semi-proletariat cause geographical displacement and weaken their connection to the land.[97]

In terms of the rural semi-proletariat, Akram-Lodhi and Kay argued that "a significant and increasing proportion of the global rural population... [are] seeking, day by day, refuge in their small plot of land, producing agricultural products for food security reasons while simultaneously engaged in selling their power to capitalist farmers, richer proto-capitalist peasants, or non-farm capitalists."[98] The interests of the rural semi-proletariat are often strongly related to those of the broader peasantry when they act as farmers, and under the proletariat when they are wage laborers. The greater the dependence on wage labor for subsistence, the less significant rural issues become in terms of their overall interests, and the more their class interests become more closely aligned with the proletariat in general. In this context, Akram-Lodhi and Kay note that this group is "straddling farm and off-farm activity, [and] have

---

96   Kay, "Latin America's Agrarian Transformation," 132.
97   Y. Haberfeld, R.K. Menaria, B.B. Sahoo, and R.N. Vyas, "Seasonal Migration of Rural Labor in India," *Population Research and Policy Review* 18 (1999); Alan De Brauwa, *Seasonal Migration and Agriculture in Viet Nam,* ESA Working Paper No. 07-04, Agricultural Development Economics Division, The Food and Agriculture Organization of the United Nations (2007); Priya Deshingkar and John Farrington, "Rural Labour Markets and Migration in South Asia: Evidences from India and Bangladesh," for the World Development Report, 2008, London, Overseas Development Institute; Hugo, "Circular Migration in Indonesia." *Population and Development Review* 8, No 1 (1982); Tran Quang Lam, John R. Bryant, Aphichat Chamratrithirong, and Yothin Sawangdee, "Labour Migration in Kanchanaburi Demographic Surveillance System: Characteristics and Determinants," *Journal of Population and Social Studies* 16, No 1 (2007); Blessing Uchenna Mberu, "Internal Migration and Household Living Conditions in Ethiopia," *Demographic Research* 14, no. 21 (2006); Xiushi Yang, "Temporary Migration and its Frequency from Urban House-Holds in China," *Asia Pacific Population Journal* 7, no. 1 (1992).
98   Akram-Lodhi and Kay, "Surveying the Agrarian Question," 273–274; and Kay, "Latin America's Agrarian Transformation."

become increasingly reliant on income arising from the sale of their commodified power as waged."[99]

8   Contemporary Peasant Struggles

In order to qualify this discussion, it should be noted that while the overall trend is toward the urbanization of the global South, it is not a linear process, and due to various historical and subjective factors, there are some cases of repeasantization where peasants have been able to gain control over land.[100] Notable examples of this include *Movimento dos Sem Terra* in Brazil, the Zapatista movement in Mexico, and the land reforms carried out in Zimbabwe.[101] These, however, are not generalizable examples, with the Zimbabwean movement being carried out in response to the particular circumstances of settler colonialism, and the rise of MST being strongly connected to the end of Brazil's military dictatorship and the influence of the Catholic Church in the countryside.[102]

Both the Zapatista movement and MST are united by a common, but specific, historical experience. Vergara-Camus notes that,

> Peasantries in Latin America have participated in guerrilla movements since the 1960s in Colombia, Guatemala, Nicaragua, El Salvador and Peru. Over a period of several decades, while guerrilla movements were frequently able to destabilize local oligarchic regimes, they never managed to defeat them completely. As a consequence, peasant movements in Central America have accepted that their demand must remain within the limits of liberal representative democracies instead of challenging them like the MST and the EZLN do.[103]

---

99   Akram-Lodhi and Kay, "Surveying the Agrarian Question," 271.

100   Jan Douwe Van der Ploeg, "The Third Agrarian Crisis and the Re-emergence of Processes of Repeasantization," *Rivista di Economia Agraria* LXII, no. 3 (2007).

101   Vergara-Camus, "The MST and the EZLN," 381; Mario Zamponi, "Farewell to the Third World? Farewell to the Peasantry? Primitive Accumulation and the Rural World in the Contemporary Development Discourse," Working Paper No 5 (2011), 11.

102   Lúcio Flávio de Almeida and Félix Ruiz Sánchez, "The Landless Workers' Movement and Social Struggle Against Neoliberalism," *Latin American Perspectives* 27, no. 114 (2000): 11–32, 14; Anne-Laure Cadji, "Brazil's Landless Find their Voice," NACLA *Report on the Americas* 33, no. 5 (2000): 32; and Zander Navarro, "Breaking New Ground Brazil's MST," NACLA *Report on the Americas* 33, no. 5 (2000): 37.

103   Leandro Vergara-Camus, *Land and Freedom: The MST, The Zapatistas and Peasant Alternatives to Neoliberalism* (London: Zed, 2014), 372.

Unlike other states in Latin America, the Brazilian and Mexican states were successful in suppressing guerilla movements in the early 1960s and 1970s, and establishing corporatist structures, which have only recently been challenged by neoliberalism, leading to the radicalization of peasant politics in these contexts.[104]

In a similar fashion, struggles against land grabs are a meaningful expression of the peasant and rural semi-proletarian politics, which have been important in recent times. The peasant resistance against land acquisition in India's Singur and Nandigram regions in West Bengal are a notable example of how peasants have organized to resist the use of state power to acquire land on behalf of powerful domestic capitalist interests. While this movement was opportunistically co-opted by both the Trinamool Congress and the Communist Party of India (Maoist) and ultimately declined as a result, its impact on Indian politics was felt due to the contribution it made in ending more than thirty years of Left Front government in West Bengal and the entrenchment of the Trinamool Congress within parliamentary politics.

This type of struggle is roughly consistent with James Scott's understanding of peasant revolts as "defensive reactions" in response to some kind of "sharp moral departure from norms of reciprocity."[105] The Left Front had depended on, and received, the support of the peasantry in West Bengal for its electoral success ever since the implementation of the *Operation Barga* land reforms in the late 1970s.[106] Its policy of land acquisition for special economic zones tarnished this longstanding relationship.

The present struggle in the Philippines between the *Kilusang Magbubukid ng Pilipinas* (Peasant Movement of the Philippines), an arm of the Communist Party of the Philippines, and the Lapanday Corporation can also be highlighted as an example of successful repeasantization, with the farmers being granted land that was illegally acquired by the corporation.[107] The Duterte government appears to be making some concessions to the land reform demands raised by the Communist Party of the Philippines (CPP) in order to maintain a broad enough base of support in light of both international and domestic criticism of the anti-drug campaign, which has disproportionately impacted poor people

---

104   Ibid.

105   James Scott, *The Moral Economy of the Peasant: Rebellion and Subsistence in Southeast Asia* (New Haven: Yale University Press, 1976), 10, 194.

106   Suhas Chattopadhyay, "Operation Barga: A Comment," *Economic and Political Weekly* 49, no. 8 (1979).

107   Telesur, *Militant Filipino Farmers Force Duterte to Seize Oligarchs' Land in Agrarian Reform Push*, (2017). http://www.telesurtv.net/english/news/Filipino-Farmers-Force-Duterte-to-Redistribute-Oligarchs-Land-20170517-0033.html.

from various social classes across the Philippines. The government also has the objective of ensuring the continuation of the peace process between the government and the CPP. It is these specific factors that have generated a positive land reform outcome.

These examples demonstrate that within certain historically contingent circumstances, peasants, particularly when aligned with the rural semi-proletariat, continue to be important social actors, fueling the development of new movements and new politics. They will continue to play an important role in the global class structure in the short to medium term despite the declining importance of the peasantry and of rural struggles in the wake of world urbanization.

9   Conclusion

This section has argued that agriculture in the global South has been subject to important and wide-ranging changes in the twentieth and early twenty-first centuries. The primary change has involved the decline of semi-feudal relations of production and the development of capitalist agriculture. These developments have occurred despite the ability of imperialism to extract surplus from the agricultural sectors of the global South.

A broad survey of twentieth-century revolutionary politics shows that with the singular exception of the Russian Revolution, peasants and the rural semi-proletariat have been the leading forces behind social transformation. In most cases, the proletariat played the role of the junior partner. This chapter has argued that the overall world trend is one of rapid urbanization. While the peasantry will remain important, over the course of the twenty-first century, these roles will be reversed. Urbanization is shifting the terrain of future political struggles, and as a result, the third world proletariat and semi-proletariat are expected to be the leading forces in future struggles.

A final note of caution, this analysis should not be interpreted as the "death of the peasantry," a conclusion that this analysis finds to be premature.[108] This analysis has merely argued that, for economic and demographic reasons, the importance of the peasantry is declining. Additionally, this analysis has argued that the increasing separation of peasants from the land is making the semi-proletariat into a much more important class, particularly as it migrates

---

108   Eric Hobsbawm, "Age of extremes: the short twentieth century, 1914–1991" (London: Michael Joseph, 1994); Vanhaute, *From Famine to Food Crisis: What History Can Teach Us About Local and Global Subsistence Crises* (2009). http://www.ccc.ugent.be/file/115.

to major cities in search of wage labor and comes into contact with the urban proletariat, and it is these class forces which will rise in their significance in the twenty-first century. Fanon's contributions to revolutionary theory are manifold. However, his analysis of the peasantry was questionable and debatable even at the time he made it, let alone in an urbanizing world.

Bibliography

Akram-Lodhi, A. Haroon, and Cristobal Kay. "Surveying the Agrarian Question (Part 2): Current Debates and Beyond." *The Journal of Peasant Studies* 37, no. 2 (2010).

Almeida, Lúcio Flávio de, and Félix Ruiz Sánchez. "The Landless Workers' Movement and Social Struggle Against Neoliberalism." *Latin American Perspectives* 27 no. 114 (2000): 11–32.

Amin, Samir. "Modes of Production and Social Formations." *Ufahamu: A Journal of African Studies* 4, no. 3 (1974).

Araghi, Farshad. "The Great Global Enclosure of our Times: Peasants and the Agrarian Question at the End of the Twentieth Century." in *Hungry for Profit: The Agribusiness Threat to Farmers, Food, and the Environment*, edited by F. Magdoff, F.H. Buttel and J. Bellamy Foster, New York: Monthly Review Press, 2002.

Araghi, Farshad. "The Invisible Hand and the Visible Foot: Peasants, Dispossession and Globalization." in *Peasants and Globalization: Political Economy, Rural Transformation and the Agrarian Question*, edited by A.H. Akram-Lodhi and C. Kay. London: Routledge, 2009a.

Araghi, Farshad. "Accumulation by Displacement: Global Enclosures, Food Crisis, and the Ecological Contradictions of Capitalism." *Review (Fernand Braudel Center)*. 2009b.

Avakov, R., and G. Mirskii, "Class Structure in the Underdeveloped Countries." *Mirovaia Ekonomika I Mezhdunarodnye Otnosheniia* no. 4 (1962).

Baran, Paul. *The Political Economy of Growth*. New York: Monthly Review Press, 1957.

Barros, Carlos Pestana, Ari Fransisco Araujo, Jr., and Joao Ricardo Faria. "Brazilian Land Tenure and Conflicts: The Landless Peasants Movement." *Cato Journal* 33, no. 1 (2013).

Basole, Amit and Dipankar Basu. "Relations of Production and Modes of Surplus Extraction in India: An Aggregate Study." *Sanhati.* http://sanhati.com/wp-content/uploads/2009/05/india_surplus_may_11.pdf (2009).

Basole, Amit and Dipankar Basu. "Relations of Production and Modes of Surplus Extraction in India: Part 1 – Agriculture." *Economic and Political Weekly* 46, no. 14 (2011).

Bernstein, Harry. "Is There an Agrarian Question in the 21st Century?" *Canadian Journal of Development Studies/Revue canadienne d'études du* développement 27, no. 4 (2006).

Bernstein, Harry. "Agrarian Questions Then and Now." *The Journal of Peasant Studies* 43, no. 3 (1996).

Biao, Lin. "Long Live the Victory of People's War." 1965. https://www.marxists.org/reference/archive/lin-biao/1965/09/peoples_war/ch07.htm.

Brauwa, Alan De. *Seasonal Migration and Agriculture in Viet Nam.* ESA Working Paper No. 07-04, Agricultural Development Economics Division, The Food and Agriculture Organization of the United Nations (2007).

Byres, Terence J. "Political Economy, the Agrarian Question and the Comparative Method." *The Journal of Peasant Studies* 22, no. 4 (1995).

Cadji, Anne-Laure. "Brazil's Landless Find their Voice." *NACLA Report on the Americas* 33, no. 5 (2000).

Chandrasekhar, C.P., and Jayati Ghosh. "Recent Employment Trends in India and China: An Unfortunate Convergence." Paper presented at JNU-IIAS conference "Making Growth Inclusive with Reference to Employment Generation," Jawaharlal Nehru University, New Delhi, June 28–29, 2007.

Chattopadhyay, Suhas. "Operation Barga: A Comment." *Economic and Political Weekly* 49, no. 8 (1979).

Coquery-Vidrovitch, Catherine. "Research on an African Mode of Production." in *African Social Studies,* edited by P Gutkind, and P Waterman. London: Heinemann, 1977.

Davis, Mike. 2007. *Planet of Slums.* New York: Verso, 1977.

Deshingkar, Priya and John Farrington. "Rural Labour Markets and Migration in South Asia: Evidences from India and Bangladesh." Background paper for the World Development Report, London, Overseas Development Institute, 2008.

Fahri, Farideh. "States and Urban-Based Revolutions: Iran and Nicaragua." Champaign: University of Illinois Press, 1990.

Fanon, Frantz. *The Wretched of the Earth.* New York: Grove Press, 1965.

Fay, Marianne. *The Urban Poor in Latin America.* Washington DC: The World Bank, 2005.

Guevara, Ernesto Che. *Guerilla Warfare.* Lincoln: University of Nebraska Press, 1998.

Haberfeld, Y., R.K. Menaria, B.B. Sahoo, and R.N. Vyas. "Seasonal Migration of Rural Labor in India." *Population Research and Policy Review* 18 (1999).

Harris, Nigel. "The Revolutionary Role of the Peasants." *International Socialism* no. 41 (1970).

Hobsbawm, Eric. *Age of Extremes: The Short Twentieth Century, 1914–1991.* London: Michael Joseph, 1994.

Hugo, Graeme J. "Circular Migration in Indonesia." *Population and Development Review* 8, no. 1 (1982).

Joes, Anthony James. *Urban Guerilla Warfare.* Lexington: University of Kentucky Press, 1982.

Kar, Guruprasad. "The Semi-Feudal Character of Indian Agriculture." *Sanhati,* translated by Ipsita Samanta, from article, "Bharatiya Krishir Adhasamantatantrik charitra." *Aneek,* 2012. http://sanhati.com/excerpted/8197/.

Kay, Cristóbal. "Rural Latin America: Exclusionary and Uneven Agricultural Development." in *Capital, Power and Inequality in Latin America,* edited by Sandor Halebsky and Richard Harris, 21–51. Boulder, CO: Westview Press, 2012.

Kay, Cristóbal. "Latin America's Agrarian Transformation: Peasantization and Proletarianization." in *Disappearing Peasantries? Rural Labour in Africa, Asia and Latin America,* edited by D Bryceson, Kay, and Mooij, London: ITDG Publishing, 2000.

Kerswell, Timothy. "Samir Amin." in *The Palgrave Encyclopedia of Imperialism and Anti-Imperialism,* edited by Immanuel Ness and Zak Cope, Basingstoke: Palgrave MacMillan, 2016.

Lam, Tran Quang., John R. Bryant, Apichat Chamratrithirong, and Yothin Sawangdee. "Labour Migration in Kanchanaburi Demographic Surveillance System: Characteristics and Determinants." *Journal of Population and Social Studies* 16, no. 1 (2007).

Lenin, Vladimir Ilich. *Collected Works, Vol 24.* Moscow: Progress Publishers, 1964. 21–26.

Lerche, Jens. "Agrarian Crisis and Agrarian Questions in India." *Journal of Agrarian Change* 11, no. 1 (2011).

Lerche, Jens. "The Agrarian Question in Neo-liberal India: Agrarian Transition Bypassed?" *Journal of Agrarian Change* 13, no. 3 (2013).

Li, Minqi. "China's Changing Class Structure and National Income Distribution 1952–2015." *Journal of Labor and Society* 20, no. 1 (2017).

Lin, Justin Yifu "Rural Reforms and Agricultural Growth in China." *The American Economic Review* (1992): 34–51.

Ma, Licheng. *Leading Schools of Thought in Contemporary China.* Singapore: World Scientific, 1992.

Mafeje, Archie. *The Agrarian Question, Access to Land, and Peasant Responses in Sub-Saharan Africa.* Geneva: UNRISD, 2003.

Marks, Thomas A., and Paul B. Rich. "Back to the Future–People's War in the 21st Century." *Small Wars and Insurgencies* (2017): 409–425.

Marx, Karl. The Eighteenth Brumaire of Louis Napoleon. https://www.marxists.org/archive/marx/works/subject/hist-mat/18-brum/ch07.htm Moscow: Progress Publishers, 1937.

Mazoyer, Marcel and Laurence Roudart. *A History of World Agriculture: From the Neolithic Age to the Current Crisis.* New York: Monthly Review Press, 2006.

Mberu, BU. Internal Migration and Household Living Conditions in Ethiopia. *Demographic Research* 14, no. 21 (2006).

McMichael, Philip. "Peasants Make Their Own History, but Not as They Please." *Journal of Agrarian Change* 8, no. 2–3 (2008).

Meillassoux, Claude. *L'Anthropologie Economique des Gouro de Cote D'Ivoire*. Paris: Mouton and Cie, 1964.

Moyo, Sam. "Land in the Political Economy of African Development: Alternative Strategies for Reform." *Africa Development* 32, no. 4 (2007).

Moyo, Sam, Praveen Jha, and Paris Yeros. "The Classical Agrarian Question: Myth, Reality and Relevance Today." *Agrarian South: Journal of Political Economy* 2, no. 1 (2013).

Mulumbu-Mvuluya, F. "Introduction a l'etude du role des payans dans les changements politiques," in *Cahiers Economiques et Sociaux* 8, no. 3 (1970): 439–442.

National Bank for Agriculture and Rural Development. "Agricultural Land Holdings Pattern in India." *NABARD Rural Pulse 1* (January-February, 2014) https://www.nabard.org/Publication/Rural_Pulse_final142014.pdf.

Navarro, Zander. "Breaking New Ground Brazil's MST." *NACLA Report on the Americas*, 33, no. 5 (2000).

Omvedt, Gail. "Capitalist Agriculture and Rural Classes in India." *Economic and Political Weekly* 16, no. 52 (1981).

Ortiz, Sutti, Susana Aparicio, and Nidia Tadeo. "Dynamics of Harvest Subcontracting: The Roles Played by Labour Contractors." *Journal of Agrarian Change* 13, no. 4 (2013).

Palmeira, Moacir and Sérgio Leite. "Debates econômicos, procesos sociais e lutas políticas." in *Política e reforma agrária*, edited by Raimundo Santos and Luiz Flávio Carvalho Costa, Rio de Janeiro: MAUAD Consultoria e Planejamento Editorial, 1998.

Patnaik, Utsa. "Development of Capitalism in Agriculture-I," *Social Scientist* 1, no. 2 (1972a): 15–31.

Patnaik, Utsa. "Development of Capitalism in Agriculture-II," *Social Scientist* 1, no. 3 (1972b): 3–19.

Patnaik, Utsa. "Class Differentiation within the Peasantry: An Approach to Analysis of Indian Agriculture," *Economic and Political Weekly* 11, no. 39 (1976).

Patnaik, Utsa. "Empirical Identification of Peasant Classes Revisited," *Economic and Political Weekly* 15, no. 9 (1980).

Patnaik, Utsa. "The Agrarian Question and Development of Capitalism in India," *Economic and Political Weekly* 21, no. 18 (1986).

Perinbam, B. Marie. "Fanon and the Revolutionary Peasantry – The Algerian Case." *The Journal of Modern African Studies* 11, no. 3 (1973).

Petras, James and Henry Veltmeyer. "Are Latin American Peasant Movements Still A Force for Change? Some New Paradigms Revisited." *The Journal of Peasant Studies* 28, no. 2 (2001).

Pomfret, James. *Freedom Fizzles in China's Rebel Town.* Reuters, February 28, 2013. http://reuters.com.

Ramachandran, V.K. "Classes and Class Differentiation in India's Countryside." *World Review of Political Economy* 2, no. 4 (2011).

Ray, P.P. "The Lineage Mode of Production." *Critique of Anthropology* 2, no. 2 (1975).

Scott, James. *The Moral Economy of the Peasant: Rebellion and Subsistence in South-East Asia.* New Haven: Yale University Press, 1976.

Taylor, Alan. *Rising Protests in China.* 2012. http://www.theatlantic.com/photo/2012/02/rising-protests-in-china/100247/.

Telesur, TV. *Militant Filipino Farmers Force Duterte to Seize Oligarchs' Land in Agrarian Reform Push.* 2017. http://www.telesurtv.net/english/news/Filipino-Farmers-Force-Duterte-to-Redistribute-Oligarchs-Land-20170517-0033.html.

United Nations. *World Urbanization Prospects.* 2014. https://esa.un.org/unpd/wup/Publications/Files/WUP2014-Highlights.pdf.

Van der Ploeg, Jan Douwe. "The Third Agrarian Crisis and the Re-emergence of Processes of Repeasantization." *Rivista di Economia Agraria* LXII, no. 3 (2007).

Vanhaute, Eric. *From Famine to Food Crisis: What History Can Teach us About Local and Global Subsistence Crises.* 2009. http://www.ccc.ugent.be/file/115.

Vergara-Camus, Leandro. *Land and Freedom: The MST, The Zapatistas and Peasant Alternatives to Neoliberalism.* London: Zed, 2014.

Vergara-Camus, Leandro. "The MST and the EZLN Struggle for Land: New Forms of Peasant Rebellions." *Journal of Agrarian Change* 9, no. 3 (2009).

Vergara-Camus, Leandro and Cristóbal Kay. "Agribusiness, Peasants, Left-Wing Governments, and the State in Latin America: An Overview and Theoretical Reflections." *Journal of Agrarian Change* 17 (2017).

Wallerstein, Immanuel. *The Capitalist World Economy.* Cambridge: Cambridge University Press, 1979.

Warren, Bill. *Imperialism: Pioneer of Capitalism.* London: Verso, 1980.

Xu, Zhun, Wei Zhang, and Minqi Li. "China's Grain Production: A Decade of Growth or Stagnation?" *Monthly Review* 66, no. 1 (2014).

Yang, X. "Temporary Migration and its Frequency from Urban House-Holds in China." *Asia Pacific Population Journal* 7, no. 1 (1992).

Young, Jason. *Markets, Migrants and Institutional Change.* Basingstoke: Palgrave MacMillan, 2013.

Yuen, Samson. "China's New Rural Land Reform? Assessment and Prospects." *China Perspectives* no. 1 (2014).

Zamponi, Mario. "Farewell to the Third World? Farewell to the Peasantry? Primitive Accumulation and the Rural World in the Contemporary Development Discourse." Working Paper No 5. 2011.

Zedong, Mao. *Analysis of Classes in Chinese Society*. 1926. https://www.marxists.org/
reference/archive/mao/selected-works/volume-1/mswv1_1.htm.

Zhou Tian. *Anhui Experiments with Sales of Rural Land in 20 Counties*. 2013. http://
english.caixin.com/2013-11-15/100605583.html.

CHAPTER 9

Frantz Fanon in Ali Shariati's Reading: Is it Possible to Interpret Fanon in a Shariatian Form?

Seyed Javad Miri

Is there a Shariatian reading of Frantz Fanon? What kind of interpretation of Fanon does Ali Shariati present? In other words, what are the features of Fanon that Shariati portrays in his own work? It should be noted that in this discussion, I am not interested in Frantz Fanon as a revolutionary or an ideologue, rather I am looking for aspects that are respected in "social theory" and post-colonial theories, within the broader framework of sociological theories. Thus, in this discussion, certain aspects of Fanon in Shariati's interpretation are of significance, while other areas of Fanon are out of my theoretical consideration. Thus, if we want to examine Shariati's interpretation of Fanon, we must do so from within the framework of sociological theory.

In his book, *History and Recognition of Religions*, Shariati refers to Frantz Fanon. It should be noted that Shariati did not write a specific book on Fanon's ideas and opinions; however, throughout the thirty-six volumes of his collected works, he often cites Fanon, and attempts to express his interpretation of the Caribbean thinker in various ways. Shariati claims that he introduced Fanon to the Iranian intellectual community for the first time. In the book, *The History of Civilization* he writes, "nobody can accuse me of not knowing Fanon, because I am the first person in Iran who has known Fanon, translated his works, spoken of him, and written and published all his thoughts."[1]

Of course, this claim is questionable in-and-of-itself, because Fanon's works exceed the number of those Shariati refers to in his books. The current existing works written by Fanon are as follows:

1. *The Wretched of the Earth*
2. *Black Skin, White Masks*
3. *A Dying Colonialism*
4. *Concerning Violence*
5. *The Fact of Blackness*
6. *Alienation and Freedom*

---

1 Ali Shariati, *Collected works no.12. Tarikh tamaddon* (The History of Civilization) Vol. 2. (Tehran: Ghalam, 2015), 122.

7.   *Decolonizing Madness: The Psychiatric writings of Frantz Fanon*
8.   *Toward the African Revolution*

Decolonizing Madness is a collection of Fanon's writings in the field of psychiatry, which did not exist as a book in Fanon's time. This invalidates Shariati's claim that "I have translated his works."[2] *Decolonizing Madness* was translated into English by Lisa Damon, edited under the supervision of Nigel Gibson, and published by McMillon's Publications in the United States, only in 2014. In other words, as far as I know, this collection of Fanon's psychiatric writings had not been published as a book by Fanon during his lifetime. Nigel Gibson categorized these essays into the following eleven sections:

1.   The North African syndrome
2.   Mental disorders and neurological disorders
3.   Aspects of psychiatric care in Algeria today
4.   Social therapy in a ward for Muslim men
5.   The conduct of "Confession" in North Africa
6.   Ethno-psychiatric Considerations
7.   The T.A.T. (Thematic Apperception Test) and Muslim women: The sociology of perception and imagination
8.   The phenomenon of agitation in psychiatry
9.   Letter to the resident minister (during the colonial period)
10.   The benefits and limitations of daily hospitalization in psychiatry
11.   The encounter of society with psychiatry

Indeed, Nigel Gibson wrote an extensive introduction to this 2017 book, and Roberto Beneduce, an Italian psychiatrist and anthropologist, who has produced important writings in the field of anthropology and psychiatry, wrote "The Last Words." With this explanation, one can argue that Ali Shariati's claim about Fanon, that claim to have "translated his works" is questionable. However, it is notable that Shariati says, "I am the first person in Iran who has known Fanon... [and] ... I have spoken of him."[3] This must be analyzed. Unfortunately, this part of Shariati's thoughts has not been seriously considered in Iran, and we do not know what this "reconstruction" of Fanon looks like, i.e. the Fanon that Shariati knew and published about. Consequently, we are presented not with the factual Fanon, or the Fanon that Gibson or Beneduce talk about, but are rather faced with a "Shariati-like reconstruction" that needs to be seriously addressed.

Shariati argues that the world is divided into two areas: "subject" and "object." The *subject* is the European (Western and white) human, while non-Western

---

2   Ibid.
3   Ibid.

indigenous people are the *object*. Anchored within such a conceptualization, he regards Fanon as being one of the greatest contemporary thinkers, whom he "sincerely thinks about and believes in."[4] The question is: what has Fanon written to make Shariati regard him as "a great man"?[5] Fanon states,

> Friends! (by friends, he does not mean Algerians, Africans, the people of the South American Antillean Islands, but all the people of the Third World, all the people who were humiliated and looted) Let's not turn Africa into a third Europe, the experience of America is enough for us. What the US did was to build itself like Europe and [consequently] Europe became two. That means people and humanity were suffering from one pain, and that pain became two, and if the struggle of the people of Africa, the intellectuals and the mujahidin leads Africa to become a France, an England, a Western Europe, and so on, we will have three Europes. Do we want to turn Asia, Africa, and Latin America into another America and Europe?[6]

In other words, Shariati deems Fanon as an important person not because he was the ideologue of an anti-Western revolution, rather Shariati finds other reasons in Fanon to elevate him in his own work. What are the reasons? Shariati says that, from Fanon's point of view, if we

> want to turn Asia, Africa, and Latin America into another America and Europe [then it is better to]... give our nation's fate to colonial Europe, because they deserve more to make such a civilization than we do.[7]

Therefore, why does the non-Western person want to take control of his fate? In Shariati's interpretation of Fanon, if "we"

> want to take control of our fate ourselves, we should not try to bring in the French, English, and Americans through the window, while we ousted them out of Africa and Asia through the door. While we are throwing them out, we are returning [to them] their views, rights, structures, civilization, and opinions. Just be happy about what France and America have done; now we are doing it on our own.[8]

---

4   Ibid., 123.

5   Ali Shariati, *Collected Works no. 14. Tarikh shenakht e adyan* (History and Recognition of Religions) Vol. 1. (Tehran: SahamiEnteshar, 2009), 206.

6   Ibid., 206–207.

7   Ibid., 207.

8   Ibid.

In other words, "we" in

> Asia and Africa do not fight for a catastrophe called civilization, so that
> we merely change people's places to replace an Asian with a European.
> We, the third-world intellectuals, have not risen up to just throw out colo-
> nization, to just replace people; we will not rise to renew the civilization
> of the West in the East.[9]

Why have "we" not risen up to "renew western civilization" in the East? Why did
Shariati, in his interpretation of Fanon, despise "Western civilization renewal"
and consider it a failure? Why is "the renewal of Western civilization," which
mesmerized the world, useless and absurd in Shariati's opinion? Did Fanon not
look to "renew Western civilization"? Is the "renewal of Western civilization" in
the East a simple and petty matter underestimated by the Fanonist Shariati?
Shariati says that Fanon considers "the renewal of Western civilization,"

> not for Africa and the slaved Asia... and not for humanity, [because] then
> humanity will vomit once more what it has once eaten up. If we [the
> Third World intellectuals] turn Africa and Asia into another America
> and another Europe, Europe and America would see their vomit with a
> metamorphosed face of their own, and this is neither a service to the
> colonized nor a service to Europe and civilization, nor a service to hu-
> manity. Because we know that the greatest victim of Western civilization
> is humanity... Third World intellectuals should not follow the path that
> leads to human metamorphosis.[10]

To put it in other words, Shariati's interpretation of Fanon assumes that Fanon's
approach will come to the following:

> We create a new world, a new system and civilization. And we try to cre-
> ate a new human, a new race, and a new thought, not a human who has
> become metamorphosed in this fast-paced competitive Western produc-
> tive system.[11]

The question that arises here is why do Third World intellectuals want to create a "new human," a "new race," a "new thought," a "new system," and a "new
civilization"? Why is the "competitive Western productive system" introduced

---

9   Ibid.
10   Ibid.
11   Ibid.

as a human-metamorphosing system? Is a comradely system preferred against this "competitive system," or does Shariati call out the "competitive system" for failing to pursue an ideal that has neither the disadvantages of the competitive capitalist system nor the restrictions of the comradely feudalist system? With his interpretation of Fanon, it seems that Shariati has come to the conclusion that the Western competitive system, with its tremendous speed and efficiency, places humans in a state of imposition, as these humans are constantly thinking about further pursuits. He writes, "at the same time, nobody asks the person near to them how they feel, nor does any human being see the person next to him. We must abandon this crazy race and [attempt] to build and recognize humanity and [thus] save humanity."[12]

In other words, the relations that produced America as another Europe, which produced colonization in the East, should be eliminated, so that not only the human of the East can be saved, but also so that the human colonialist of the West can be saved from his metamorphosed self. For such a project, the imposed relations must be transformed so that we can reconstruct anew in order to gain a novel recognition. This new reconstruction will be the way of human liberation in the future. It will not turn Africa or the East into another Europe. But an important question remains: what should be done to create such a new human? Shariati presents the following interpretation of Fanon on that issue:

> for this new human to be built, and this new skin [to be made into] a new race – no longer white, black, yellow and red – and whose name will be human race... we need Noah's Deluge, the deluge within which every corruption, civilization, and inhuman building made on the ground drowns, [resulting in a] clean and pure generation. This will begin humanity's true evolution.[13]

Here we clearly see that the Shariati-reconstructed Fanon speaks in the form of an apocalyptical prophet who, in his own mind, begins to develop mankind's true evolution.

> The great responsibility of the Third World intellectuals... is not only to bring about independence and freedom through an anti-colonial struggle, but a mission for posterity... For this purpose, today's human should

---

12   Ibid.
13   Ibid., 208.

be saved, not to save them from European colonization, [only] to then take them [back] to Europe; this is not ideal.[14]

Many critics of the Islamic Republic of Iran believe that Shariati has nothing to do with the Islamic Republic system, rather he is only "the teacher of the revolution." Yet, one can see traces of the system in his thoughts that cannot be easily restricted to a "movement." In other words, the macro-policies that are being proposed today in the Islamic Republic in opposition to "Westerniza-tion," and the attempt to develop an "Islamic human," are rooted in the desire to create a new race against the "socialist human" and "capitalist human." The Islamic Republic, in today's different interpretations (such as Islamic humani-ties), is in line with this "new race." However, this term should not be concep-tualized in the classical sense of "race." Shariati has beautifully portrayed this "new race," he asks: "What kind of race is this new race that should be con-structed and become the successor to the White and Red, Yellow and Black race?"[15] Shariati believes that Fanon's assumption is correct and that "we" should not turn Asia, Africa, and Latin America into another America and Eu-rope, but now we, as Eastern intellectuals, must think about building this "new race." However, the question remains: how should we build this "new race?" Shariati argues that we have, "the materials for building this human. Those ma-terials are the civilization of the West as the body... the culture of the East, and the pure religion, which is now buried under superstitions, which intellectuals hate, as the soul. These two can make that human."[16] In other words, in his interpretation of Frantz Fanon, Shariati concludes that the reconstruction of Eurocentric modernism in Iran (and in the rest of the non-Western world), is the re-establishment of the metamorphosing relations of Western civilization, which has constrained both the West and the East; and to get out of the ma-trix of these affiliations is needed in order to find a future for humanity. "We," Shariati believes, "as those who are attached to a great religious culture – one of the greatest religions of history," must also make a substantial contribution to that cause.[17] In other words, the West is the body, and the East is the soul, and upon that the true intellectual must rebuild and create this center.

   There are a few key points here: The first is whether the true intellectual can move fluidly between contexts and settings, in order to view the West as a body from an indexicalist position? That is to say, is the subject-object relation only

14   Ibid.
15   Ibid.
16   Ibid.
17   Ibid., 15.

based on mental relations or on objective *and* mental relations? The neglected point in Shariati's thought is that he assumes power is not involved in relations between the subject and object, and "we" can, when we reach self-awareness, turn the "West" into the object of the "East."

The second point is that Eastern culture is not limited to religion, but rather contains other dimensions that are contradictory, opposite, or even parallel to religion. Therefore, to divest the East from its plurality and reduce it to religion will not only damage its history, but also depicts a rather totalitarian future for it.

The third point is the following: if the assumption is true, that the East has a "pure religion," i.e. one freed from superstition, what then is the guarantee that the "pure East" would be able to become the holistic absolute subject and recruit the West in the mode of objectivity?

A fourth concern, which Shariati and his interpretation of Fanon seem to be unaware of, is whether "Western materials" (such as technology and science) are "neutral objects," that under the Eastern soul, and in its pure state, could be employed in the Third World intellectual's project to rebuild that "new race."

It seems that these major drawbacks in Shariati's interpretation of Fanon require a pause for more reflection. Without considering these questions, we might assume that there is no organic connection between Shariati's ideals and political philosophy, and that Shariati's *Ummah and Imam* (the Peoples and the Imam) as a roadmap are separable.

Another important question concerns the "new race" that Shariati proposes: what characteristics does this human have? In other words, when the Third World intellectuals integrate Western civilization and Eastern religion, what kind of future for humanity is being imagined? Shariati puts forth such a vision in the following way:

> a strong and a scientific human, whose virtue is not trampled under the power of civilization, but the power of civilization is at the service of the human spirit and evolution; the human who is not a slave, who is not sub-missive, and who is not trampled under consumptive capitalism, and the human whose machine has not become a tool to crush him, but rather the human is the master of the machine... At that time, the evolved and self-aware human being, who has human spirit and human feelings, even if he utilizes machines, instead of ten hours of work a day, two hours of work in a day would be enough for him. The remaining eight hours, for the human who is self-aware and utilizes machines, would be free for reflection, evolution, evolving spirituality, and building a more human history.[18]

---

18   Ibid., 208.

Nevertheless, the question that can be posed here is whether this future is possible by combining the materials proposed by Shariati in his interpretation on Fanon? Is it possible, in essence, to reduce Western civilization (with all its equipment, both material and spiritual) to the "body" and refine the Eastern religion (with all its dimensions) of "the buried superstitions," and exalt it to the level of "spirit," and then establish the future of humanity on this godly creation?[19]

It seems that beyond this assumption, there is a creative mentality that derives from religious myth (the soul and the body that God creates) and is conceptualized within the framework of the divine *Kon Fa Yakun* ("Be, and it is"), which Shariati has not paid attention to. Mystics and the scholars of the East make a distinction between "God's will" and "human limitation" in the form of the letter "*Fa*" in the phrase "*Kon + Fa + Yakun.*" Additionally, they have said that a universe lies beneath this "*Fa*," and one of its most important components is that humans should avoid repeating the great Deluge of Noah on earth in their attempts to create a "new race." In other words, "divine providence" in religious literature refers to the same human constraints in order to remind humanity that it does not possess the powers of divinity. In my opinion, Shariati's divine ambitions are not derived from religion; rather it belongs to the "modern age" (especially the world of Nietzsche), which attempts to transcend the world in various ways. In other words, if we want to prevent the construction of another Europe in the East, perhaps the most important step is not to see ourselves in the position of divinity and/or holistic absolute subjectivity, contrary to what Shariati says: "If... we want not to turn Asia, Africa, and Latin America, into another America... so... we should not bring back their ideology."[20]

It seems that within a more complex view, Shariati incorporates Eurocentric thinking into an Eastern Dialogue, and this "return of Eurocentric thinking," despite its anti-colonial appearance, is evident in the deeper layers of Shariati's thought. His idea of human divinity coupled with holistic absolute subjectivity, is fundamentally opposed to the religious spirit. Because the main characteristic of the human is to "worship," and human divinity can only be understood in the "*Fa*" [*Kon FaYakun*] (i.e. the gradual world based on choice, consciousness, self-awareness, understanding, and avoidance of violence, as well as compulsion to reach the position of exaltation), and the exit from it, means that we drove the

---

19   Ibid.
20   Ibid., 207.

French, English, and Americans out of Africa and Asia, but... we ourselves
again, have let them in through the [metaphysical] window into [our
mind's] house... [that is, not only did] we return to their views, rights,
constructions, civilization, and thoughts, but we [accepted] Eurocentric
metaphysics, which transposed the [position of humanity] from worship
to divinity as a measure.[21]

However, the question that should be asked is to what extent have these
thoughts influenced Fanon? In other words, how does Fanon view such deifi-
cation of humanity? Is this only Shariati's interpretation of Fanon, or are there
foundations for such an approach within Fanon's thought itself?

1   Civilization and Modernism

In a discussion entitled *Civilization and Modernity*, Shariati argues that intellectuals should be sensitive to such above issues, and in this discussion, he
represents his own interpretation of Fanon. He says:

One of the most sensitive issues, but also the most vital issue that must
be posed today... is the issue of modernity, which we face today in all non-
European societies as well as in Islamic societies.[22]

In other words, Shariati, by distinguishing the concepts of "civilization" and
"modernity," invokes an important debate, often referred to in sociological discussions as "Diverse Modernities." It is argued that either modernity has a fixed
global pattern, or the ways to achieve modernity are fundamentally linked to
the history, religion, culture, and the behavioral patterns of any given society,
with the understanding that one cannot impose a pattern consistent with
the "lived experience of Europe" in all existing contexts. This way of entering
into the debate and proposing diverse modernities, initiated the critique, rejection, and abandonment of the "modernization plans" that were made by
the International Monetary Fund (IMF) and other international institutions,
which were influenced by the Eurocentric models of development. Within this
discussion, a methodological distinction between the concepts of "modernization" and "Westernization" was born. In this context, Shariati states:

---

21   Ibid., 207.
22   Shariati, *Civilization and Modernity*, 361–362.

The most fundamental issue... that we face, as people in this century – a phenomenon that directly deals with our everyday lives, our own destiny and our society, as well as with our beliefs, thoughts, and souls – and also the most sensitive issue for us as Muslims – who are dependent on religion, which has commitment, goal, and direction in the issue of civilization and modernity, human culture, and the worldly life of human – is [to distinguish between] modernity and civilization, [which]... unfortunately... in these [two centuries] modernity, in the name of civilization, has been fed to non-European societies.[23]

In other words, the form of modernity that is "fed to non-European societies" in the name of civilization has created "one of the greatest sufferings [and deviations] ... in today's [non-European] society": "the psychological deviation of non-European personalities."[24] Shariati believes that "we" (i.e. all non-European societies) are suffering from a kind of psychological deviation in our personality structure. But what does this "deviation" mean in Shariati's conceptual system, and how does he interpret this deviation? He says "deviation" can be interpreted as the following:

our realities are something else, but... we feel something else... we feel somebody else; whereas twenty years ago, they were the same non-European countries, but when we entered those societies, although they may not have today's European civilization, they each were themselves: their feelings, their aspirations, their way of working, their spirituality, their delectation, their pleasures, their tastes and their worship, all their work, their arts and their beauties, their religious and philosophical mentality... either good or bad, all in all, were their own.

And when I entered India, for example, or an African country, I knew that it was an African country or India, its taste is its own, it has its own building, the painter paints like a Hindi, a poet writes poetry like himself and has his own Indian pain and his own country's mentality; they have their own sufferings, diseases, aspirations and religion, all of which are their own; while they were weak in terms of the level of civilization and material possessions, all things were their own; they were not sick, although they were poor, and illness is other than poverty.[25]

---

23   Ibid., 362–363.
24   Ibid., 263, 371.
25   Ibid., 371.

Therefore, the deviation in the mind and language of Shariati is that we, instead of taking the Western civilization as the "body," and taking the Eastern culture and religion – erased from superstitions – as "the heart," have acted in the opposite way, that is, we had taken "Western civilization" as the only form of civilization; we have named it "modernity" and ignored the spirit of our Eastern self, and also the religion we adhered to is nothing but superstition and is far from the "pure religion" that once had a heart and movement.[26] In other words, the West,

> to the extent that it has been able to bring manifestations of its own civilization into non-European societies... it has, to the same extent, been able to deliver a philosophical way of thinking, [as well as] beliefs, tastes, and particular behaviors from its society to these societies, societies that are never consistent with those behaviors, mentalities, tastes, and attachments... Thus, outside of European civilization, societies emerged – such as our societies – that are mosaic societies.[27]

These incoherent societies, with the advent of modernity in the "form of civilization" – which essentially means "Westernization," not the possibility of modernity based on the conditions of various subjects – have reached a situation effortlessly controllable by the dominant Western subject, and are manipulated towards the Western markets. Shariati describes this "change situation," or the "rotation of the indigenous people," as follows:

> here European thinkers... have to come up with a certain plan, first of all... to change these non-European peoples' tastes and thoughts; secondly... to change their lifestyle... not that they want to change themselves, because they may change in such ways that they do not become consumers of commodities, but... to change their tastes, favors, sufferings, sorrows and aspirations, ideals and beauties, traditions, recreation, social relationships, and leisure, and so on, in ways that they become consumers... of European goods only. The great producers and great capitalists of Europe in the 18th and 19th centuries gave the plan to the thinkers. The plan is that all people on the planet should be uniform, live in the same way, think in the same way; but it isn't possible that all nations think uniformly.[28]

---

26   Shariati, *History and Recognition of Religions*, 308.
27   Shariati, *Civilization and Modernity*, 371–372.
28   Ibid., 376.

Shariati seeks to provide a framework in which to explain the alienation of non-European cultures and nations, and in this context, poses the following question: "which materials shape the way of thinking in a nation?"[29] In Shariati's view, six fundamental components play a crucial role in shaping social identity: (1) Religion, (2) Culture, (3) History, (4) Past civilization, (5) Education, and (6) Tradition. These are "the factors that shape the personality, mental and intellectual quality, as well as the life of a human, and these are different in every society and region."[30] These components, "each of which have made a kind of society, [produced] a distinct nation [with] distinct tastes, flairs, sufferings, desires and sensitivities, [and created] distinct religions and social relationships."[31] European experts on the other hand, in Shariati's view, define each of these societies within a Euro-centric standpoint, as they attempt, under the name of "modernity," "to [diminish] all non-European societies and the non-European individual in every form and in every way of thinking... our only task as Europeans is to generate the temptation for modernization in those societies."[32] In other words, what Shariati says about the distinction between "civilization" and "modernity" is derived from Fanon's interpretation of the same. But what does Fanon say about the modernization of indigenous people? In Shariati's interpretation of Fanon, we come to the idea that, "Europe wanted to captivate all people... by [way of the] machine; but is it possible that a human [individual] or human society be captivated by a machine or by a particular product of Europe before it has first erased their personality?"[33] The Fanon that Shariati reconstructed gives a considerable answer to this question. It is that every society has an independent identity, which forms the personality of that society and has the constituents of religion, society, history, culture, and tradition. For non-European societies to be captive and subjugated, they must first be "depersonalized."[34] As such, Fanon argues that, in order to subjugate non-Western societies, there must be processes of de-religionization, de-traditionalization, de-civilization, de-educationalization, deculturization, and de-historicization from the essential components of which personalities are constructed. This is precisely because,

> in the 19th century, as an Iranian person, I felt that I am dependent on a great civilization in the 4th, 5th, 6th, 7th and 8th centuries of Islam,

---

29   Ibid., 376.
30   Ibid., 377.
31   Ibid.
32   Ibid.
33   Ibid., 382.
34   Ibid.

which was unique in the world. The whole world was influenced by our civilization. I felt that I was affiliated with a culture of several centuries... that in various forms had created... a new culture, new spirituality, new art and literature; ...and in the name of the human I could feel human personality in myself, against the world, and in front of everyone.[35]

What is the meaning of the last sentence in the paragraph above, which Shariati says in a Fanonian form? Fanon speaks of "depersonalization strategy," and Shariati argues that this strategy is only effective when the personality components of a society are erased and consequently, "I" no longer feel in myself the human personality, with the result that I become reduced from "human" to "indigenous," or from "the subject" to "the object." Therefore, a person who has a sense of belonging and relies on the core constituents – not the imaginary and superficial – withstands subjugation. From that, we must ask the following question: "How such an 'I' can become... something that only consumes new commodities?"[36]

2　　Fanon's Original Theses

In order to understand Fanon, Shariati refers to three of his works. The first, which Shariati introduces as the first book of Fanon, is *Black Skin, White Masks*; the second work is the *Fifth Year of Algerian Revolution*, which "is about the effects of the revolution on commercial and familial relationships, religious ideas, insights, and thoughts about the people."[37] Fanon's third book, from Shariati's point of view, is *The Wretched of the Earth*, in which Fanon says:

> as there are scales to assess the actions of people, a number of them will be sent to heaven, and a number of them to hell on doomsday. In the present earth, we have doomsday as well, as there are 500 million saviors and 1.5 billion wretched people [the world's population was 2 billion at that time], and this wretched majority comes from the third world countries.[38]

35　　Ibid., 383.
36　　Ibid., 383.
37　　Ibid., 417.
38　　Ibid., 420.

Based on these three books, Shariati attempts to interpret Fanon and re-construct the Fanon who put forward the above classifications. Based on these classifications, Shariati evaluates issues regarding "the cultural aspect[s] of colonization."[39] Perhaps one can claim that such a critique is one of the most important dimensions of Shariati's post-colonial theory. At this point, we should review Shariati's interpretation of Fanon in order to identify to what extent it can be included in his overall sociological framework. The reason for this statement is that many sociologists in Iran claim that Shariati is not a soci-ologist, and in their minds a sociologist is one who considers social issues, such as in the translated literature of Emile Durkheim, Max Weber, and Anthony Giddens, despite the fact that there are sociological paradigms more compli-cated that can be analyzed rather than reduced to the views of Durkheim, We-ber, or Giddens. For example, after the 1960s, we encountered the new trio of sociological classics that turned to Marx-Durkheim-Weber, instead of dealing with Weber, Durkheim, Pareto and Smalls. But in Iran, scholars still interpret Marx through the ideology of Marxism, even in Leninist, Stalinist, and Maoist forms, which are very different from the Marxist/ Left/ Post-Left paradigms. In other words, the phrase "Ali Shariati is not a sociologist" requires serious exam-ination. To find out whether Shariati was a sociologist, we first need to know what sociological paradigms are, and what the basic features of the "sociologi-cal pantheon" are, as well as how a theorist can be regarded as a sociologist.

In his works, Shariati addresses the works of Marx, Weber, and Durkheim, as well as other sociologists and academic paradigms of alternative sociology. One of the most prominent of these sociologists is Frantz Fanon and the post-colonial paradigms in sociology, which deal with social affairs in the form of "cultural colonization."

Due to the similarities that may exist in the official discourse of the Islamic Republic and Fanon from a "rhetorical standpoint," this paradigm has created a kind of "theoretical fear" among the scholars of the human sciences, in order to prevent sociology from falling into "the service of the official power," which could reduce its critical nature. This cross-relation is a kind of simplistic re-ductionism that requires a critical analysis. It also constitutes a cross-relation that I reject. To articulate it in a more expressive way, Shariati's interpretation of Fanon enables us not only to restore the Shariatian Fanon, but also allows us the chance to discuss Shariati within a postcolonial existentialist sociological paradigm, and thus move beyond the "non-sociologist Shariati myth."

There are three key theses in Shariati's interpretation of Fanon that form the foundation of Fanon's theory. The first thesis is the idea of "revolution" and

---

39   Ibid., 415.

its effects on the matrix of business and family affiliations, as well as religious beliefs and public opinion. Revolution is one of the most effective components of change. Fanon believes that:

> the impact of social transformation in social relations, especially family and social traditions [has a deep connection with revolution], including the impact on religious and familial traditions, which had been solid and frozen over the centuries and had religious sanctity... If the society wanted to eliminate those traditions by educating and reforming the thought of the society, it needs continuous effort for four to five generations because those traditions took root over the centuries, and such an old tradition cannot be eliminated within one or two generations, and generations must come and pass, in order to gradually eliminate that tradition, and replace it with another tradition, whether good or bad.[40]

Of course, Fanon puts forward *"the originality of the revolution for social transformations"* in this thesis, and Shariati conceptualizes it in "revolutionary self-creation," and even describes the "advent of the prophet" in the Arabian Peninsula, following Fanon's original thesis. Through a Fanonian interpretation of the advent of Islam, Shariati, in his book *The Covenant with Abraham*, says:

> Fanon does not pose the issue of revolution in an epic and heroic manner, rather he represents a detailed analysis of the people of Algeria, who suddenly lose all their old-fashioned and highly-frozen traditions in less than half of a generation, as a result of the spiritual revolution and this change of direction. He believes that due to the length of the historical events, and the history of a nation that continued for two thousand years or more, weaknesses and deviations may be inherent in the nation. Education, training, admonition and advice do not have the potential to eliminate these deviations, but with a sudden change, all people of the nation change their minds and believe in a particular direction... [They] turn to that direction and mobilize, and it is in this mobilization that suddenly, after three to four years, psychological weaknesses, corrupt relationships, and moral degeneration, which has accumulated in their souls for centuries, miraculously disappears.[41]

---

40   Ibid., 420.
41   Ali Shariati, *Collected Works no. 29. Miaad ba Ebrahim* (Covenant with Abraham). (Tehran: Didar publication, 2012), 524–525.

In other words, the Medina community

> is organized under the leadership of Muhammad and his followers, a
> society full of human weakness and corruption; because the forming ele-
> ments are tribal – people who have no civilization and culture except pil-
> lage and war – from the psychological point of view, these menial people
> cannot form a superior composite, but they were able to... These deca-
> dent tribes and people, when they found a certain social orientation and
> ideology, [having been mobilized], eliminated all the moral weaknesses,
> all deviations, and corruptions that their society accepted throughout
> the ages. After ten years they [were] excellent humans [with an] excel-
> lent society.[42]

In other words, Shariati accepts the thesis *"the originality of the revolution for
social transformations"* in his analysis, and remarks that "Fanon provides examples of some of these traditions which will not be lost over the course of
several centuries."[43] What are the examples that Fanon provides? Is the method by which a sociologist confronts a theory the same as the one that Shariati
shows us? In other words, should a sociologist first talk about a theory and
list its main components and then list examples that empirically corroborate
the theory? Shariati explains the examples that Fanon provides to bolster his
"originality of the revolution for social transformation" thesis:

> Before 1954, families in North Africa maintained strong traditions, which
> were established by history, religion, or both. History means the passing
> of from generation to generation... the spirit of the society, the social con-
> ditions, and the set of factors that make the society. Religion is, keeping
> herself away from the eyes of the father after the ages of seven to eight,
> which, of course, has various degrees: in some families they do not see
> each other at all, and in some others, the daughter should wear a hijab
> in front of her father and her brother, and even in some cases in front
> of her mother, and this is because of the shame and modesty which is
> placed like a slave between a father and an adolescent daughter. This is
> a tradition that cannot be easily changed. It is easy to change the way of
> thinking, reasoning, and even enlightenment, but it is difficult to change
> the taste, tradition, spirit and habit, which has taken deep roots... over
> generations. However, these traditions can change rapidly – even in a few

---

42   Ibid., 525.
43   Ibid.

years, that is, one generation – when all people try to achieve a common goal and believe in it.[44]

In other words, by accepting the thesis of the *originality of the revolution* in a Fanonian form, and interpreting this originality as "having a common goal and pursuing it," Shariati concludes that:

> There are other societies... in which everything (tradition, morality, social relations, etc.) have degenerated and it seems they never change, or a society that is aging and ill [wherein] the causes of its destruction [are many]. But a social miracle changes all these predictions in a way that was not conceivable, by having a common goal and pursuing it. In the meantime, all those effects, which have been ingrained in the spirit of the nation, disappear like a social miracle, once they face a phenomenon that was not only unpredictable, but was not even imaginable.[45]

Shariati tries to assess the samples provided by Fanon with other samples, and then conceptualizes the specific examples in a generalized format. This is what all sociologists employ in the human sciences. Shariati takes the distinction Fanon makes between "reasoning" and "taste" seriously, and believes that it might be possible to influence the first through learning, school, training, and education, and change it in a short period of time, but "taste" cannot be easily changed precisely because they are old habits and traditions that dominate people's soul, and therefore do not easily change. This Fanonian distinction, which Shariati has reconstructed and accepted in his social transformation theory, is one of the most important components of the theory of the *originality of the revolution*, which has not been dealt with adequately in the context of Iranian sociology. This, in my opinion, is significant, and can be studied in order to understand the historical changes in contemporary Iranian society, in the "constitutional" and "Islamic" revolutions, and the changes in Iranian society after the establishment of the Islamic Republic. For instance, the point Shariati puts forward pertaining to Fanon's example of the northern African families' approach to the girls' adolescence, has striking similarity to the fatwā by Shi'i authorities on women's social roles in the years leading to the revolution in 1357A.H. (1979 CE), in which some argued that a woman's presence alongside men in the demonstrations against the Pahlavi Regime was not permissible

---

44   Shariati, *The History of Civilization,* 417–418.
45   Ibid., 418.

"according to Shari'a." But the revolution changed many of the consolidated traditions. For example, in Fanon's instance, it is clearly obvious that,

> All these rooted traditions (hiding the girls from their fathers between the ages of sixteen and twenty) change fast and intensively, and the opposite becomes the order of the day. In a way that the same girls who become the Mujahidin lose whatever love they have for their country, and not only do their families not disapprove of their actions, but their actions and the sufferings... appear to be their pride; they [actually] encourage them. We can easily see how their way of thinking changed in a short period of time (during one generation), a matter that takes several generations in normal times.[46]

It seems that Shariati does not follow the distinction Fanon makes between "reasoning" and "taste" in a coherent and logical way. In the above reference, Shariati says "we could easily see how their way of thinking changed in a short time," but earlier in the same reference, he states, "it is easy to change the way of thinking... but it is difficult to change the taste."[47] Because that is within the same line of thought, the following questions might be raised: Do revolutions only temporarily change already established ways of thinking? Are they incapable of transforming tastes? If the people do not resist changing their way of thinking for a short period of time, is it just because of the particular revolutionary situation? Last, once the "revolutionary fever" has subsided, will the rooted traditions come back? In my opinion, this is the question that Fanon and the Shariatian Fanon should answer, and those who believe in "*the originality of the revolution for social transformations*," should answer with references with historical examples.

The second thesis of Fanon, within Shariati's interpretation, which is an extract from the book *The Wretched of the Earth*, is the concept of "childhood." Shariati does not consider this concept under Fanon's *universal* theory, but interprets it as a *socially bound* theory. In other words, the second thesis, "of Fanon is that childhood and the child boy is eliminated by social transformations."[48]

What does this concept mean? What does Fanon want to say? What is meant by the phrase "social transformations eliminate childhood," and from Fanon's thesis, what conclusion has Shariati obtained for his sociological

---

46   Ibid., 417–418.
47   Ibid.
48   Ibid., 419.

understanding?[49] Shariati argues that in order to understand Fanon's concept of "childhood," which stands in relation to social changes, attention should be paid to the following matter:

> The child is very sweet for parents and relatives up to the age of six or seven, and captures everyone's attention and affection. Gradually, as they approached the ages of eight or nine, they receive less attention and are left on their own until they reach puberty; this means that they go through an interim period in which the child is forgotten. Not that they leave them alone, but they are no longer the center of attention, that is, they are neither sweet nor sufficiently taken seriously. The ages of six or seven are the period of childhood, after which they find themselves talking to adults. This means they become a real audience: a real speaker or listener, but on a lower level.[50]

In other words, Shariati maintains that Fanon

> investigates this [conception] of childhood, which can be seen in the West. [He notes that it] increases the more one goes from the south to the north. This period takes ten, twelve, or thirteen years in European and American societies. In the north of Europe, it takes thirteen to fourteen years, and in the south of Europe, nine to ten years. It takes four, five, or six years for the under-developed countries.[51]

In my opinion, this is a very interesting point. For those who argue that Shariati was not a sociologist, Shariati's approach to the problem of "childhood," from a comparative perspective, and in the framework of Fanon's theory, should be studied. Shariati, through his interpretation of Fanon, seemingly "de-biologizes" a biological theme, thus posing the issue of childhood within a sociological framework. He says that if we look at the issue of childhood and its relation to the interim period between "childhood" and "puberty," then we will see that,

> The cause [of difference between developed and under-developed countries in relation to childhood] ... is that in an under-developed country, the child works from the age of 9, and therefore they cannot be neglected and/or forgotten because there is no time to be forgotten: the child is

---

49   Ibid.
50   Ibid.
51   Ibid.

not only a little boy but is also a worker and a brother who has a unique relationship to society, as he financially contributes to the family. A child who, for example, weaves carpets, is not in an interim period, he feels everything, poverty, distress, impecuniousness; He knows suffering, deprivation, ignorance, and oppression; He suffers from the difference between his class and the employer's class. He knows there are many things he has never seen or eaten, and there are many things he does and others do not do. This is the level of his thought; one has to talk to him because he is serious and he feels all the bitter issues of life deep down in his existence.[52]

Nonetheless, due to social differences, seemingly biological structures undergo fundamental changes. In Europe, for example, compared to North Africa, "a child at the age of [nine]... has a non-serious spirit and doesn't understand anything of the world. Eighteen to Nineteen-years-old girls and boys play with toys and are childish."[53]

Shariati derives interesting results from Fanon's thesis: First, the border between "the sociological matter" and "the biological matter" is not biologically solvable; rather it is "bound culturally." Second, social problems are not merely analyzable in the form of "universal matter," rather general matters should be studied dialectically in relation to particular matters. Third, more so (and earlier) than many Western, African, and Indian scholars, Shariati concluded that Fanon was not merely "a psychiatrist," but rather that his ideas contained important sociological perspectives, which he began to develop more than 50 years ago. Thus, it is not mistaken to speak of "Shariati's interpretation" of Fanon's "sociological discourse" today. As such, Shariati believes that "childhood" is not merely a biological matter, but also a social one. He says, that according to the Fanon's theory,

> [childhood] is shortened in poor families, and in the same society, when it comes to social and political self-awareness, it is almost eliminated... [once in puberty] the child can feel that there are things which he does not have, while others have them, even though he is no less talented... this makes him... feel impoverished.[54]

---

52   Ibid., 419–420.
53   Ibid., 420.
54   Ibid.

The feeling of poverty "is beyond poverty itself, like a sense of ignorance that is other than ignorance itself. The feeling of poverty and backwardness has a social value, not poverty itself."[55] Therefore, for societies that are in a state of poverty, backwardness, colonialism, ignorance, and exploitation, the mission of the intellectual "is to distinguish between the feeling of poverty and poverty itself, so that people can understand correctly the border between reality and the feeling of reality."[56]

Fanon's third thesis, within Shariati's interpretation, which appears to be based on his interpretation of the book *The Wretched of the Earth*, refers to the ways in which system formations occur in *wretched* societies (the Third World countries which were colonized). In other words, Fanon's third thesis, "which strongly influenced Africa, is that all societies in the Third World must come under a system of industrial unity, with a unified lifestyle, and their intellectuals must strive to make them a unified race."[57] Of course, this aspect of Fanon's statements requires serious critique. Yet, it is necessary to first refer to Shariati's political philosophy, which is beautifully depicted in the book *Ummah and Imam* (the Peoples and the Imam), in order to understand this statement. Many followers of Shariati argue that this work is marginal and should not be taken seriously. However, to respond to these approaches, those critics should refer to Shariati's concept of the "the third way," which he developed out of his interpretation on Fanon.

In other words, Fanon in his third thesis presents an exquisite concept: "A unified lifestyle." This notion must be taken as the basis of the "unified race" as well as the "anti-capitalist society," while the "industrial" must be created under the leadership of the intellectuals, because "the role of the intellectuals in these societies is greater."[58] In Shariati's view, based on his interpretation of Fanon, the basic duty of the intellectual is "to build the Third World on the basis of 'the unified race,' but the concept of 'race' in relation to 'the Third World' should not be conceptualized in a biological sense. The 'Third World' (*tiers monde*) refers to 'all the countries of the world that have not reached industry-derived wealth via capitalism,' and for the same reasons, "they have common characteristics."[59] In other words, the concept of "the unified race" must be understood in relation to these "common characteristics," not in relation to the color of the skin or race in a biological sense. This point can be found in both

---

55   Ibid.
56   Ibid.
57   Ibid., 419–421.
58   Ibid., 420.
59   Ibid., 421.

Fanon's and Shariati's thought. It is from Fanon, reconstructed through Shariati's mind and language, that,

> The shared aspect of the nations is neither religion, nor language... But rather a common painful situation. Therefore, since the painful situation is shared, and the Third World countries are subject to a common danger (the incursion of capital and industry), they must be united.[60]

Yet, the question that arises here is: "how can the commonality and unity of these very different countries, with a diverse history, culture, nationality, ethnicity, language, and civilization, take shape? Is such a coalition even possible?"[61] To answer this question, Shariati poses another question: "how does this... unity develop? Essentially, it arises when they face their opposition."[62]

When we talk about the Third World and its relation to colonization, we must always be aware that the underdeveloped countries have a common painful situation that places them against the capitalist world in a similar fashion. Now, as Shariati explains,

> The industrial and capitalist world is rapidly moving towards its path, and the movement is so fast that no matter how much the Third World strives and moves forward, the distance increases day by day... Therefore, the Third World countries are influenced by [industrial capitalism], and the Third World's destiny is in their hands, as they are stronger in terms of both spirituality and wealth.[63]

The result of Fanon's third thesis as interpreted by Shariati is that we should make a fundamental distinction between "industrialization" and "capitalization," and do not endanger the "unified race" that will be born in the future with the pernicious lie, which states that "in order to industrialize, we must be capitalist," because capitalism is "dangerous." That is why Fanon says: "We should not turn Africa into another America; the ill experience of America is enough for us. That is, these countries [or the future race] should become industrialized in a way other than through capitalism."[64]

---

60   Ibid.
61   Ibid.
62   Ibid.
63   Ibid.
64   Ibid.

Shariati, indeed, argues that this thesis of Fanon "strongly influenced Africa."[65] But today it has been revealed to us that the distinction between "industrialization" and "capitalism" is not commensurate to the reality of the existing world order. In other words, if we do not adopt capitalism, our industry will not flourish. Africa's slow course of industrialization may be attributed to the effects of this Fanonian thesis, which proved not to be conducive for attracting capital.

We might criticize Shariati for the same reason in regards to Iran; did his interpretation of Fanon place Iranian society on the same "no industrialization" and "no capitalism" path? This is because, in my opinion, his idea of a "unified race," with its "common painful situation," is not solely based on ontology and anthropology, but on "political economy." The logic for this economy can be examined in Shariati's own works. In other words, when Shariati, in his interpretation of Fanon, says that we should not turn Africa into another America, he certainly speaks of Iranian society as a part of the Third World, which has the same "common painful situation" and is faced with a common threat by industrial capitalism. He clearly tells Iranians not to turn Iran into the United States, because the exploitation derived from American capitalism "is extremely violent."[66] Therefore, in order to establish the Third World and its "unified race," which can serve as the savior of humanity, there must be an economic design that leads to industrialization, "under a unified industrial system and a unified lifestyle," without causing this savior race to embrace capitalism.

What strategy should the Third World have? How should the political economy of the Third World, along with its different ontologies and anthropologies, be designed?

Indeed, there are many similarities between the Shariatian/Fanonian discourse and post-Pahlavi discourses in contemporary Islamic Republic of Iran, and these discourses should be examined. In this regard, I disagree with the scholars who, in both positive and negative manners, claim that there is no connection between Shariati's discourse and a post-Pahlavi discourse. I also contend that there is a deep affinity between Shariati's discourse and the idea of a new Islamic civilization in the Islamic Republic that requires critical review.

On the original question – Shariati's proposed economic policies for the Third World – we will consider the prospects he prescribes for Third World industrialization without capitalism. In his interpretation of Fanon, Shariati maintains that, "We should not turn Africa into another America; the ill

---

65   Ibid., 420.
66   Ibid., 423.

experience of America is enough for us; that is, these countries should become industrialized in a way other than capitalism."[67] The question posed here is: what should be done? If industrialization without capitalism is possible and desirable, what pattern does Shariati conceive? Is Shariati's model a kind of socialism on the "Soviet model," which existed in the Soviet Union, the Eastern bloc, or in countries like China, Cuba, and Latin America? Or, does Shariati envision other models? Was Shariati envisioning something closer to the "Scandinavian model"? Or did Shariati intend none of these models. I contend that he sought "synthetic models" that could meet the needs of the complex society of Iran as well as the rest of the Third World?

In my opinion, Shariati's approach to economic and matters of political-economy could be a separate inquiry. However, I am going to highlight the following point: The relationship between Shariati's philosophy of politics and his perspectives on political-economy on one hand, and his anthropology and ontology debates on the other, is very deep, therefore, it is impossible to claim that these discussions are not connected. Additionally, if Shariati had said a word on this in *Ummah and Imam* (The Peoples and the Imam), it could be regarded as an immature facet of Shariati's political philosophy, which can essentially be interpreted in the context of "committed democracy." Thus, we should not associate Shariati's anthropological and ontological dimensions with these political arguments and philosophies, or even political economy. I disagree with the above-mentioned opinions; as I mentioned in my 2016 book *Shariati and Heidegger.* Shariati's was concerned with the conceptualization of a "different kind" of social living and ecosystem of civilization, and in order to create this, he tried to portray all possible dimensions of human life within a general schema.[68]

With the Fanonian distinction between "industrialization" and "capitalism," Shariati accepted Fanon's conclusion, considering "industrialization" as the path forward, while considering capitalism as "modern savagery." His strategy for the industrialization of the Third World, including Iran, is that, "A country with small industries... cannot become industrial... because (in such a situation) it will always be in need of other countries."[69]

What then is to be done? What steps should the Third World take to industrialize and prevent capitalism from spreading into non-capitalist societies? Shariati, in his interpretation of Fanon, which is based on the "unified industrial system," states that one of the first steps for the Third World is to move

---

67   Ibid., 421.
68   Seyed Javad Miri, *Shariati and Heidegger,* Tehran: Naghd Farhang, 2016.
69   Shariati, *The History of Civilization,* 422.

"in the way of the heavy industry."[70] Thus, the Third World has to turn to "the basic industries and primary production" in order to avoid relying on other countries.[71] Of course, Shariati is aware of the limitations of this thesis in the context of liberal capitalism and the Cold War, and argues that the Third World must take steps towards instituting basic industries and primary production. Yet, it is almost impossible from a strategic perspective, because,

> The social form of these countries (as they are now) is limited in two ways: the quantity of consumer acceptance and the quality of consumer acceptance. The quantity of consumer acceptance, the number of people who buy, is not high enough for heavy industry to work and for marketing opportunities, because heavy industry is constantly producing and the market should absorb it. The quality of consumer acceptance is also limited, that is, of the same potential purchasers and consumers, only a minority are buyers and consumers. A place may have a population of 300 million, but not all have the purchasing power of such industries. The quality of consumption acceptance means the buyer's power.[72]

Because of this, the Third World would face fundamental challenges in the capitalist world, and it would not be easy to escape the intra-system constraints. In his interpretation of Fanon, Shariati is trying to find a way out of this paradox, but his strategy requires a serious overhaul.

Of course, it is worth mentioning that Fanon had visited the Soviet Union, and that he was closely acquainted with the Soviet Union's common market system. In my opinion, the solution that Shariati puts forward in his interpretation of Fanon is based on the distinction between "industrialization" and "capitalism." He also speaks about the "one system, one industrial unity, and a unified lifestyle," which was closely linked to the "Soviet form" that had a special place in the mind of Fanon, which Shariati had internalized.[73]

Is this impression correct or based on speculation? It seems that Shariati, in the book *The Features of the New Century,* in the chapter on Third World "pioneers of returning," has made clear indications towards this "Soviet form," which requires serious consideration. In order to overcome the problems of

---

70   Ibid., 420.

71   Ibid., 422.

72   Ibid.

73   William W. Hansen, "Another side of Frantz Fanon: Reflections on Socialism and Democracy," *New Political Science* 19, no. 3 (1997): 89–111.

quantity and quality in consumer acceptance, Shariati refers to a key point: He argues that this challenge is serious and the Third World must find a solution to overcome these problems. He writes, "firstly, the [Third World's] goods are expensive, and then they become classical (that is, like the old times); they are forced to purchase cheaper goods from the outside, as it was with airplane manufacturing."[74] What should we do if we want to "industrialize," thus freeing us of the "need [for] other countries," while avoiding becoming involved in capitalism, while also creating "a unified race," so that we are no longer among "the wretched of the earth"? How could we achieve these goals? In Shariati's view, a system of manufacturing and exchange between Third World countries must be established, wherein the products of heavy industries within Third World countries find markets outside of Europe. As one nation within this system produces a particular heavy industry, the others do not. Shariati says, "In this way, they can both have heavy industry and have no need for the Western capitalist system."[75]

This seems to be the "Soviet model," which was set up in the fifteen republics of the Soviet Union. The reason for the existence of this system was that Russia had been able to shatter the sovereignty of other countries. In other words, these republics were settled as autonomous oblasts under the central Russ state of the Soviet Union. Otherwise, without damaging the sovereignty of the Third World countries, there was no possibility of managing these countries, as it was impossible for any one country to tell another country not to establish an industry because it was already established in another, or that the markets of the Third World have no need for European markets and goods.

In other words, Fanon defined the Soviet model as a model of socialism and democracy, and Shariati, disregarding the concept of "national sovereignty," naively presented it as a solution to industrialization and capitalism. It would supposedly liberate peoples from colonial rule and establish the "savior race." Nevertheless, it was in fact Soviet-style communism, which has nothing to do with the "Social Democracy of Scandinavia." Some in Iran, of course, claim that Shariati's perception of the "Left Movement" has been a Social-Democratic interpretation in the mold of Scandinavia, but I consider this claim to be dubious, because the solution that Shariati offers in his new century strongly resembles the "Soviet model," not the "Scandinavian model."

---

74   Shariati, *The History of Civilization*, 422.
75   Ibid.

3   The Colonized and the Colonizer

One of the most important concepts in Ali Shariati's social theory is the concept of "colonialism/colonization." In this context, Shariati's interpretation
of Fanon has a special place, since Fanon used the concepts of "colonialism,"
"alienation," and "race" in a cohesive fashion in his theoretical framework. Unlike Karl Marx, Max Weber and Emile Durkheim, Fanon does not ignore the
relationship between "race" and "ethnicity" within colonialism, but rather sees
a decisive relationship between colonial culture and the "race" issue. In *The
History of Civilization*, Shariati makes a point that is worth noting:

> A quarter of the century ago, a new human, culture, era, and religion
> began... We are at the threshold of a new insight that... begun in our
> world; it shows that if the Renaissance was the new beginning of culture
> and civilization in Europe, the new Renaissance is the culture of an era
> which is to found outside of Europe, and that Europe itself is affected by
> this movement.[76]

In other words, the era of Eurocentrism is nearing its end. The post-colonial
movements have opened up space in a Post-Eurocentric world, and in doing so
have given humanity new possibilities. Yet, one must not forget that there are
serious obstructions to the emergence of the "new race" or "new human." What
are the obstructions facing the Post-Eurocentric human? In Shariati's view,

> one of the signs of the alienation illness is degeneration and self-
> depreciation of a human against another human, or even another civi-
> lization, which the second-hand human neither has the courage to
> recognize nor the ability to recognize, because the ability of recognize
> depends on the individual's brain power to understand a scientific issue,
> and the courage to recognize [such a reality] depends on the bravery and
> the spiritual and moral independence of a person.[77]

In the above quote, Shariati aptly refers to the "degeneration of civilization,"
and argues that one of the serious obstructions to creating the Post-Eurocentric
civilization is the state of the internalized objectivity that the non-European
human has been entangled in. According to Shariati, based on this modality,
the non-European has lost both the "ability for recognition" and the "courage

76   Ibid., 252.
77   Ibid.

for recognition." Nevertheless, the question is, in what context, and within what relations, has this lack of personality and lack of courage been created? It is essential to mention that Shariati poses the non-Europeans' objectivity within the framework of "alienation," but his interpretation of alienation is closer to Fanon's. In the book, *The History of Civilization,* in his discussion on "self-discovering," Shariati refers to Fanon's essay *Racism and Culture,* and argues that Fanon puts forward a distinct theoretical interpretation of alienation in the framework of post-colonial theory.

As far as I have been able to find, Fanon never wrote a book entitled *Racism and Culture.* However, Shariati, in the book *History of Civilization,* Volume II, in the chapter on the issue of "self-discovering," refers to such a book. "According-ing to Fanon," he quotes, "in the book *Racism and Culture,* in order to alienate, restrict, tame, and be imitative, one must introduce them to themselves as an inferior race via racism."[78]

Now, before I begin the discussion on the content of Fanon, or Shariati's interpretations of Fanon, on degeneration and self-depreciation, I will briefly reflect on the book *Racism and Culture.* In September of 1956, Frantz Fanon delivered a lecture (in French) in Paris at the First Congress of Negro Writ-ers and Artists, and this speech, entitled "Racism and Culture," was published in the Special Issue of the *Presence Africaine* journal in the June/November 1956 issue. Later, in 1980, the lecture was published by an authorized publisher in London, as a preface to the book *Toward the African Revolution.* This key speech, however, went on another path, which has caused paradoxical confu-sions in the context of Shariati's references.

Based on my research, in Iran, a researcher named Manouchehr He-zarkhani, a member of the *Mojâhedin-e khalq Organization* (MKO) (Peoples' Mujahedin of Iran), was a translator of works from French to Persian, who seems to have had close literary ties with Jalal al-Ahmad.[79] Hezarkhani had collected four articles from Aliouin Deep, Frantz Fanon, Aymah Henus, and Jacques Rabemananjara, and published these articles in a book titled *Racism and Culture* 1968 by Ibn Sina publications in Tabriz. Thus, Fanon neither wrote a book called *Racism and Culture* in French, nor a book originally existed with this title in French; nevertheless, there are a collection of articles with differ-ent titles that have been published in Persian by Manuchehr Hezarkhani with the title derived from Frantz Fanon's lecture. The translator in the preface of this book explicitly states that,

---

78   Shariati, *The History of Civilization,* 252.

79   The MKO joined Saddam Hussein's Front against Iran under Masoud Rajavi's leadership, after the Islamic Revolution and the 1960s confrontations.

In his first global congress with the writers, poets and black men of culture, which was held in Paris in 1956, while discussing the specific cultural issues of black people, he addressed and examined this issue, which afflicted the whole colonized world. The translation of these reports and analyses are collected in this booklet.[80]

This booklet was a collection of lectures by four key personalities in the "Negritude" movement, who established the philosophy of the black anti-discourse. But Shariati's re-interpretation of this discourse in the context of Iran seems to require a critical interpretation. "Race" and "skin color," in the framework of the Iranian discourse against colonialism, as opposed to the discourse of the Black African struggle in Africa, Latin and North America, as well as in Madagascar and the Caribbean, despite significant similarities in the political and economic areas, had fundamental differences.

Of course, Shariati, in his book *Eslamshenasi* (Islamology) (V.2), mentions the existing differences in the global anti-colonization front. He states:

> This was a matter of three private letters between me and Frantz Fanon. Then he criticized this issue, the reliance on religion, and his criticism is like many of the great, committed, and truly human and libertarian intellectuals, who believed that in the anti-colonization world, in which all intellectuals should try to get all the fronts of thought in one orientation, and with one insight, and enter one path of thought (for their common and united struggle, which is the rejection of colonization, take place in the world scale), the reliance on religion will infect this great unity with sectarian and religious divisions.[81]

It seems that Shariati has neglected one important point, and that is if we consider the distinctions "unimportant," the formation of a united front is not possible arising from the failure to focus on the fundamental differences that exist in the confrontation with colonization. For example, Fanon considered "religion" as an obstruction, and Shariati completely ignored the "Negritude Discourse" in Fanon's philosophy, thus generalizing the "racism experience" (against the black race) to other cultural aspects of colonization. In other words, careless generalizations can seriously damage our theoretical frameworks, and

---

80   Hezarkhani, Manouchehr. *Nezhadparasti va farhang* (Racism and Culture). Tabriz: Ibn Sina Publications, 1968.

81   Ali Shariati, *Collected Works no. 17. Eslamshenasi* (Islamology Vol. 2.) (Tehran: Ghalam, 2011), 193–194.

therefore we must try to critically examine the variant dimensions of Shariati's interpretation of Fanon so that we can attain the results that can develop and amplify the existentialist post-colonial discourse in Iranian sociology and post-colonial social theory, without being trapped in careless generalizations.

Now, after this brief introduction, we turn to Shariati's interpretation of Fanon's theory about the colonized and the colonizer. Shariati states that, according to Fanon,

> In order to make someone alienated, restricted, tame, and imitative, one must introduce them to themselves as an inferior race via racism. Once they feel that they belong to an inferior race, an "escape from themselves" shapes them, and all the efforts will shift to shunning away from their race... In order to reach the level of the superior race, in every possible way, they will imitate everything from the superior race.[82]

In other words, Europeans humiliate others in terms of race, culture, and humanity; the reaction by the humiliated is to "get away from themselves to immunize themselves from the humiliated 'self,' and reject themselves by pretending to be European in order to escape their own self-contempt."[83]

There is a kind of dialectic in this matter; because of the predominance of the culture of colonization, the humiliated self of the "Black" (or everyone else against the European) "escapes from themselves," and to the extent that they get away from their real identity, it is in direct proportion to that caused by the colonialism. Shariati considers the relationship between, "the colonized and... the colonizer [as] the dialectical relationship of the child and the mother. The mother attacks the child and the child takes refuge in the mother's arm to protect itself from the mother's attack, and [in doing so] embraces her."[84]

How can "Dominique Sourdel's dialectic" be removed? If we want to consider Shariati's interpretations of Fanon as a base, and from this perspective consider "the civilizational degeneration" of Iran (the Islamic world and the broader non-European world), what is the solution?

Shariati contends that in order to free a person (and a civilization) from alienation, restriction, taming, and imitation, we cannot rely on "science, industry, politics, and... war," or "work.... and economics," because they are not components that create human civilization, but they are the cause of other

---

82   Shariati, *Covenant with Abraham*, 252–253.
83   Ibid. 253.
84   Ibid.

transformations.[85] Nonetheless, the question is: what kind of transformation should be done to change the ruling relations between "the colonized" and "the colonizer," which would allow for the colonized human to become free from alienation, restrictiveness, timidity, and imitativeness? Shariati, with his interpretation of Fanon, argues that,

> I believe that since a quarter of a century ago, a new civilization has been in the process of evolving, and a new human being is being born... and... tomorrow's civilization will arise... not [from] North America, not [from] France and England, or Germany and Italy... but from the depths of the Third World, Asia, Africa, and Latin America. [It will rise] not from the Sorbonne, Harvard, and Cambridge universities... but from the primitive tribes of the Black Africa, the yellow hungry peasants, and the illiterate intellectuals emerging from the heart of the people, they grow like patient and assertive trees from the heart of infernal deserts; as this is how prophethood gives birth to new history, culture, and civilization.[86]

In other words, Shariati claims that what builds civilization and brings about transformations of human history is not "work tools" or "economic tools," but a more important component must be transformed in order to see more fundamental changes in social relations. But the question is: what is the key component that Shariati has derived from Fanon's view? Shariati states:

> What makes civilization and culture is not science, not industry, not politics, not war, not work, not economics, but new insights. In every era, when the insight has changed, a civilization has arisen. Therefore, the emergence of a civilization and a new movement is due to the emergence of a new insight.[87]

Shariati believes that de-colonization movements are the preludes to these new insights that have gone on to shape the foundations of the "new race" against the "capitalist human" and the "Soviet human." Moreover, he seems to be involved in the rhetoric of "Post-Marxist Left," in the form of Fanon's Negritude philosophy, by what he refers to as "cultural prophethood," which has no close sense to the religious understanding of prophethood; rather, it represents

---

85   Ibid., 254.
86   Ibid., 254–255.
87   Ibid., 254.

the semantic system of Post-Marxist discourse in the framework of Negritude philosophy, which requires serious critique and analysis.

Is it possible today, in the depths of the Third World, to find universities similar to the Sorbonne, Harvard, and Cambridge? Would "the new race" thrive among the isolated tribes of Black Africa, or among the hungry Asian peasants and illiterate intellectuals? Shariati brings to the surface a correct point, and that is the importance of "new insights" and their relevance to the "era," which requires serious conceptualization. The rhetorical internalization of the "Negritude Movement" (the Black Movement) does not help to expand Shariati's theoretical framework, but leads to "Poesy" poetry, rather than to a kind of "awareness."

In conclusion, in order to overcome the alienation of colonialism, and the transformation of colonial relations, we need to critique the internalized Post-Marxist discourses that have entered Shariati's discourse in both poetic and epic forms. It seems that Shariati's interpretation of Fanon, and Fanon's thesis that "we should not turn the Third World into another Europe (like America)," has led to Shariati's indulgence towards "the primitive tribes" as "the creators of new history, culture, and civilization, and the cultivators of a new human race."[88]

Bibliography

Al-e-Ahmad, Jamal. *Noun Val Ghalam*. 8th edition. Tehran: Meyar Andisheh, 2016.

Bauman, Zygmunt. *Modernity and the Holocaust*. Ithaca, NY: Cornell University Press, 1989.

Fanon, Frantz. *Toward the African Revolution*. London: Writers and Readers Publishing Cooperative, 1980.

Gibson, Nigel C. and Roberto Beneduce. *Frantz Fanon, Psychiatry and Politic: Creolizing the Canon*. Rowman & Littlefield Publishers Inc., 2017.

Hansen, William W. "Another side of Frantz Fanon: Reflections on Socialism and Democracy." *New Political Science* 19, no. 3 (1997): 89–111.

Hezarkhani, Manouchehr. *Nezhadparasti va farhang* (Racism and Culture). Tabriz: Ibn Sina Publications, 1968.

Miri, Seyed Javad. *Azadi vatarikh: tamoli bar nagah e ensanshenasi Shariati* (History and Freedom). Tehran: Naghdefarhang, 2017.

Miri, Seyed Javad. *Shariati and Heidegger*. Tehran: Naghd Farhang, 2016.

----

88   Ibid., 255.

Shariati, Ali. *Collected Works no. 14. Tarikh shenakht e adyan* (History and Recognition of Religions) Vol. 1. Tehran: SahamiEnteshar, 2009.

Shariati, Ali. *Collected Works no. 17. Eslamshenasi* (Islamology Vol. 2.). Tehran: Ghalam, 2011.

Shariati, Ali. *Collected Works no. 24. Ensan* (Human). Tehran: Elham, 2011.

Shariati, Ali. *Collected Works no. 29. Miaad ba Ebrahim* (Covenant with Abraham). Tehran: Didar publication, 2012.

Shariati, Ali. *Collected Works no. 28. Raveshibarayeshenakht e eslam* (An approach to the understanding of Islam). Tehran: Chabakhsh publication, 2014.

Shariati, Ali. *Collected works no.12. Tarikh tamaddon* (The History of Civilization Vol. 2.). Tehran: Ghalam, 2015.

Shariati, Ali. *Collected Works no. 31. Vizhegihayeghoroun e jaded* (Characteristics of Contemporary Century). Tehran: Chabakhsh publication, 2015.

Tabatabaei, Seyyed Javad. *Ibn Khaldunvaolum e ejtemaei* (Ibn Khaldun and Sociology). Tehran: Saleth publication, 2011.

Tabatabaei, Seyyed Javad. *Khaje Nezamol Molk Tousi.* (Sir Nezam al-Molk Tousi). Tehran: Minouye kherad publication, 2013.

Tabatabaei, Seyyed Javad. *Zeval e andisheye siasi dar Iran* (Decline of Political Thought in Iran). Tehran: Kavir publication, 2015.

CHAPTER 10

Fanon and Biopolitics

Pramod K. Nayar

This chapter argues that biopolitics as engendered in Fanon's work mobilizes injury, vulnerability, affect, and risk, in order to foreground the possibilities for the reclamation of the black body: a rehumanization. Proceeding from the discussion of the loss of a form-of-life and embodied dignity to the public insurgencies of voluntary exposure, Fanon maps a trajectory for the dehumanized colonized native.

1 The Black Body and its Dignity

Throughout *Black Skins, White Masks*, Fanon argued that the black man is increasingly "locked" into his body. As Laura Chrisman observes, "pain," in Fanon's reading of the black body, "results from the loss of connection to that black body, or more specifically, from the loss of corporeal self-possession."[1] Racial difference, plotted on the skin, determines everything else: "distinctions of bare and good life... allows for the possibility and production of difference and the enactment of violence in the form of conflict and terror/antagonism asymmetrically."[2] Fanon would famously describe his separation from his objectified black self in biomedical terms: "an amputation, an excision, a hemorrhage that spattered my whole body with black blood."[3] Alan Ramón Ward would gloss this Fanon passage, directing us to the objectification of the body for the black man: "Fanon's black man, as a unified subject, experiences his own constitutive desire as externalised, and calcified in material objects – as the object – that experience."[4] Stephanie Clare's incisive essay on Fanon focuses on his biopolitics, where even he "locates the beginnings of decolonization within

---

1 Laura Chrisman, "The Vanishing Body of Frantz Fanon in Paul Gilroy's *Against Race* and *After Empire*," *The Black Scholar* 41, no.4 (2011): 18–30, cited from 21.
2 Ibid., 117.
3 Frantz Fanon. *Black Skin, White Masks*, trans. Charles Lam Markmann (London: Pluto, 2008), 185.
4 Alan Ramón Ward, "Redefining Resistance: Seeking Fanon's Subject Between 'the Unified' and 'the Dispersed,'" *Culture, Theory and Critique* 56, no. 2 (2015): 170–186, cited from 175–176.

life itself."[5] This life, as Clare reads it, "is... tied to movement and action."[6] Clare will then demonstrate that in Fanon there is a link between this vital life and the land, but treats this as an instantiation of Fanon's insistence on the decolonizing process. In one sense, Clare is correct.

For the black man, there is no escaping the body – "the black man is locked into his body," writes Fanon in *Black Skin, White Masks* – and therefore, no escaping colonial biopolitical regimes.[7] Elsewhere he would explicitly link the body and the world:

> slow composition of my*self* as a body in the middle of a spatial and temporal world – such seems to be the schema. It does not impose itself on me; it is, rather, a definitive structuring of the self and of the world – definitive because it creates a real dialectic between my body and the world.[8]

But this "corporeal schema" does not adequately explain the dialectic for the black body. Fanon would elaborate:

> Below the corporeal schema I had sketched a historico-racial schema... by the other, the white man, who had woven me out of a thousand details, anecdotes, stories. I thought that what I had in hand was to construct a physiological self, to balance space, to localize sensations, and here I was called on for more.[9]

Fanon has already indicated in these passages that there is something that undergirds the black body: the historico-racial scheme.[10] In *Wretched,* he would show us exactly this schema operates upon the black body:

---

5   Stephanie Clare, "Geopower: The Politics of Life and Land in Frantz Fanon's Writing," *Dia-critics* 41, no. 4 (2013), 60–80, cited from 62.
6   Ibid., 63.
7   Fanon, *Black Skin, White Masks*, 175.
8   Ibid., 83.
9   Ibid., 84.
10   Achille Mbembe offers a summary of Fanon's reading of the colonial effect on the native, colonized: "Colonial violence aimed not only to evacuate the colonized people's history of all substance but also to foreclose on their future. It similarly attacked the colonized body, causing muscles to cramp, provoking stiffness and aches. The psyche was not spared; this violence aimed for nothing less than destruction of the mind. Sores, wounds, and scars striped the body and the conscience of the colonized." Mbembe, "Frantz Fanon's *Oeuvres: A Metamorphic Thought,*" NKA *Journal of Contemporary African Art* 32 (2013): 8–16, cited from 12.

For a colonized people, the most essential value, because it is the most meaningful, is first and foremost the land: the land, which must provide bread and, naturally, dignity. But this dignity has nothing to do with "human" dignity. The colonized subject has never heard of such an ideal. All he has ever seen on his land is that he can be arrested, beaten, and starved with impunity; and no sermonizer on morals, no priest has ever stepped in to bear the blows in his place or share his bread.[11]

Here Fanon suggests that the native has no *dignity* on his native land, because he only receives blows and beatings from the white master. Fanon does of course link the politics of domination of land and bodies in the above passage, and the loss of control in one domain leads to a similar loss in another. There is no dignity, Fanon suggests, for/in the broken, beaten body. Several points about Fanon's focus on the broken/beaten body call out for attention. The laboring, broken, and beaten body has no possibilities in life. "Starved with impunity," the black body is scarcely a recognizable body – even the priest does not intervene. The broken, beaten body implies a non-human state, simply because it does not fit in with the normative human form.[12] That is, the colonial regime dehumanizes the colonized by targeting the body in such a way that it is no longer recognizably human. Fanon clearly aligns the dignity of the human with the integrity of the human form here – and it is this integrity that colonialism's biopolitical regime takes apart. If, as Elaine Scarry has theorized, torture reduces the human to a primal state of pain and screams, then Fanon's colonized body is mere primal matter.[13]

What does it mean for the black body to have, or not have dignity? What is dignity itself? "The essence of revolution is not the struggle for bread; it is the struggle for human dignity," writes Fanon in *A Dying Colonialism*.[14] In *Black Skin, White Masks* he would state "When it encounters resistance from the other, self-consciousness undergoes the experience of *desire* – the first milestone on the road that leads to the dignity of the spirit."[15] In *The Wretched of*

---

11   Frantz Fanon, *The Wretched of the Earth,* trans. Richard Philcox. (New York: Grove Press, 2004), 9.

12   Elizabeth Anker, *Fictions of Dignity: Embodying Human Rights in World Literature*. (Ithaca, NY: Cornell UP, 2012); Judith Butler, *Precarious Life: The Powers of Mourning and Violence*. (London: Verso, 2004) and *Precarious Life: The Powers of Mourning and Violence*. (London: Verso, 2009).

13   Elaine Scarry, *The Body in Pain: The Making and Unmaking of the World*. New York: Oxford University Press, 1985.

14   Frantz Fanon, *A Dying Colonialism*, trans. Haakon Chevalier. New York: Grove Press, 1965.

15   Fanon, *Black Skin, White Masks*, 169.

the Earth, Fanon would declare: "For a colonized people, the most essential value, because it is the most meaningful, is first and foremost the land: the land, which must provide bread and, naturally, dignity."[16] Dignity, then, is central to the Fanonian vision of both, the wretched of the earth as well as the emancipated.

The term dignity itself has been debated endlessly in philosophy and the field of Human Rights. Etymologically, the word dignity comes from the Latin word for "worthiness." "Dignity" implies a dual meaning: worthiness in one's own eyes, and a social evaluation of worthiness. The second meaning is linked to another etymological origin of "dignity": "worthy, proper, fitting" and "to accept." This is our cue to examine the question of dignity and cultural discourses around it.

There appears in many 20th century texts an implicit or explicit link between rights and dignity. For instance, the German Constitution (1945) begins Article 1 with the declaration: "human dignity is inviolable. To respect and protect it shall be the duty of all state authority." In Article 2 it adds: "The German people *therefore* acknowledge inviolable and inalienable human rights as the basis of every community, of peace and of justice in the world."[17] The Helsinki Accords (1975) claim that human rights "derive from the inherent dignity of the human person."[18] And, of course, the Preamble to the Universal Declaration of Human Rights (1948) says in its opening line: "whereas recognition of the inherent dignity and of the equal and inalienable rights of all members of the human family is the foundation of freedom, justice and peace in the world."[19] Later this Declaration would add:

> Whereas the peoples of the United Nations have in the Charter reaffirmed their faith in fundamental human rights, in the dignity and worth of the human person and in the equal rights of men and women and have determined to promote social progress and better standards of life in larger freedom...[20]

The Preamble to the Indian Constitution speaks of "fraternity, assuring the dignity of the individual" but does not examine the idea of dignity in any

---

16   Fanon, *The Wretched of the Earth*, 9.
17   https://www.constituteproject.org/constitution/German_Federal_Republic_2012.pdf.
18   https://berkleycenter.georgetown.edu/quotes/helsinki-accords-article-7.
19   Universal Declaration of Human Rights, http://www.un.org/en/universal-declaration
      -human-rights/.
20   http://www.un.org/en/universal-declaration-human-rights/.

sustained manner.[21] Examining the philosophical issues around dignity, Marcus Düwell writes:

> The scope of ascription of human dignity is *universal* in the sense that it applies to all human beings, it is *egalitarian* insofar as each human being is equal with regard to his dignity and references to human dignity are justifying *duties towards others* that have the form of *categorical obligations*.[22]

Josiah Ober attempting to theorize dignity writes:

> Dignity can be defined as *non-humiliation* and *non-infantilization*. We suffer indignity – humiliation and/or infantilization – when our public presence goes unacknowledged, when we cringe before the powerful, when we are unduly subject to the paternalistic will of others and when we are denied the opportunity to employ our reason and voice in making choices that affect us.[23]

For Human Rights scholars, there is an implicit and intrinsic link between "dignity" and the human body or form. For Elizabeth Anker, the dignified body, she argues, is a coherent, autonomous and agential body: "the dignified individual in possession of rights is imagined to inhabit an always already fully integrated and inviolable body: a body that is whole, autonomous and self-enclosed."[24] Corporeality, she writes, is "a baseline condition that precedes the ascription of dignity and rights to an individual."[25] The body as the embodiment of dignity is the point of departure for this essay as well.

---

21   https://www.india.gov.in/my-government/constitution-india/constitution-india-full-text. I have elsewhere examined the question of dignity in Dalit writing – writings by subalterns, of the so-called "untouchable" castes in India – through a similar lens. See Nayar, "Marginality, Suffering, Justice Questions of Dalit Dignity in Cultural Texts," *eSocial Sciences*, October 2017.

22   Marcus Düwell, "Human Dignity: Concepts, Discussions, Philosophical Perspectives," in *The Cambridge Handbook of Human Dignity: Interdisciplinary Perspectives*, ed. Marcus Düwell et al (Cambridge: Cambridge UP, 2014), 23–49. Cited from 27. Emphasis in original.

23   Josiah Ober, "Meritocratic and civic dignity in Greco-Roman antiquity," in *The Cambridge Handbook of Human Dignity: Interdisciplinary Perspectives*, ed. Marcus Düwell et al (Cambridge: Cambridge UP, 2014), 53. Emphasis in original.

24   Elizabeth S. Anker, *Fictions of Dignity: Embodying Human Rights in World Literature*. (Ithaca and London: Cornell UP, 2012), 3–4.

25   Anker, *Fictions of Dignity*, 4.

The black man's very form-of-life that has been significantly altered in the colonized state. The phrase/concept "form-of-life" is Giorgio Agamben's. Agamben writes:

> With the term *form-of-life*, by contrast, we understand a life that can never be separated from its form, a life in which it is never possible to isolate and keep distinct something like a bare life... A life that cannot be separated from its form is a life for which, in its mode of life, its very living is at stake, and, in its living, what is at stake is first of all its mode of life. What does this expression mean? It defines a life – human life – in which singular modes, acts, and processes of living are never simply *facts* but always and above all *possibilities* of life, always and above all potential.[26]

Fanon suggests that any possibilities of life the black man may have had, have been destroyed by colonialism. Throughout *Wretched* he would list this loss of possibilities: "But the fellah, the unemployed and the starving do not lay claim to truth. They do not say they represent the truth because they are the truth in their very being."[27] Starvation is central to Fanon's troping of the material conditions of the colonized bodies.

Wretched is replete with images of starving bodies and even a starving nation.[28] Indeed, Fanon would use the corporeal image to describe the entire continent:

> Africa must understand that it is no longer possible to advance by regions, that, like a great body that refuses any mutilation, she must advance in totality, that there will not be one Africa that fights against colonialism and another that attempts to make arrangements with colonialism.[29]

Colonial history, he would go so far as to declare, is this history of starving the colony.[30] In *A Dying Colonialism* he notes how, after the father is taken away or killed, "The women are then left to find ways of keeping the children from starving to death."[31] Elsewhere Fanon would write:

---

26   Giorgio Agamben, *The Uses of Bodies. Homo Sacer IV.2*, trans. Adam Kotsko (Stanford, CA: Stanford UP, 2016), 207. Emphasis in original.
27   Fanon, *Wretched*, 13.
28   Ibid., 15, 23, 48, 61, 113, 130.
29   Frantz Fanon, *Towards the African Revolution*, trans. Haakon Chevalier (New York: Grove, 1967), 192.
30   Fanon, *Wretched*, 15.
31   Fanon, *Dying Colonialism*, 99.

Who are they, those creatures starving for humanity who stand buttressed against the impalpable frontiers (though I know them from experience to be terribly distinct) of complete recognition?[32]

In *Black Skin, White Masks*, he would refer to his "bad nigger's hunger."[33] Fanon's use of starvation and the starving native body directs us to the draining of nutrition/nutrients from the native/national body, thus depriving it of its strength and, more importantly, of its possibilities. Starvation is the form-of-life for the native/colonized. This form-of-life is beneath and bereft of human dignity. David Lloyd, in his study of the representations of nineteenth century Irish famines, writes:

> The excessive spectacle of these starving bodies forces the viewer to the very threshold of humanity, to the sill that divides the human and the nonhuman, or, rather, to the boundary that marks the division between the human and the nonhuman within the human... the famine victim becomes the index of the always imminent and immanent lapse of the subject into object, of the autonomous spirit into the dependence of corporeal existence, that act of distancing can never ultimately be achieved; the boundary between the spectator and the still human object seems constantly to dissolve, with profoundly disturbing, haunting effects.[34]

When Fanon foregrounds the emaciated *and* beaten black body he does not only speak of the violence of the colonizer in terms of directed assaults on the colonized, but also the violence of denial and deprivation. Colonial biopolitics does not only beat the colonized body into the dead or dying, it renders through slow, protracted violence of denial, the descent of the human into the nonhuman. Fanon is speaking not of instantly transformative violence, not of violent events, but *sustained* violence. Lloyd's insistence on the "constantly dissolv[ing]" and "haunting effects" suggests continuities and continuums rather than one isolated instance. Fanon too understands that this is a *process*.

The loss of dignity, wherein the African becomes unrecognizable as a human, objectifies the human. Writing about torture, Adriana Caverero says: "[The] centre of the scene is occupied by a suffering body, a body reduced to a totally available object, or, rather, a thing objectified by the reality of pain,

---

32   Fanon, *African Revolution*, 3.
33   Fanon, *Black Skin, White Masks*, 102.
34   David Lloyd, "The Indigent Sublime: Specters of Irish Hunger," *Representations* 92, no. 1 (2005): 152–185, cited from 163.

on which violence is taking its time about doing its work."[35] Cavarero suggests that "horrorism" is the slow erosion of corporeal integrity (dismemberment, mutilation, or in this case, starvation), aimed at "nullifying human beings even more than at killing them."[36]

Fanon's explication of the starving African body focuses on the loss of capability and capacity on the part of the black body to assert agency, and implicitly signals the collapse of its (the African body's) dignity. The inability of the black to acquire enough food, aligned with the inability to work or own land in the colonial scheme of things, is the progressive loss of dignity, proceeding outward from the body. That is, the body is the centre from which the dehumanization and loss of dignity proceeds.

2   The Black Body, "Corpsing" and the New *Bíos*

As is now well established in Fanon studies, Fanon sees the hope and prospects of a decolonization in the native turning to violence, putting his body to violent use. In *Wretched* he would say: "The lumpenproletariat, this cohort of starving men, divorced from tribe and clan, constitutes one of the most spontaneously and radically revolutionary forces of a colonized people."[37] He would declare: "The colonized, who took up arms not only because they were dying of hunger and witnessing the disintegration of their society but also because the colonist treated them like animals."[38]

Fanon is theorizing a new form-of-life, built around the very starving bodies that were produced by the colonial system. The revolutionary starving body explores a new form-of-life: by *performing* the act of dying. Appropriating the work of David Marriott on African Americans, I shall term this "corpsing." The word "corpsing" (verb) signifies a blunder occurring when, in the performance of a role, an actor is "put out" of his part. A role that is corpsed is one that exposes the limits of performance and, depending on the metaphor, denotes the "death" of theatre, *as* theatre. Such a role, which is something contrary to the usual performance of a part, is one that evidently does away with an actor's mastery (of illusion) and no more clearly than when the disjoin between

---

35   Adriana Cavarero, *Horrorism: Naming Contemporary Violence,* trans. William McCuaig (New York: Columbia UP, 2011), 31.
36   Cavarero, *Horrorism,* 9.
37   Fanon, *Wretched,* 81.
38   Ibid., 89.

persona and part is exposed.[39] "Corpsing" is also evident outside theatre; we see it when people fail to live up to or grasp their social roles.[40] The question Marriott asks is:

> What if one's role is to be socially that of failure or if one is ordered and commanded to perform a role through one's corpse-like obliteration, would this not mean that corpsing can only occur when one refuses that spur and its contagious pleasure? Would this not be an example of a "death" of death?[41]

African Americans, Marriott argues,

> live under the command of death (as citizens, parents, siblings, and subjects); consequently, those who obey this rule are said to live under a law of symbolic death and are regarded as subjects who are already dead. Social death has to do with how rules of life are connected to the symbolically dead.[42]

With Algerians, Fanon sees the colonized, living under the command of death, refusing to lie down and die. Instead, the dying, the wounded and the traumatized – the symbolically dead – become the *life* of the revolution in the colonies. In other words, revolution, anti-colonial struggles and nationalist movements find their life in the symbolically dead, starving colonized bodies. The "performance" of dying, in the form of starving black bodies, but participating in the wholesale violence and resistance that is the anti-colonial struggle resignifies the body in Fanon's view. My argument here is consonant with Anna Agathangelou's, who argues,

> The 'rupture of antagonism' or the disinvestment of the colonial subject from the colonial world allows the structurally impossible and socially

---

39   This "corpsing" is *not* to be taken as the image of the settler's corpse about which Fanon would offer comments in *Wretched*: "The arrival of the colonist signified syncretically the death of indigenous society, cultural lethargy, and petrifaction of the individual. For the colonized, life can only materialize from the rotting cadaver of the colonist." (50) For a reading, see Ben Grant, "'Inhuman voices': Reflections on the place of Ancestors in the Work of Frantz Fanon," *Textual Practice* 28, no.4 (2014): 593–610.

40   David Marriott, "Corpsing; Or, the Matter of Black Life," *Cultural Critique* 94 (2016): 32–64, cited from 32.

41   Ibid., 34.

42   Ibid., 34.

dead body to acquire a new symbolic form, thereby pushing for the possibility to reformulate once and for all the violence that has been the foundation of black non-being without ever entering into a sacrificial logic of any social contract.[43]

The biopolitical regime which rendered the colonized body symbolically dead and starving is inverted when, from within this same symbolically dead body, life rather than death emerges – the life of the native identity, the life of the community, race and even, perhaps, the nation. The corpsing by the native colonized African is thus a performance that refuses and refutes the colonial law: of being a dead native. The starving body, which should be, logically speaking, headed towards annihilation – starvation results not in the broken or injured body, but the slowly dissolving, disappearing one – becomes the wellspring of life. Corpsing by the native body then is a refusal to *play the role proper to it*: of the dying native.

Corpsing is the afterlife of colonial violence, even when the violence is ongoing and continuous. Violence indicates "an ongoing transformation and acknowledgement of devastation and damage."[44] For Fanon, commentators have noted, violence is regenerative, redemptive and reconstructive. I suggest, following Yasmeen Arif, that *bíos* (as opposed to Giorgio Agamben's *zoe*, or bare life), is a "form of life that is qualified and constructed by the pathos of an afterlife, one that emerges in the life-worlds after violence."[45] Arif even proposes that

> Political violence can itself be framed within a biopolitical paradigm, the apparatus of violence can be understood as one that has power over life... one that leads to a politics of death or a thanatopolitics.[46]

Arif goes on to suggest that when the

> *ethnic targets* of genocide, the *queer recipients* of gendered violence, the *colored* in the racially oppressed, the *Dalits* in caste hegemonies... stand for... be resilient toward, or even retaliate on behalf of those who occupy those forms of life [they] share in the group, yet... are individuated

43   Anna M. Agathangelou, "Fanon on Decolonization and Revolution: Bodies and Dialectics," *Globalizations* 13, no.1 (2016), 110–128, cited from 121.

44   Yasmeen Arif, *Life, Emergent: The Social in the Afterlives of Violence* (Minneapolis and London: University of Minnesota Press, 2016), 5.

45   Arif, *Life, Emergent*, 23–24.

46   Ibid., 24.

carriers, in [their] biological flesh and blood the signifieds of a process of individuation that recognizes us only through our politicized social relations... there will be renewed individuation that will emerge from our belief of life as shared but will find form in the specificities of our political and social relations.[47]

She goes on to suggest that "an experience and articulation of life's vulnerability come to the fore" in this afterlife of violence.[48] Arif's insistence on the tension and dialectic, in the afterlife of violence, between individuation and politically charged, or defined, social relations is a useful way of thinking through Fanon's focus on the biopolitics of resistance and revolution.

One notes Fanon's invocation of an *embodied* revolutionary "feeling" in *Wretched*, appositely, in the chapter "On Violence":

The colonized subject thus discovers that his life, his breathing and his heartbeats are the same as the colonist's. He discovers that the skin of a colonist is not worth more than the "native's." In other words, his world receives a fundamental jolt, The colonized's revolutionary new assurance stems from this. If, in fact, my life is worth as much as the colonist's, his look can no longer strike fear into me or nail me to the spot and his voice can no longer petrify me. I am no longer uneasy in his presence. In reality, to hell with him. Not only does his presence no longer bother me, but I am already preparing to waylay him in such a way that soon he will have no other solution but to flee.[49]

And elsewhere:

The raging wolf, rabid with hunger, and the whirlwind, blowing in a genuine wind of revolt, may be rendered completely unrecognizable if the struggle continues, and it does continue.[50]

Fanon clearly sees the new *bíos*, and the inversion of the colonizer's biopolitical paradigm, as an *embodied* condition. If we read Fanon via Arif, we can posit the new *bíos* as a retrieval of the individuated sense of self within a set of social and political relations, both (individuation and collective identity)

---

47   Ibid., 29. Emphasis in original.
48   Ibid.
49   Fanon, *Wretched*, 11.
50   Ibid., 90.

derived from the violence itself. Fanon calls for a violence that brings the injured together, as already noted, but in the process, willy-nilly, also calls for a
willing confrontation ("waylay," in the above passage) of the injured with their
oppressors.

I suggest that for Fanon, it is the *physical* assembly of the injured that enables individuation and the afterlife of violence. It is in the embodied confrontation, and the resultant emotional stresses and visceral responses, with
the oppressor and perpetrator, that the new *bíos* will emerge. It is the putting
to risk the already injured and the vulnerable – Fanon speaks of the starving
peasants as revolutionaries – that generates the *bíos*. To return to Arif again:

> The politics of and in life that emerges in the aftermath of suffering
> emerges as one that necessarily collectivizes the life-worlds in the after-
> math and makes it social, just as much as it makes the social articulate an
> individuated sense of a form, a guise of life, within that social.[51]

The physical assembly that collectivizes and individuates is revolutionary and
constitutes what Judith Butler terms "public insurgencies of grief."[52] When
Fanon suggests that the starving, dying, and injured natives gather for a revolution, he is speaking in Butler's resonant phrasing. Butler would explore the
mobilization of the injured further. The gathered bodies are "nascent and pro-
visions of popular sovereignty." The body "in its struggle with precarity and
persistence is at the heart of so many demonstrations, it is also the body that
is on the line ... enacting, by the embodied form of the gathering, a claim to
the political." Further, "when bodies assemble on the street, in the square, or
in other public venues is the exercise – one might call it a performative – of
the right to appear, a bodily demand for a more livable set of lives."[53] The revolutionaries, then are "overcoming unwilled conditions of bodily exposure" as
a political act.[54] It is the exposure of what they unwillingly endured – injury,
starvation – an "exposure [of their vulnerability] to power."[55] It is their vulnerability acting "in concert."[56] Butler writes:

---

51   Arif, *Life, Emergent,* 29–30.
52   Judith Butler, *Notes Towards a Performative Theory of Assembly* (Cambridge, MA: Harvard
      University Press, 2015), 197.
53   Butler, *Notes,* 16, 18, 24–25.
54   Ibid., 126–127.
55   Ibid., 22.
56   Ibid., 151.

When the bodies of those deemed 'disposable' or 'ungrievable' assemble in public view ... they are saying, 'we have not slipped quietly into the shadows of public life: we have not become the glaring absence that structures your public life.'[57]

The corpsing now turns into a public insurgency of voluntary exposure to (further) injury, to power and oppression. It enacts an inversion of the biopolitical paradigm by exposing, voluntarily, the injured to further injury, thus making a mockery of the very idea of the vulnerable native.

3   Conclusion

When vulnerability is harnessed into revolutionary states of being, with accompanying violence, it becomes a mark of re-humanization. For Fanon, everything begins in the biopolitical – the quest for identity, dignity, self-affirmation and eventually the decolonized state. Even without accounting for his psychiatric practice and writing, Fanon's canonical works do clearly indicate this biopolitical theme, as we can see.

Bibliography

Agamben, Giorgio. *The Uses of Bodies. Homo Sacer IV.2.* Translated by Adam Kotsko. Stanford, CA: Stanford UP, 2016.

Agathangelou, Anna M. "Fanon on Decolonization and Revolution: Bodies and Dialectics." *Globalizations*, vol. 13, no. 1 (2016), 110–128.

Anker, Elizabeth S. *Fictions of Dignity: Embodying Human Rights in World Literature.* Ithaca and London: Cornell UP, 2012.

Arif, Yasmeen. *Life, Emergent: The Social in the Afterlives of Violence.* Minneapolis and London: University of Minnesota Press, 2016.

Butler, Judith. *Precarious Life: The Powers of Mourning and Violence.* London: Verso, 2004.

Butler, Judith. *Precarious Life: The Powers of Mourning and Violence.* London: Verso, 2009.

Butler, Judith. *Notes Towards a Performative Theory of Assembly.* Cambridge, MA: Harvard UP, 2015.

---

57   Ibid., 152.

Cavarero, Adriana. *Horrorism: Naming Contemporary Violence.* Translated by William McCuaig. New York: Columbia UP, 2011.

Chrisman, Laura. "The Vanishing Body of Frantz Fanon in Paul Gilroy's *Against Race* and *After Empire.*" *The Black Scholar* vol. 41, no. 4 (2011): 18–30.

Clare, Stephanie. "Geopower: The Politics of Life and Land in Frantz Fanon's Writing." *Diacritics* 41, no. 4 (2013), 60–80.

Constitution of India: https://www.india.gov.in/my-government/constitution-india/ constitution-india-full-text.

Düwell, Marcus. "Human Dignity: Concepts, Discussions, Philosophical Perspectives." In *The Cambridge Handbook of Human Dignity: Interdisciplinary Perspectives.* Edited by Marcus Düwell et al. Cambridge: Cambridge UP, 2014.

Fanon, Frantz. *A Dying Colonialism.* Trans. Haakon Chevalier. New York: Grove, 1965.

Fanon, Frantz. *Black Skin, White Masks.* Translated by Charles Lam Markmann. London: Pluto, 2008.

Fanon, Frantz. *Towards the African Revolution.* Translated by Haakon Chevalier. New York: Grove, 1967.

Fanon, Frantz. *The Wretched of the Earth.* Translated by Richard Philcox. New York: Grove, 2004.

German Federal Republic Constitution: https://www.constituteproject.org/constitu tion/German_Federal_Republic_2012.pdf.

Grant, Ben. "'Inhuman voices': Reflections on the place of Ancestors in the Work of Frantz Fanon." *Textual Practice* 28, no. 4 (2014): 593–610.

Helsinki Accords: https://berkleycenter.georgetown.edu/quotes/helsinki-accords-arti cle-7.

Lloyd, David. "The Indigent Sublime: Specters of Irish Hunger." *Representations* 92, no. 1 (2005): 152–185.

Marriott, David. "Corpsing; Or, the Matter of Black Life." *Cultural Critique* 94 (2016): 32–64.

Mbembe, Achille. "Frantz Fanon's *Oeuvres:* A Metamorphic Thought." *NKA Journal of Contemporary African Art* 32 (2013): 8–16.

Nayar, Pramod K., "Marginality, Suffering, Justice Questions of Dalit Dignity in Cultural Texts." *eSocial Sciences*, October 2017.

Ober, Josiah. "Meritocratic and civic dignity in Greco-Roman antiquity." In *The Cambridge Handbook of Human Dignity: Interdisciplinary Perspectives.* Edited by Marcus Düwell et al. Cambridge: Cambridge UP, 2014.

Scarry, Elaine. *The Body in Pain: The Making and Unmaking of the World.* New York: Oxford University Press, 1985.

Universal Declaration of Human Rights: http://www.un.org/en/universal-declaration -human-rights/.

Ward, Alan Ramón. "Redefining Resistance: Seeking Fanon's Subject Between 'the Unified' and 'the Dispersed.'" *Culture, Theory and Critique* 56, no. 2 (2015): 170–186.

CHAPTER 11

The Secret Life of Violence

Elena Flores Ruíz

1 Structural Witnessing

In the state of Michigan where I teach, it is illegal for incarcerated people to read the work of Frantz Fanon. The Michigan Department of Corrections places texts like Fanon's *Black Skin, White Masks* alongside Adolf Hitler's *Mein Kampf* as a threat to the order of the institution for "advocating racial supremacy."[1] Fanon scholars have argued publicly against the ban, noting that whoever made the decision did so without having read a word of what they were censuring.[2] Fanon, after all, had a deep commitment to democratic humanism but without the structural contradictions that disenfranchise people of color or debase them as subhuman; he sought equality, not supremacy.

As of this writing, the ban remains in place. If it is lifted, another one, morphed in form but similar in function, will likely take its place. As a structural feminist thinker, this is one way I engage with productive aspects of Fanon's work: structural witnessing.

Structural witnessing is the ability to acknowledge the systematicity of power asymmetries hidden in society without the supporting conventions of language and official history to aid one. It has an epistemological and existential component. First, the knowledge generated about one's situation is not dependent on dominant hermeneutic resources (or licensed meanings) that are readily available to structurally advantaged communities. Second, the sense of asymmetrical worldhood generated by this knowledge is itself rooted in bodily experience and its social interstices. It is, in less scientific terms, the tragic gift of the not-yet killed to know with one's whole body what the dominant world around you says you cannot know, cannot witness, name, and take your rightful place in adjudicating or bringing into balance. It is a knowledge practice rooted in the diverse lineages and long traditions of witnessing

---

1 Michigan Department of Corrections, "Restricted Publication List," Revised November 2014. I wish to thank Axelle Karera, Kristie Dotson, and Nora Berenstain for their support.

2 Alec Shea, "Banning Black Liberation," Accessed July 22, 2018. https://www.muckrock.com/news/archives/2017/aug/04/michigan-doc-fanon/.

in Black, Latinx, indigenous, and women of color writings in the aftermath of colonialism.

Fanon's structural witnessing had visionary strengths and severe limitations. Despite his stances on women's key role in revolutionary society, he remained blind to many of the forces bearing down on the lives of the women he wrote about. He had no intersectional consciousness. His strengths, like those of anti-colonial thinkers before him, honed in on the tacit operations of colonial systems in Abya Yala, Turtle Island, Aotearoa, Alkebulan and other ancestral lands dispossessed by settler logics of the bourgeois nation-state. What is distinct in Fanon's vision of structural oppression is the particular shape it takes in identifying the systemic and latticed nature of colonial power through the function of race and its rationalization in society. Racism, he believed, is *structural.* As such, "the habit of considering racism as a mental quirk, a psychological flaw, must be abandoned."[3] He built a revolutionary program on the idea that social change requires radical breaks and transformations, especially at the ontological level. This flows from the (almost biological) necessity he saw as constitutive of structures of oppression and the day-to-day operations of colonial violence. But Fanon could not abandon his own role in the abiding colonial systems of gendered oppression; he failed to witness the ways gender-based violence flows through the basic mechanisms of colonial violence and his own body. He failed to see how the habit of considering *racist sexism* a mental quirk must also be abandoned if the colonial system is to be challenged at the roots. This failure, which still bedrocks many strains of anti-colonial thinking today, demands an accounting.

This chapter proceeds in two ways. First, I argue that Fanon's structural witnessing of racism yields important insights about the nature of violence that challenges the settler colonial concept of violence as the extra-legal use of force. Second, I argue that his analysis of violence is insufficient for combating colonial racism and violence because, using the terms of his own analysis, it leaves intact logics and mechanisms that allow racism to structurally renew itself in perpetuity: violence against women. Without a critical feminism that tracks the alterities of structural violence against women, and women of color in particular, Fanonianism is just another lifeline of colonialism. I thus caution against uncritical uses of Fanon's structural account of violence for any emancipatory social theory that fails to acknowledge the attendant alterities, asymmetries, and axes of coordinated subordination involved in racialized violence against women.

---

3   Fanon, "Racism and Culture" in *Toward the African Revolution*, Trans. Haakon Chevalier (New York: Grove Press, 1967), 38.

2   Fanon on Violence

Fanon is generally seen as an icon of anti-colonial revolutionary strategy and ardent supporter of armed violence in national struggles for liberation. He has become synonymous with African independence and justifications for the ethical suspension of moral universals in defense of one's freedom: "as soon as you and your fellow men are cut down like dogs," he writes, "there is no other solution but to use every means available to reestablish your weight as a human being."[4] At the time of his death, little had been written about his extensive psychiatric writings and humanitarian work as a medical doctor, much less his plays, philosophical engagements with existentialism and phenomenology, or even his public support of non-violent strategies in anti-colonial independence movements.[5] Instead, the posthumous image crafted in the Anglo-European world was that of a radically politicized writer and rising architect of Black liberation in the Third World – "the Jean-Jacques Rousseau of the Algerian Revolution" – one who posed a significant threat to the order and stability of western nations' interests abroad.[6] He was called "the disciple of violence" and his works indexed under subjects suited more to the study of military combat and organized warfare between nations than cultural or philosophical confrontations with the legacies of colonialism. The historical reception of his view of violence was, needless to say, shaped by colonialism itself.

3   Les Damnés de la Terre

Much of what is known today about Fanon's view of violence comes from the historical reception of the section entitled "On Violence" that makes up the

---

4   Frantz Fanon, *The Wretched of the Earth*. (New York: Grove Press, 2005), 221.
5   Fanon expressed public support of Dr. Kwame Nkrumah's non-violent strategies for gaining Ghanaian independence; for related documents see Jean Khalfa and Robert J.C. Young's *Frantz Fanon: Alienation and Freedom*. London: Bloomsbury Publishing, 2018.
6   This image was partly due to the dominance of European periodicals, editors and publishers on African affairs. Editorial descriptions rarely captured the complexity of Fanon's ideas and generally reduced them to political dogma for the FLN, particularly as international tensions in cold war politics heightened. It is often forgotten that the publication of *The Wretched of the Earth* coincided with the publication of Che Guevara's *Guerrilla Warfare* and the Cuban Revolution; this contributed to the heightening of securitization discourses against perceived leftist uprising and populist insurgency. In this context, *The Wretched of the Earth* easily became mythologized as nationalist war manual, "un livre de guerre" on par with Guevara's *Warfare*. See Robert Schwenger, *Review of The Wretched of the Earth*, Monthly Labor Review 86, no. 2 (February 1963): 185–198; and Jean-Marie Domenach, "Les Damnés de la Terre" *Esprit*, Nouvelle série 305, no. 4 (AVRIL 1962): 634–645.

first part of *Les Damnés de la Terre* (1961) [trans. as *The Wretched of the Earth* in 1963]. In this section, Fanon justifies the use of armed violence by colonized peoples in ways historically limited to legitimate use by Anglo-European nation states and peoples: in defense of one's freedom. But Fanon had a more nuanced, structural account of violence that the predominantly colonialist reception of *The Wretched of the Earth* obscured. Swiftly dictated on his deathbed, the work tolls Fanon's most basic bearing on the life he inhabited; it is his resounding *no* to the kind of world he most feared would outlive his efforts. It is his great refusal to succumb to the fire, famine, and misery that the colonial system cast on native peoples across generations, continents, and seas. It gives a noticeably different impression of the fate of the colonial system than some of his early writings, which tended to render very clinical, cultural diagnoses of French colonialism at the micrological (psychological) levels of experience: what it is, how to treat it, what treatments might work under what conditions... the agonism in these early writings was both personal and detached, measured and conceptual. As a doctor, he rejected the systematic dehumanization of native peoples under French colonialism and its appending cultural apparatuses – foremost, colonial psychiatry in Algeria. However, by the time he tackles in-depth analyses of macrological (political, economic, cultural) features of colonialism – from the writings that make up *A Dying Colonialism* to the section on violence in *The Wretched of the Earth* – what is militant in his refusal is existential, not measured and conceptual. It is a clue to the toll colonialism takes, not in the abstract but in the flesh.

While I don't think *Wretched* is a good indicator of the complexity of Fanon's structural views on violence, owing both to the conditions of its writing and its historical reception, I do think it illuminates some of his most important structural commitments to understanding oppression. He notes, for instance, that "challenging the colonial world is not a rational confrontation of viewpoints" in the sense of western systems of rational thought that unilaterally derive from Greek logic.[7] No amount of interpersonal confrontations with racial bias will dismantle the inveterate mechanisms of racist prejudice and colonial violence without a transformation of the supporting infrastructural conditions in society. Fanon, a trained psychiatrist, famously resigned from his post as medical director of the psychiatric hospital at Blida-Joinville on these grounds:

> If psychiatry is the medical technique that aims to enable man no longer to be a stranger to his environment, I owe it to myself to affirm that the Arab, permanently an alien in his own country, lives in a state of absolute

---

7   Fanon, *The Wretched of the Earth*, 6.

depersonalization... *The social structure existing in Algeria was hostile to any attempt to put the individual back where he belonged.* ...The events in Algeria are the logical consequence of an abortive attempt to decerebralize a people... The function of a social structure is to set up institutions to serve man's needs. A society that drives its members to desperate solutions is a non-viable society, a society to be replaced.[8]

Sartrean interpretations of Fanon often overlook this point. While Fanon clearly had an ontological commitment to existential humanism through his approach to psychiatry, he thought the pervasive dissemination of racism in the colonial world constituted a prior violence to identity that western humanism, even in the existential tradition, was structurally complicit in.[9] Concrete social and historical structures therefore come first in Fanon's philosophical imagination – if physical violence is a defensively necessary "desperate solution," brought about by historical conditions against colonized peoples, then the revolt is ultimately not against individual colonizers but against the colonial structure.

This move to *preconditions for existence* allows Fanon to bring in temporal dimensions to his account of structural violence that western discourses of temporality do not attend to. Because the colonized are operating in the ontologically abject zone-of-non-being, the bi-directional folding of past and futurity into the present is not a smooth, continuous event. It is ruptured at every moment of possible existence, thus constituting an ontological harm (one Fanon thinks is worked out in dreams and aggression) and is yet another layer of settler violence to the colonized's sense of worldhood. Upturning this is of primary importance. Thus, as Fanon sees it, anti-colonial violence is not a purely destructive, backwards looking phenomenon that attempts to right past wrongs. That's simply the level at which western ethics evaluates anti-colonial violence at (rather than seeing it as the struggle for a livable future).

For Fanon, anti-colonial violence is also part of a postcolonial *world-building* move motivated towards a multi-level restructuring of culture and its social structures, including the very agency of the colonized subject (who is always implicitly male for Fanon). A large part of *Wretched* is dedicated to the idea that a widespread restructuring of social, individual, material, and economic relations will be necessary to build a truly postcolonial world – a world where equality is not based on the structural contradictions that allow racial

---

8   Fanon, "Letter to the Resident Minister" in *Towards the African Revolution*, 53.
9   Elena Ruíz, "Existentialism for Postcolonials: Fanon and the Politics of Authenticity," *APA Newsletter on Hispanic /Latino Issues in Philosophy* 15, no. 2 (Spring 2016).

prejudice to exist seamlessly alongside democratic institutions. But, as we will later see, the future Fanon dreams of bringing into being through revolutionary violence is limited to a particular kind of colonized subject; without attending to the alterity of violences against women, Fanon is unable to build a vision of a world where colonized women are also free of colonial violence. This criticism is lost in the colonial reception of Fanon's texts. Instead, the focus remains on a narrow analytic judgment of whether retributive violence can ever be a feature of a just act. It is well known that Fanon is often charged with being as dualist, reductive, Manichean, and divisive about "what species, what race one belongs to" as the settler colonial racists he denounces, so that he may be dismissed as a racial nationalist.[10] In 1959, he wrote the following:

> The new [post-revolutionary] relations are not the result of one barbarism replacing another barbarism, of one crushing of man replacing another crushing of man. What we Algerians want is to discover the man behind the colonizer; this man who is both the organizer and the victim of *a system* that has choked him and reduced him to silence... we want an Algeria open to all, in which every kind of genius may grow.[11]

But it does not really matter that Fanon disavowed dualistic thinking when abstracted from the operations of colonial systems. As a structural thinker, Fanon himself presaged the ways this failure of audibility is set up in advance, how it was always destined to fail due to the unique stronghold of colonial violences in culture. It is not universal Reason that will heal but the collective *and infrastructural* recognition of the existence of a deeper unreason that allows racism to continue as a rationalized process in culture. Fanon's structural witnessing saw the power of what I'm describing here as "revolutionary reabsorption" – the neutralizing of anti-revolutionary potential by reabsorbing challenges to authority back into a system in scalable versions that can be redeployed in non-revolutionary ways. Fanon shared this idea with Latin American liberation thinkers – in fact, this is a core thesis in *Guerilla Warfare*, published the same year as *Wretched* – as well as with critical theorists and, of course, generations of women of color who theorized oppression as complex systems and their intersections.

Despite the colonial reception of *Wretched,* I contend that Fanon held the view that violence is not a simple act – a physical discharge of force reducible to a moment in time. This seems patently false for readers of *Wretched*, as

---

10   Fanon, *The Wretched of the Earth*, 5.
11   Ibid., 32.

Fanon often speaks of the discrete distension and contraction of the human musculature – of the need to exert oneself in space by force – in response to the horrors and abuses of colonial repression. But he regards this as a consequence, outcome, or better yet, a reflexive *symptom* of a prior violence that certainly includes physical violence, widespread torture and confinement, but is not reducible to it. Violence to flesh is irreducible. But without other supporting forms of violence to shroud colonial authority in mystery and create the status quo, colonialism simply could not have been carried out in its historical manner – whether as the systemic torture of flesh or the background gaslighting of a whole collective in our daily interactions with public structures. On this view, *violentus*, the use of force in excess of normative limits relative to a given time and place, is not an objective, universal phenomenon. It is a *cultural production* that serves a normative function relative to power differences in society. As I read him, violence under colonialism is a deeper, cultural, epistemic, and discursive phenomenon that supports the internal consistency of colonial power by *limiting the domain of intelligibility* – what violence can *appear as* – to settler colonial logics.[12] As a hermeneutic reading of Fanon's project, this suggests that people who experience colonial violence must learn to redescribe experience through the lens of languages and logics historically devoid of cultural meanings adequate for capturing one's experiences (a point he makes in "The Negro and Language"). This is why structural witnessing becomes important for unraveling structural aspects of colonial violence, and why critical feminist practices of witnessing must also be attendant in this narrative.

4   Structural Violence as Organized Domination

In 1956, Fanon gave a speech in Paris at the First Congress of Negro Writers and Artists that helps us understand his structural views on violence. This speech first appeared in print in the June-November issue of *Présence Africaine* in 1956 and later as the essay "Racism and Culture" in *Pour la Révolucion Africaine* (1964, trans. 1967 as *Towards the African Revolution*). In it, Fanon lays the groundwork for a theory of "organized domination" that helps explain the longevity, intractability, and resilience of European colonialism as a structural phenomenon.

---

12   This framing of Fanon's work is most visible in his discussion of colonial medicine. See his 1952 essay, "The North African Syndrome."

Organized domination, according to Fanon, is made up of positive and negative oppressions. It is not like the bivalent distinctions of positive and negative liberty, as in freedom *to* and freedom *from*. For Fanon, positive oppressions include physical enslavement and even more intangible phenomena like economic indenture because they can emerge as intelligible phenomena in the discursive domains of settler culture. They are brutalizing and annihilating experiences. The fact that they *can* come to be seen, acknowledged, or written about in history textbooks, however, does not help colonized peoples much, as this in no way lessens the functioning of white European cultural supremacy as the arbiter of moral history. Just as they can be seen, they can be denied at any point; making racism and enslavement legitimate objects of scientific observation does not preclude the emergence of scientific arguments in support of racial supremacy, or historical theses that challenge the facticity of enslavement (as we've seen in recent times). Because this logic shows up as a necessary feature of the most legitimate instruments of generating truth in the West – deliberative principles based on falsifiability of truth claims – it does not come to be seen as a problem by settlers in settler colonial cultures. This is not an epistemic accident. It is the product of a deeper violence that operates in synchronicity with positive oppressions. Fanon understands this next register as negative oppression.

One way to understand negative oppression is as the multi-level suppression of cultural alternatives to European settler supremacy. It is an ongoing undoing, unmaking, erasing, "decerebralization," whitewashing and structured forgetting of non-European cultural traditions for the purposes of *organizing domination as a logical affair.* He refers to negative oppression as *deculturation:* "the enterprise of deculturation turns out to be the negative of a more gigantic work of economic, and even biological enslavement."[13] He suggests that for positive oppressions to work long term, enslavement has to look like positive oppression but function on the basis of negative oppressions. A culture can regenerate, resist, renew itself if it has "fertile lines of force," as in resources of meaning and interpretation to organize resistance and communication around.[14] Dispossessing native peoples of cultural resources of interpretation like language is thus intimately linked to the dispossession of lands, territories, and bodies. Colonialism is a long game, and for this, a native culture's "systems of reference have to be broken," and ultimately liquidated.[15] "Expropriation, spoliation, raids, objective murder, are matched by the sacking of cultural

---

13   Fanon, "Racism and Culture," 31.
14   Ibid., 34.
15   Ibid., 33, 38.

patterns, or at least condition such sacking. The social panorama is destructed; values are flaunted, crushed, emptied."[16] I call this hermeneutic violence. Hermeneutic violence occurs when violence is done to structures of meaning and interpretation, such as language.[17] Because meaning is relational and lived, hermeneutic violence includes violence done to rivers, lands, temples, textiles, gender, and other constitutive social relations that sustain the referential network of a culture's social panorama. It immobilizes peoples and communities, and that *is a tactic of war*. On this view, it is nonsensical to talk about epistemic "bad luck" or accidental cases of hermeneutic injustice against people of color, unless, of course, one is operating under a settler colonial logic and supportive infrastructural economy.

Although it is not perfectly clear in his writings, there seem to be at least two kinds of negative oppression for Fanon: deculturation and *acculturation*. They are interrelated. Acculturation is the *imposition* of European conceptual orthodoxies as the universal basis for meaning-making and legitimate knowledge practices in culture. As deculturation deteriorates native epistemic resources, "in their stead a new system of values is imposed, not proposed but affirmed by the heavy weight of cannons and sabers."[18] Acculturation shows that the lingua franca of a settler culture is always already based on violence: "thus we witness the setting up of archaic, inert institutions, functioning under the oppressor's supervision and patterned like a caricature of formerly fertile institutions," such as a government-run Bureau of Native Affairs.[19] *Acculturation is needed to organize domination as a logical affair* because it provides the official (i.e., carrying salience in institutions) ordering domains for talking about and thinking through experiences of domination; it naturalizes the appearance of oppression as the routine ordering of reality and mystifies challenges to it. First among these ordering domains is universal thinking since it allows colonial logics to operate as *the* epistemic standpoint that acknowledges the existence *of* difference. One culture structures what counts as "cultural difference" and develops official languages internal to its system, like "multiculturalism." Acculturation makes it so that, eventually, the first thing one thinks of to resist positive oppressions is based on the limits set forth by negative oppressions. On this view, rights-based claims to progressive emancipation have been filtered by (a) settler logics of European political traditions (capitalist heteropatriarchy

---

16   Ibid., 33.
17   Language here is not reducible to speech acts. Fanon extends this idea in "The Negro and Language," in *Black Skin, White Masks.*
18   Fanon, "Racism and Culture," 34.
19   Ibid.

and white supremacy) that limit *the emancipatory futurity* of people of color, and (b) a prior/ongoing deculturation of non-western political alternatives. Negative oppressions thus seem to be a two-fold move that make their way to positive registers in an ideological manner. This, again, is not totally clear; Fanon seems to be relying on Marxist models of a superstructure, where negative oppressions for the base/relations of production and an Hegelian dialectic freed from ideal theory as Eurocentric history and Reason. What Fanon is clear on, however, is that the goal of negative oppressions is to preempt cultural resistance to colonialism by allowing it to regenerate – to form new bloodlines – in less and less visible ways. This is why he states that "the specificity of neocolonialism is to pre-empt revolutionary situations by introducing scalable methods into its system" that are internal to the system itself.[20] Acculturation is thus about *power*, including the power to retain control over the very means of interpretation in culture.[21] I call this *interpretive power* and, relatedly, the hermeneutic accumulation of *interpretive wealth* as a structural basis for settler epistemic standpoints – interpretive power, among other things, produces internally consistent claims to innocence and epistemic ignorance *while perpetuating the conditions for the futurity of colonial violence.*

One clue to Fanon's understanding of the interrelations of colonial violence is his training as a medical doctor. Morphology seems to be central to the processes he describes, especially when seen in the transitions from colonialism to neocolonialism to neoliberalism and so forth.[22] One of his concerns is that, over time, through morphology, acculturation works to produce empirical claims that correlate diminished visibility of violence with a material reality of diminished violence when that's clearly not the case for people of color.

---

20   Frantz Fanon, "National Independence: The Only Possible Outcome," *El Moudjahid*, No. 10, September, reprinted in Khalfa and Young, *Frantz Fanon: Alienation and Freedom*, 552.

21   One of the ways it does this is through logical universalism. When applied to culture, it promotes an understanding of culture as an organic, value-free phenomenon that results in the natural development, contraction or decay of cultural formations. This hides the instrumental function of universality, wherein one is "concerned about Man but strangely not about the Arab" (Fanon, "Letter to a Frenchman," 48).

22   Part of Fanon's lexical imaginary for this process of structural self-regeneration comes from his medical training. Fanon often speaks of deculturation as a "sclerosis" or hardening of cultural arteries, and of colonial violence as a morphological process or angiogenesis that leads to cultural malignancies, yet simply recedes into the background unnoticed. Angiogenesis is the formation of new blood vessels in the body; it involves the growth, migration, but also differentiation of certain kinds of cells that line blood vessel walls. While angiogenesis inhibitors were not yet a standard part of treatment protocols for hematologic malignancies like leukemia, it is remarkable to see the linkages between Fanon's thinking about structures, his own experience of illness, and the regenerative of qualities he attributes to colonialism as a kind of cancer.

Alternatively, he writes, "the truth is that the rigor of the system made the daily affirmation of a [European cultural] superiority superfluous."[23]

The metonymic power of structural violence mystifies our experiences with it. This suggests that one way of retaining control over the means of interpretation in culture is precisely by *blurring* the connections and interdependencies between positive and negative oppressions and their violences. Fanon's main example of this interdependency is the colonial phenomenon of racism.

5   Racism as Structural

Fanon saw structures as more than biological patterns that organize life forms in determinate ways, such as molecular structures. His views on how things fit together in terms of functional (automated) patterns – especially those that are not always visible to colonial clinicians – had multiple influences that included Marxism, psychoanalysis, and his own embodied experience of racism. His main idea was that racism is not reducible to a mental habit or psychological feeling controlled by individual will. Racism is a structural phenomenon that serves a critical function in the maintenance of colonialism through its morphological processes. One of the ways racism shows up *is* as an individual prejudice, but that is the product of settler cultural dominance itself. As such, "it is... not as a result of the evolution of people's minds that racism loses its virulence. No inner revolution can explain this necessity for racism to seek more subtle forms, to evolve."[24] That is why it is not possible to eradicate racism at the individual level; it doesn't operate the way it always seems to "show up." Negative oppressions are thus critical in the emergence of racism as a structural phenomenon that includes positive oppression manifestations of racism, *but can persist without them* (as in a "post-racial" society).

To explain this, it is helpful to remember that Fanon thinks colonialism is a *process,* not a historical event that came and went. As a process, colonialism has no "endpoint" or terminus to conquest; the telos of manifest destiny is inherent in its structure. The colonist will thus never be satisfied with settling or taking native lands as a political act, for to settle is to reign as if *futurity* itself belongs to settlers. This means the possibility of non-futurity, a world in which Anglo-European culture is not in charge, is constantly guarded against:

---

23   Fanon, "Racism and Culture," 37.
24   Ibid., 35.

In the colonialist perspective, a minimum of terror has to be upheld on the land being occupied. Police, racist administrators and prevaricators, colons of abominable dishonesty and perverse enjoyment, weave over the entire colonized country a very tight network within which the native comes to feel literally immobilized.[25]

Whenever settler futurity is challenged a recirculation of racism will emerge in form and proportion to its challenge, even when some forms of racism have been thought surpassed. This is because the main function of racism is to immobilize colonized peoples – whether as a structural, psychological, or physical paralytic. The goal of colonialism is thus to find ways for social reorganizations of colonialism to emerge in tandem with cultural, economic, and technological changes without ever changing the very culture of coloniality. On this view, the burden will always fall on people of color to show how, precisely, the prison system is an extension of slavery; one will have to become an expert on their own oppression to make the case for the reality of oppression. This is why Fanon writes, "racism has not managed to *harden*. It has had to *renew* itself, to adapt itself, to change its appearance. It has had to undergo the fate of the cultural whole that informed it...[it] is only one element of a vaster whole: that of the *systematized oppression* of a people."[26] Acculturation allows for the rationalization of the idea that racism is an interpersonal bias at its core – that it's ultimately a fight over hearts and minds, not land or bodies. It also provides the visibility for frameworks for thinking about violence as the extra-legal use of force that will always criminalize resistance to uses of force that *can* be litigated as "legal" (because the infrastructural support is colonial), such as police, military, or state violence against people of color. This definition of violence, as the extra-legal use of force, was forged in Roman law and its intersections with enslavement and territorial expansion; when coupled with the universal rationalism of Enlightenment legal thinking, it easily came to provide the bedrock for legal thinking in settler, colonial, and imperial nations. The goal of the standard view of violence is thus to have an innocence-effect of scientific neutrality and impartiality on par with Newtonian laws of motion, but with the actual effect of securing settler futurity.

As a negative oppression that is the Janus-head of deculturation, acculturation produces what Fanon calls *rational racism*. Rational racism differs from the forms of racism made visible by positive oppression, such as "vulgar

---

25   Frantz Fanon, "The Cavalry of a People," *El Moudjahid,* No. 13, November 1958, reprinted in Khalfa and Young, *Frantz Fanon: Alienation and Freedom,* 617.

26   Fanon, "Racism and Culture," 32–33, emphasis added.

racism."[27] Vulgar racism, "in its biological form corresponds to the period of crude exploitation of man's arms and legs," but given that racism is a functional component of organized domination, Fanon thinks its formulations will morph alongside the developing means of exploitation in culture. Thus, "the perfecting of the means of production inevitably brings about the *camouflage* of the techniques by which man is exploited, hence the forms of racism."[28] This camouflage does not erase the reality of racism for people of color, but it does shroud it in "verbal mystification." Organized domination suggests that settler ignorance is a structural benefit of colonial violence; settlers remain subjects of and in their own history. Meanwhile, "exploitation, tortures, raids, racism, collective liquidations, rational oppression take turns at different levels in order literally to make of the native an object in the hands of the occupying nation."[29] This multi-level approach to domination is critical for recognizing that "the setting up of the colonial system does not of itself bring about the death of a native culture."[30] Positive oppression is only one – albeit brutalizing – feature of colonial violence.

Ultimately, for Fanon, the experience of racism is never accidental but made possible by an interlocking web of material, social, economic, and epistemic conventions rooted in the Anglo-European colonial project, with colonial violence playing a central role. According to Fanon, racism has had *and will continue to have* a unique stronghold on cultures whose infrastructures and institutions are rooted in colonial violence. By colonial violence he means a multifaceted, "poly-dimensional," sustained cultural project of positive and negative oppressions aimed at maintaining a doctrine of cultural hierarchy through organized practices of domination, like racism. Racism is therefore not a logical concept (in the sense of timeless universals) or mental habit. It did not antedate the rise of colonialism depicted in the Cantino planisphere. Racism functions by helping to sustain organized domination as the uncoupling of the power of the dominated to resist from the resources that might help them do so, including their own sense of themselves and their lands. Colonial culture instrumentalizes universal frames of reference so that it is easy to maintain that racists and anti-racists are both violent in the same ways without contradiction, as in Donald Trump's 2017 account of "violence on both sides" in Charlottesville, Virginia. This suggests that whoever wields the parameters for defining, conceptualizing, and prohibiting violence wields the socio-economic

---

27 Ibid., 35.
28 Ibid. Emphasis added.
29 Ibid.
30 Ibid., 34.

engine of culture. It also suggests that progressive emancipation, the idea that "with time all this will disappear," is not a historical force but a colonial meta-function; a grand narrative that abjures what it promotes in name.[31] As such, it will continue to generate contradictions in our lives whenever we run up against the poly-dimensional reemergence of colonial racism in so-called post-racial, multicultural democracies.

6   The Secret Life of Violence

6.1   *Structural Complicity*

Fanon's structural witnessing was no prophetic gift. The capacity to identify the structural inner-workings of colonial violence is prevalent in the long quill-work of anti-colonial women of color feminist and indigenous theorizing, as in the work of Audre Lorde and Lee Maracle. One of the reasons I think Fanon has risen to the scale of historical audibility in the commonwealth of screams against colonial violence is that his voice can operate in some of the same co-lonial registers he critiques. He was incontrovertibly homophobic, denying the existence of homosexuality in his native Martinique and expressing "revul-sion" at the thought of hearing one man say to another, "he is so sensual!"[32] His sexism and misogynoir knew few bounds; in "Algeria Unveiled," he instrumen-talized women's bodies in revolutionary struggle as collateral sites of actual detonation of violence. While black men could, obliquely, regain their human-ity through the physical violence pummeled into their oppressors, women paid with their lives to say *their* "no more." Unsurprisingly, his analysis of sexual vio-lence almost always triangulated with men's experiences and women's alleged failures. He was especially critical of black women's intellectual production when it challenged his theories, even if (or because) they were trailblazers, as was the case with Mayotte Capécia's *Je suis Martiniquaise* (I am a Martinican Woman) (1948). While he pathologized the psychological narrative of a black woman's confrontation with being abandoned, with child, by a white man, he makes no mention of his own abandonment of a woman and their child for a white Frenchwoman. These are not contradictions; these are *complicities*. As such, they give him interpretive access to domains of intelligibility that carry

---

31   Ibid., 39.

32   Denean Sharpley-Whitting, *Frantz Fanon: Conflicts and Feminisms.* (Lanham, MD: Row-man and Littlefield, 1997), 10; Also see Kobena Mercer, "Decolonization and Disappoint-ment: Reading Fanon's Sexual Politics," in *The Fact of Blackness,* ed. Alan Read (Seattle: Bay Press, 1996), 114–131.

salience in the epistemic registers of western European history and intellectual traditions. This does not erase the facticity of racism and colonial violences he writes about, but rather complicates it. It shows that colonial structural dominance is an even more powerful phenomenon because it performs its own critique, allowing the most salient features of the colonial panorama to be transmitted from generation to generation via challenges to it by colonized subjects: racism, sexism, homophobia, classism, casteism, and their intersections with sexual violence are very often administered by racialized men, even if the toxicity of what they administer did not originate with them but with settler colonial culture. Fanionianism without anti-colonial feminism is thus another lifeline of colonialism.

Recently, the fieldwork of Félix Germain has confirmed what some of us have long suspected about Fanon's relationship to women: he was a very violent man. As Germain reports,

> During my fieldwork in Paris, I discovered that Fanon's private life, especially his relationship with his partner [Josie Fanon], was punctuated by violence. When I interviewed Paulin Joachim...[who] knew Fanon very well, he admitted witnessing a disturbing event during a social gathering at a cafe Mr. Joachim, who had gone out with Fanon and his partner, saw the couple arguing. Eventually the argument escalated into a violent outburst. According to Mr. Joachim, Fanon lost his temper and slapped the woman in the face. Apparently, this was not an isolated incident. Mr. Joachim asserts, 'He used to hit his wife in the bedroom; he once did it in front of me, Ibrahim Seïd, and Ado Maurice. He did it to humiliate her, and he would say 'I avenge myself.' He was violent. He was a very violent man.' Professor Maryse Condé, who I later interviewed, also mentioned hearing similar stories from the mouths of his family members. Fanon's behavior, however, did not surprise her. She claimed, 'I am not surprised because we've learned to disassociate men's private relationships with their partner(s) from their intellectual accomplishments. Sometimes we expect these things.'[33]

Josie Fanon committed suicide in Algiers in 1989, shortly after the public riots and uprisings that led to the fall of the *Front de libération nationale* (FLN) and the start of civil war. David Macey, perhaps the most noted of Fanon's biographers, is largely silent on this, adding only that Josie "was always very reluctant

33   Félix Germain, *Decolonizing the Republic: African and Caribbean Migrants in Postwar Paris, 1946–1974*. (East Lansing: Michigan State University Press, 2016), 90.

to talk about her private life, and especially her life with Fanon, and their relationship has never really been described."[34] This inattention is not accidental;
one only thinks to look for what one already suspects to be missing. Anten-
nas for detecting silences surrounding women's lives *and the circumstances
that produce them* are critical components of anti-colonial theory. Without
them, one can underwrite a tacit commitment to violences that support other
violences – ones we sometimes track and make visible – but do not get at the
root of the processes of automation and systemic violence that constitute colonial oppression. This is particularly important for tracking and identifying
violences against racialized women – especially indigenous women – who are
perpetually made sub-audible by colonial violence.

7   The Alterity of Violence

Alterity describes what escapes articulation in dominant cultural registers, yet
forms an indelible feature of experience. When applied to violence, it does
not mean violence is not a physical force, only that femicides and epistemi-
cides alike take a toll on our collective bodies, spirits, and chances of survival;
we should have tools that tackle the wide spectrum of harms and forces that
interlock in support of coloniality and its multiple blows to our lived bodies.
But there are limits to alterity as a way to organize our thinking about structural violence against women of color. Using alterity to talk about violence can
be dangerous; it can be used to prioritize interpretive dilemmas and incom-
mensurabilities at a time when the only thing left to interpret are corpses and
causes of death. It can also be used to suggest people who endure violence are
unclear about the nature of what is happening to them.[35] While the traumatic
impact of violence can register in profoundly different ways for each of us,
I do not think that people who bear out the logics of colonial violences are
generally in the dark about what is happening to them, or that one is in need

---

34   David Macey, *Frantz Fanon: A Biography*. (New York: Verso, 2012), 132.
35   I think Fanon was guilty of this on many levels, like when he used western psychiatric
        methods to critique colonialism (medicalizing the effects of racism as a psychological
        disorder at the individual level), or in his critique of Capécia's work. It denies the pos-
        sibility that the black Martinican woman, *Lucette Ceranus* – not her pseudonym, Mayotte
        Capécia – is strategically or performatively controlling a narrative. That is to say, no one
        questions Soren Kierkegaard (or attributes bad faith to him) through his many pseud-
        onyms when they exemplify the aesthetic sphere he so loathed *because he is afforded the
        epistemic credibility* of self-awareness seldom given to women of color. Fanon did not op-
        erate at this register, famously writing "as for the woman of color, I know nothing about
        her." Frantz Fanon, *Black Skin, White Masks*. (New York: Grove Press, 2008), 50.

of a generational seer, scientist, or structural account to make sense of things. I think violence is experienced and understood by those who live it; it is never so radically incommensurable that it is nothing. My bones know this. However, it is possible to become estranged from one's bodily knowledge when one seeks confirmation of one's experience amidst the public structures of settler colonial cultures. This confirmation is not existential or heuristic but motivated by the need to seek justice in an unjust world – to get help, quite literally, from a domestic violence shelter, a legal statute, or an institutional policy. Women of color all too often seek assistance from anti-violence advocacy organizations only to find that the supporting conventions of colonialism answer the doorbell. Caught in a web of violent responses to violence, you begin to question the trustworthiness of your own experience. So my concern is not with individual difference in the experience of violence but with the subordinated role our sense-making plays in the social institutions, discourses, and public logics most tied to colonial power (law, medicine, politics, education). This is where alterity can be useful as a conceptual tool – by linking lived experiences with their social *silencing*. It is also where Fanon's structural witnessing can *appear* to be helpful, since it looks at practices of silencing from the standpoint of the role they play in organized domination.

I think we can still make critical use of Fanon in a broader emancipatory social theory, but for this we have to read Fanon *against Fanon* through the alterity of violence. We can use alterity to show that what gets annihilated in the production (Mayotte Capécia, racialized women, indigenous and non-binary identities, for example) of anti-colonial narratives like Fanon's, which is critically important for understanding that the *functional asymmetries* produced through structural violence in settler colonial societies rest on their *reproducibility*, not their identification. We can show, for example, that colonial institutions are built to give explanatory priority to commensurable differences – things that can be made intelligible if that difference has a *positive* valence – so that in the moment one speaks to power *through that power*, hospitable domains are identified as sites for colonial reproducibility. The secret life of violence thus tacitly rests on networks of negative valences – on the structural unintelligibility of cultural power as, for example, non-normative bodies, voices, corporeal connections to waterways, native plants, and lands. Structural justice, as a rejection of the organized failure of understanding that prevents infrastructural support for non-dominant peoples and communities, thus begins with a deep *refusal*.[36]

---

36   See Audra Simpson. "Ethnographic Refusal: Indigeneity, 'Voice,' and Colonial Citizenship," *Juctures: The Journal for Thematic Dialogue* 9 (2007): 67–80.

8   Refusing Violence

Historically, anti-colonial theories of harm and violence that obscure the particularities of racialized and indigenous women's realities are the standard, not
the exception. Women's interests have been consistently subsumed under the
broader goals of liberation struggles for generations; Fanon's structural witnessing of racism is no different.[37] Fanon saw how there is a range of harms
produced when violence is held hostage to functions and definitions borne to
only one cultural tradition – violence's secret life as an instrument of cultural
power – yet he could not see it working in his own body. He was able to see the
replication of *lytic* cycles of colonial violence, but not the *lysogenic* cycles. The
latter would have required an epigenetic, intergenerational perspective that
points to one's own embeddedness and incorporation into the host genome.
The lysogenic view pushes one to see that one's witnessing of dispossession
takes place on epistemic positionalities complicated by colonialism. To the
fact, for example, that I write this as both a colonized subject resisting colonization and a settler living on (and theorizing from) indigenous land (Pot-
tawatomie, Ottawa, Ojibwe) in Michigan. Colonial violence has levels, and so
should its examination.

There was a time in the so-called colorblind society of the post-civil rights
era that tremendous energy was spent sounding the alarm of structural racism and the continuation of Jim Crow by other means: in schools, health care
systems, prisons, and legal system. What has changed is the alleged "reappearance" (because it is not new to many) of vulgar racism in culture and the corre-
sponding need to make the same case. This alone should alarm. Vulgar racism
is not foundational, an aberration located in "in the hearts and minds" of those
who espouse it. There is nothing new about Trumpism. We do not need Fanon
to see that violence (codified as the extra-legal use of force) has been a cultural
good reserved for those who *already participate in the system that systematizes
violence* – its secret life in our lives as people of color living in settler colonial
societies.

One does not need to have read Fanon to sense there is something strategi-
cally amiss in an institutional logic that censures the liberational consciousness of those it disproportionately institutes and extracts cheap labor from.
That it is unsurprising, in the age of Michelle Alexander's *The New Jim Crow*
and *Black Lives Matter,* that Fanon remains on the list of prohibited books
alongside *The Black People's Prison Survival Guide* and *Independent Black Leadership in America.* The question is: what structures the sense of surprise in the

---

37   See Ofelia Schutte, *Cultural Identity and Social Liberation in Latin American Thought.* New
        York: State University of New York Press, 1993.

first place? What logic engineers the social imagination to reveal fracture and discontinuity – the "I can't believe this is so!" – where, from the standpoint of so many, it is mundanely so. Given the renewed force of racism and white supremacy, once thought to have been surpassed in colorblind multicultural democracies, Fanon's work is poised for another renaissance, one I worry about in the context of structural violence against women of color.

Bibliography

Domenach, Jean-Marie. "Les Damnés de la Terre" *Esprit*, Nouvelle série 305, no. 4 (AVRIL 1962), 634–645.

Fanon, Frantz. *Black Skin, White Masks*. New York: Grove Press, 1952 [2008].

Fanon, Frantz. "The Cavalry of a People, *El Moudjahid*, No. 13, November 1958." In *Frantz Fanon: Alienation and Freedom*, edited by Jean Khalfa and Robert J.C. Young. Translated by Steven Corcoran, 617–623. New York: Bloomsbury Academic, 2018.

Fanon, Frantz. "A Democratic Revolution, *El Moudjahid*, No. 12, November 15, 1957." In *Frantz Fanon: Alienation and Freedom*, edited by Jean Khalfa and Robert J.C. Young. Translated by Steven Corcoran, 569–573. New York: Bloomsbury Academic, 2018.

Fanon, Frantz. "Letter to a Frenchman." In *Toward the African Revolution: Political Essays*, Translated by Haakon Chevalier, 47–51. New York: Grove Press, 1967.

Fanon, Frantz. "Letter to the Resident Minister (1956)." In *Toward the African Revolution: Political Essays*, Translated by Haakon Chevalier, 52–54. New York: Grove Press, 1967.

Fanon, Frantz. "National Independence: The Only Possible Outcome. *El Moudjahid*, No. 10, September, 1957." In *Frantz Fanon: Alienation and Freedom*, edited by Jean Khalfa and Robert J.C. Young. Translated by Steven Corcoran, 549–555. New York: Bloomsbury Academic, 2018.

Fanon, Frantz. "The North African Syndrome." In *Toward the African Revolution: Political Essays*, Translated by Haakon Chevalier, 3–16. New York: Grove Press, 1967.

Fanon, Frantz. "Racism and Culture." In *Toward the African Revolution: Political Essays*, Translated by Haakon Chevalier, 29–45. New York: Grove Press, 1967.

Fanon, Frantz. *The Wretched of the Earth*. New York: Grove Press, 2005.

Germain, Félix. *Decolonizing the Republic: African and Caribbean Migrants in Postwar Paris, 1946–1974*, East Lansing: Michigan State University Press, 2016.

Khlafa, Jean and Robert J.C. Young. *Frantz Fanon: Alienation and Freedom*. London: Bloomsbury Publishing, 2018.

Macey, David. *Frantz Fanon: A Biography*. New York: Verso, 2012.

Mercer, Kobena. "Decolonization and Disappointment: Reading Fanon's Sexual Politics." In *The Fact of Blackness*, edited by Alan Read. Seattle: Bay Press, 1996: 114–31.

Ruíz, Elena. "Existentialism for Postcolonials: Fanon and the Politics of Authenticity." *APA Newsletter on Hispanic /Latino Issues in Philosophy* 15, no. 2 (Spring 2016).

Schutte, Ofelia. *Cultural Identity and Social Liberation in Latin American Thought*. New York: State University of New York Press, 1993.

Schwenger, Robert. "Review of *The Wretched of the Earth*" *Monthly Labor Review* 86, no. 2 (February 1963): 185–198.

Sharpley-Whitting, Denean. *Frantz Fanon: Conflicts and Feminisms*. Lanham, MD: Rowman and Littlefield, 1997.

Shea, Alec. "Banning Black Liberation," https://www.muckrock.com/news/archives/2017/aug/04/michigan-doc-fanon/.

Simpson, Audra. "Ethnographic Refusal: Indigeneity, 'Voice,' and Colonial Citizenship." *Juctures: The Journal for Thematic Dialogue* 9 (2007): 67–80.

CHAPTER 12

Fanon's New Humanism as Antidote to Today's Colonial Violence

Majid Sharifi and Sean Chabot

The vast majority of political scientists, sociologists, and philosophers continue to label Frantz Fanon as an "apostle of violence."[1] In the process, they deny his deep commitment to revolutionary humanism and mutual recognition among colonizer and colonized. This chapter argues that Fanon is highly relevant for understanding and confronting colonial violence in the contemporary world-system. It starts by discussing Fanon's analysis of total violence in colonial contexts, before considering his original approach to decolonizing counter-violence. Then it examines Fanon's concept of "new humanism" and illustrates the latter's significance. We propose that "stretching Fanon" allows us to make sense of how today's wretched of the earth struggle against and beyond conditions of colonial annihilation.

1   Colonialism's Total Violence

For Fanon, violence is inherent in the colonial system itself, shaping all relationships among the colonizer and the colonized. *The Wretched of the Earth*, therefore, starts by showing how "the colonial world is a world divided into compartments," juxtaposing the "zones of being," where the colonizers live, with "the zones of non-being," of the colonized.[2] The social spaces of white settlers are prosperous, clean, comfortable, and safe, while the social spaces of black natives are dilapidated, dirty, crowded, and dangerous. The colonial police officers and soldiers are the officials who use the colonial state's monopoly of violence to establish and defend the "lines of force" between the two worlds. The colonial teachers and missionaries serve as the benign intermediaries

---

1   For examples, see Hannah Arendt, "A Special Supplement: Reflections on Violence," *The New York Review of Books*, February 27, 1969, https://www.nybooks.com/articles/1969/02/27/a-special-supplement-reflections-on-violence/; Barbara Deming, *Revolution and Equilibrium*. New York: Grossman Publishers, 1971; Aristide Zolberg and Vera Zolberg, "The Americanization of Frantz Fanon," *National Affairs* (Fall 1967).

2   Frantz Fanon, *The Wretched of the Earth* (New York: Grove Press, 1963), 37–41.

seeking to civilize the colonized nonbeings. And the colonial capitalists and elites benefit by freely exploiting the colony's resources, labor, and morality. In short, colonialism is a system of total violence where violence infuses and destroys every aspect of colonized people's way of life, while enriching the colonizing people at the expense of their own humanity.

Besides sketching the basic contours of colonial violence, Fanon uses the concept of violence in three specific ways. He first uses violence to describe the coercive physical power of "the colonizer" to force "the colonized" to obey and submit. Such repressive force reduces the colonized to an object, a thing, a direct or indirect instrument of the Other. According to Fanon, colonial rule "is the bringer of violence into the home and into the mind of the native."[3] The colonized feel compelled to give up their agential power as colonizers establish control over their bodies and souls – their subjectivities. In other words, the colonized do not own their bodies or control how their bodies are perceived, evaluated, and recognized by colonizers. As objects in the eyes of colonizers, the colonized cannot see or experience their self-worth, neither can they enjoy social status or social recognition as full human beings.

The second dimension of violence is institutionalized violence that allows colonizers to use their monopoly of violence to regulate and protect sovereign order. Fanon shows how, in the process, this "legalized violence" eradicates all indigenous institutional rules, practices, and juridical norms on the one hand, and builds pseudo-traditions that enable the colonial system to persist on the other hand. In his book *Subject Citizens*, Mahmood Mamdani details the violence of such slash, burn, and build policies, resulting in the erasure of colonized history, rule, traditions, and in effect, selfhood.[4] Fanon also shows how such social reordering normalizes divisions between the colonizer's and colonized's worlds, often with the collaboration of native chiefs, clerics, warlords, entrepreneurs, intellectuals, and others. The colonial world is a world of conquerors over conquered, occupiers over occupied, and privileged settlers over dehumanized natives. The overall effect of institutionalized violence is to create a juridical, educational, political, and economic order that controls the social body of the colonized, leaving them powerless, voiceless, confused, and fearful of an alien order. Every institution in this order works toward advancing the science of domination.

And finally, the third dimension of violence is epistemic, cultural, and psychological. In this dimension, the structure of colonial violence produces its

---

3 Fanon, *The Wretched of the Earth*, 38.
4 Mahmood Mamdani, *Citizen and Subject : Contemporary Africa and the Legacy of Late Colonialism*. Princeton, NJ: Princeton University Press, 1996.

own hegemonic superstructure (culture) "with the help of books, newspapers, schools... texts, advertisements, films, and radio." This cultural production "slowly and subtly" penetrates the body and the mind of the colonized and the colonizer, shaping their interiorized subjectivities accordingly. For Fanon, this cultural condition is deeply violent in itself: "Colonialism is not a thinking machine, nor a body endowed with reasoning faculties. It is violence in its natural state."[5] It is in this cultural violence where the psychology of the colonized develops, creating cultural traumas for native communities. In *Toward the African Revolution*, Fanon writes, "We witness the destruction of cultural values, of ways of life. Language, dress, techniques are devalorized... The social panorama is destructed; values are flaunted, crushed, emptied... a new system of values is imposed."[6] Hegemonic institutions such as colonial media, schools, hospitals, and churches reinforce colonized people's sense of inferiority by classifying Black traditions as backward, irrational, and evil. At the same time, they glorify and normalize Western cultural domination by enabling white educators and humanitarians to fulfill the colonial "civilizing mission."[7]

For Fanon, violence affects the psychological make up of both the colonized and colonizers, although in different ways. As a psychiatrist, Fanon examines psychological effects of colonialism on both the colonized and colonizers. Given the space, a brief review of a few cases might be demonstrative of his thinking. In one case, he shows the case of French policemen violently raping an Algerian woman to force her to reveal her husband's whereabouts. The event leads to her husband, a militant nationalist, to abandon his wife, leaving her to fend for herself. But the unbearable guilt of abonnement affects the physical and psychological health of the husband, making him, among other things, impotent.[8] In this particular case, Fanon does not examine the violence of repeated gang raping on the wife, as a direct victim, or the French policemen, as the victimizer. But in other cases, he shows that that violence affects both the physical and psychological, not only the perpetuators and direct victims of violence, but also bystanders and their community. Other empirical studies done since then verified Fanon's finding to the effect that violence has physical, psychological, and what Fanon calls atmospheric effects.

Fanon shows the same phenomenon in another case study, where he examines the effects of violence on the victimizer rather than the victims of direct

---

5   Quoted from, Gibson, *Fanon: The Postcolonial Imagination*, 106.
6   Frantz Fanon, *Toward the African Revolution* (New York: Grove 1967), 33–34.
7   Ibid.
8   Fanon, *The Wretched of the Earth*, 185.

or atmospheric victims. In an examination of a French interrogator, Fanon describes the story of a French police inspector who seeks treatment because he finds himself torturing his wife and his three children when he goes home.[9] In the process of examination, Fanon finds out that the police inspector is an interrogator who routinely tortures suspected insurgents to force them to betray their comrades, their families, and their lifelong mission. Not surprisingly to Fanon, the torturer becomes the tortured victim of his own victimization in the process. During his treatment, the psychotic detachment of the patient from reality becomes obvious. On the one hand, the inspector does not understand why he has become a simple "foot soldier" in a war the government says does not exist. On the other hand, he feels obligated to perform his duty as effectively as possible, even though he says the job wears him out. "Sometimes I torture for ten hours straight," he admits. And in a blind loyalty to his duty, he tortures his victims as efficiently as Adolf Eichmann did in transporting Jews to concentration camps with total detachment from the ethical implication of his actions. In a sense, he has lost his autonomous, ethical conscience and become a non-reflective, non-being as Eichmann was. In fact, the performance of his duty becomes a sign of his personal success. "Our problem" in forcing prisoners "to squeal" is a "matter of personal success," as officers compete to beat the person to talk, he confesses. "We eventually mess up our fists... so we bring the Senegalese. But they either hit too hard and mess up the guy, or not enough and nothing happens... That is why it's best to do your own work, so you can judge better how you're doing." This ethical detachment extends beyond his torture chambers, when he begins to torture his wife and children. Rationalizing his violent behavior at home, he confesses that he does not understand why his wife thinks he is being too harsh with the children. In other cases, Fanon shows how dehumanization of the Other in effect turns into the dehumanization of Selfhood. The reverse is also true for Fanon, as he argues that Selfhood cannot be complete without the arduous process of humanizing the Other. Since then, others in the medical field have verified Fanon's clinical findings.[10]

Thus, the three specific dimensions of violence affect the psychological, sociological, and cultural context of both the colonized and colonizers. As such, Fanon uses violence to connote the organizing principle of the colonial order. This principle revolves around different dimensions of violence. It is violence that totalizes relationships between the occupier and the occupied, thereby distorting and dehumanizing their psyches. "The Negro enslaved by his inferiority,

9   Ibid., 197.
10   For example, M.D. James Gilligan, *Violence*. New York Vintage Books, 1997.

the White man enslaved by his superiority alike behave in accordance with a neurotic orientation," Fanon contends.[11] This relational opposition gives those endowed with means of violence a sense of narcissistic superiority and those without such means a masochistic feeling of inferiority. Regardless of one's position, however, colonialism is a psychopathic order that produces two opposing species – colonizing beings and colonized non-beings – at war with each other and their humanity.

In this violent order, the colonizer sees Self as the extension of the universalizing metropole, the owner of imperial law, truth, history, and order. Endowed with the responsibility of maintaining imperial rule, colonizers make history. Their lives are active and heroic: "We made this land. If we leave, all will be lost, and the land will return to the Dark Ages."[12] In contrast, the colonized's lives lack meaning and existence, and are devoid of law, truth, history, and responsibility. This is a totalizing world, where the colonized "is declared impervious to ethics, representing not only the absence of value but also the negation of values. He is... the enemy of values... Values are, in fact, irreversibly poisoned and infected as soon as they come into contact with the colonized."[13] In other words, colonial violence is necessary for civilized peace.

What the colonizer ultimately seeks is the total disappearance, expulsion, and annihilation of what is seen as the absolute evil – the backward, inferior, deprived, lazy, irrational, and violent people of colonies. Yet without the colonized, there would be no colonialism, nor any cheap labor, slaves, peasants, and servants. Out of this contradiction emerges a Manichean order designed to rule two different species living under the same world system but experiencing life in two separate zones. Therefore, any threat to transcend or break down these walls of separation is a threat to the whole system. Without the use of instrumental, institutional, and epistemic violence, the whole system falls apart. In fact, violence functions not only as the glue that keeps the order together, but also as the engine that drives it, and the rationality that justifies its ends. That is why Fanon insists that colonialism, as well as neocolonialism, cannot exist or survive without its instrumental, institutional, and epistemic violence. Immersed in this psychopathic order, violence is everywhere and affects everybody in an atmospheric way. For Fanon, violence is not reducible to individual acts and responsibilities defined by the law. Stated differently, Fanon does not define violence in juridical terms, such as breaking the law. For him, colonizing law is always violent and its enforcement is even more violent.

---

11   Fanon, *Black Skin, White Masks* (New York: Grove Press, 1967), 42.
12   Fanon, *The Wretched of the Earth*, 14–15.
13   Ibid., 6.

For Fanon, colonial violence is produced systemically; so its effects are atmospheric, as both the colonizer and colonized breathe the same toxic social air. But the effects on their bodies are not the same, because they do not experience or understand violence in the same way. For colonizers, colonial violence is required for protection and progress. For them, the violent nature of the system appears as the necessary means, natural laws, institutional rules, and moral force of the righteous sanctioned by biblical laws. For them, the violence of segregation is not only a means of protecting their racial purity, but also their class interest. For colonizers, discrimination serves their rational, just, and purposeful interests and values. For them, policing, schooling, surveillance, control, punishment, and "zero tolerance" for infractions of rules are preventive measures to maintain the order. For them, the system is not violent; only evil individuals are. Thus, colonizers interpret the violence of abject poverty as the natural, personal, biological, or cultural characteristic of their "territorial enemies," the violence of state repression as reasonable protection from the evil nature of "black, brown, and yellow hordes." For the colonizers of the old and new, the psychotic temptation to obliterate the colonized enemy into total submission is strong and ever present.

Such temptations are put on display on many occasions, as happened in the nuclear annihilation of Hiroshima and Nagasaki, in the indiscriminate bombings of Vietnamese villages, in the shooting of an Iranian passenger airplane. In all these cases, the psychotic temptation to kill is a better explanation than any military justification offered. Otherwise, no military justification can possibly explain what, for example, Israeli occupiers call *mowing operations*, when once every few years they attack Palestinians into submission. In the 2014 *mowing* operation, the world witnessed how bright burning explosives rained down from the sky on Gazans: how bombs knock on their buildings' rooftops just before the jetfighter unloaded their *real bomb*, pulverizing huge apartment complexes. As Palestinians were escaping from their burning buildings, they would come to the crosshair of Israeli target shooters. Fanon understood this colonizing *death wish*. In *Dying Colonialism*, Fanon wrote about how the French military, French Navy, French jet fighters, and French paid militias boastfully slaughtered an uncounted number of Algerians. Members of the European settler communities were heard saying, "Let's each one of us take ten of them and bump them off and you'll see the problem solved in no time."[14]

Yet the temptation to totally obliterate the colonized contradicts the nature of colonialism, or for that matter, neocolonialism. After all, colonialism without the colonized does not function. Neither does capitalism without the

---

14   Fanon, *A Dying Colonialism* (New York: Grove Press, 1967), 56.

concept of absolute ownership. At the conceptual level, then, those who own the state also own the means of violence. And those who own the best means of violence can and do speak for it as a legitimate *cleansing force* against the evil nature of their common enemies, who in effect want what the colonizers own: their homelands, their possession, their privileges, their wives, their cities, and their civilization. In other words, the legitimacy of violence has much to do with who owns what and whom. For colonizers, therefore, the ultimate goal is to maintain their racial and class supremacy, as well as total control over everything in it, including the body and mind of the colonized.

But the colonized see themselves as the main target of colonial violence in all its forms. Their bodies experience the pain of hunger, segregation, discrimination, and punishment. Their feelings, neglected by the colonizers, are deeply hurt by the indignity of abject poverty. Under constant surveillance, control, and *zero tolerance* policing, they live in an occupied world, where their "breathing is an observed, occupied breathing. It is a combat breathing," as Fanon puts it.[15] Mis-educated and mystified by a world they do not own, control, or even understand, they are reduced to caged animals traumatized by the violence of existence, which they often direct at themselves and their communities. Embodied in the violence of their existence, the colonized remain alienated from self, culture, and history. And as they see themselves in the gaze of their occupiers, they develop a series of inferiority complexes and lose their self-confidence.

Yet, the colonized cannot help but resist the system in any way they can. After all, they are in daily combat in which they are over-powered, caged, and disoriented, but not completely tamed, Fanon contends. "He is treated as an inferior, but he is not convinced of his inferiority."[16] They are not allowed to express their agential power, but their desire for freedom remains part of their dreams, despite the darkened reality. In Fanon's words, "During the period of colonization, the native never stops achieving his freedom from nine in the evening until six in the morning."[17] The natives dream about action, muscular prowess, aggression, freedom of movement, and joy of living. They find outlets for existential violence in various forms of rituals, for example dancing, where they release their pent-up aggression, as they expresses their muscular prowess, desire for freedom, and joy for love of life. For Fanon, these dream-actions represent two interrelated phenomena. First, they represent the uncrushable desire of the subaltern for freedom. Second, they represent how colonial

---

15   Fanon, *Toward the African Revolution*, 65.
16   Fanon, *The Wretched of the Earth*, 16.
17   Ibid., 15.

violence fails to tame, let alone convince, the colonized into complete docility. As such, the colonized never stop resisting, resenting, and defying their dehumanization. This insight is crucial for understanding Fanon's revolutionary strategy of counter-violence.

2   Fanon on Counter-violence

In Fanon's eyes, the best colonialism or neocolonialism can ever achieve is a hegemonic empire founded on violence. The conclusion is that an empire of violence "lives by the sword and dies by the sword." For Fanon, therefore, the verdict is clear: the colonized must break down the colonizer's monopoly of violence by resorting to what he calls counter-violence of anti-colonial violence. Fanon uses both terms. We prefer the use of counter-violence, as opposed to anti-colonial violence, because it reflects Fanon's dynamic thinking, which by no means is binary. In any case, Fanon argues that for the caged colonized, counter-violence is a necessary force to break out of their shackles, allowing them to breathe the detoxifying air of freedom at the individual, local, and national levels. But as a psychiatrist working with colonizers and colonized patients in an Algerian hospital, Fanon is keenly aware of the potential as well as danger of subjective violence in response to systemic colonial violence.

Far from glorifying violence, or seeing it as an end in itself, Fanon realizes that within a colonial society dying from total violence, counter-violence is often the only imaginable first step in the long struggle toward decolonization. As Fanon writes in the early pages of *The Wretched of the Earth*:

> Decolonization is always a violent phenomenon. At whatever level we study it ... decolonization is quite simply the replacing of a certain 'species' of men by another 'species' of men... Decolonization, which sets out to change the order of the world, is, obviously, a program of complete disorder... Decolonization is the meeting of two forces, opposed to each other by their very nature... Their first encounter was marked by violence and their existence together – that is to say the exploitation of the native by the settler – was carried on by the dint of a great array of bayonets and cannons.[18]

In other words, for decolonization to actually replace and transform the order of the colonial world, it must initially violate the submissive subjectivity of the

---

18   Fanon, *The Wretched of the Earth*, 36.

colonized (suffering from internalized inferiority complexes) as well as violate
the dehumanizing subjectivity of the colonizers (unable to see the ethical contradictions of their actions). More concretely, the native must use violence (the
last available tool in the violent colonial system) to directly confront the settler
(whose violence is routine and "civilizing") on an equal footing, as two human
beings fighting for survival and existence. For colonized individuals suffering
from "crushing objecthood," this violent act can be "cleansing" in the sense that
it allows for self-recognition, opening the way for realizing self-worth.[19] Such
active subjectivities are then ready to step toward decolonization. For Fanon,
therefore, this temporarily "cathartic" violence serves the larger purpose of
self-realization among the colonized and, in the long run, mutual ethical recognition among the colonized and colonizers.[20]

Fanon's approach to the ethics of recognition begins with the view that colonialism negates the being of black people by excluding them from the Self-
Other encounters shaping identity-formation. With no Other to validate them,
the colonized, be they in black and brown or white, lack the means to create
their own Self, reducing them to inanimate objects. What the colonized, or occupied bodies of the oppressed, want, in the first place, is "to be considered,"
to experience "reciprocity of recognition" as equally valuable human beings –
something that is completely lacking in colonial relationships.[21] Only such reciprocal recognition can enable people of color to gain self-consciousness and
interact with white colonizers with self-confidence. While cleansing violence
is one way that colonized non-beings can become decolonizing revolutionaries, retrieval of native cultural traditions and aesthetic practices – as favored
by the literary movement *negritude* – is another. Thus, decolonization relies on
the capacity of both colonizers and colonized to recognize and respect each
other's differences in their interactions.[22]

We suggest that Fanon's concept of counter-violence has two distinct yet related meanings. Initially, it refers to counter-*violence* by the colonized in reaction to the total violence of colonialism. Such decolonizing violence is different
from colonial violence, because it arises from conditions of desperation and
potentially turns passive non-beings with inferiority complexes into revolutionary makers of history. But Fanon does not deny the seductive and destructive tendencies of such violence. He witnesses and experiences the horrors of

---

19   Fanon, *Black Skin, White Masks*, 82.
20   Pramod K. Nayar, "Frantz Fanon: Toward a Postcolonial Humanism," *The IUP Journal of
      Commonwealth Literature III*, No.1 (January 2011): 22.
21   Fanon, *Black Skin, White Masks*, 170.
22   Nayar, "Frantz Fanon," 23–24.

violence everyday among the colonizers and colonized he treats at the mental hospital. For him, therefore, violence is never an end in itself or something to glorify. Fanon highlights the contradictions faced by armed revolutionaries: "The militant who faces the colonialist war machine with the bare minimum of arms realizes that while he is breaking down colonial oppression he is building up yet another system of exploitation."[23] Without careful planning and discipline, counter-violence is likely to reproduce the colonial system and merely replace foreign with domestic oppressors. Violent revolution is insufficient for constructing alternative material realities and significantly improving the lives of colonized people.[24]

According to Fanon, counter-violence is only productive to the extent it allows the colonized to experience and struggle for freedom. It is in freedom that the colonized begin recognizing themselves as humans endowed with agential power, right to self-determination, and self-respect at the individual and community level. It is in freedom that they begin to unveil their Selfhood from a life of mis-education, mystification, and violent physical and conceptual borders. It is in freedom that they become political and begin developing a unified sense of community. The internalized, self-directed violence dissipates and they become actional political beings, aware of their relationships with fellow community members. In the process, their debilitating fear of the colonial master disappears, as does their inferiority complex. Suddenly, they emerge as human subjects with independent consciousness, as opposed to objectified things occupied by the consciences of their masters. It is in their independence where they learn how to build a decolonized political community. For Fanon, this is the beginning of the decolonization struggle.

As the decolonization struggle grows, the emphasis shifts toward counter-violence. Fanon argues that the "fighting phase" leads to "radical mutation" of colonized people's consciousness and capacity to act. The colonized start to meet in local communities to talk politics, develop theories, decide on resistance strategies, and envision the "real task of reconstruction."[25] In their interactions, they become a social movement: they tune in to the same radio stations, read or hear about battles against colonizers, and imagine shared destinies. By engaging in social dialogue and building social relationships, they create a new national consciousness based on recognition of unity-in-diversity and protagonism of the people rather than native elites. In the practice of becoming a liberated nation, the colonized begin to realize that national independence is not a gift to be given by the colonizer, a deal to be negotiated

---

23   Fanon, The Wretched of the Earth, 145.
24   Ibid., 81.
25   Fanon, A Dying Colonialism, 86.

by reformist parties, an award to be discovered by Westernized intellectuals, or a model to be dictated or copied from another empire of violence. Instead, freedom must be taken and made through speech-actions. During this phase, the decolonization movement focuses on constructing alternative ways of life that go *against-and-beyond* the total violence of colonialism.

From Fanon's perspective, therefore, the lessons for the wretched of the earth should be loud and clear: *counter-violence* is instrumental in the first stage of liberation. However, instrumental violence is exactly that: it is a temporary means, not an end. In that, Fanon considers counter-violence as an organized push back against being choked to death. It is a push back when the colonized are being thrown against the wall and shot. It is a mere means to free the Self from the physical daily abuse, suspicion, arrest, labor encampment, and ghettoization. Counter-violence has the psychological effect of liberating the occupied body of the colonized from internalized fear, their inferiority complex, and self-directed violence. It is a catalyst in coercing the oppressor to recognize the will and desire, as well as the potential threat, of the oppressed. Counter-violence spurs the national (collective) consciousness of the colonized, empowering them to speak of their demands, desires, and expectations.

3   Fanon's New Humanism

Despite being known as an apostle of violence, Fanon's ultimate goal is a world order built on mutual recognition and love of humanity among former colonizers and the colonized. Throughout his writings, Fanon makes it clear that *counter-violence* in and of itself is not enough to create a "new man" or another world that goes beyond the violence of Manicheanism, racism, militarism, poverty, and inequality. Lamenting how some revolutionaries use violence without critically questioning their goals, he writes:

> Because we want a democratic and renovated Algeria, because we believe one cannot rise and liberate oneself in one area and sink in another, we condemn with pain in our hearts those brothers who have flung themselves into revolutionary action with the almost physiological brutality that centuries of oppression give rise to and feed.[26]

This lamentation is despite the fact that Fanon believes that *counter-violence* is inevitable at the beginning of the Algerian revolution. Yet he insists that such violence must be limited, reasoned, and measured. He argues that hatred

---

26   Ibid., 25.

cannot be an agenda, and the use of violence in and of itself cannot constitute a constructive political program or a strategy for liberation, aiming to end colonialism, not to renew it in ethno-nationalistic or sectarian forms. Fanon also maintains that every decolonization situation is contextually different. Therefore, the way Algerians use *counter*-violence cannot be a universal model for other people. For Fanon, praxis dictates how other people should go through the process of liberation in their own ways, using counter-*violence* in the first stage of decolonization and *counter-violence* in the long struggle toward human emancipation.

All in all, Fanon's writings make three crucial points concerning *counter-violence* that are particularly relevant in today's world. First, *counter-violence* used in the process of liberation is a "double-act" in response to colonialism's total violence that must be proportionate to the intensity of violence used to maintain the colonial order. Second, the use of *counter-violence*, as a strategy in the liberation phase of decolonization, cannot in and of itself stop the reemergence of neocolonialism in the postcolonial era. And finally, decolonization is an unfinished project that requires ongoing experiments with *counter-violence* as means and end. After establishing national independence, decolonized leaders and people must end colonialism by first and foremost dismantling its physical, institutional, and epistemic violence.

Fanon's complex understanding of colonial violence and decolonizing counter-violence informs his approach to a new humanism that envisions a world in which "the last shall be first and the first last."[27] He does not mince words in his criticism of liberal Western humanism that prevails in the imperial world-system:

> Leave this Europe where they are never done talking of Man, yet murder men everywhere they find them, at the corner of every one of their own streets, in all the corners of the globe... That same Europe where they were never done talking of Man, and where they never stopped proclaiming that they were only anxious for the welfare of Man: today we know with what sufferings humanity has paid for every one of their triumphs of the mind.[28]

Fanon recognizes that Western humanism is toxic because it has been used instrumentally. But he does not give up on the revolutionary potential of a new and decolonized formation of humanism, which should be made to serve the greatest majority of humans, not the few with special rights and privileges.

---

27   Fanon, *The Wretched of the Earth*, 37.
28   Ibid., 311–312.

That is why he invokes the idea of the *damned of the earth,* not the plight of Algerians or the oppression of blacks or the demonization Arabs. What Fanon wants is to go beyond any form of racial, ethnic, cultural, or territorial nationalism. For Fanon, new humanism is about giving voice to the *last,* which constituted the multitudes, not the *first,* who dominate the rest. For Fanon, humanism is not about following in the footsteps of Western, liberal humanism, which was born out of the womb of colonialism, mercantilism, racism, and civilizing missions. New humanism for Fanon starts as an initiative to imagine and build a new world order, not to reconstitute the *white man's burden* in its liberal humanitarian forms.

Instead of imitating the West, Fanon's new humanism sets out to move in new directions, enabling new ways of thinking, living, and being in the world. He believes that colonized people awakening from the slumber of non-being and struggling to forge relationships of mutual recognition are capable of transforming humanity *without* depending on Western modernity and leadership. Contrary to the elitist and imperialist perspective of Western humanism, Fanon proposes a participatory and revolutionary humanism shaped by new human beings who no longer seek to destroy each other in the name of national, racial, or economic domination:

> No, we do not want to catch up with anyone. What we want to do is to go forward all the time, night and day, in the company of Man, in the company of all men. The caravan should not be stretched out, for in that case each line will hardly see those who precede it; and men who no longer recognize each other meet less and less together, and talk to each other less and less. It is a question of the Third World starting a new history of Man... [If] we want humanity to advance a step further, if we want to bring it up to a different level than that which Europe has shown it, then we must invent and must make discoveries.[29]

In short, Fanon's new humanism both opposes and goes beyond the Eurocentric humanism that continues to normalize and justify colonial violence in today's world-system. This new humanism highlights how the colonial Western gaze constructs violent divisions between nations, communities, races, classes, and other social groups. But it insists that oppressed people suffering from these divisions are capable of imagining new concepts and experimenting with new practices that avoid the hostilities and brutalities associated with Western liberal humanism.

---

29   Ibid., 314–315.

Fanon's new humanism also opens up alternative perspectives on violence and nonviolence, namely Western neocolonial humanism, which uses enlightened reason to condone what it defines as "legitimate" use of violence, while opposing what it names as "illegitimate" violence. While it reserves the right to name, judge, and execute what it calls "legitimate" violence, by extension it defines what is "illegitimate." Similarly, it projects itself as the promoter of nonviolence as the only legitimate means of social resistance. As such, it claims to support people's nonviolent resistance, yet decides what to name as nonviolent or violent resistance. From the perspective of liberal humanism, the distinction between "legitimate" and "illegitimate" use of violence, or the difference between violence and nonviolence becomes a matter of who has the power to name it. In so doing, liberal humanism creates a series of flawed binaries, which define "legitimate" or "illegitimate" use of violence in reductive juridical terms. As such, it can name what legal and thus legitimate use of violence is, what is not legal, and therefore what is an illegitimate use of violence. These flawed binaries have pervaded the discourse of liberal humanism, in which Western imperial states are represented as the gold standard against which other communities are evaluated. Fanon rejects this colonizing orientation promoted by Westoxificated intellectuals – a term used by Jalal Al-e Ahmad, an Iranian intellectual influenced by Fanon's thinking.

Instead, Fanon problematizes the conventional binary between violence and nonviolence, as well as other Manichean classifications of good and evil. On the one hand, he shows that some forms of *counter-violence* can set the stage for social change from the bottom up and *beyond* colonial violence. On the other hand, he draws attention to the possibility that even popular nonviolent resistance movements might reproduce violent neocolonial systems.[30] For example, if nonviolent movements were to merely change one colonizing regime for another nothing has in effect changed. Therefore, Fanon's new humanism calls for revolutionary struggles seeking political, cultural, and ethical transformation.

4   Examples of Fanon's Relevance Today

The need to counter colonial violence and realize Fanon's vision of new humanism remains as urgent and unfulfilled as during the Algerian decolonization movement. Fanon feared that post-colonialism may not necessarily mean

---

30   Sean Chabot and Majid Sharifi, "The Violence of Nonviolence: Problematizing Nonviolent Resistance in Iran and Egypt," *Societies Without Borders* 8, no. 2 (May 2013).

the end of colonialism, let alone the end of Eurocentric coloniality as the governing rationality of global domination. Sadly, his worst fears have come true. Whereas today's world-system is supposed to be based on the concept of national sovereignty of all states, in reality this promise is a legal fiction everywhere. Neoliberal globalization has turned Western as well as non-Western states into loyal servants of global capitalism and corporations, while imperial as well as subaltern states primarily serve national elites instead of popular freedom and social equality.[31] The hierarchical ordering of the world population into a compartmentalized world order also continues. As we speak, Fanon's Manichean walls of separation are taller, harder, and more pervasive than ever. Nowadays, human beings are categorized as two different species: one that makes and implements all the rules, including decisions concerning who deserves to have human rights and who does not. The other species must obey given rules and live precarious or even disposable lives, whether they officially enjoy human rights or not. For example, many populations around the world must pay the price for the "humanitarian wars" of Western states and their allies, aimed at global control over resources, forms of government, and cultural norms. Thus, Fanon's insights into differences between colonized and colonizing people can easily describe two different species living under the neocolonial order in the present. On one side are those very few residing in manicured mansions and guarded communities while they collectively own and control almost all the world's capital, whether they reside in the poor global South or the rich global North. And then there are the rest of the wretched of the earth who own nothing except perhaps their cheap labor, which is increasingly harder to sell. While the former lay down the law, the latter follow. While the former freely travel and buy citizenship of any country they desire, the latter remain chained to the tyranny of poverty at home or to the mirage of a better life abroad, often facing the indignity of living as a nonbeing in a perpetual state of foreignness.

The condition of alienation is not exclusive to immigrants. It has become a permanent feature of the neocolonial order, afflicting people everywhere and in every language. As in Fanon's time, the youths of the world have never stopped dreaming of freedom "from nine in the evening until six in the morning." But their dreams of freedom are often made in Hollywood type productions, where the lifestyles of celebrities and billionaires pervade their desires. By definition, such dreams contradict the lived experiences of the damned of the earth. Lured by unreachable dreams, the life of the wretched of the earth is

---

31   Majid Sharifi, *Imagining Iran: The Tragedy of Subaltern Nationalism.* Lanham: Lexington Books, 2013.

a life of violence, insecurity, depravation, and alienation. The manifestation of such interiorized violence appears in pent up frustration in non-state groups and actors everywhere. The interiorized violence ranges from suicidal to homicidal tendencies, from black on black violence in American to sectarian violence in the Middle East, from the rise of racist nationalism in the heart of the liberal empire to organized violence by terror groups like Daesh (ISIS).

The expression of such estrangement from society and self appears in various forms of art throughout the world, including in the heart of the liberal Empire. African-American poet, rapper, and actress Lauryn Hill, for example, sings about the institutionalized injustice in the American justice system. In her 2002 song, "It's the Mystery of Inequity," Hill describes the system as politically correct but morally corrupt. She compares the courtroom with an arena where crooked lawyers, unethical judges, paid expert witnesses, bailiffs, legal extortionists, and professional liars perform injustice in the name of the law and the truth, while the victim sits in a fog of confusion. She calls this the "mystery of inequity." Drawing on the biblical meaning of the mystery as a phenomenon that humans are incapable of understanding, Hill points to a moral crisis in the system:

> How long will you sleep, troubled by the thoughts that you keep. The idols you heap. Causing the destruction you reap. Judgement has come… renounce all your thoughts; Repent and let your mind be re-taught; You'll find what you sought; Was based on the deception you bought; A perception of naught where the majority remains caught, in loving their lies.

In other words, Hill shows that various forms of colonial violence and division persist in the twenty-first century – not only in formerly colonized societies, but also in societies that dominate today's colonizing world-system.

In another song, Lauryn Hill draws on Carter G. Woodson's book, *Mis-Education of the Negro,* to question how life is squeezing her so tight that she can't breathe because of "what someone else has taught her to be and achieve."[32] In this song, she alludes to the pervasive epistemic violence of the system. This frustration, and analogy to "combat breathing," also shows up in a song by popular hip-hop artist Kendrick Lamar:

> What if a dream was reality and reality was a dream? And as complicated as it seems, if things we imagined actually happened? And real-life

---

32   Carter Godwin Woodson, *The Mis-Education of the Negro.* Trenton: Africa World Press, 1933.

situations was artificial... They say we only living to die... Imagine if we're already dead, waiting to live, living in hell. Trying to cross over to heaven we're confusing ourselves. Planet earth's like Oceans 11, we're plottin' for the getaway... When my childhood friends get sent away to prison on their first offense. It's fucked up but listen, we study God but don't know him.... Criticize people that work on Sundays, two jobs just to feed their kids... Well, momma's scratching lottery tickets knowing that it's just a fairy tale.... Every time that she's bubblin' in, it feels like the devil's holding a pen... Don't mind me I'm just thinking again. Thinking out loud, thinking the opposite of proud. Cus' I'm disappointed at myself sometimes. Self-esteem gets lower than night strippers.... [Only] if dreams was reality!

Here, a Black American man expresses in heart-breaking language the lived experience of every existence in a world where dreams of freedom remain just that: dreams. A world order that claims to be free yet pushes ever-growing millions of people into colonizing conditions of misery and indignity.

It is important to recognize, however, that Fanon's influence spreads far beyond music and popular culture. Although the forms of colonial rule have evolved since the 1960s, colonial situations and hierarchies remain pervasive in today's world-system, making Fanon's revolutionary analysis and calls to action as relevant as ever. We examine two different places where Fanonian ideas and practices are particularly significant: occupied Palestine and occupied Ferguson, Missouri. But bear in mind that there are many other places in the global South as well as North where colonial violence prevails and decolonizing counter-violence emerges.

The recent Great March of Return in Gaza clearly shows that the colonial violence depicted by Fanon persists in the contemporary world. This campaign draws on the *Nakba* (catastrophe) Day demonstrations in 2011, when Palestinian refugees, who were forced to live in overcrowded camps and open-air prisons in the region, approached the border with Israel to symbolize their demand to return to the lands from which they were evicted, as well as to highlight the horrific living conditions in their current places of residence. Similar to Fanon's description of colonial spaces in the beginning of *The Wretched of the Earth*, Palestinian refugees are calling into question "a world cut in two," with Israeli colonizers living in relatively clean and prosperous territories and colonized Palestinians pushed to survive in the poorest and least dignified territories. They also directly confront "the policeman and the soldier who are the official, instituted go-betweens, the spokesmen of the settler and his rule of oppression," who ruthlessly attack peaceful demonstrators and harmless rock-throwers, and openly celebrate the killing of Palestinian children and mothers.[33] Palestinian refugees and inhabitants of occupied territories experience the instrumental, institutional, and epistemic forms of colonial violence on a daily basis – not only during dramatic events like the Great March of Return. Besides deliberate military invasions and strikes, they also experience a legal system that turns them into non-beings and refuses to punish brutal acts by Israeli soldiers or citizens. Additionally, Israel's colonial regime largely controls global discourse on its war with the Palestinian people, preventing mainstream media and elites around the world from opposing Israeli propaganda and crimes against humanity. Thus, Fanon's words paint an eerily accurate picture of the colonial situations and mentalities experienced by millions of Palestinians today.

Palestinian people have engaged in various forms of counter-violence since the birth of Israel in 1948, especially since the Israeli war known as *Nakba* in 1967. They have used violent tactics like throwing rocks and Molotov cocktails, suicide attacks, and air strikes to resist Israeli occupation and militarism. But they have also enacted peaceful tactics like mass marches, boycotts, rallies, and hunger strikes. Palestinians have relied on *sumud* ("steadfastness") as a way of life that demonstrates their capacity to exist and resist despite constant Israeli efforts to evict them from their homes, make them give up their struggle for liberation, abandon their cultural traditions and artistic modes of expression, and submit to the inevitability and superiority of Israel's colonial rule. In other words, the Palestinian people have adopted both counter-*violence* and nonviolence to survive and imagine alternatives to the colonial violence of Israel's domination. They have not only drawn attention to Israel's neocolonial project, but also experimented with new humanist concepts and new forms of social life that, according to Fanon, might decolonize human beings and communities among the wretched of the earth.[34]

Colonial violence occurs in the periphery as well as the center of the contemporary world-system. Like the Palestinians, poor Black people in American cities also often live in occupied territories that are reminiscent of *The Wretched of the Earth*. Take for example the 2014 police shooting of Michael Brown, an unarmed Black teenager, in Ferguson, Missouri. While mainstream media focused on the warzone in the wake of this event, many Black residents experienced various forms of violent rule in their predominantly Black neighborhoods. They encountered police officers eager to give them tickets for minor offenses like jaywalking or driving with broken taillights, and threaten

---

33   Fanon, *The Wretched of the Earth*, 37–40.

34   Nick Rodrigo, "Fanon in Palestine," *Middle East Monitor*, October 19, 2015, https://www
      .middleeastmonitor.com/20151019-palestine-through-the-lens-of-frantz-fanon/.

or use violence whenever they face a lack of subservience. This lack of freedom and security is a structural problem in Ferguson and other cities, producing so-called "debtor's prisons." Large numbers of poor Black people unable to pay the fees get arrested and end up in prison, which further hurts their employment, housing, and financial prospects, while the (predominantly white) city government benefits economically and politically. Besides such forms of instrumental and institutional violence, Black residents of Ferguson also suffer from epistemic violence that castigates them as dangerous, disposable, and exploitable, thereby exacerbating their own sense of inferiority.[35]

Like their Palestinian counterparts, Black people in Ferguson have responded with a mix of counter-*violence* and nonviolence techniques. Right after the murder of Michael Brown, riots broke out that involved looting, arson, and broken windows. Besides such expressions of rage by the oppressed and unheard, many Black rebels also analyzed the political situation and struggle in their own language, demonstrating the kind of critical consciousness valorized by Fanon. One participant in the standoff between the people and the militarized police stated: "We keep giving these crackers our money, staying in their complexes, and we can't get no justice. No respect! No respect! They're ready to put you out [if you] miss a bill... You got to be fed up!"[36]

But since these initial days of "cleansing violence," Black people – in alliance with the wider Black Lives Matter movement – have initiated and organized many activities aimed at constructing alternatives to the violent spaces, relationships, and structures in Ferguson and beyond. Participants in nearby St. Louis, for instance, created The Truth Telling Project, which "implements and sustains grassroots, community-centered truth-telling processes to amplify our voices about structural violence."[37] By sharing stories of Black youth and adults, they seek to contribute to personal healing, public education, and restorative justice that transform deep-seated structural violence through joint struggles and coalitions. Far from imitating conventional strategies of protest and politics in white communities, they are inventing new ways of articulating their colonial experiences and forging new connections with other oppressed communities – locally, nationally, and globally. It is not surprising therefore that Palestinians expressed their solidarity during the so-called Ferguson riots. Several Black Lives Matter activists recently visited occupied Palestine. Today's

---

35   Whitney Benns and Blake Strode, "Debtor's Prison in 21st Century America," *The Atlantic*, February 23, 2016, https://www.theatlantic.com/business/archive/2016/02/debtors-prison/462378/.

36   Robert Stephens II, "In Defense of the Ferguson Riots," *Jacobin*, August 14, 2014, https://www.jacobinmag.com/2014/08/in-defense-of-the-ferguson-riots/.

37   The Truth Telling Project, http://www.thetruthtellingproject.org/.

wretched of the earth are increasingly recognizing that only transnational networks and resistance can open cracks in the colonial-capitalist world-system.

5   Conclusion

Fanon's Manichean world order lives on, but in its nationalized and personalized forms, which appear gender sensitive, politically correct, color-blinded, and culturally fitted, in accordance with liberal neocolonialism. As Manicheanism continues in its neocolonial form, so does the violence of militarism, racial inequity, national disparity, and social inequity at every local, national, and global level. Breathing once again has become difficult in the neocolonial world, which declares itself to be color blind and politically correct. Yet, various forms of discrimination occur even in the heart of the empire. In a sense, Eric Garner's last words, "I can't breathe, I can't breathe" ring true to billions of people around the world who find themselves in a systematic police chokehold, as Garner did. They can neither free themselves, nor can they breathe freely. They are seduced by the glory of living in a free-market of things, people, and ideas, but they are held by the "invisible hand" of global corporatism combined with the iron fist of governments that keep them locked in a state of perpetual depravation.

Rife with these internal contradictions, however, the neocolonial world order appears incapable of managing its self-created crises. It is at this historical juncture, when the contemporary significance of Fanon's vision of humanism is more relevant than during the height of the national liberation movements of the 1950s or 1960s. Obviously, Fanon's revolutionary hope that a world order of free, independent nation-states will lead a nonviolent humanist order has failed. Yet Fanon's vision of decolonization of national sovereignty, decolonization of juridical order, and decolonization of the mind is still relevant to emerging liberation movements in a postcolonial era. If there is any hope for the redemption of humans, it is in the liberation of the mind from the instrumental, institutional, and epistemic violence of neocolonialism. A world beyond the total violence of colonialism is indeed the organizing philosophy and practice of Fanon's new humanism.

Bibliography

Arendt, Hannah, "A Special Supplement: Reflections on Violence," *The New York Review of Books*. February 27, 1969.

Benns, Whitney, and Blake Strode, "Debtor's Prison in 21st Century America," *The Atlantic*, February 23, 2016.

Case, Benjamin Steinhardt. "Decolonizing Jewishness: On Jewish Liberation in the 21st Century." Tikkun https://www.tikkun.org/nextgen/decolonizing-jewishness-on-jewish-liberation-in-the-21st-century.

Chabot, Sean and Sharifi, Majid, "The Violence of Nonviolence: Problematizing Nonviolent Resistance in Iran and Egypt." *Societies Without Borders* 8, no. 2 (May 2013).

Cox, Robert W. "Social Forces, States and World Orders: Beyond International Relations Theory." In *Neorealism and Its Critics*, edited by Robert O. Keohane. New York: Columbia University Press, 1986.

Deming, Barbara, *Revolution and Equilibrium*. New York: Grossman Publishers, 1971.

Duffied, Mark. *Development, Security, and Uneding War: Governing the World of People*. Cambridge: Polity Press, 2007.

Evans, Brad, and Terrell Garver. *Histories of Violence*. London: Zed Books, 2017.

Fanon, Frantz. *Black Skin, White Masks*. London: Pluto Press, 1952.

Fanon, Frantz. *A Dying Colonialism*. New York: Grove Press, 1965.

Fanon, Frantz. *Toward the African Revolution*. New York: Grove, 1967.

Fanon, Frantz. *The Wretched of the Earth*. Translated by Richard Philcox. New York: Grove Press, 1963/2004.

Galula, David. *Counterinsurgency Warfare: Theory and Practice*. Westpost, CT: Praeger Security International, 1964.

Gibson, Nigel C. *Fanon: The Postcolonial Imagination*. United Kingdom: Polity Press, 2003.

Gilligan, James. *Violence*. New York: Vintage Books, 1997.

Mamdani, Mahmood. *Citizen and Subject : Contemporary Africa and the Legacy of Late Colonialism*. Princeton, NJ: Princeton University Press, 1996.

Nandy, Ashis. *The Intimate Enemy: Loss and Recovery of Self under Colonialism*. New York: Oxford University Press, 1983.

Nayar, Pramod K., "Frantz Fanon: Toward a Postcolonial Humanism." *The IUP Journal of Commonwealth Literature III*, No. 1 (January 2011).

Penny, James. "Passing into the Universal: Fanon, Sartre, and the Colonial Dialectic." *Paragraph, Edinbufgh University Press* 27, no. 3 (November 2004).

Rodrigo, Nick. "Fanon in Palestine," *Middle East Monitor*, October 19, 2015.

Stephens II, Robert, "In Defense of the Ferguson Riots." *Jacobin*, August 14, 2014.

Veer, Peter van der. *Imperial Encounters: Religion and Modernity in India and Britain*. Princeton, NJ: Princeton University Press, 2001.

Woodson, Carter G. *The Mis-Education of the Negro*. Trenton: Africa World Press, 1933.

Zolberg, Aristide and Vera Zolberg. "The Americanizatin of Frantz Fanon." *National Affairs* (Fall 1967).

CHAPTER 13

The Pathology of Race and Racism in Postcolonial Malay Society: A Reflection on Frantz Fanon's *Black Skin, White Masks*

Mohamed Imran Mohamed Taib

> There is a fact: White men consider themselves superior to black men. There is another fact: Black men want to prove to white men, at all costs, the richness of their thought, the equal value of their intellect. How do we extricate ourselves?
>
> ~ FRANTZ FANON[1]

1 Introduction

Every society that manages to extricate itself from colonial domination has to grapple with a set of new problems. The nature of these problems includes (1) the physical and material, such as agriculture, communications, and housing; (2) organizational, such as economic relations, political administration, education, social welfare, and industrialization; and (3) socio-psychological and moral problems, such as values and modes of thought. According to Syed Hussein Alatas, the third set of problems is the most formidable, since it forms "the greatest damage occasioned by colonialism" and "hampers the solution to other difficulties."[2]

A similar concern was raised by Frantz Fanon when he wrote: "To tell the truth, the proof of success [of decolonization] lies in a whole social structure being changed from the bottom up. The extraordinary importance of this change is that it is willed, called for, demanded. The need for this change exists in its crude state, impetuous and compelling, in the consciousness and in the lives of the men and women who are colonized."[3] Fanon was a revolutionary

---

1   Frantz Fanon, *Black Skin, White Masks* (New York: Grove Press, 1967), 10.
2   See Syed Hussein Alatas. "Some Fundamental Problems of Colonialism." *Eastern World* (Nov., 1956).
3   Frantz Fanon, *The Wretched of the Earth* (New York: Grove Press, 1963), 35.

thinker and psychiatrist whose writings had a tremendous influence on anticolonial and postcolonial movements worldwide and continues to inspire scholars and activists working on issues of race and domination. He was among
the first to link the issue of class domination with the race question, which
Marxists tend to ignore. In one of his major works, *The Wretched of the Earth*,
he wrote:

> In the colonies the economic substructure is also a superstructure. The
> cause is the consequence; you are rich because you are white, you are
> white because you are rich. This is why Marxist analysis should always be
> slightly stretched every time we have to do with the colonial problem.[4]

It is this relationship between racism and colonial domination that became
the primary concern in many of Fanon's analyses. This essay seeks to discuss
some of these analyses and argues that Fanon's thoughts are particularly
useful and insightful in diagnosing racist ideology, albeit in subtler forms,
which continue to dominate postcolonial Malay society. As highlighted by
Hansen,

> One important reason Fanon claims our attention as a subject of seri-
> ous inquiry is the issues of his writings and the way he deals with them.
> He presents a serious commentary on significant human problems. The
> question of the psychological alienation of the black man in a white-
> dominated world, his inferiority complex, the quest for whiteness, the
> depersonalization, the feeling of hopelessness, of nonbeing, that Fanon
> deals with are all current problems of people living in the underdevel-
> oped countries.[5]

Two recurring themes will be dealt with specifically: The first is the psychopathological condition of the colonized people. The second is the problem of
alienation observed in their cultural and intellectual life. Both of these problems are observably found in segments of Malay society, emerging out of the
postcolonial trauma. Although Fanon's writings covered many other themes,
this essay will restrict itself to these two central themes as found primarily in
the collected essays of his book *Black Skin, White Masks*.

---

4 *Ibid., 40.*
5 Emmanuel Hansen, *Frantz Fanon: Social and Political Thought* (Columbus, OH: Ohio State
   University Press, 1977), 8.

2   Psychopathology of the Colonized

In *Black Skin, White Masks*, Fanon seeks to explain the pathology that besets the man of color. Informed by his training in psychology and psychiatry, as well as deeply influenced by the writings of his mentor, Aime Cesaire,[6] Fanon highlighted the psychological problems that oppressive colonial situations wrought upon "negros."[7] Through observing the interactions between "negros" and "whites," and the manner in which these interactions occur, he delved into the *collective unconscious* operating within the colonial society. This collective unconscious, according to Fanon refers primarily to essentialized notions of the Negro – "the sum of prejudices, myths, collective attitudes of a given group" – which were repressed, but emerged back into consciousness in a different form: a *catharsis* or release.[8]

To the racist whites, Blacks often symbolizes the negative: "whether concretely or symbolically, the black man stands for the bad side of the character" – a symbol of "evil," "sin," and the "archetype of the lowest values" in every civilized and civilizing countries, particularly Europe.[9] At the same time, the essence of Blacks has often been reduced to the *biological*: singularly eroticized as being sexually powerful and athletic.[10] This essentialized notion of the "negro" is invariably tied to the idea that "negroes are animals." Fanon captured this racist element well, when he wrote:

> As for the Negroes, they have tremendous sexual powers. What do you expect, with all the freedom they have in their jungles! They copulate at all times and in all places. They are really genital. They have so many children that they cannot even count them. Be careful, or they will flood us with little mulattoes.[11]

---

6   Cesaire, like Fanon, was born in Martinique and received his education in Paris. A former member of the French Communist Party, he spent much of his life as a writer, poet and politician and served as President of the Regional Council of Martinique from 1983 to 1988. Cf. Cesaire (2001), *Discourse on Colonialism*. Fanon himself once remarked: "I wish that many black intellectuals would turn to him for their inspiration." See Fanon, *Black Skin, White Masks*, 187.

7   Fanon's analyses were based upon his observations and diagnoses of the Antilleans and Martiniquais of the Caribbean colonies, as well as the Negroes living in France. Much of his reflections were also closely linked to his own subjective life experiences.

8   Fanon, *Black Skin, White Masks*, 188. Fanon adopts these concepts from psychoanalysts, especially Sigmund Freud and Carl Jung. Also see Fanon, *Black Skin, White Masks*, 144–145.

9   Ibid., 188–189.

10 Fanon notes that a prostitute once told him that the mere thought of going to bed with a negro would bring on an orgasm. Fanon, *Black Skin, White Masks*, 158.

11 Ibid., 157.

Such notions, Fanon argued, soon entered into the consciousness, suppressed into the realm of the subconscious, and eventually emerged as a collective catharsis in a neurotic form. Trapped in these racial images of the black man, the "negro" began displaying symptoms of neurosis: *anguish, aggression* and *devaluation of self*.[12] Eventually, a debilitating form of psychopathological tendency develops: *lactification*, a word Fanon employs in *Black Skin, White Masks* to denote the attempt by the black to become white through assimilation. "Out of the blackest part of my soul," Fanon explicates, "across the zebra striping of my mind, surges this desire to be suddenly white. I wish to be acknowledged not as black but as white," for "the black man cannot take pleasure in his insularity. For him there is only one way out, and it leads into the white world."[13]

Such desires to be white have a dialectical relationship with a phobic attitude towards anything black/negro. Fanon gave many examples, particularly in his analysis on the colored person's desire to marry or have sexual relations with whites: for the black woman to feel accepted; for the black man to have a sense of conquest. Both are manifestations of a deep-seated contempt for their own fact of blackness imposed upon them by a culture of racism.[14]

Language is another important component in Fanon's analysis of the Black psychopathology. He writes:

Every colonized people – in other words, every people in whose soul an inferiority complex has been created by the death and burial of its local cultural originality – finds itself face to face with the language of the civilizing nation; that is, with the culture of the mother country. The colonized [individual] is elevated above his jungle status in proportion to his adoption of the mother country's cultural standards. He becomes whiter as he renounces his blackness, his jungle.[15]

Observing the Antillean "negro," Fanon notes that those who express themselves well and have mastered the language of their colonial master, are inordinately feared and respected: "Keep an eye on that one, he is almost white," or "He talks like a white man," as they would comment.[16] This tendency to put the language of the colonizer (in the Antillean case, French language) above the local dialects is a sign of cultural dislocation. In Fanon's analysis, such dislocation

---

12   Ibid., 73.
13   Ibid., 63, 51.
14   See Chapters 2 and 3 of *Black Skin, White Masks*.
15   Ibid., 18.
16   Ibid., 20–21.

is to be found in the racist social relation between the Antillean negro and their white French master. He notes that:

> A white man addressing a Negro behaves exactly like an adult with a child and starts smirking, whispering, patronizing, cozening. It is not one white man I have watched, but hundreds; and I have not limited my investigation to any one class but, if I may claim an essentially objective position, I have made a point of observing such behavior in physicians, policemen, employers.[17]

This syndrome of "talking down" is, in fact, a display of the white's own pathological behavior that corresponds with an inhuman psychology of the racist mind. In addition, there is an ideological function in talking "*pidgin-nigger*" to a black man: to remind them of their position in the human hierarchy. According to Fanon, "To make him talk pidgin is to fasten him to the effigy of him, to snare him, to imprison him, the eternal victim of an essence, of an appearance for which he is not responsible."[18]

Such were the effects of colonial racism that bred psychopathological conditions within the colonized people. In other words, the "negro" "did not have as his purpose the formulation of a healthy outlook on the world; he had no striving toward the productiveness that is characteristic of psychosocial equilibrium, but sought rather to corroborate his *externalizing* neurosis."[19]

3   Cultural and Intellectual Alienation

The psychopathology displayed by the colonized people as a result of racist social relations can be viewed also as a form of alienation. "The wearing of European clothes, whether rags or the most up-to-date style; using European furniture and European forms of social intercourse; adorning the Native language with European expressions; using bombastic phrases in speaking or writing a European language; all these contribute to a feeling of equality with the European and his achievements."[20]

---

17   Ibid., 31.
18   Ibid., 35.
19   Ibid., 81.
20   Ibid., 18. Fanon quoted from D.H. Westermann, a German missionary, linguist and Africanist.

Two processes are at work, in producing the alienation suffered by colonized Blacks. Firstly, he/she is constantly humiliated. As it is, they are told that they have no culture, no civilization and no long historical past.[21] Whatever they have is deemed inferior vis-à-vis that of the colonizer. Secondly, everything that they learn and absorb themselves in since their youth is that of the colonizer's world. Little wonder then that, as Fanon pointed out, the black schoolboy in the Antilles "in his lessons is forever talking about "our ancestors, the Gauls," identifies himself with the explorer, the bringer of civilization, the white man who carries truth to savages – an all-white truth." In addition,

> There is identification – that is, the young Negro subjectively adopts a white man's attitude... Little by little, one can observe in the young Antillean the formation and crystallization of an attitude and a way of thinking and seeing that are essentially white.[22]

Such alienation is most observable among the educated middle-class. Fanon observes that the black middle-class perpetuates a form of intellectual alienation that rigidify black society in "predetermined forms, forbidding all evolution, all gains, all progress, all discovery."[23]

4   The "Malay Problem"

Much of the symptomatic neuroses as discussed above are not peculiar to the negro or black community. They can be found within postcolonial Malay society. Given the similar colonial conditions imposed upon Malay society since the early 19th century, it is not surprising that postcolonial Malay society is still suffering from many of the psychopathologies identified by Fanon in the mid 20th century. As Fanon himself would put it, these are symptomatic of a structural racism that dominates every colonial situation.

According to Fanon, the sense of inferiority suffered by Blacks is an outcome of a "double process": primarily economic (exploitation and deprivation), and the subsequent internalization of this sense of inferiority ("epidermalization" or the struggle to "become white").[24] This "double process" existed and was

---

21   Ibid., 34.

22   Ibid., 147–148.

23   Ibid., 224. Fanon discussed this issue further in his essays, "The Pitfalls of National Consciousness" and "On National Culture" in *The Wretched of the Earth*.

24   Fanon, *Black Skin, White Masks*, 11.

experienced by the Malays throughout the period of colonization. At the root of it is the image of "the indolent, dull, backward and treacherous native," which transforms into "that of a dependent native requiring assistance to climb the ladder of progress."[25]

Lily Zubaidah Rahim argues the following: the "cultural-deficit" argument, which accords an inferior status to marginalized Malays in Singapore (once a British colony), may explain some obvious pathological symptoms.[26] Suratman's research has also revealed how Malay local newspapers portray the dominant image of Malays as (1) "being slow in adapting to changes" in the 1960s; (2) "old fashioned and traditional" in 1970s; (3) "still lagging behind and not integrating" in 1980s; (4) "progressing but cannot be satisfied yet" in 1990s; to (5) "progressing but are distancing themselves" in 2000s.[27] The existence of structural marginalization and perpetuation of the image of the "problematic Malays" can be seen as causes for the emergence of the "neurotic Malay."

Often, the Malay becomes a repository of everything negative. At the most basic level is his skin color, akin to Fanon's revealing statement: "[I am] a slave of my own appearance... When people like me, they tell me it is in spite of my color. When they dislike me, they point out that it is not because of my color. Either way, I am locked into the infernal circle."[28] The reference to skin color is apparently common in many conversations that this author has encountered in the teaching profession. For example, a schoolteacher once remarked: "She's Malay but she's beautiful." When a Malay student achieves academic distinction, it is said to be despite of being Malay; when he fails, it is to be expected since he is Malay after all.

Certain policies, although introduced for good reasons, such as integration of the races, could have the unintended consequence of reinforcing negative stereotypes of the Malays – particularly when one is unconscious of the "double process" at work. For example, the Ethnic Integration Policy (EIP) was introduced in 1989 to prevent ethnic enclaves in housing estates in Singapore.[29] Then-prime minister, Mr Lee Kuan Yew, remarked that the mixing in

---

25   Syed Hussein Alatas, *The Myth of the Lazy Native: A Study of the Image of the Malays, Filipinos and Javanese from the 16th to the 20th Century and Its Function in the Ideology of Colonial Capitalism* (London and New York: Frank Cass Publishers, 1977), 8.

26   Lily Zubaidah Rahim, *The Singapore Dilemma: The Political and Educational Marginality of the Malay Community* (Selangor: Oxford University Press, 2001).

27   Suriani Suratman, "'Problematic Singapore Malays': The Making of a Portrayal." *Seminar Paper* No. 36, Dept. of Malay Studies, National University of Singapore, 2005.

28   Fanon, *Black Skins, White Masks*, 116.

29   National Library Board, 2014. "National Integration Policy is implemented"; http://eresources.nlb.gov.sg/history/events/d8fea656-d86e-4658-9509-974225951607#1.

every estate is needed so that Malays can mix more with the Chinese and be more competitive "by example and interaction."[30] Similarly, a school principal once remark to the author that a school with too many Malays is not desirable because the performance of the school will be affected. This sentiment is found in Malay parents too who seek to dissociate their children from other Malay children in what Michael Schwalbe describes as "defensive othering."[31] In school textbooks, it is subtly implied that the Malay and Indian boys will run around the class while their Chinese counterpart will write and draw attentively; and a Malay man is depicted as being a bus driver while his Chinese counterpart is a teacher.[32]

It would seem that the racial neuroticism that emerged out of structural and everyday racism is abound.[33] In a workshop organized by the Islamic Religious Council of Singapore (Muis), which this author participated in and observed in 2011, a prominent youth leader of a Muslim organization derided the Malays as being "problematic," and remarked that Malays are blind to problems that are "right in front of their nose." When queried by another participant whether he is himself a Malay, the leader replied: "My mother is Chinese." Such examples are not rare. In fact, similar to Fanon's observations, the tendency to deny and denigrate anything associated with "Malayness" is most common among the middle-class intelligentsia and Malay leadership. As Lily Zubaidah Rahim puts it:

> Having attained high educational credentials, material success, and social mobility, the meritocratic discourse advocated by the PAP leadership serves to flatter their [i.e. the Malay middle-class] achievements and accords them the esteemed status as role models of exceptional qualities. Their socio-economic distance from the general Malay community and their ethnic difference from the non-Malay community places them in a position of double alienation. This profound level of alienation has rendered the Malay middle class socially vulnerable and susceptible towards

30   "Integrate or separate: Malays' pick" *The Straits Times*. March 4, 2001. Also see Michael Schwalbe, Sandra Godwin, Daphne Holden, Douglas Schrock, Shealy Thompson, and Michele Wolkomir. "Generic Processes in the Reproduction of Inequality: An Interactionist Analysis." *Social Forces* 79 no. 2 (2000).

31   Annas Bin Mahmud, *Internalized Racism and Malay Youths: Responding to Stereotypes of Malays in Singapore*. Unpublished Honor's Thesis (Department of Malay Studies, National University of Singapore, 2014), 29.

32   Michael D. Barr and Zlatko Skrbis, *Constructing Singapore: Elitism, Ethnicity and the Nation-Building Project* (Copenhagen: NIAS Press., 2008), 162–167.

33   Selvaraj Velayutham, "Everyday Racism in Singapore," in *Everyday Multiculturalism*, eds. Amanda Wise and Selvaraj Velayutham. London: Palgrave Macmillan, 2009.

uncritically accepting the cultural deficit thesis which gratifies their ego for having extricated themselves from the negative cultural attributes afflicting the Malay community.[34]

Thus, clichés such as *Melayu malas* (Malays are lazy), *Melayu kurang berusaha* (Malays lack efforts), *Melayu tidak ada sifat keusahawanan* (Malays lack entrepreneurial skills), *Melayu perlu pertingkat diri* (Malays must upgrade their selves), and *Melayu harus mengubah sikap dan minda* (Malays must change their attitude and mindset), are often heard and quoted in the Malay daily, *Berita Harian*.[35] Such clichés serve to entrench further the cultural deficit notion, as much as they reveal the level of alienation that segments of the Malay intelligentsia and leadership suffers from.[36] Such alienation points to structural marginality and the persistent ideological use of the "meritocracy thesis."[37] However, the root of the problem may lie deeper in the subconscious of the social psychological domain. They may have resulted from an initial colonial domination that resulted in the victimhood mentality compounded by racial divisions that postmodern societies like Singapore fail to confront adequately.[38] In other words, the very structures of racism introduced by the British masters remain intact and continue to be perpetuated uncritically even after the end of the colonial period. The notion of the "natural" hierarchy of races – upon which Europeans used to justify their "civilizing mission" to the world – are now turned towards the races present in former colonies. This was aptly observed in Albert Memmi's notion of "dialectical racism": If one race is seen inferior, the opposing race will by default be superior.[39] This is similar to Fanon's own observation that "the feeling of inferiority of the colonized is the correlative to the European's feeling of superiority."[40]

In Malaysia, examples of the neurotic syndrome can be found in many writings, particularly written by the corporate and ruling elites. In 1971, the ruling party United Malays National Organization (UMNO), published *Revolusi*

---

34   Rahim, *The Singapore Dilemma*, 59.
35   Ibid., 187; Fadli Bin Fawzi, "Moving Beyond Racialised Health Narratives in Singapore," *Yahoo News*, Mar 4, 2015.
36   Such syndrome is similar to the experience of the black middle class in America as E. Franklin Frazier identified in his book *Black Bourgeoisie*. New York: Simon and Schuster, 1997.
37   Rahim, *The Singapore Dilemma*; Barr and Skrbis, 2008.
38   Collin Abraham, *The Naked Social Order: The Roots of Racial Polarisation in Malaysia*. Selangor: Pelanduk Publications, 2004.
39   Albert Memmi. *Racism*. Minneapolis: University of Minnesota Press, 1991.
40   Fanon, *Black Skin, White Masks*, 93.

Mental, that reflects the dominant elites' utilization of the cultural deficit notion to explain Malay underdevelopment.[41] Ignoring historical, political, and structural factors for the Malay underdevelopment, the authors called instead for a "mental revolution" or a mindset change. Three decades later, the argument still holds sway and is employed in several popular works dominating the Malay masses. One such example is the book, *The Malays Par Excellence... Warts and All*, written by two corporate leaders linked to the ruling elites.[42] In several passages, the authors render the Malay character as problematic: "In the course of history, the Malays may appear to be divisive and vehemently at odds with each other, even to the extent of appearing to wreck each other's credibility and livelihood in the process."[43]

In another book, *The Malay Ideals*, the author asserts that all forms of Malay underdevelopment were due to the Malay mindset, character or attitude.[44] On the Malay's poor educational achievement vis-à-vis other ethnic groups, for example, the author attributes it to "the nature of Malay people themselves and their attitude towards success." He wrote:

> The Malay attitude does not contribute favourably towards being a successful student. For instance, the Malays do not usually view the successes of others as something to look up to. Success, to a Malay breeds contempt and jealousy. If a Malay person is successful, other Malays would frequently feel uneasy. They would then focus upon the less positive side of that person's character, in order to find fault.[45]

It is interesting to note that in these examples, there is a tendency to denigrate the Malays in a homogenizing way and attribute essentialist traits in them, while attempting to "diagnose" their problems. This is a common characteristic of neuroticism that dominates segments of the Malay intelligentsia and elites. As explained by Hansen,

> The intellectuals, politicians and bureaucrats in the underdeveloped countries, in spite of the rhetoric of populism, have a low opinion of the

---

41   For a critique of this book and the cultural deficit notion in general, see the books of Syed
      Hussein Alatas, *Siapa Yang Salah: Sekitar Revolusi Mental dan Peribadi Melayu*. Singapore:
      Pustaka Nasional, 1972; and *Intellectuals in Developing Societies*. London: Frank Cass, 1977.
42   Ismail Noor and Muhammad Azaham. *The Malays Par Excellence...Warts and All*. Selan-
      gor: Pelanduk Publications, 2000.
43   Ibid., 33.
44   Asrul Zamani, *The Malay Ideals*. Kuala Lumpur: Golden Books Centre, 2002.
45   Ibid., 144–145.

country people and the masses generally, and sometimes treat them with disdain. They regard them in the same way as the colonial officials did: lazy, superstitious, apathetic, passive, and lacking in understanding of the issues and problems of politics.[46]

Thus, to be able to speak English well is a sign of "sophistication" and a symbol of being "modern" and "educated," as one Malay bureaucrat remarked to this author. According to him, the Malay language is "kampungan" (literally: "village," denoting backwardness) and to use the language shows that we have not "integrated" into the larger cosmopolitan, modern, and globalized Singapore. The neuroticism displayed by him is best captured in the following passage by Fanon, albeit referring to the case of the Black Antillean:

> The black man wants to be like the white man. For the black man there is only one destiny. And it is white. Long ago the black man admitted the unarguable superiority of the white man, and all his efforts are aimed at achieving a white existence.[47]

On another level, there is also a sign of neuroticism in the Malay elites' clarion call of "ketuanan Melayu" (Malay supremacy), as seen in post-1969 Malaysian politics.[48] One the one hand, the Malay ruling elites view their own people with contempt and blame their culture for problems that are structural in nature.[49] On the other hand, they employed the idea of "Malay supremacy" to justify their leadership positions. The ultra-nationalist sentiment that asserted the supremacist position of the Malays was a sign of a deep-rooted sense of insecurity, which could only be explained through centuries of colonial subjugation. Thus, upon independence, the tendency was to prove their worth at all cost. The dominant sentiment of wanting to revive the "Golden Age" of Malaccan Sultanate, and to romanticize the feudal era, is an example of such

---

46   Hansen, *Frantz Fanon*, 189.

47   Fanon, *Black Skin, White Masks*, 228.

48   Malaysia experienced one of the worst racial riots on 13 May 1969, involving the Malays and Chinese. The aftermath led to the introduction of the New Economic Policy – seen as an affirmative action to lift up the socioeconomic conditions of the Malays – but ended up being utilized as an ideological move to assert Malay supremacy vis-à-vis other races, particularly the Chinese. See Leon Comber, *13 May 1969: A Historical Survey of Sino-Malay Relations*. Kuala Lumpur: Heinemann Asia, 1983.

49   An example is Mahathir Mohamed's *The Malay Dilemma* (1970). Mahathir was the 4th prime minister of Malaysia (1981–2003) and made a comeback again as the 7th prime minister in 2018 after a momentous defeat of the ruling coalition Barisan Nasional in the 9 May general election.

neuroticism.[50] Having been emptied of any history, the Malay elites wanted to prove the existence of a Malay civilization to the white world at all costs, as Fanon observed in the case of the black middle class.[51] Underneath that desire is the trauma of being told that Malays are a people without civilization, that is, until the Europeans came with their "civilizing mission."

5   Conclusion

One important aspect of Fanon's work is that it displays a unique combination of sociological and psychological understanding in addressing the problem of racism. By way of social psychology, Fanon highlights the dynamics operating between social structures (colonial aggression, domination, exploitation in social, economic, and political life) and mental states (pathological behaviors and thinking). The combination of structural and psychological factors then explains why the relationship between the colonizer and the colonized is *always* that of violence.[52] Thus, it is not enough to merely denounce racism. One must also target the very structures that embed, nurture, and perpetuate racism. "If society makes difficulties for him because of his color, if in his dreams I establish the expression of an unconscious desire to change color," wrote Fanon, "my objective will not be that of dissuading him from it by advising him to "keep his place"; on the contrary, my objective, once his motivations have been brought into action (or passivity) with respect to the real source of the conflict – that is, toward the social structures."[53]

Last but not least, Fanon was struggling against the enslavement of man by man, and for such an enslavement to cease forever. His appeal to humanity is for them to (re)discover and to love fellow humans, wherever they may be from. "A negro is not any more than the white man."[54] Thus, the antidote to white supremacy is not to assert black supremacy. Only through equal acceptance of each other can authentic communication occur. To achieve this, man must struggle for freedom. And freedom requires efforts toward *dis*-alienation.

---

50   Sharifah Maznah Syed Omar, *Myths and the Malay Ruling Class.* Singapore: Times Academic Press, 1993; Azhar Ibrahim, *Historical Imagination and Cultural Responses to Colonialism and Nationalism.* Selangor: Strategic Information and Research Development Centre, 2017.
51   Fanon, *Black Skin, White Masks,* 34.
52   See, in particular, Fanon, *The* Wretched *of the Earth*; Frantz Fanon, *Toward the African Revolution.* New York: Monthly Review Press, 1967b.
53   Fanon, *Black Skin, White Masks,* 100.
54   Ibid., 231.

It is for this reason that we ought to pay close attention to the perspectives provided in Fanon's insightful work. To conclude, the following quote best exemplifies the overall project of Fanon's discourse on and against racism:

> I find myself suddenly in the world and I recognize that I have one right alone: That of demanding human behavior from the other. One duty alone: That of not renouncing my freedom through my choices.[55]

In reading Fanon, Malay society and the postcolonial states of Malaysia and Singapore can reveal their hidden and embedded colonial mental structures, and move towards the unfinished process of decolonization that Fanon envisioned for a truly free and equal world.

Bibliography

Abdul Rahman, Senu, ed. *Revolusi Mental*. Malaysia: Penerbit Utusan Melayu, 1971.

Abraham, Collin.*The Naked Social Order: The Roots of Racial Polarisation in Malaysia*. Selangor: Pelanduk Publications, 2004.

Alatas, Syed Hussein. "Some Fundamental Problems of Colonialism." *Eastern World* (Nov., 1956).

Alatas, Syed Hussein. *Siapa Yang Salah: Sekitar Revolusi Mental dan Peribadi Melayu*. Singapore: Pustaka Nasional, 1972.

Alatas, Syed Hussein. *The Myth of the Lazy Native: A Study of the Image of the Malays, Filipinos and Javanese from the 16th to the 20th Century and Its Function in the Ideology of Colonial Capitalism*. London and New York: Frank Cass Publishers, 1977.

Alatas, Syed Hussein. *Intellectuals in Developing Societies*. London: Frank Cass, 1977.

Barr, Michael D. and Jevon Low "Assimilation as Multiracialism: The Case of Singapore's Malays." *Asian Ethnicity* 6, no. 3 (Oct. 2005).

Barr, Michael D. and Zlatko Skrbis, 2008. *Constructing Singapore: Elitism, Ethnicity and the Nation-Building Project*. Copenhagen: NIAS Press, 2008.

Cesaire, Aime. *Discourse on Colonialism*. USA: Monthly Review Press, 2001.

Comber, Leon. *13 May 1969: A Historical Survey of Sino-Malay Relations*. Kuala Lumpur: Heinemann Asia, 1983.

Fanon, Frantz. *The Wretched of the Earth*. New York: Grove Press, 1963.

Fanon, Frantz. *Black Skin, White Masks*. New York: Grove Press, 1967.

Fanon, Frantz. *Toward the African Revolution*. New York: Monthly Review Press, 1967b.

---

55   Ibid., 229.

Fawzi, Fadli Bin. "Moving Beyond Racialised Health Narratives in Singapore." *Yahoo News*, March 4, 2015.

Frazier, E. Franklin. *Black Bourgeoisie*. New York: Simon and Schuster, 1997.

Hansen, Emmanuel. *Frantz Fanon: Social and Political Thought*. USA: Ohio State University Press, 1977.

Ibrahim, Azhar. *Historical Imagination and Cultural Responses to Colonialism and Nationalism*. Selangor: Strategic Information and Research Development Centre, 2017.

Mahmud, Annas Bin. *Internalised Racism and Malay Youths: Responding to Stereotypes of Malays in Singapore*. Unpublished Honours Thesis, Department of Malay Studies, National University of Singapore, 2014.

Memmi, Albert. *Racism*. Minneapolis: University of Minnesota Press, 1991.

Mohamed, Mahathir. *The Malay Dilemma*. Singapore: Times Books International, 1970.

National Library Board 2014. "National Integration Policy is implemented"; http:// eresources.nlb.gov.sg/history/events/d8fea656-d86e-4658-9509-974225951607#1.

Noor, Ismail and Muhammad Azaham. *The Malays Par Excellence...Warts and All*. Selangor: Pelanduk Publications, 2000.

Rahim, Lily Zubaidah *The Singapore Dilemma: The Political and Educational Marginality of the Malay Community*. Selangor: Oxford University Press, 2001.

Schwalbe, Michael, Sandra Godwin, Daphne Holden, Douglas Schrock, Shealy Thompson, and Michele Wolkomir. "Generic Processes in the Reproduction of Inequality: An Interactionist Analysis." *Social Forces* 79 no. 2 (2000).

Suratman, Suriani. "'Problematic Singapore Malays': The Making of a Portrayal." *Seminar Paper* No. 36, Dept. of Malay Studies, National University of Singapore, 2005.

Syed Omar, Sharifah Maznah *Myths and the Malay Ruling Class*. Singapore: Times Academic Press, 1993.

The Straits Times. "Integrate or separate: Malays' pick." March 4, 2001.

Velayutham, Selvaraj "Everyday Racism in Singapore," In *Everyday Multiculturalism*, edited by Amanda Wise and Selvaraj Velayutham. London: Palgrave Macmillan, 2009.

Zamani, Asrul. *The Malay Ideals*. Kuala Lumpur: Golden Books Centre, 2002.

CHAPTER 14

Re-reading Fanon: Language, Literature, and Empire

Esmaeil Zeiny

It is no easy task to add to the already existing scholarship on Frantz Fanon, but re-reading his thoughts and concepts is a *sine qua non* and gains momentum in the light of events that conjure up colonialism in the current postcolonial climate. Fanon's works are by far the most influential source in the production of postcolonial criticism and have been used for discussions of colonizer/ colonized relationship and decolonization, involving issues as varied as violence, revolution, political actions, ethics, love, humanism, intellectualism, language and literature. This chapter, however, seeks to continue the debate over the significance of Fanonian perspectives on the language of empire and national literature. Fanon discusses the role of colonial language in colonization and argues that it leads to subjugation and feelings of dependency and inadequacy. He also proposes the idea that native writers should return to tradition and write the national literature in indigenous language to "shake" the natives in order to battle colonialism. While closely examining his thoughts on colonial language and national literature, this chapter presents how postcolonial African writers return to tradition and what language they choose in writing their national literature.

1   Introduction

Before delving into Fanon's thoughts on the colonizer's language and the colonized literature, I feel it is significant to commence this chapter with two key points so that my re-reading of Fanon's thoughts and perspectives is deliberated and purposeful. The first point is Fanon's relevance to today's world, which has been a topic of many scholarly debates and studies. Scholars are obsessed with making Fanon's work relevant to the current world in order to place him within contemporaneity. More often than not, this is carried out by simply wresting him from the past into the present without taking into account the need to differentiate the two contexts. The question "is Fanon still relevant?" relies upon what is indeed translated into the present as relevant. In order to re-enact Fanon's project in present terms, one has to think both with and against him as the contemporary world is no longer the same as his. This takes us one step further when speaking of Fanon's relevance to the contemporary world. Fanon's relevancy is no longer just about discovering his works that correspond to the current world, rather it is also looking for the moments where Fanon's works do not speak to the contemporary world, which brings up the urge to ask how Fanon would think and act if faced with current issues. The second point, drawing upon Mota-Lopes (2007), is that Fanon's thoughts and perspectives on various issues should be studied by considering the two fundamental traits of his works that are not oftentimes taken into interpretive consideration: (a) his works were written within the context of the liberation movement of Algeria.[1] This means that his contemplation about colonialism and national liberation resulted from the observation of a politically involved cadre of the liberation movement in the particular context of armed struggling, and (b) his writings were produced from the early 1950s to the early 1960s, which is indicative of a short span in terms of intellectual development. This suggests that his writings must be read as an "incomplete work that was cut short by his untimely, sudden death in 1961."[2] The contention here is that Fanon might have responded differently to neo-colonialism and contemporary imperialism by adopting a different strategy, or he would have developed his thoughts further if he had lived longer. For instance, his earlier works, such as *Black Skin, White Masks* (1952), epitomize the assertions upon which he began his revolutionary career, but later in his career he modified those assertions and principles in view of his realization of the Third World's conditions. Modifying one's perspectives is a fundamental part of an intellectual's movement and dynamism, and Fanon is no exception. Thus, it is safe to argue that his writings are works in progress and can be completed and developed further. If these two key points are not taken into consideration while reading Fanon, and if the space and time that exists between us and him is overlooked, the reading is bound to be a rehash or, what I call, a reiterative reading.

Having said this, it is no easy task to add to the already existing scholarship on Frantz Fanon, but re-reading his thoughts and concepts in the light of the two above-mentioned key points is a *sine qua non*, which gains momentum in today's context of post-colonialism, capitalism, and globalization, wherein "democracy" and "development" enforce similar versions of colonial rules. Fanon's

---

1   Jose da Mota-Lopes, "Re-Reading Frantz Fanon: Language, Violence, and Eurocentrism in the Characterization of Our Time," *Human Architecture: Journal of The Sociology of Self-Knowledge*, v. Especial Double issue, 2007.

2   Ibid., 47.

works are by far the most influential source in the production of postcolonial criticism and have been used for discussions of colonizer/colonized relationship and decolonization, involving issues as varied as violence, revolution, political actions, ethics, love, humanism, intellectualism, language and literature. This chapter, however, seeks to continue the debate over the significance of Fanonian perspectives on the colonial language and the national literature. Fanon discusses the role of colonial language in colonization and argues that it leads to subjugation and feelings of dependency and inadequacy. He illustrates that the colonial language is the instrument of power that colonizes, traumatizes, and decentralizes the role of native languages in the cultural and historical imagination of the local people. He also suggests that native intellectuals should return to tradition and native writers should write their national literature in an indigenous language to "awaken" the people in order to battle colonialism. Whereas a number of authors, such as Ngugi wa Thiong'o, follow Fanon's path and reject the hierarchy of languages and cultures, and thus write in their local languages as opposed to the colonial English, authors like Chinua Achebe seize the colonial language, as Fanon did, and produce anticolonial discourses in an attempt to reverse and subvert colonial accounts. Considering that the role colonial language played in Fanon's time is different from the current role the imperial language plays, we must ask "what language would Fanon have written in had he lived longer?" What would he think of those writers writing in the imperial language? While closely investigating Fanon's thoughts on colonial language and national literature, this chapter seeks to answer these questions in the light of the two key points mentioned earlier.

2   Language and (De)colonization

Central to the concept of decolonization is the historical and cultural continuum of the colonial legacy. One of the most controversial issues in this continuum is the status of a colonial language in the context of newly independent nations and the Third World in a broader context. If a language possesses a colonial history and was a tool of colonization, what is its current status in relation to the task of nation-building and resisting contemporary imperialism? This correlation between language and decolonization is addressed by many social thinkers and revolutionary writers, especially in Africa, where many countries experienced ruthless colonization by Europeans. It is no coincidence that Fanon begins his work *Black Skin, White Masks* (1952) with language, where he explores the dynamics of language as a practical way to understand the ill effects of colonialism and racism on society. What probably impelled Fanon to write *Black Skin, White Masks* (1952) was the novel *I am a Martinican Woman* (1948) by Mayotte Capécia. Yet, his desire to present a historical critique of the impacts of racism and dehumanization inherent in situations like colonial dominations, and bring a conscious cognizance of subtler forms of colonial dominations, was also impellent.[3] However, what most probably prompted Fanon to write on language, and begin his first important work with it, besides his observation of the power of language and the locals' attempt to master the colonial language, was the recollection of his school years at lycée where speaking Creole (a mix of French and African languages) was prohibited. Only French was accepted. Recalling this linguistic hierarchy, Fanon underscores the centrality of language to colonialism in *Black Skin, White Masks* (1952).

In the first chapter "The Negro and Language," Fanon says: "I ascribe a basic importance to the phenomenon of language. That is why I find it necessary to begin with this subject, which provides the readers with one of the components in the colored man's comprehension of the dimension of the other. For it is implicit that to speak is to exist absolutely for the other."[4] Fanon explores how a feeling of inferiority is subtly internalized in the colonized people via the colonial language. He argues that the identity of the colonized people relies on their ability to acquire fluency in the colonizer's language. He writes: "The Negro of the Antilles will be proportionately whiter – that is, he will come closer to being a real human being – in direct ratio to his mastery of the French language."[5] Fanon believes that when the colonized person encounters the language of the colonizers, he is raised above his "heathenism," and he affirms the cultural standard of the colonialists and becomes whiter as he rejects his own cultural heritage. He states that "the more the colonized has assimilated the cultural values of the metropolis, the more he will have escaped the bush. The more he rejects his blackness and the bush, the whiter he will become."[6] Fanon situates language at the center of the predicament of colonization, marginalization, and servitude, and he theorizes that language is a vital element of culture; it shapes and structures cultures and mediates social intercourse. The acquisition of the colonial language represents the acquisition of its culture. The Antillean who masters the French language becomes more French, whiter, and less black.

---

3 Mayotte Capécia, *I am a Martinican Woman*, Correa, 1948.
4 Frantz Fanon, *Black Skin, White Masks*. (New York: Grove Press, 2008), 8.
5 Ibid., 8.
6 Ibid., 2–3.

Mastery of the colonial language, according to Fanon, makes the colonized feel "whiter" and in doing so "come[s] closer to being a real human being."[7] Therefore, language use is not simply an act of accepting its formal linguistic requirements but also acquiring the accompanying culture implied by the language. As a primary mode of expression, language determines one's values and value within the said cultural system. Fanon writes that "to speak means to be in a position to use a certain syntax, to grasp the morphology of this or that language, but it means above all to assume a culture, to support the weight of a civilization."[8] Concomitant with language acquisition is an entire set of cultural underpinnings. Language mirrors the speakers' culture, Fanon declares, and a man who uses the language possesses the worldview implied by that language.[9] Those who have taken up the language of the colonizers are vulnerable to internalizing the perspectives and the cultural assumptions of the colonizers. That language is considered as a repository of culture, conjures up Benjamin Lee Whorf's (1959) idea that "each language is encoded with a particular mode of thought, a [cultural] metaphysics that affects the speaker's experience at the level of perception."[10] Fanon is, indeed, referring to the potency of language in constructing the lens through which meaning and understanding take place. He writes that "mastery of language affords remarkable power" through which he criticizes the fact that the French language assumed a particular privilege over the dialects of the natives.[11] Fanon is of the idea that this valorization of a European language in Africa (or anywhere else) by the native intellectuals further subordinates the colonized subjects and legitimizes French language privilege.

Fanon argues that as the colonized become proficient in the language of the colonizer, they become estranged from their native language and culture. Therefore, central to Fanon's idea of the colonized mind is the importance of language in the alienation of the colonized, an ugly colonial process Fanon aimed at reversing via disalienation. He is especially pondering on the moment when the Martinican returns to his homeland after having gone to France and brushed up on his French: "The black man who has been to the metropole is a demigod."[12] With this concentration on language at the point where literary and cultural vicinity to the white world enables and authorizes the colored

---

7   Ibid., 3.
8   Ibid., 8.
9   Fanon, *Black Skin, White Masks*.
10   Alamin Mazuri, "Language and the Quest for Liberation in Africa: The Legacy of Frantz Fanon," *Third World Quarterly*, 14 (2) (1993): 351.
11   Fanon, *Black Skin, White Masks*, 9.
12   Ibid., 3.

person, Fanon asserts that "all colonized people – in other words, people in whom an inferiority complex has taken root, whose local cultural originality has been committed to the grave – position themselves in relation to the civilizing language, i.e. the metropolitan culture."[13] That colonized people constantly mimic the colonizer is a sign of their yearning and striving to receive recognition from the white masters. The goal to speak a different linguistic register is "the hopes to be like, and therefore, *liked by*, the colonizer."[14] This is what Fanon calls "putting on the white world" through which the colonized seek to deracinate himself, lose his color, his language and his very identity.[15] But no matter how well the colonized speak the colonial language and how far they distance themselves from their local culture, the colonized never reach the level of the whites in the eyes of the colonizers, and they are never treated on equal grounds as the whites either.[16]

These few paragraphs, which encapsulate Fanon's perspectives on the colonial language, oftentimes drive scholars to reduce him to a revolutionary theorist who negates and rejects French language and culture in its entirety in favor of dis-alienation and decolonization. On the other side of the spectrum, Fanon is always dragged to different contexts and his thoughts on language are criticized sometimes to the level of rejection. For instance, it has been argued that within the context of the liberation movements of the former Portuguese colonies "the language problem denounced and discussed by Fanon concerned what historically and sociologically no more than very small colonized minorities, those *assimilated* by the colonial system."[17] In other words, a great majority of the Portuguese colonies population did not speak or even adequately understand the colonizer's language and therefore, language could not alienate the population. What has been overlooked here is the particular context in which Fanon produced his work. With the exception of some parts of *Black Skin, White Masks* (1952), Fanon's work was written and published within the context of the anti-colonial armed struggle of the Algerian National Liberation Front (FLN). Fanon wrote for "his comrades of struggle within the FLN, by those outside who supported the on-going anti-colonial struggle (particularly in French Left), and by those within Africa who were feeling the first post-colonial abuses from their own decolonized elites in power."[18] To read Fanon in a non-Algerian situation of anti-colonial armed struggle, argues Mota-Lopes,

---

13   Ibid., 2.
14   Pramod K. Nayar, *Frantz Fanon*, (London & New York: Routledge, 2013), 44.
15   Fanon, *Black Skin, White Masks*, 23.
16   Ibid.
17   Mota-Lopes, "Re-Reading Frantz Fanon," 51.
18   Ibid., 50.

is to read it within an identical context to the one in which it was written and produced.[19]

Drawn from individual or collective experiences, Fanon's writings are proposals, assertions, testimonials, and discussions that belong to situations that were historically located and specific. Although Fanon's thoughts on language transcend his time and context, simply wresting him from his own specific context to apply his thoughts in a different context and later reject them is not decent. Another major criticism, put forward by Mota-Lopes, is that language as a problem had not been much of an issue within the Southern African liberation movements, particularly after the early 1970s.[20] He argues that the language of the colonizers was adopted by various liberation movements in Namibia, as well as today's Zimbabwe, where much of the population spoke English. He further argues that in other countries, such as Angola and Mozambique, the language of the colonizers was also adopted and transformed into an instrument of liberation. The idea that the colonizer's "language *did not belong to him"* became dominant in these countries.[21] It is true that Fanon asserts in taking on a language, one takes a particular symbolic order, the community and its culture, but he also puts forward, upon a closer reading, another feasibility of a colonial language used by the colonized. He recognizes that learning the French language is "the key that can open doors" for the natives if they are able to use it effectively.[22] Knowing the language and using it to their advantage is a step in the right direction in making them aware of their own condition. What Fanon rejects is the colonized man's wish to disown his own origin, language and culture to adopt the identity and culture of the French. He lambasts those men who internalized, what Chateerjee (1994) terms as, the rule of colonial difference.[23] It is precisely this black man who speaks the language incognizant of the conditions it brings with it that irritates Fanon. The language of the colonizers affects the cognitive and social orientation of the oppressed only if the colonized are alienated in the first place, and they will be whiter as they acquire "greater mastery of the cultural tool that language is."[24] This greater mastery of the colonial language puts the colonized, who believe in the superiority of colonial language, in the state of further alienation. Those who consciously use the colonizer's language cannot be influenced by

---

19   Ibid.
20   ibid.
21   Ibid., 52.
22   Fanon, *Black Skin, White Masks*, 25.
23   Partha Chatterjee, *The Nation and its Fragments.* Princeton, N.J.: Princeton University Press, 1994.
24   Fanon, *Black Skin, White Masks*, 25.

the conditions that language brings with it. Thus, Fanon's position on language and decolonization is not an exclusion of the colonial language and culture but involves a critical re-thinking of the role of colonial language that played a fundamental role in the process of colonization.

3   Language and National Literature

Fanon propounds the concepts of national literature and national culture in a chapter entitled "On National Culture" in his 1961 *The Wretched of the Earth*. He recognizes the importance of cultural nationalism that leads to national consciousness in reclaiming national history and culture as a process of liberation even after decolonization. He argues that a national culture in the context of Africa must take recourse to the African myths and cultural practices. He formulates three phases in which the national culture is formed. In the first phase, the native intellectuals seek to emulate and assimilate the colonizers' culture by jettisoning their own culture. Fanon calls this stage "the period of unqualified assimilation."[25] In the second phase, the intellectual is perturbed and concerned, and acknowledges the disparity that makes them want to return to study their own culture. The writings of this phase are called the "literature of just-before-the-battle," which is dominated by humor and allegory.[26] Aesthetics suited to colonial powers are still used in reinterpreting the recollection of childhood memories and old native legends. The third phase is the "fighting phase," in which the native intellectual truly becomes anti-colonial, out of which "comes a fighting literature, a revolutionary literature, and a national literature."[27] This is the stage where the native intellectuals "awaken" and "shake" the people.[28] During this stage, a great number of people who "would never have thought of producing a literary work, now... feel the need to speak to their nation, to compose the sentence which expresses the heart of the people and become the mouthpiece of a new reality in action."[29] This is the stage where initially the native writers still make use of the colonizers' language and techniques.

Fanon says that when "the native intellectual is anxiously trying to create a cultural work he fails to realize that he is utilizing techniques and language

---

25   Frantz Fanon, *The Wretched of the Earth*. (New York: Grove Press, 1963), 222.
26   Ibid., 222.
27   Ibid., 222, 223.
28   Ibid., 223.
29   Ibid.

which are borrowed from the stranger in his country."[30] The way the native intellectuals are creating their cultural work, he continues, is "strangely reminiscent of exoticism."[31] However, as time goes by, the native intellectuals obtain the ability to develop a new aesthetics suited to their mother country. These native intellectuals should dismiss the colonizers' language and culture, and set out to rediscover the dignity and glory of African civilization as that is the true national culture. This is how native intellectuals progressively acquire the habit of addressing their own people. It is only from this moment, argues Fanon, that "we can speak of national literature."[32] Fanon labels this national literature a "literature of combat, in the sense that it calls on the whole people to fight for their existence as a nation."[33] According to Fanon, it is the literature of combat because "it molds the national consciousness, giving it form and contours and flinging open before it new and boundless horizons," and he continues, it is a literature of combat because "it assumes responsibility, and because it is the will to liberty expressed in terms of time and space."[34] To substantiate and further consolidate his "literature of combat," Fanon cites the revival of epic poetry in Algeria and the poetry of revolt in Africa and elsewhere. He references the Guinean poet Keita Fobeda's poem *African Dawn*, which is, to him, a "true invitation to thought, to de-mystification, and to battle."[35] Thus, as Fanon describes, true national literature approves of and adores revolutionary efforts; and it spawns and shapes the national consciousness that makes a revolution at the national level possible.[36]

It is beyond doubt that Fanon's thought on national literature has relevance. National literatures usually evolve in stages and share similar features such as connection with and rootedness in tradition, existence of indigenous components, and the ability to unite the nation. However, the need for a literature of one's nation alters in accordance with the political situation of the nation in question. It, indeed, changes according to the moment the nation is experiencing. His ideas of "National Literature" were meant to "arouse" the people in Algeria and need not be appropriated in every context haphazardly. Today's national literatures usually reflect themes and morals of the ruling ideology of that nation. This sort of national literature grows oftentimes at the cost of

30   Ibid.
31   Ibid.
32   Ibid., 240.
33   Ibid., 240.
34   Ibid., 240.
35   Ibid., 227.
36   Imre Szeman, *Zones of Instability: Literature, Postcolonialism, and the Nation*. Baltimore, MD: Johns Hopkins University Press, 2003.

excluding ethnic literature. I have no intention of continuing debates on the conflict between "national literature" and "ethnic literature," as it is beyond the scope of this chapter, but what these two kinds of literature have in common is their return to tradition. In looking for tradition in the past to produce national literature, Fanon cautions the native intellectual to be wary of the past that colonialism turns to in order to "distort, disfigure and destroy" it.[37] Ostensibly repudiating the colonizers' culture in favor of a return to tradition bears peril. Whoever adopts this strategy, according to Ranger, "faces the ironic danger of embracing another set of colonial inventions instead."[38] Perhaps Fanon should have put "tradition" into a very detailed perspective and should have accentuated the fact that much of what passes for "tradition" in Africa is "the result of a conscious determination on the part of the colonial authorities to 're-establish' order and security and a sense of community by means of defining and enforcing 'tradition.'"[39] The most pervasive "inventions of tradition in colonial Africa took place when the Europeans believed themselves to be respecting age-old African custom. What were called customary law, customary land-rights, customary political structure and so on, were in fact *all* invented by colonial codification."[40] As the production of colonial laws, codifications, and boundaries, this tradition affects much of the thinking about precolonial Africa. Tradition may be a crucial component and part and parcel of a national culture, but it is not easy to obtain it from the past, especially by those whose thoughts have been formed and impacted by Western education.[41]

Fanon seems to develop an ambivalent feeling towards the role of native intellectuals who are tasked to attain tradition from the past and write the national literature. On the one hand, he rejects "any easy connection between the writing of nationalist literature by an intellectual elite and the creation of the nation or of national culture."[42] On the other hand, they are given an important role in the revolutionary anti-colonial struggle, and are expected to produce "national consciousness" through the writing of literature of combat. In so many of his works, Fanon expresses what Szeman describes as a "deep

37   Fanon, *The Wretched of the Earth*, 210.

38   Terence Ranger, "The Invention of Tradition in Colonial Africa," in *The Invention of Traditions*, eds. Eric Hobsbawm and Terence Ranger (Cambridge: Cambridge University Press, 1983), 262.

39   Ibid., 250.

40   Ibid.

41   Roy Armes, *Third World Film Making and the West*. Berkeley: University of California Press, 1987.

42   Imre Szeman, *Zones of Instability*, 39.

suspicion about the third-world intellectual."[43] These native intellectuals easily compromise and are usually positioned between worlds that make Fanon suspicious of their contribution to the anti-colonial struggle. They are estranged from the public, and they must resolve and do away with this estrangement by addressing the people genuinely. And yet, "it must also be recognized that it is only the intellectual's estrangement that makes possible the introduction of this largely foreign concept – 'literature' – into the midst of the revolutionary struggle in the first place."[44] In Fanon's view, these native intellectuals can also disentangle themselves from estrangement by ceasing to use the "language and techniques" of the colonizers in writing the national literature. Fanon rejects the colonizers' "language and techniques" at a time "when not only the then new concepts of nationalism, political independence, and the nation-state but also the very definitions of tradition itself are shaped by Western concepts."[45] His plea for the third stage of political commitment by the native intellectuals seems to be at odds with the African leaders and theorists' task in liberating their nation through seeking "alternative in Marxism."[46] Mazuri argues that it is "a socio-linguistic impossibility" for Africans to be sophisticated Marxists as Marxist manuscripts were not available in African languages.[47]

A significant change can be pointed out in Fanon's thoughts on language. Whereas in *Black Skin, White Masks* (1951), Fanon recognizes that using the colonizers' language can be "the key that can open doors"[48] if used effectively, in *The Wretched of the Earth* (1961), he warns the African native intellectual against using it. This change of thought is certainly the result of observing the situations in Algeria when it was at the verge of gaining independence in the early 1960s, not to mention his learnings from Albert Memi's *The Colonizer and the Colonized* (1957), wherein Memi maintains that "the most urgent claim of a group to revive is certainly the liberation and restoration of its language."[49] Fanon seems to suggest that avoiding the use of the colonizers' language can be commonly applied throughout Africa. This is suggestive of his inclination to use the Algerian model for the decolonization of the rest of Africa. Although points of common struggle for cultural nationalism and cultural identification in Africa were clear, conditions in Algeria were in significant ways different

---

43 Ibid., 39.
44 Ibid.
45 Armes, *Third World Film Making*, 28.
46 Ibid., 28.
47 Mazuri, "Language and the Quest for Liberation in Africa."
48 Fanon, *Black Skin, White Masks*, 25.
49 Albert Memi, *The Colonizer and the Colonized*, trans. Howard Greenfeld (London: Earthscan Publications Ltd, 2003), 154.

from those that pertained in most of Africa. Before the propagation of French (1830–1954), Algerians primarily spoke Arabic.[50] Thus, Fanon's suggestion to write in the native language, in the context of Algeria, means going back to the Arabic language. However, it is a different scenario for most multi-lingual African countries such as Kenya, Zimbabwe, and Nigeria, where writing in indigenous languages usually gives rise to the conflict over what ethnic language should be the language of national literature. In the new post-independence Africa, many African writers concur that national literature must be written by drawing on the tradition and the lives of the natives. They are aware that they should produce rehabilitative works to restore African values and dignity and to reconstruct events in colonial history from the African viewpoint. They feel the responsibility to produce a national literature that transforms the African people to a self-affirming subject in charge of their destiny, which would mobilize an African collective conscious. However, many of these native writers respond differently to the question "what language can best support the national literature?" As it is central to debates about postcolonial African identity and postcolonial writing in Africa, language choice has produced heated debates amongst African writers. The bilingual or multilingual African writers have to choose a language to express and negotiate the power dynamics related to "colonizer-colonized and indigenous-alien." Therefore, the choices are either to reject the colonial language and write in a local language, or use the language of the colonizers to write back to the Empire.

Ngugi wa Thiong'o, the Kenyan writer, has been one of the major voices in this debate. For Ngugi, the unavoidable threat as a writer is linguistic castration. European "writing came to be considered the norm" during the colonization of Kenya, and it continues to be the popular language in literature after independence.[51] Following Fanon, Ngugi Wa Thiongo also proposes a program of radical decolonization through the rejection of colonial language, as he views writing in the colonizers' language to be the current "neo-colonial linguistic policies" and a means of cultural control.[52] By continuing to write in European languages, Ngugi argues, native writers would perpetuate colonial and neo-colonial forms of enslavement. In his 1986 *Decolonising the Mind: The Politics of Language,* he points to specific ways that the language of African literature is indicative of the dominance of the empire. Ngugi further argues

---

50   Berber is the only other language with which a small percentage of Algerians communicate.
51   Ngugi wa Thiong'o, *Something Torn and New: An African Renaissance.* (New York: Basic Civitas books, 2009), 92.
52   Ngugi wa Thiong'o, *Decolonising the Mind: The Politics of Language in African Literature.* (Harare: Zimbabwe Publishing House, 1986), 85.

that language is a means through which one can make sense of the world and understand oneself. He builds a cogent argument for African writers to use the native languages of Africa rather than European languages. He realizes that those who need to receive the messages through literature the most are the poor and uneducated people who could not read in the colonial languages but could read and understand the native languages. Although he had a very successful career writing novels in English, he decided to write in Gikuyu to rejuvenate the history and tradition of Gikuyu. Anthony Appiah points out that what has led Ngugi to write in Gikuyu is "cultural nationalism" and he characterizes this decision as "linguistic nativism."[53]

Following Fanon, Ngugi believes that language "carries culture, and culture carries, particularly through orature and literature, the entire body of values by which we perceive ourselves and our place in the world."[54] Ngugi's decision to write in Gikuyu is by no means unique; African literature has been produced in all of the languages of Africa. The decision to write in his native language stems from Ngugi's participation in the widespread reconceptualization of language and in the restoration and reconstitution of African literature, which has represented the postcolonial era.[55] Before Ngugi, the language question in writing the national literature of Africa was raised by Obi Wali in 1963. He argues that African literature and culture would not progress if African writers adopt an uncritical attitude towards colonial languages. Obi Wali maintains that African literature must be written in African languages, otherwise it "would be pursuing a dead end."[56] Audre Lorde, in her *Sister Outsider: Essays and Speeches* (1984) had also developed a similar thought on language, to which she points out that "the master's tools can never dismantle the master's house."[57] For Ngugi, national literature written in European languages is not African literature, he rather terms them as "Afro-European literature," no matter how well they capture and reinvigorate the African tradition. To him, writers who write in European languages are continuing at the level of cultural practice, the neo-colonialism they are criticizing. He argues that writers of African literature should align themselves with the masses and use their language.[58] He rejects

53   Kwame Anthony Appiah, *In My Father's House: Africa in the Philosophy of Culture*. (Oxford: Oxford University Press, 1992), 199.

54   Ngugi, *Decolonising the Mind*, 16.

55   Kathrine Williams, "Decolonizing the Word: Language, culture, and the self in the Works of Ngugi wa Thiong'o and Gabriel Okara," *Research in African Literatures*, 22 (4). (p. 53–61). 1991.

56   Quoted in Ngugi, *Decolonising the Mind*, 24.

57   Audre Lord, *Sister Outsider: Essays and Speeches*. (Berkeley: Ten Speed Press, 1984), 110.

58   Ngugi, *Decolonising the Mind*.

the colonial language, English in his case, as the language of choice for African writers and embraces his mother tongue as an act of self-realization and empowerment.

Thus, he advocates turning to tradition and using the native language in African literature. Ngugi's thoughts on national literature rhyme well with Fanon and Obi Wali, who argue that revolutionary literature cannot contribute to decolonization if written in a colonial language. To Ngugi, the task of liberating Africans from neocolonialism has to be done in African native languages. Although he advocates linguistic decolonization in writing African literature, he seems to have developed a love-hate relationship towards English. His novels and other literary works written in Gikuyu language are easily available in authorized English translation or even translated by Ngugi himself. That he authorizes translations or translates his works himself is suggestive of his desire to tap into the language of the colonizers. Ngugi calls translation a "dialogue between the literatures, languages and cultures of different nationalities within any one country – forming the foundations of a truly national literature and culture, a truly national sensibility."[59] He preserves his native culture by preserving his language, but translation bridges the gap between his local language and universal communication. Just like Fanon's, his so-called "radical linguistic decolonization" does not seem to reject the language of the colonizers completely. Ngugi has unease with the normalization of the colonizers' language as the language of power, intelligence, and intellectuality. For him, writing the national literature in the language of the colonizers equals to an acceptance of the superiority of the colonizers' language.

On the other end of the spectrum, in regards to the question of language in national literature, there are writers such as Chinua Achebe, Ken Saro-Wiwa, Wole Soyinka, Gabriel Okara, Ama Ata Aidoo, Derek Walcott and Chimamanda Adichie, who use English for their literary productions. Considering what Fanon and Ngugi thought of the colonial language in producing national literature, one might wonder if these writers are collaborating with neo-colonialism, out of which emerges the question "Aren't they betraying their indigenous language and culture?" To begin with, many of these writers argue that they are using English as a means to challenge and subvert the colonial accounts of their motherland. Like other writers who write in indigenous languages of Africa, these writers are also reclaiming their heritage and at the same time indicating directions for constructive change. They have been "writing back" to colonial texts and have been countering the colonial accounts of traditions that have denigrated African cultures and populations. For instance,

---

59   Ibid., 85.

Saro-Wiwa recognizes that "literature in a critical situation such as Nigeria's cannot be divorced from politics... literature must serve society" and that writers "must play an interventionist role."[60] The English many of these writers use differs from standard English. They have, indeed, developed a hybrid language that contains elements of their indigenous languages. For instance, Chinua Achebe incorporates elements of the Igbo language and tradition into his literary writings. By incorporating Igbo words such as *chi, egwugwu, ogbanje*, and *obi* in his *Things Fall Apart* (1958), and by his frequent citation to the traditional Igbo proverbs and tales, Achebe creates an authentic African story through the transformed English.[61] His carefully orchestrated usage of Igbo elements in an English novel pushes the boundaries of the definition of English fiction.

The Jamaican writer, Louise Bennett is another such writer who inserts native words such as *boonoonoonoos* for "pretty," and *boogooyagga* for "worthless," into her texts in English.[62] To cite a further example, Uwem Akpan, the Nigerian writer, enjoys inserting indigenous words such as *randa* and *chrome* in his writings and treats them as if they are English words by turning indigenous verbs into gerunds. Wole Soyinka, the Nigerian poet "yorubizes English language poetry" using the indigenous language grammar.[63] Another prominent African writer is Ken Saro-Wiwa, who creates a voice for the voiceless by producing a language that he terms "Rotten English," which he defines as "a mixture of Nigerian pidgin English, broken English and occasional flashes of good, even idiomatic English."[64] Gabriel Okara infuses the English of his novel with African language patterns and syntax. In writing his 1964 novel *The Voice*, Okara describes the intricate process by means of which he contemplated his way into a revitalized English by leaving it completely.[65] He states, "in order to create the vivid images of African speech, I had to eschew the habit of expressing my thoughts first in English."[66] This way he produces an English in which idiom and syntax are thoroughly modified. The reordering of syntax, language patterns, and structures, blur the literal meaning and bring to the surface an allegorical reading. This marriage of African language-phrasing with English is

---

60   Scott Pegg, "Review: Ken-Saro Wiwa: Assessing the multiple legacies of a literary interventionist," *Third World Quarterly* 21(4), 2000, (p. 703).

61   Chinua Achebe, *Things Fall Apart*. Portsmouth, NH: Heinemann, 1958.

62   Jahan Ramazani, "Contemporary Postcolonial Poetry," in *A Companion to Twentieth Century Poetry*, ed. Neil Roberts (Malden, MA: Blackwell Publishing Ltd, 2001), 596.

63   Ibid., 606.

64   Ken Saro-Wiwa, *Sozaboy*. (London: Longman African Writers, 1994), Author's Notes.

65   Gabriel Okara, *The Voice*. New York: Africana, 1970.

66   Patrick Scott, "Gabriel Okara's The Voice: The Non-Ijo Reader and the Pragmatics of Translingualism *Research*," *African Literatures*, 21 (1990): 78.

successfully indigenizing the standard English and the English literary forms. The introduction of new forms and language into traditional English modifies standard English as well as literary structures.

Their English is now "purely local... [and] expresses the experiences of the African... authentically."[67] This is the "new English, still in full communion with its ancestral home but altered to suit its new African surroundings."[68] Achebe argues that this transformed English should be enough to express the African peculiarities.[69] This transformed English or the hybrid English emerges from the linguistic reconstruction of what Humboldt (1988) terms, *energia* (activity) which is a "force borne out of the peculiar energy of each culture, an unceasingly creative process that has been indelibly marked by the culture that created it."[70] This sort of literature would reach a wider audience, including both the colonized and the colonizers. This literature challenges the empire in two respects: first of all, as this sort of writing gains entry to the field of literature, it challenges the colonial ideologies of superiority, especially when Africans are no longer treated as the object. Second, this literature, written in hybrid language, questions the authorization of the empire in determining what constitutes standard English. This English, according to Arjuna Parakrama, "dehegemonizes language standards and creates new directions."[71] This English is the "most accessible means of 'natural' resistance, and, therefore, one of the most sensitive indices of dehegemonization."[72] This way they dismiss Ngugi's accusation that those writers who write in the former colonial language imitate the West, continue the dominance of imperial language and adhere to cultural imperialism. The hybrid language in literature allows them to reject the hierarchy of languages and cultures and embrace a network of languages and cultures. This literature shatters the center/periphery binary and offers a postcolonial version of English that can function along with literary works written in standard English in a non-hierarchical fashion.

---

67   Lee Nicholas, *African Writers as the Microphone.* (Washington, D.C.: Three Continents Press, 1984), 124.

68   Chinua Achebe, "The African Writer and the English Language," in *African Intellectual Heritage: A Book of Sources,* eds. Molefi Kete Asantre and Abu Shardow Abarry (Philadelphia: Temple University Press, 1996), 384.

69   Ibid.

70   Wilhelm von Humboldt, *On Language,* trans. Peter Heath. Cambridge: Cambridge University Press, 1988; Williams, "Decolonizing the Word," 56.

71   Arjuna Parakrama, *De-Hegemonizing Language Standards: Learning from (Post) Colonial Englishes about "English,"* London: Palgrave, 1995.

72   Ibid., xii.

4   Conclusion

That Fanon is as important and relevant today as he was during his time in
the 1950s and 1960s is undeniable. Fanon wrote both *Black Skin, White Masks*
(1952) and *The Wretched of the Earth* (1961) when decolonization was taking
place in Africa and Asia. This indicates that Fanon had a direct experience with
colonialism, liberation movements, independence, and their accompanying
problems. His thoughts on these issues resonate with the current neocolonialism and globalization that leads many scholars to appropriate him collectively.
The current configuration of the world corroborates the idea that his thoughts
and perspectives still hold validity. However, snatching him from the past and
incorporating his thoughts into the present may lead to a generalized and reductionist reading. What Fanon addresses several decades ago applies, mutatis
mutandis, to the contemporary world; yesteryears' colonial cruelty and atroc-
ity have just changed their shapes and forms; it is still called inhumanity. But
what Fanon proposes as solutions might not always work within every context.
For instance, his ideas about language that in taking on a language, one assumes the cultural underpinnings; and the wish to speak a colonial language
alienates the colonized are not controversial claims. However, his take on
abandoning the colonial language in national literature deserves to be studied in its particular context. Fanon's suggestion to return to the indigenous
language emanates from his idea that national literature had to revolutionize
the Algerian people in order to gain independence from French colonialism.
Two issues need to be taken into consideration here: (a) The French impact
on native society was greater than elsewhere in Africa, and the colonial regime was far more discriminatory and repressive; (b) the primary language of
Algerians before French colonialism was Arabic. On the one hand, this could
not function as the best solution for most African countries due to the existence of the multiplicity of ethnic languages. On the other hand, in proposing
this Fanon has only the native people in mind as the audience of the national
literature. Decolonization has never been a domestic issue and it involves negotiation with the colonizers as well to making them aware of the inhumanity
they brought upon the colonized. While this national literature in indigenous
languages "awakens" the people, it excludes any possibility of negotiation with
the colonial powers. Can't a "fighting literature" or "national literature" address
both the colonized and colonizers? Who is the intended audience of his own
writings? In *The Wretched of the Earth* (1963), Jean-Paul Sartre argues in the
preface of the text that Fanon writes this book to be read by the colonized,
but this is the point I would like to depart from, and add that this book and his
other writings, which illustrate the realities of the colonial and postcolonial

world, are addressed to both the colonized and colonizers. Wouldn't he also write in a language different than French such as Martinique Creole (as a mark of national pride) or Arabic if he just wanted to address the colonized?[73] The fact that he did not write in any other languages suggests that he would not exclude the formerly colonial language in its entirety. Had he lived longer, he would have probably invented a new form of French.

Bibliography

Achebe, Chinua. *Things Fall Apart*. Portsmouth, NH: Heinemann, 1958.

Achebe, Chinua. "The African Writer and the English Language." In *African Intellectual Heritage: A Book of Sources*, edited by Molefi Kete Asantre, Abu Shardow Abarry. Philadelphia: Temple University Press, 1996.

Appiah, Kwame Anthony. *In My Father's House: Africa in the Philosophy of Culture*. Oxford: Oxford University Press, 1992.

Armes, Roy. *Third World Film Making and the West*. Berkeley: University of California Press, 1987.

Capécia, Mayotte. *I am a Martinican Woman*. Correa, 1948.

Chatterjee, Partha. *The Nation and its Fragments*. Princeton, NJ: Princeton University Press, 1994.

Fanon, Frantz. *Black Skin, White Masks*. New York: Grove Press, (1952) 2008.

Fanon, Frantz. *The Wretched of the Earth*. New York: Grove Press, 1963.

Humboldt, Wilhelm von. *On Language*. Translated by Peter Heath. Cambridge: Cambridge University Press, 1988.

Lorde, Audre. *Sister Outsider: Essays and Speeches*. New York: Ten Speed Press, 1984.

Mazuri, Alamin. "Language and the Quest for Liberation in Africa: The Legacy of Frantz Fanon." *Third World Quarterly* 14, no. 2 (1993).

Memi, Albert. *The Colonizer and the Colonized*. Translated by Howard Greenfeld. New York: Earthscan Publications Ltd. (1957), 2003.

Mota-Lopes, Jose. "Re-Reading Frantz Fanon: Language, Violence, and Eurocentrism in the Characterization of Our Time." *Human Architecture: Journal of The Sociology of Self-Knowledge*, v. special Double issue (Summer 2007).

Nayar, Pramod K. *Frantz Fanon*. London & New York: Routledge, 2013.

Ngugi wa Thiong'o. *Decolonising the Mind: The Politics of Language in African Literature*. Zimbabwe Publishing House, 1986.

---

73   Although his knowledge of Arabic was rudimentary, he could still have his works translated.

Ngugi wa Thiong'o. *Something Torn and New: An African Renaissance*. New York: Basic Civitas Books, 2009.

Nicholas, Lee. *African Writers as the Microphone*. Washington, D.C.: Three Continents Press, 1984.

Okara, Gabriel. *The Voice*. New York: Africana, (1964) 1970.

Parakrama, Arjuna. *De-Hegemonizing Language Standards: Learning from (Post) Colonial Englishes about "English."* London: Palgrave, 1995.

Pegg, Scott. "Review: Ken-Saro Wiwa: Assessing the multiple legacies of a literary interventionist." *Third World Quarterly* 21 no. 4 (2000): 701–708.

Ramazani, Jahan. "Contemporary Postcolonial Poetry." In *A Companion to Twentieth Century Poetry*, edited by Neil Roberts. Malden, MA: Blackwell Publishing Ltd., 2001.

Ranger, Terence. "The Invention of Tradition in Colonial Africa." In *The Invention of Traditions*, edited by Eric Hobsbawm and Terence Ranger. Cambridge: Cambridge University Press, 1983.

Saro-Wiwa, Ken. *Sozaboy*. London: Longman African Writers, 1994.

Scott, Patrick. "Gabriel Okara's The Voice: The Non-Ijo Reader and the Pragmatics of Translingualism." *Research in African Literatures*, 21 (1990).

Szeman, Imre. *Zones of Instability: Literature, Postcolonialism, and the Nation*. Baltimore, MD: Johns Hopkins University Press, 2003.

Williams, Kathrine. "Decolonizing the Word: Language, Culture, and the Self in the Works of Ngugi wa Thiong'o and Gabriel Okara." *Research in African Literatures* 22 no. 4 (1991).

Index

CPSIA information can be obtained
at www.ICGtesting.com
Printed in the USA
LVHW041134240820
664015LV00002B/2